AFTER
THE
FACT

The Art of
Historical
Detection

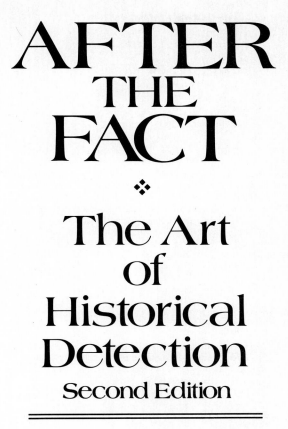

AFTER
THE
FACT

❖

The Art
of
Historical
Detection

Second Edition

James West Davidson

Mark Hamilton Lytle

Bard College

Alfred A. Knopf   New York

For
Gretchen, Mike, and Rug
(first readers)
and Jesse and Kate
(future prospects)

❖

Second Edition   987654321   *Copyright © 1982, 1986 by Alfred A. Knopf, Inc.*

Library of Congress Cataloging in Publication Data

Davidson, James West.
  After the fact.

  Includes bibliographies and index.
    1. United States—Historiography—Addresses, essays,
lectures. 2. United States—History—Addresses, essays,
lectures. I. Lytle, Mark H. II. Title.
E175.D38 1985   973'.072   85–23087
ISBN 0–394–35475–3 (pbk.)
ISBN 0–394–35476–1 (v. 1)
ISBN 0–394–35477–X (v. 2)
ISBN 0–394–55287–3

Manufactured in the United States of America

Cover photo: Doug Fornuff

PHOTO CREDITS

Courtesy of CBS, Inc.: 387, 389. The Huntington Library, San Marino, California: 88 (right).
Library of Congress: xviii, xxvii, xxxi, 5, 7, 23, 41, 65, 66, 95, 99, 104, 109, 148, 151, 152, 154,
168, 171, 178, 183, 207, 218, 221, 223, 228, 241, 243, 245, 247, 249, 252, 267, 273, 282, 293,
322, 325, 341. *Life* magazine, © 1947 Time Inc.: 366. Museum of the City of New York: 230,
232, 234, 235, 236. Collection, The Museum of Modern Art, New York: Ben Shahn, *Bartolomeo
Vanzetti and Nicola Sacco.* From the Sacco-Vanzetti series of twenty-three paintings (1931–32).
Tempera on paper over composition board, 10½ × 14½. Gift of Abby Aldrich Rockefeller: 297.
National Archives: 63, 192, 200, 225, 284, 305, 314, 331, 350, 353, 356, 361. New-York
Historical Society: 140. Stark Museum of Art, Orange, Texas: 125. *The Saturday Evening Post:* 370,
377. Sterling Memorial Library, Yale University: xxvii, 43. Collection of the University of Wiscon-
sin-Madison Archives: 88 (left). Walters Art Gallery, Baltimore: 123, 137. Wide World Photos:
396, 399, 409, 422.

INTRODUCTION

This book began as an attempt to bring more life to the reading and learning of history. As young historians we have been troubled by a growing disinterest in or even animosity toward the study of the past. How is it that when we and other historians have found so much that excites curiosity, other people find history irrelevant and boring? Perhaps, we thought, if lay readers and students understood better how historians go about their work—how they examine evidence, how they pose questions, and how they reach answers—history would engage them as it does us.

As often happens, it took a mundane event to focus and clarify our preoccupations. One day while working on another project, we went outside to watch a neighboring farmer cut down a large old hemlock that had become diseased. As his saw cut deeper into the tree, we joked that it had now bit into history as far back as the Depression. *"Depression?"* grunted our friend. "I thought you fellas were historians. I'm deep enough now, so's Hoover wasn't even a gleam in his father's eye."

With the tree down, the three of us examined the stump. Our wood-cutter surprised us with what he saw.

"Here's when my folks moved into this place," he said, pointing to a ring. "1922."

"How do you know without counting the rings?" we asked.

"Oh, *well*," he said, as if the answer were obvious. "Look at the core, here. The rings are all bunched up tight. I bet there's sixty or seventy —and all within a couple inches. Those came when the place was still forest. Then, you notice, the rings start getting fatter all of a sudden. That's when my dad cleared behind the house—in '22—and the tree started getting a lot more light. And look further out, here—see how the rings set together again for a couple years? That's from loopers."

"Loopers?" we asked cautiously.

"Sure—*loopers*. You know. The ones with only front legs and back." His hand imitated a looping, hopping crawl across the log. "Inchworms. They damn near killed the tree. That was sometime after the war—'49 or '50." As his fingers traced back and forth among the concentric circles, he spoke of other events from years gone by. Before we returned home, we had learned a good deal about past doings in the area.

Now, it occurs to us that our neighbor had a pretty good knack for putting together history. The evidence of the past, like the tree rings, comes easily enough to hand. But we still need to be taught how to see it, read it, and explain it before it can be turned into a story. Even more to the point, the explanations and interpretations *behind* the story often turn out to be as interesting as the story itself. After all, the fascination in our neighbor's account came from the way he traced his tale out of those silent tree rings.

Unfortunately, most readers first encounter history in school textbooks, and these omit the explanations and interpretations—the detective work, if you will. Textbooks, by their nature, seek to summarize knowledge. They have little interest and less space for looking at how that knowledge was gained. Yet the challenge of doing history, not just reading it, is what attracts so many historians. Couldn't some of that challenge be communicated in a concrete way? That was our first goal.

We also felt that the writing of history has suffered in recent years because some historians have been overly eager to convert their discipline into an unadulterated social science. Undeniably, history would lose much of its claim to contemporary relevance without the methods and theories it has borrowed from anthropology, psychology, political science, economics, sociology, and other fields. Indeed, such theories make an important contribution to these pages. Yet history is rooted in the narrative tradition. As much as it seeks to generalize from past events, as do the sciences, it also remains dedicated to capturing the uniqueness of a situation. When historians neglect the literary aspect of their discipline—when they forget that good history begins with a good story—they risk losing that wider audience which all great historians have addressed. They end up, sadly, talking to themselves.

Our second goal, then, was to discuss the methods of American historians in a way that would give proper due to both the humanistic and scientific sides of history. In taking this approach, we have tried to examine many of the methodologies that allow historians to unearth new evidence or to shed new light on old issues. At the same time, we selected topics that we felt were inherently interesting as stories.

Thus our book employs what might be called an apprentice approach to history rather than the synthetic approach of textbooks. A text strives to be comprehensive and broad. It presents its findings in as rational and programmatic a manner as possible. By contrast, apprentices are much less likely to receive such a formal presentation. They learn their profession from artisans who take their daily trade as it comes through the front door. A pewter pot is ordered? Very well, the pot is fashioned. Along the way, an apprentice is shown how to pour the mold. An engraving is needed? Then the apprentice receives his first taste of etching. While this method of teaching communicates a broad range of knowledge over the long run, it does so by focusing on specific situations.

So also this book. Our discussion of methods is set in the context of specific problems historians have encountered over the years. In piecing the individual stories together, we try to pause as an artisan might, and point out problems of evidence, historical perspective, or logical inference. Sometimes, we focus on problems that all historians must face, whatever their subjects. These include such matters as the selection of evidence, historical perspective, the analysis of a document, and the use of broader historical theory. In other cases, we explore problems not encountered by all historians, but characteristic of specific historical fields. These include the use of pictorial evidence, questions of psychohistory, problems encountered analyzing oral interviews, the value of decision-making models in political history, and so on. In each case, we have tried to provide the reader with some sense of vicarious participation—the savor of doing history as well as of reading it.

Given our approach, the ultimate success of this book can be best measured in functional terms—how well it works for the apprentices and artisans. We hope that the artisans, our fellow historians, will find the volume's implicit as well as explicit definitions of good history worth considering. In choosing our examples, we have naturally gravitated toward the work of those historians we most respect. At the same time we have drawn upon our own original research in many of the topics discussed; we hope those findings also may be of use to scholars.

As for the apprentices, we admit to being only modest proselytizers. We recognize that, of all the people who read this, only a few will go on to become professional historians. That is only natural. We do hope, however, that even casual readers will come to appreciate the complexity and excitement that go into the study of the past. History is not something that is simply brought out of the archives, dusted off, and displayed as "the way things really were." It is a painstaking construction, held together only with the help of assumptions, hypotheses, and inferences. Readers of history who push dutifully onward, unaware of all the backstage work, miss the essence of the discipline. They miss the opportunity to question and to judge their reading critically. Most of all, they miss the chance to learn how enjoyable it can be to go out and do a bit of digging themselves.

NOTE TO THE
SECOND EDITION

Our neighbor's surviving trees have added four more circles since the first edition, and the girth of this book, too, has expanded slightly, in hopes of providing readers with additional topics of interest. Since we discuss the question of visual evidence in Chapter 8 (on photography and Jacob Riis), we have replaced Chapter 5 from the first edition (on Indian portraits) with a new topic: the importance of ecology and epidemiology for understanding the settlement of the western frontier. We have also added a chapter on the image of women in the 1950s and how that image was shaped by the mass media, particularly television.

Many thanks are due to readers who have written us or to students who have suggested comments and corrections in person; in particular, we appreciated the counsel of Jack Wilson, Kit Collier, Carol Karlsen, and David Detzer, even if we proved unable to carry out all of their advice. In addition to the changes noted above, we have revised our Additional Readings to take into account new materials and have updated sections of other chapters. But the basic thrust of the book remains: that doing history, as well as simply reading it, is both a challenge and fun.

May 1985

ACKNOWLEDGMENTS

Because this book is as much about doing history as about history itself, we have drawn heavily on the research and methods of those scholars we most respect and whose history seems to us to provide excellent working models for any apprentice. These historians, past and present, demonstrate how exciting the pursuit of history can and ought to be. Because our narrative is written for lay readers and students as much as for professional scholars, we have omitted extensive footnotes and instead tried to acknowledge our many specific debts in the bibliographical essays that follow each chapter. These essays should provide scholars with the data needed to track down any specific points or issues of interest, as well as direct general readers and students to the primary and secondary sources needed for beginning their own investigations.

For the lay reader or student who comes to history only to sample the discipline or to fulfill distribution requirements, a confession of sorts is in order. Neither of us entered college with the idea of majoring in history, much less making a profession out of it. In the end it was good teachers who lured us into the vineyard. We had the fortune as undergraduates to study under some unusually exciting historians. At Cornell University, Donald Kagan made the ancient world come alive in a way that convinced Mark Lytle that history offered an indispensable way of organizing human knowledge. Walter LaFeber persuaded him that historians could have deep convictions, a powerful grasp of critical issues, and basic human decency. David Davis and Michael Kammen astonished him with the breadth and depth of their intellectual interests.

Jim Davidson's undergraduate years at Haverford College brought him the guidance and friendship of Wallace MacCaffery, whose judicious and eloquent lectures served as models not only for the department but for the rest of the college. In American history, Roger Lane's insights were by turns laconic (Vermont-style) and oratorical (the Irish mode), but always keenly analytical. And then there was William Smith—a colonial historian unaccountably serving in the English department and refusing to be digested by it. He taught unsuspecting freshmen the art of expository prose, a job he performed with more hard-nosed rigor (and consequent effect) than most of his suspicious colleagues.

Graduate school brought the authors together under the tutelage of many exceptional historians. To Edmund S. Morgan, David Davis, John Blum, Gaddis Smith, David Hall, Sydney Ahlstrom, Lawrence Chisolm,

Donald Kagan, Firuz Kazemzadeh, Steven Ozment, C. Vann Woodward, and others who taught at Yale, we owe our belief that historians can adopt all manner of methodologies and still write with precision and eloquence. They demonstrated the value of imaginative approaches to evidence, at the same time insisting that history ought to be literate as well as accurate. To the extent that we have followed their precepts, we owe them our gratitude. Where we have not succeeded in following, we can at least say that the spirit was willing, if the flesh a little weak.

We have been fortunate, too, to have had graduate school friends who researched, wrote, kibitzed, and shared lunches along the way. Glenn May, Sherm Cochran, Alan Williams, Bill Gienapp, Jon Clark, Marie Caskey, Allan Winkler, Alexis Pogerlskin, Jim Crisp, Steve Wiberley, Ellen Dwyer, Hal Williams, Rick Warch, and Elsa Dixler have now scattered across the nation, but they all contributed to the authors' present respect for the teaching and writing of history. Among our present colleagues, friends, and wife (only one of the latter), we would like to thank Gretchen Lytle, Mike Stoff, Mary Keller, John Rugge, Avi Soifer, Christine Stansell, James Lytle, Tom Frost, Geoff Linburn, Eric Berger, Doug Baz, Sam Kauffmann, Irene Solet, Ellen Boyce, Ken Ludwig, Adrienne George, Robert Koblitz, Stephen Andors, David Pierce, Peter Skiff, John Fout, and Fred Crane. All of them responded generously with advice and comment, sharpened the authors' focus, lampooned their pretensions, and generated ideas and criticism that have kept this book alive. To them all we say, *wea culpa* but thanks.

To Angus Cameron, editor at Alfred Knopf, goes our gratitude for early and continuing interest in the project. Professor Jack Wilson of Smith College provided many perceptive comments that improved the final draft substantially. He is one of those rare critics who not only pinpoints the flaws in a manuscript but also comes up with concrete and creative remedies. At the College Department, David Follmer and Marilyn Miller of Alfred Knopf patiently superintended the manuscript through the hurdles of writing, editing, and production. At Bard College, Ann McTigue and Curt Crane found time, amidst the mounting requests for "yesterday if not sooner," to type and retype the many drafts of chapters.

There are many names here. But then, history has not proved a lonely business. For that, too, we remain grateful.

JIM DAVIDSON
MARK LYTLE

June 1981

CONTENTS

The Strange Death of Silas Deane

The writing of history is one of the most familiar ways of organizing human knowledge. And yet, if familiarity has not always bred contempt, it has at least encouraged a good deal of misunderstanding. All of us meet history long before we have heard of any of the social science disciplines, at a tender age when tales of the past easily blend with heroic myths of the culture. In Golden Books, Abe Lincoln looms every bit as large as Paul Bunyan, while George Washington's cherry tree gets chopped down yearly with almost as much ritual as St. Nick's Christmas tree goes up. Despite this long familiarity, or perhaps because of it, most students absorb the required facts about the past without any real conception of what history is. Even worse, most think they do know and never get around to discovering what they missed.

"History is what happened in the past." That is the everyday view of the matter. It supposes that historians must return to the past through the surviving records and bring it back to the present to display as "what really happened." The everyday view recognizes that this task is often difficult. But historians are said to succeed if they bring back the facts without distorting them or forcing a new perspective on them. In effect, historians are seen as couriers between the past and present. Like all good couriers, they are expected simply to deliver messages without adding to them.

This everyday view of history is profoundly misleading. In order to demonstrate how it is misleading, we would like to examine in detail an event that "happened in the past"—the death of Silas Deane. Deane does not appear in most American history texts, and rightly so. He served as a distinctly second-rate diplomat for the United States during the years of the American Revolution. Yet the story of Deane's death is an excellent example of an event that cannot be understood merely by transporting it, courier-like, to the present. In short, it illustrates the important difference between "what happened in the past" and what history really is.

AN UNTIMELY DEATH

Silas Deane's career began with one of those rags-to-riches stories so much appreciated in American folklore. In fact, Deane might have made a lasting place for himself in the history texts, except that his career ended with an equally dramatic riches-to-rags story.

He began life as the son of a humble blacksmith in Groton, Connecticut. The blacksmith had aspirations for his boy and sent him to Yale College, where Silas was quick to take advantage of his opportunities. After studying law, Deane opened a practice near Hartford; then continued his climb up the social ladder by marrying a well-to-do widow, whose inheritance included the business of her late husband, a merchant. Conveniently, Deane became a merchant. After his first wife died, he married the granddaughter of a former governor of Connecticut.

Not content to remain a prospering businessman, Deane entered politics. He served on Connecticut's Committee of Correspondence and later as a delegate to the first and second Continental Congresses, where he attracted the attention of prominent leaders, including Benjamin Franklin, Robert Morris, and John Jay. In 1776 Congress sent Deane to France as the first American to represent the united colonies abroad. His mission was to purchase badly needed military supplies for the Revolutionary cause. A few months later Benjamin Franklin and Arthur Lee joined him in an attempt to arrange a formal treaty of alliance with France. The American commissioners concluded the alliance in March 1778.

Deane worked hard to progress from the son of a blacksmith all the way to Minister Plenipotentiary from the United States to the Court of France. Most observers described him as ambitious: someone who thoroughly enjoyed fame, honor, and wealth. "You know his ambition —" wrote John Adams to one correspondent, "his desire of making a Fortune. . . . You also know his Art and Enterprise. Such Characters are often useful, altho always to be carefully watched and contracted, specially in such a government as ours." One man in particular suspected Deane enough to watch him: Arthur Lee, the third member of the

American mission. Lee accused Deane of taking unfair advantage of his official position to make a private fortune—as much as fifty thousand pounds, some said. Deane stoutly denied the accusations and Congress engaged in a heated debate over his conduct. In 1778 it voted to recall its Minister Plenipotentiary, although none of the charges had been conclusively proved.

Deane embroiled himself in further controversy in 1781, having written friends to recommend that America sue for peace and patch up the quarrel with England. His letters were intercepted, and copies of them turned up in a New York Tory newspaper just after Cornwallis surrendered to Washington at Yorktown. For Deane, the timing could not have been worse. With American victory complete, anyone advocating that the United States rejoin Britain was considered as much a traitor as Benedict Arnold. So Deane suddenly found himself adrift. He could not return to America, for no one would have him. Nor could he go to England without confirming his reputation as a traitor. And he could not stay in France, where he had injudiciously accused Louis XVI of aiding the Americans for purely selfish reasons. Rejected on all sides, Deane took refuge in Flanders.

The next few years of his life were spent unhappily. Without friends and with little money, he continued in Flanders until 1783, when the controversy had died down enough for him to move to England. There he lived in obscurity, took to drink, and wound up boarding at the house of an unsavory prostitute. The only friend who remained faithful to him was Edward Bancroft, another Connecticut Yankee who, as a boy, had been Deane's pupil and later his personal secretary during the Paris negotiations for the alliance. Although Bancroft's position as a secretary seemed innocent enough, members of the Continental Congress knew that Bancroft was also acting as a spy for the Americans, using his connections in England to secure information about the British ministry's war plans. With the war concluded, Bancroft was back in London. Out of kindness, he provided Deane with living money from time to time.

Finally, Deane decided he could no longer live in London and in 1789 booked passage on a ship sailing for the United States. When Thomas Jefferson heard the news, he wrote his friend James Madison: "Silas Deane is coming over to finish his days in America, not having one *sou* to subsist on elsewhere. He is a wretched monument of the consequences of a departure from right."

The rest of the sad story could be gotten from the obituaries. Deane

Drawn from the life by Du Simitier in Philadelphia.   *Engraved by B. L. Prevost at Paris.*

"You know his ambition—his desire of making a Fortune. . . . You also know his Art and Enterprise. Such
Characters are often useful, altho always to be carefully
watched and contracted, specially in such a government
as ours."   —John Adams on Silas Deane

boarded the *Boston Packet* in mid-September, and it sailed out of London
down the estuary of the Thames. A storm came up, however, and on
September 19 the ship lost both its anchors and beat a course for safer
shelter, where it could wait out the storm. On September 22, while
walking the quarter deck with the ship's captain, Deane suddenly "com-

plain'd of a dizziness in his head, and an oppression at his stomach." The captain immediately put him to bed. Deane's condition worsened; twice he tried to say something, but no one was able to make out his words. A "drowsiness and insensibility continually incroached upon his faculties," and only four hours after the first signs of illness he breathed his last.

Such, in outline, was the rise and fall of the ambitious Silas Deane. The story itself seems pretty clear, although certainly people might interpret it in different ways. Thomas Jefferson thought Deane's unhappy career demonstrated "the consequences of a departure from right," whereas one English newspaper more sympathetically attributed his downfall to the mistake of "placing confidence in his [American] Compatriots, and doing them service before he had got his compensation, of which no well-bred Politician was before him ever guilty." Yet either way, the basic story remains the same—the same, that is, until the historian begins putting together a more complete account of Deane's life. Then some of the basic facts become clouded.

For example, a researcher familiar with the correspondence of Americans in Europe during 1789 would realize that a rumor had been making its way around London in the weeks following Deane's death. According to certain people, Deane had become depressed by his poverty, ill-health, and low reputation, and consequently had committed suicide. John Cutting, a New England merchant and friend of Jefferson, wrote of the rumor that Deane "had predetermin'd to take a sufficient quantity of Laudanum [a form of opium] to ensure his dissolution" before the boat could sail for America. John Quincy Adams heard that "every probability" of the situation suggested Deane's death was "voluntary and self-administered." And Tom Paine, the famous pamphleteer, also reported the gossip: "Cutting told me he took poison."

At this point we face a substantial problem. Obviously, historians cannot rest content with the facts that come most easily to hand. They must search the odd corners of libraries and letter collections in order to put together a complete story. But how do historians know when their research is "complete?" How do they know to search one collection of letters rather than another? These questions point up the misconception at the heart of the everyday view of history. History is not "what happened in the past;" rather, it is *the act of selecting, analyzing, and writing about the past.* It is something that is done, that is constructed, rather than an inert body of data that lies scattered through the archives.

∠'NB

The distinction is important. It allows us to recognize the confusion in the question of whether a history of something is "complete." If history were merely "what happened in the past," there would never be a "complete" history of Silas Deane—or even a complete history of the last day of his life. The past holds an infinite number of facts about those last days, and they could never all be included in a historical account.

The truth is, no historian would *want* to include all the facts. Here, for example, is a list of items from the past which might form part of a history of Silas Deane. Which ones should be included?

Deane is sent to Paris to help conclude a treaty of alliance.
Arthur Lee accuses him of cheating his country to make a private profit.
Deane writes letters which make him unpopular in America.
He goes into exile and nearly starves.
Helped out by a gentleman friend, he buys passage on a ship for America as his last chance to redeem himself.
He takes ill and dies before the ship can leave; rumors suggest he may have committed suicide.

      •   •   •

Ben Franklin and Arthur Lee are members of the delegation to Paris.
Edward Bancroft is Deane's private secretary and an American spy.
Men who know Deane say he is talented but ambitious, and ought to be watched.

      •   •   •

Before Deane leaves, he visits an American artist, John Trumbull.
The *Boston Packet* is delayed for several days by a storm.
On the last day of his life, Deane gets out of bed in the morning.
He puts on his clothes and buckles his shoes.
He eats breakfast.
When he takes ill, he tries to speak twice.
He is buried several days later.

Even this short list of facts demonstrates the impossibility of including all of them. For behind each one lie hundreds more. You might mention that Deane put on his clothes and ate breakfast, but consider also: What color were his clothes? When did he get up that morning? What did he have for breakfast? When did he leave the table? All these things "happened in the past," but only a comparatively small number of them can appear in a history of Silas Deane.

It may be objected that we are placing too much emphasis on this process of selection. Surely, a certain amount of good judgment will suggest which facts are important. Who needs to know what color Deane's clothes were or when he got up from the breakfast table?

Admittedly this objection has some merit, as the list of facts about

Deane demonstrates. The list is divided into three groups, roughly according to the way common sense might rank them in importance. The first group contains facts which every historian would be likely to include. The second group contains less important information, which could either be included or left out. (It might be useful, for instance, to know who Arthur Lee and Edward Bancroft were, but not essential.) The last group contains information that appears either too detailed or else unnecessary. Deane may have visited John Trumbull, but then, he surely visited other people as well—why include any of that? Knowing that the *Boston Packet* was delayed by a storm reveals little about Silas Deane. And readers will assume without being told that Deane rose in the morning, put on his clothes, and had breakfast.

But if common sense helps to select evidence, it also produces a good deal of pedestrian history. The fact is, the straightforward account of Silas Deane we have just presented has actually managed to miss the most fascinating parts of the story.

Fortunately, one enterprising historian named Julian Boyd was not satisfied with the traditional account of the matter. He examined the known facts of Deane's career and put them together in ways common sense had not suggested. Take, for example, two items on our list: (1) Deane was down on his luck and left in desperation for America; and (2) he visited John Trumbull. One fact is from the "important" items on the list and the other from items that seem incidental. How do they fit together?

To answer that, we have to know the source of information about the visit to Trumbull's, which is the letter from John Cutting informing Jefferson of Deane's rumored suicide.

> A subscription had been made here chiefly by Americans to defray the expense of getting [Deane] out of this country. . . . Dr. Bancroft with great humanity and equal discretion undertook the management of the *man* and his *business.* Accordingly his passage was engaged, comfortable cloaths and stores for his voyage were laid in, and apparently without much reluctance he embarked. . . . I happen'd to see him a few days since at the lodging of Mr. Trumbull and thought I had never seen him look better.

We are now in a better position to see how our two items fit together. And as Julian Boyd has pointed out, they don't fit. According to the first, Deane was depressed, dejected, almost starving. According to the second, he had "never looked better." An alert historian begins to get nervous when he sees contradictions like that, so he hunts around a little more. And finds, among the collection of papers published by the Connecticut and New York historical societies, that Deane had been writing letters of his own.

One went to his brother-in-law in America, who had agreed to help pay Deane's transportation over and to receive him when he arrived—something that nobody had been willing to do for years. Other letters reveal that Deane had plans for what he would do when he finally returned home. He had seen models in England of the new steam engines, which he hoped might operate gristmills in America. He had talked to friends about getting a canal built from Lake Champlain in New York to the St. Lawrence River, in order to promote trade. These were not offhand dreams. As early as 1785, Deane had been at work drumming up support for his canal project. He had even laboriously calculated the cost of the canal's construction. ("Suppose a labourer to dig and remove six feet deep and eight feet square in one day. . . . 2,933 days of labour will dig one mile in length, twenty feet wide and eight feet deep. . . .") Obviously, Deane looked forward to a promising future.

Lastly, Deane appeared to believe that the controversy surrounding his French mission had finally abated. As he wrote an American friend,

> It is now almost ten years since I have solicited for an impartial inquiry [into the dispute over my conduct]. . . . that justice might be done to my fortune and my character. . . . You can sufficiently imagine, without my attempting to describe, what I must have suffered on every account during so long a period of anxiety and distress. I hope that it is now drawing to a close.

Other letters went to George Washington and John Jay, reiterating Deane's innocence.

All this makes the two items on our list even more puzzling. If Deane was depressed and discouraged, why was he so enthusiastic about coming back to build canals and gristmills? If he really believed that his time of "anxiety and distress" was "drawing to a close," why did he commit suicide? Of course, Deane might have been subject to dramatic shifts in mood. Perhaps hope for the future alternated with despair about his chances for success. Perhaps a sudden fit of depression caused him to take his life.

But another piece of "unimportant" information, way down on our third list, makes this hypothesis difficult to accept. After Deane's ship left London, it was delayed offshore for more than a week. Suppose Deane did decide to commit suicide by taking an overdose of laudanum. Where did he get the drug? Surely not by walking up to the ship's surgeon and asking for it. He must have purchased it in London, before he left. Yet he remained on shipboard for more than a week. If Deane bought the laudanum during a temporary "fit" of depression, why did he wait a week before taking it? And if his depression was not just a sudden fit, how do we explain the optimistic letters to America?

This close look at three apparently unrelated facts indicates that perhaps Deane's story has more to it than meets the eye. It would be well, then, to reserve judgment about our first reconstruction of Silas Deane's career, and try to find as much information about the man as possible—regardless of whether it seems relevant at first. That means investigating not only Deane himself but also his friends and associates, like Ben Franklin, Arthur Lee, and Edward Bancroft. Since it is impossible in this prologue to look closely at all of Deane's acquaintances, for purpose of example we will take only one: his friend Bancroft.

SILAS DEANE'S FRIEND

Edward Bancroft was born in Westfield, Massachusetts, where his stepfather presided over a respectable tavern, the *Bunch of Grapes.* Bancroft was a clever fellow, and his father soon apprenticed him to a physician. Like many boys before him, Edward did not fancy his position and so ran away to sea. Unlike many boys, he managed to make the most of his situation. His ship landed in the Barbadoes, and there Bancroft signed on as the surgeon for a plantation in Surinam. The plantation owner, Paul Wentworth, liked the young man and let him use his private library for study. In addition, Bancroft met another doctor who taught him much about the area's exotic tropical plants and animals. When Bancroft returned to New England in 1766 and continued on to London the following year, he knew enough about Surinam's wildlife to publish a book entitled *An Essay on the Natural History of Guiana in South America.* It was well received by knowledgeable scholars and, among other things, established that an electric eel's shock was actually caused by electricity, a fact not previously recognized.

A young American bright enough to publish a book at age twenty-five and to experiment with electric eels attracted the attention of another electrical experimenter then in London, Ben Franklin. Franklin befriended Bancroft and introduced him to many influential colleagues, not only learned philosophers but also the politicians with whom Franklin worked as colonial agent for Pennsylvania. A second trip to Surinam produced more research on plants used in making color dyes; research so successful that Bancroft soon found himself elected to the prestigious Royal Society of Medicine. At the same time, Franklin led Bancroft into the political arena, both public and private. On the public side, Bancroft published a favorable review of Thomas Jefferson's pamphlet, *A Summary View of the Rights of British America;* privately, he joined Franklin and other investors in an attempt to gain a charter for land along the banks of the Ohio River.

Up to this point it has been possible to sketch Bancroft's career without once mentioning the name of Silas Deane. Common sense would suggest that the information about Bancroft's early travels, his scientific studies, his friends in Surinam, tell us little about Deane, and that the story ought to begin with a certain letter Bancroft received from Deane in June 1776. (Common sense is again wrong, but we must wait a little to discover why.)

The letter, which came to Bancroft in 1776, informed him that his old friend Silas Deane was coming to France as a merchant engaged in private business. Would Bancroft be interested in crossing over from England to meet Deane at Calais to catch up on news for old time's sake? An invitation like that would very likely have attracted Bancroft's curiosity. He did know Deane, who had been his teacher in 1758, but not very well. Why would Deane now write and suggest a meeting? Bancroft may have guessed the rest, or he may have known it from other contacts; in any case, he wrote his "old friend" that he would make all possible haste for Calais.

The truth of the matter, as we know, was that Deane had come to France to secure military supplies for the colonies. Franklin, who was back in Philadelphia, had suggested to Congress's Committee of Secret Correspondence that Deane contact Bancroft as a good source of information about British war plans. Bancroft could easily continue his friendship with English officials, because he did not have the reputation of being a hot-headed American patriot. So Deane met Bancroft at Calais in July and the two concluded their arrangements. Bancroft would be Deane's "private secretary" when needed in Paris and a spy for the Americans when in England.

It turned out that Deane's arrangement worked well—perhaps a little too well. Legally, Deane was permitted to collect a commission on all the supplies he purchased for Congress, but he went beyond that. He and Bancroft used their official connections in France to conduct a highly profitable private trade of their own. Deane, for instance, sometimes sent ships from France without declaring whether they were loaded with private or public goods. Then if the ships arrived safely, he would declare that the cargo was private, his own. But if the English navy captured the goods on the high seas, he labelled it government merchandise and the public absorbed the loss.

Deane used Bancroft to take advantage of his official position in other ways. Both men speculated in the London insurance markets, which were the eighteenth-century equivalent of gambling parlors. Anyone who wished could take out "insurance" against a particular event which might happen in the future. An insurer, for example, might quote odds on the chances of France going to war with England within the year. The insured would pay whatever premium he wished, say £1,000, and if France did go to war, and the odds had been five-to-one against it, the insured would receive £5,000. Wagers were made on almost any public event: which armies would win which battles, which politicians would fall from power, and even on whether a particular lord would die before the year was out.

Obviously, someone who had access to inside information—someone who knew in advance, for instance, that France was going to war with England—could win a fortune. That was exactly what Bancroft and Deane decided to do. Deane was in charge of concluding the French alliance, and he knew that if he succeeded Britain would be forced to declare war on France. Bancroft hurried across to London as soon as the treaty had been concluded and took out the proper insurance before the news went public. The profits shared by the two men from this and other similar ventures amounted to approximately ten thousand pounds. Like most gamblers, however, Deane also lost wagers. In the end, he netted little for his troubles.

Historians know these facts because they now have access to the papers of Deane, Bancroft, and others. Acquaintances of the two men lacked this advantage, but they suspected shady dealings anyway. Arthur Lee publicly accused Deane and Bancroft of playing the London insurance game. (Deane shot back that Lee was doing the same thing.) And the moralistic John Adams found Bancroft's conduct distasteful. Bancroft, according to Adams, was

> a meddler in stocks as well as reviews, and frequently went into the alley, and into the deepest and darkest retirements and recesses of the brokers and jobbers . . . and found amusement as well, perhaps, as profit, by listening to all the news and anecdotes, true or false, that were there whispered or more boldly pronounced. . . . This man had with him in France, a woman with whom he lives, and who by the French was called La Femme de Monsieur Bancroft. At tables he would season his foods with

such enormous quantities of cayenne pepper which assisted by generous burgundy would set his tongue a running in the most licentious way both at table and after dinner. . . .

Yet for all Bancroft's dubious habits, and for all the suspicions of men like Lee and Adams, there was one thing that almost no one at the time suspected, and that not even historians discovered until the records of certain British officials were opened to the public more than a century later. Edward Bancroft was a double agent.

At the end of July 1776, after he had arranged to be Deane's secretary, Bancroft returned to England and met with Paul Wentworth, his friend from Surinam, who was then working in London for Britain's intelligence organization. Immediately Wentworth realized how valuable Bancroft would be as a spy and introduced him to two Secretaries of State. They in turn persuaded Bancroft to submit reports on the American negotiations in France. For his services, he received a lifetime pension of £200 a year—a figure the British were only too happy to pay for such good information. So quick was Bancroft's reporting that the Secretaries of State knew about the American mission to France even before the United States Congress could confirm that Deane had arrived safely!

Eventually, Bancroft discovered that he could pass his information directly to the British ambassador at the French court. To do so, he wrote innocent letters on the subject of "gallantry" and signed them "B. Edwards." On the same paper would go another note written in invisible ink, to appear only when the letter was dipped in a special developer held by Lord Stormont, the British ambassador. Bancroft left his letters every Tuesday morning in a sealed bottle in a hole near the trunk of a tree on the south terrace of the Tuileries, the royal palace. Lord Stormont's secretary would put any return information near another tree on the same terrace. With this system in operation Stormont could receive intelligence without having to wait for it to filter back from England.

Did any Americans suspect Bancroft of double dealing? Arthur Lee once claimed he had evidence to charge Bancroft with treason, but he never produced it. In any case, Lee had a reputation for suspecting everybody of everything. Franklin, for his part, shared lodgings with Deane and Bancroft during their stays in Paris. He had reason to guess that someone close to the American mission was leaking secrets—especially when Lord Stormont and the British newspapers made embarrassingly accurate accusations about French aid. The French wished to keep their assistance secret in order to avoid war with England as long as possible, but of course Franklin knew America would fare better with

The Tuileries, much as it appeared when Bancroft and Lord Stormont used the south terrace as a drop for their secret correspondence. The royal palace over-looks a magnificent formal garden which, as a modern observer has noted, "seems so large, so full of surprising hidden corners and unexpected stairways, that its strict ground plan—sixteen carefully spaced and shaped gardens of trees, separated by arrow-straight walks—is not immediately discernable."

France fighting, so he did little to stop the leaks. "If I was sure," he remarked, "that my *valet de place* was a spy, as he probably is, I think I should not discharge him for that, if in other respects I liked him." So the French would tell Franklin he *really* ought to guard his papers more closely, and Franklin would say yes, yes, he really would have to do something about that; and the secrets continued to leak. Perhaps Franklin suspected Deane and Bancroft of playing the London insurance markets, but there is no evidence that he knew Bancroft was a double agent.

What about Deane, who was closer to Bancroft than anyone else? We have no proof that he shared the double agent's secret, but his alliance with Bancroft in other intrigues tells against him. Furthermore, one published leak pointed to a source so close to the American commissioners that Franklin began to investigate. As Julian Boyd has pointed out, Deane immediately directed suspicion toward a man he knew perfectly well was not a spy. We can only conclude he did so to help throw suspicion away from Bancroft. Very likely, if Bancroft was willing to help Deane play his games with the London insurers, Deane was willing to assist Bancroft in his game with British intelligence.

Of the two, Bancroft seems to have made out better. While Deane suffered reproach and exile for his conduct, Bancroft returned to England still respected by both the Americans and the British. Not that he had been without narrow escapes. Some of the British ministry (the king especially) did not trust him, and he once came close to being hung for treason when his superiors rightly suspected that he had associated with John the Painter, a notorious incendiarist who tried to set England's navy ablaze. But Bancroft left for Paris at the first opportunity, waited until the storm blew over, and returned to London at the end of the war with his lifetime pension raised to £1,000 a year. At the time of Deane's death, he was doing more of his scientific experiments, in hopes that Parliament would grant him a profitable monopoly on a new process for making dyes.

DEANE'S DEATH: A SECOND LOOK

So we finally arrive, the long way around, back where the story began: September 1789 and Deane's death. But now we have at hand a much larger store of information out of which to construct a narrative. Since writing history involves the acts of analyzing and selecting, let us review the results of our investigation.

We know that Deane was indeed engaged in dubious private ventures; ventures Congress would have condemned as unethical. We also have reason to suspect that Deane knew Bancroft was a spy for the British. Combining that evidence with what we already know about Deane's death, we might theorize that Deane committed suicide because, underneath all his claims to innocence, he knew he was guilty as Congress charged. The additional evidence, in other words, reveals a possible new motive for Deane's suicide.

Yet this theory presents definite problems. In the first place, Deane never admitted any wrongdoing to anyone—not in all the letters he wrote, not in any of his surviving papers. That does not mean he was innocent, nor even that he believed himself innocent. But often it is easier for a person to lie to himself than to his friends. Perhaps Deane actually convinced himself that he was blameless; that he had a right to make a little extra money from his influential position; that he did no more than anyone would in his situation. Certainly his personal papers point to that conclusion. And if Deane believed himself innocent— correctly or not—would he have any obvious motive for suicide? Furthermore, the theory does not explain the puzzle that started this investigation. If Deane felt guilty enough about his conduct to commit suicide, why did that guilt increase ten years after the fact? If he did feel suddenly guilty, why wait a week aboard ship before taking the fatal dose of laudanum? For that matter, why go up and chat with the captain when death was about to strike?

No, things still do not set quite right, so we must question the theory. What proof do we have that Deane committed suicide? Rumors about London. Tom Paine heard it from Cutting, the merchant. And Cutting reports in his letter to Jefferson that Deane's suicide was "the suspicion of Dr. Bancroft." How do we know the circumstances of Deane's death? The captain made a report, but for some reason it was not preserved. The one account that did survive was written by Bancroft, at the request of a friend. Then there were the anonymous obituaries in the newspapers. Who wrote them? Very likely Bancroft composed at least one; certainly, he was known as Silas Deane's closest friend and would have been consulted by any interested parties. There are a lot of strings here, which, when pulled hard enough, all run back to the affable Dr. Bancroft. What do we know about *his* situation in 1789?

We know Bancroft is dependent upon a pension of £1,000 a year, given him for his faithful service as a British spy. We know he is hoping Parliament will grant him a monopoly for making color dyes. Suddenly his old associate Deane, who has been leading a dissolute life in London, decides to return to America, vindicate himself to his former friends, and start a new life. Put yourself in Bancroft's place. Would you be just a little nervous about that idea? Here is a man down on his luck, now picking up and going to America to clear his reputation. What would Deane do to clear it? Tell everything he knew about his life in Paris? Submit his record books to Congress, as he had been asked to do so many years before? If Deane knew Bancroft was a double agent, would he say so? And if Deane's records mentioned the affair of John the Painter (as indeed they did), what would happen if knowledge of Bancroft's role in the plot reached England? Ten years earlier, Bancroft would have been hung. True, memories had faded, but even if he were spared death, would Parliament grant a monopoly on color dyes to a known traitor? Would Parliament continue the £1,000 pension? It was one thing to have Deane living in London, where Bancroft could watch him; it would be quite another to have him all the way across the Atlantic Ocean, ready to tell—who knows what?

Admit it: if you were Bancroft, wouldn't you be just a little nervous?

We are forced to consider, however reluctantly, that Deane was not expecting to die as he walked the deck of the *Boston Packet.* Yet if Bancroft did murder Deane, how? He was not aboard ship when death came and had not seen Deane for more than a week. That is a good alibi, but then, Bancroft was a clever man. We know (once again from the letters of John Cutting) that Bancroft was the person who "with great humanity and equal discretion undertook the management of the *man* and the *business"* of getting Deane ready to leave for America. Bancroft himself wrote Jefferson that he had been visiting Deane often "to assist him with advice, medicins, and money for his subsistence." If Deane were a laudanum addict, as Bancroft hinted to Cutting, might not the good doctor who helped with "medicins" also have procured the laudanum? And having done that, might he not easily slip some other deadly chemical into the mixture, knowing full well that Deane would not use it until he was on shipboard and safely off to America? That is only conjecture. We have no direct evidence to suggest this is what happened.

But there is one other fact we do know for sure; and in light of our latest theory, it is an interesting one. Undeniably, Edward Bancroft was an expert on poisons.

He did not advertise that knowledge, of course; few people in London at the time of Deane's death would have been likely to remember the fact. But twenty years earlier, the historian may recall, Bancroft wrote a book on the natural history of Guiana. At that time, he not only investigated electric eels and color dyes, but also the poisons of the area, particularly curare (or "Woowara" as Bancroft called it). He investigated it so well, in fact, that when he returned to England he brought samples of curare with him which (he announced in the book) he had deposited with the publishers so that any gentleman of "unimpeachable" character might use the samples for scientific study.

Furthermore, Bancroft seemed to be a remarkably good observer not only of the poisons but also of those who used them. His book described in ample detail the natives' ability to prepare poisons which, given in the smallest quantities, produce a very slow but inevitable death, particularly a composition which resembles wheat-flour, which they sometimes use to revenge past injuries, that have been long neglected, and are thought forgotten. On these occasions they always feign an insensibility of the injury which they intend to revenge, and even repay it with services and acts of friendship, until they have destroyed all distrust and apprehension of danger in the destined victim of the vengeance. When this is effected, they meet at some festival, and engage him to drink with them, drinking first themselves to obviate suspicion, and afterwards secretly dropping the poison, ready concealed under their nails, which are usually long, into the drink.

Twenty years later Bancroft was busy at work with the color dyes he had brought back from Surinam. Had he, by any chance, also held onto any of those poisons?

Unless new evidence comes to light, we will probably never know for sure. Historians are generally forced to deal with probabilities, not certainties, and we leave you to draw your own conclusions about the death of Silas Deane.

What does seem certain is that whatever "really happened" to Deane 200 years ago cannot be determined today without the active participation of the historian. Being courier to the past is not enough. For better or worse, historians inescapably leave an imprint as they go about their business: asking interesting questions about apparently dull facts, seeing connections between subjects that had not seemed related before, shifting and rearranging evidence until it assumes a coherent pattern. The past is not history; only the raw material of it. How those raw materials come to be fashioned and shaped is the central concern of the rest of this book.

* As the Author has brought a confiderable quantity of this Poifon to *England*, any Gentleman, whofe genius may incline him to profecute thefe experiments, and whofe character will warrant us to confide in his hands a preparation, capable of perpetrating the moft fecret and fatal villainy, may be fupplied with a fufficient quantity of the *Woorara*, by applying to Mr. *Becket*, in the *Strand*.

—an excerpt from *An Essay on the Natural History of Guiana in South America,* by Edward Bancroft.

Additional Reading

The historian responsible for the brilliant detective work exposing the possibility of foul play on the *Boston Packet* is Julian Boyd. He makes his case, in much greater detail than can be summarized here, in a series of three articles entitled "Silas Deane: Death by a Kindly Teacher of Treason?" *William and Mary Quarterly,* 3rd Ser., XVI (1959), 165–187, 319–342, and 515–550. For additional background on Silas Deane, see the entry in the *Dictionary of American Biography* (New York, 1946). (The *DAB,* incidentally, is a good starting point for those seeking biographical details of American figures. It provides short sketches as well as further bibliographical references.) For details on additional intrigue surrounding the American mission to France, see Samuel F. Bemis, "The British Secret Service and the French-American Alliance," *American Historical Review,* XXIX (1923–1924), 474–495.

Interested readers who wish to examine some of the primary documents in the case may do so easily enough. Much of Deane's correspondence is available in *The Deane Papers,* published as part of the New York Historical Society's *Collections,* XIX–XXIII (New York, 1887–1891) and in *The Deane Papers: Correspondence between Silas Deane, His Brothers . . . 1771–1795,* Connecticut Historical Society *Collections,* XXIII (Hartford, Conn., 1930). These volumes shed helpful light on Deane's state of mind during his London years. The London obituary notices are reprinted in the *American Mercury* (Hartford, Conn., December 28, 1789), the *Gazette of the United States* (Philadelphia, Pa., December 12, 1789), and other newspapers in New York and Boston. See also the *Gentleman's Magazine* of London, LIX, Pt. ii (September 1789), 866. American colonial newspapers are available in many libraries on microprint, published by the Readex Microprint Corporation in conjunction with the American Antiquarian Society.

Edward Bancroft's role as double agent was not established conclusively until the private papers of William Eden (Lord Auckland) were made public in the 1890s. As director of the British Secret Service during the Revolution, Eden and his right-hand man, Paul Wentworth, were in close touch with Bancroft. The details of the Bancroft-Wentworth-Eden connection are spelled out in Paul L. Ford, *Edward Bancroft's Narrative of the Objects and Proceedings of Silas Deane* (Brooklyn, N.Y., 1891). Further information on Bancroft may be found in Sir Arthur S. MacNalty, "Edward Bancroft, M.D., F.R.S. and the War of American

Independence," Royal Society of Medicine *Proceedings,* XXXVIII (1944), 7–15. The Historical Society of Pennsylvania, in Philadelphia, has a collection of Bancroft's papers. And further background may be gained, of course, from the good doctor's own writings, chief among them the *Essay on the Natural History of Guiana in South America . . .* (London, 1769).

We have pointed out that no evidence in the historical record conclusively links Edward Bancroft with Silas Deane's death. In an eminently fair-minded manner, we left you to draw your own conclusions. Yet, as the lesson of this chapter makes clear, every historical narrative is bound to select facts in shaping its story—including this narrative. Given our limitations of space, we chose to concentrate on the evidence and arguments which illuminated Boyd's hypothesis most forcibly. So we suspect that most readers, if left to draw their "own" conclusions, will tend to find Bancroft guilty as charged.

Boyd's case strikes us as impressive too, but it certainly can be questioned. How sound, for instance, is the hypothesis about Deane's depression (or lack of it)? Many people who have contemplated suicide, it could be argued, do so over an extended period of time, and their moods of depression may alternate with happier periods. Perhaps Deane toyed with the idea, put it away, then returned to it in the gloomy confines of the *Boston Packet.* If Deane were a laudanum addict and had a large quantity of the drug on hand, might he not easily take an overdose during a sudden return of severe depression?

In another area, William Stinchcombe has suggested that, contrary to Julian Boyd's suggestion, Deane did not face any really hopeful prospects for success in America. If Deane continued to be destitute and down on his luck when he departed for America, then the suicide theory again becomes more probable. Stinchcombe's article, "A Note on Silas Deane's Death," may be found in the *William and Mary Quarterly,* 3rd Ser., XXXII (1975), 619–624.

We can also report with pleasure that the first edition of this book sparked an interesting counter to Boyd's thesis. Dr. Guido Gianfranceschi, a surgeon from Danbury, Connecticut, read our Prologue in a course on historical methods he was taking at Western Connecticut State College. He points out to us that a check of the standard medical reference, *Goodman and Gilman's Pharmacological Basis of Therapeutics* (Sixth Edition; New York, 1980), reveals that Deane was not likely done in by curare. Though quite toxic when entering the bloodstream, curare is "poorly and irregularly absorbed from the gastrointestinal tract. d-Tubocurarine is inactive after oral administration, unless huge doses are ingested; this fact was well known to the South American Indians, who ate with impunity the flesh of game killed with curare-poisoned arrows." (It was also known to Bancroft, who notes in his own work that, "when received by the alimentary passage," the poison "is subdued by the action of the digestive organs. . . .")

Of course, curare was only one of many poisons Bancroft learned about from the natives of Guiana. "I have spent many days in a dangerous and almost fruitless endeavor to investigate the nature and qualities of these plants," he reported in 1769, "and by handling, smelling, tasting, etc. I have frequently found, at different times, almost all the several senses, and their organs either disordered or violently affected. . . ." Could it have been another one of those deadly substances which Deane ingested? Perhaps; Boyd makes no guess what the poison might have been. But while Bancroft indicated he had brought home snake specimens, curare is the only poison he specifically mentions having in London. Furthermore, Dr. Gianfranceschi points out that the symptoms of opium overdose are similar to those Deane is said to have experienced prior to his death. Finally, for a third opinion, consult D. K. Anderson and G. T. Anderson, "The Death of Silas Deane," *New England Quarterly,* LVII (1984), 98–105. The Andersons surveyed several medical authorities and concluded that Deane may well have suffered from chronic tuberculosis and died from a stroke or some other acute attack.

Murder, suicide, stroke, or accidental overdose? We eagerly await new evidence that our readers may turn up.

Serving Time in Virginia

As has become clear, the historian's simple act of selection irrevocably separates "history" from "the past." The reconstruction of an event is quite clearly different from the event itself. Yet selection is only one in a series of interpretive acts that historians perform as they proceed about their business. Even during the preliminary stages of research, when the historian is still gathering information, interpretation and analysis are necessary. That is because the significance of any piece of evidence is seldom apparent at first glance. The historian quickly learns that the words *evidence* and *evident* rarely mean the same thing.

For historians attempting to reconstruct an accurate picture of the first English settlements in Virginia, the difficulty of taking any document at face value becomes quickly apparent. The early Virginians were, by and large, an enterprising lot. They gave America its first representative assembly, gave England a new and fashionable vice, tobacco, and helped establish slavery as a labor system in the New World. These actions raise perplexing and important questions for historians, and yet the answers to them cannot be readily found in the surviving source materials without a good deal of work.

The difficulty does not arise entirely from lack of information. Indeed, some Virginians were enterprising enough to write history as well as make it, not the least of them being Captain John Smith. Captain Smith wrote an account of the young colony entitled *A Generall Historie of Virginia,* published in 1624. Much of his history is based on eyewitness, firsthand knowledge. At a vigorous age twenty-seven, he joined the expedition sent to Virginia in 1606 by the Virginia Company of London.

3

Once there, he played a crucial role in directing the affairs of the inexperienced Jamestown colony.

Yet Smith's evidence cannot be accepted without making some basic interpretive judgments. Simplest and most obvious—is he telling the truth? If we are to believe his own accounts, the young captain led a remarkably swashbuckling life. Before joining the Virginia expedition, he had plunged as a soldier of fortune into a string of complicated intrigues in central Europe. There he waged desperate and brave warfare on behalf of the Hungarian nobility before being taken prisoner by the infidel Turk. Once a prisoner, he likely would have spent the remainder of his years as a slave had he not won the affections (so he relates) of a Greek princess with the romantic name of Charatza Trabiganza. The smitten princess helped Smith make his escape, and he subsequently worked his way back to England in time to join the expedition to Virginia in 1606.

In Virginia the adventures came nearly as thick and fast as in Hungary. While the colony's governing council quarrelled at Jamestown, Captain Smith went off on an exploring and food-gathering mission. He established the first European contact with many of the Indian tribes around Chesapeake Bay, succeeded in buying needed corn from them, and when captured by Chief Powhatan, once again managed to get himself rescued by a beautiful princess—this one, the chief's young daughter Pocahontas.

How much of this romantic adventure story do we believe? The tone of Captain Smith's narrative makes it reasonably apparent that he was not the sort of man to hide his light under a bushel. Indeed, several nineteenth-century scholars, including Henry Adams, challenged Smith's account of his Indian rescue. Adams pointed out that the Pocahontas story did not appear in Smith's earliest published descriptions of the Virginia colony. Only in 1624, when the *Generall Historie* was issued, did the public first read of the Indian maiden's timely devotion. Captain Smith, Adams argued, probably invented the story out of whole cloth, in order to enhance his reputation.

We can, of course, look for independent evidence that would corroborate Smith's claims. But in the case of the Pocahontas story no independent records survive. Yet recent historians have defended Smith, Philip Barbour prime among them. Barbour has checked Smith's tales against available records in both Hungary and England and found them generally accurate as to names, places, and dates. Smith claimed, for example, that he used an ingenious system of torch signals to coordinate a nighttime attack by his Hungarian friends, "Lord Ebersbaught" and "Baron Kisell." No other records mention Smith's role, but we do know such

The Countrey wee now call Virginia beginneth at Cape Henry distant from Roanoack 60 miles, where was S.r Walter Raleigh's plantation: and because the people differ very little from them of Powhatan in any thing, I have inserted those figures in this place because of the conveniency.

King Powhatan comands C: Smith to be slaine, his daughter Pokahontas beggs his life his thankfullnes and how he subiected 39 of their kings. reade ye histor

printed by James Reeve

"Their clubs were raised, and in another moment I should have been dead, when Pocahontas, the King's dearest daughter, a child of ten years old, finding no entreaties could prevail to save me, darted forward, and taking my head in her arms, laid her own upon it, and thus prevented my death." In Robert Vaughan's illustration for the *Generall Historie* (1624), Pocahontas apparently is pictured twice, once at Smith's side, and again, larger than life, pleading for mercy.

an attack was launched—and that it was led by two Hungarians named Sigismund Eibiswald and Jakob Khissl. Similarly, although the records show no Greek princess named Charatza Trabiganza, that seems to have been Smith's fractured pronunciation of the Greek *koritsi* [girl] *Trapedzoûndos* [from Trebizond]. Quite possibly, when he asked his captors the identity of his saviour, they merely replied, *"koritsi Trapedzoûndos"*—a "girl from Trebizond."

Yet even if we grant Smith the virtue of honesty, significant problems remain when using his account; problems common to all historical evidence. To say that Smith is truthful is only to say that he reported events *as he saw them.* The qualification is not small. Like every observer, Smith viewed events from his own perspective. When he set out to describe the customs of the Chesapeake Indians, for instance, he did so as a seventeenth-century Englishman. Behind each observation he made stood a whole constellation of presuppositions, attitudes, and opinions that he took for granted without ever mentioning them. His descriptions were thus necessarily limited by the experience and education—or lack of it—that he brought with him.

The seriousness of these limitations becomes clearer if we take a hypothetical example of what might happen were Captain Smith to set down a history, not of Indian tribal customs, but of a baseball game between the Boston Red Sox and the New York Yankees:

> Not long after, they tooke me to one of their greate Counsells, where many of the generalitie were gathered in greater number than ever I had seen before. And they being assembled about a great field of open grass, a score of their greatest men ran out upon the field, adorned each in brightly hued jackets and breeches, with letters cunningly woven upon their Chestes, and wearinge hats uppon their heades, of a sort I know not what. One of their chiefs stood in the midst and would at his pleasure hurl a white ball at another chief, whose attire was of a different colour, and whether by chance or artyfice I know not the ball flew exceeding close to the man yet never injured him, but sometimes he would strike att it with a wooden club and so giveing it a hard blow would throw down his club and run away. Such actions proceeded in like manner at length too tedious to mention, but the generalitie waxed wroth, with greate groaning and shoutinge, and seemed withall much pleased.

Before concluding any more than that Smith would make a terrible writer for the *New York Post* (we don't even know if the Yankees won!), compare the description of the baseball game with one by the real Smith, of Chesapeake Indian life:

> In this place commonly are resident seaven [7] Priests. The chiefe differed from the rest in his ornaments, but inferior Priests could hardly be knowne from the common people, but that they had not so many holes in their eares to hang their jewels at.

The ornaments of the chiefe Priest were certaine attires for his head made thus. They tooke a dosen, or 16, or more snakes skins and stuffed them with mosse; and of Weesels and other Vermines skins a good many. All these they tie by their tailes, so as all their tailes meete in the toppe of their head, like a great Tassell. Round about this Tassell is as it were a crown of feathers, the skins hang round about his head, necke, and shoulders, and in a manner cover his face.

The faces of all their Priests are painted as ugly as they can devise, in their hands they had every one his Rattle, some base, some smaller. Their devotion was most in songs, which the chiefe Priest beginneth and the rest followed him: sometimes he maketh invocations with broken sentences, by starts and strange passions; and at every pause, the rest give a short groane.

Without having read the account of the baseball game first, it would not be anywhere near as obvious just how little Smith has told us about

"**In this place** commonly are resident seaven [7] Priests. . . . The faces of all their Priests are painted as ugly as they can devise, in their hands they had every one his Rattle, some base, some smaller." Presumably, the dark figure to the right of Captain Smith is the chief priest with his headdress of snakeskins stuffed with moss. Illustration by Robert Vaughan.

the Indian rituals. Indeed, anyone who reads the *Generall Historie* or any
of the captain's writings will be impressed by their freshness, their wealth
of detail, and their perceptiveness. But that is because we, like Smith, are
unfamiliar with the rituals of the seventeenth-century Chesapeake Indians. Quite naturally—almost instinctively—we adopt Smith's point of
view as our own.

Furthermore, the perspective that is embedded in Captain Smith's
description unconsciously diverts us from asking questions to which
Smith does not have the answer. What, after all, is the point of the
communal ritual? the significance of the fur tassels covering the priest's
face? Is *priest* even the right word to use? Or is Smith choosing an English
term that distorts the Indian's status from the beginning? In addition, the
Captain's very presence has added a new dimension to the ceremony.
What effect will English culture have on Indian social structures and
belief systems? How much will the traditional tribal authority of the
"priests" be undermined by the arrival of a technologically superior
culture? These and many other questions remain unanswered or, more
to the point, unasked. They are beyond Smith's interest, his competence,
or his ken. If historians are to answer them, they must make a conscious
effort to raise the questions in the first place.

It is easy enough to see how a point of view is embedded in the facts
of an eloquent narration. Smith is, after all, not only headstrong and
unabashed, but he is also consciously writing for a wider public. He
intends his book to be read and, in being read, to convince. But consider
for a moment evidence recorded by one of the pedestrian clerks whose
jottings constitute the great bulk of history's raw material. The following
excerpts are taken from the records of Virginia's General Assembly and
the proclamations of the Governor:

> We will and require you, Mr. Abraham Persey, Cape Marchant, from this
> daye forwarde to take notice, that . . . you are bounde to accepte of the
> Tobacco of the Colony, either for commodities or upon billes, at three
> shillings the beste and the second sorte at 18*d* the punde, and this shalbe
> your sufficient dischardge.
> Every man to sett 2 acres corn (Except Tradesmen following their trades)
> penalty forfeiture of corn & Tobacco & be a Slave a year to the Colony.
> No man to take hay to sweat Tobacco because it robs the poor beasts of
> their fodder and sweating Tobacco does it little good as found by
> Experience.

Here we face the opposite of Smith's description: small bits of information dependent on a great deal of assumed knowledge. Whereas Smith
attempted to describe the Indian ceremony in some detail because it

was new to him, Virginia's General Assembly knows all too much about tobacco prices and the planting of corn. Policy is stated without any explanation, just as the scorebox in the paper lists the single line, "Yankees 10, Red Sox 3." In each case the notations are so terse, the "narratives" so brief, that the novice historian is likely to assume they contain no point of view at all, only the bare facts. But the truth is, each statement has a definite point of view that can be summed up as simple questions: (1) Did the Yankees win and if so by how much? (2) Should the price of tobacco be three shillings or eighteen pence or how much? (3) What should colonists use hay for? And so on. These viewpoints are so obvious, they would not bear mentioning—except that, unconsciously, we are led to accept them as the only way to think about the facts. Since the obvious perspective often appears irrelevant, we tend to reject the information as not worth our attention.

But suppose a fact is stripped of its point of view—suppose we ask, in effect, a completely different question of it? Historians looking back on twentieth-century America would undoubtedly learn little from baseball box scores, but at least by comparing the standings of the 1950s with those of the 1970s, they would soon discover that the Giants of New York had become the Giants of San Francisco and that the Brooklyn Dodgers had moved to Los Angeles. If they knew a bit more than Captain Smith about the economic implications of major league franchises, they could infer a relative improvement in the economic and cultural status of the West Coast. Similarly, by refusing to accept the evidence of tobacco prices or corn planting at its face value, historians might make inferences about economic and cultural conditions in seventeenth-century Virginia.

In adopting a perspective different from any held by the historical participants, we are employing one of the most basic tactics of sociology. Sociologists have long recognized that every society functions, in part, through structures and devices that remain unperceived by its members. "To live in society means to exist under the domination of society's logic," notes sociologist Peter Berger. "Very often men act by this logic without knowing it. To discover this inner dynamic of society, therefore, the sociologist must frequently disregard the answers that the social actors themselves would give to his questions and look for explanations that are hidden from their own awareness."

Using that approach, recent historians have taken documents from colonial Virginia, stripped them of their original perspectives, and reconstructed a striking picture of Virginia society. Their research reveals that life in the young colony was more volatile, acquisitive, rowdy, raw—and deadly—than most traditional accounts have assumed. Between the high ideals of the colony's London investors and the disembarkation points along the Chesapeake, something went wrong. The society that was designed to be a productive and diversified settlement in the wilderness soon developed into a world where the singleminded pursuit of one crop, tobacco, made life as nasty, brutish, and short as anywhere in the hemisphere. And the colony that had hoped to pattern itself on the free and enlightened customs of England instead found itself establishing something which the government of England had never thought to introduce at home: the institution of human slavery.

A COLONY ON THE EDGE OF RUIN

None of the English colonial ventures found it easy to establish successful and independent settlements along the Atlantic coast, but for the Virginia colony, the going was particularly rough. In the first ten years of the colony's existence, £75,000 had been invested to send around 2,000 settlers across the ocean to what Captain Smith described as a "fruitfull and delightsome land" where "heaven and earth never agreed better to frame a place for mans habitation." Yet at the end of that time, the attempt to colonize Virginia could be judged nothing less than unmitigated disaster.

Certainly most members of the Virginia Company viewed it that way. In 1606 King James had granted a charter to a group of London merchants who became formally known as "The Treasurer and Company of Adventurers and Planters of the City of London for the First Colony in Virginia." The Virginia Company, as it was more commonly called, allowed merchants and gentlemen of quality to "adventure" money in a joint stock arrangement, pooling their resources to support an expedition to Virginia. The expedition would plant a colony and extract the riches of the new country, such as gold or iron, and also begin cultivating crops that would yield a high return, such as grapes for the production of wine or mulberry trees for the production of silk. King James, a silkworm buff, even donated some of his own specially bred worms. The proceeds would repay the company's expenses, the investors (or "adventurers") would reap handsome profits, the colonists themselves would prosper, and England would gain a strategic foothold in the New World. So the theory went.

As might be expected, the practice ran rather differently. After four difficult months at sea, only 105 of the original 144 settlers reached Chesapeake Bay in April of 1607. The site chosen at Jamestown for a fort was swampy, its water unhealthy, and the Indians less than friendly. By the end of the first hot and humid summer, 46 more settlers had perished. When the first supply ship delivered 120 new recruits the following January, it found only 38 men still alive.

The company correctly blamed part of the failure on the colony's original system of government. A president led a council of 13 men, but in name only. Council members refused to take direction and continually bickered among themselves. In 1609 the company obtained a new charter providing for centralized control in a governor, but when it sent another 600 settlers across, the results were even worse. Because a hurricane scattered the fleet on its way over, only 400 settlers arrived, leaderless, in September of 1609. Captain Smith, the one old hand who had acted decisively to pull the colony together, was sent packing on the first ship home, and as winter approached, the bickering began anew.

Nobody, it seemed, had planted enough corn to last through the winter, preferring to barter, bully, or steal supplies from the Indians. And the Indians knew that the English depended on them—knew that they could starve out the newcomers simply by moving away. When several soldiers took French leave to seek food from the natives, the other settlers discovered their comrades not long after, "slayne with their mowthes stopped full of Breade, being donn as it seemeth in Contempte and skorne thatt others might expect the Lyke when they shold come to seek for breade and reliefe amongst them."

As the winter wore on, the store of hogs, hens, goats, sheep, and horses were quickly consumed; the colonists then turned to "doggs Catts Ratts and myce." Those settlers who were healthy enough searched the woods for roots, nuts, and berries, while others resorted to boiling boot leather. Conditions became so desperate that one man "did kill his wife, powdered [i.e., salted] her, and had eaten part of her" before leaders discovered his villainy and had him executed. By May 1610, when Deputy Governor Thomas Gates and the rest of the original fleet limped in from Bermuda, only 60 settlers out of 500 had survived the winter, and these were "so Leane thatt they looked Lyke Anotamies Cryeing owtt we are starved We are starved."

Grim as such tales are, we have almost come to expect them in the first years of a new colony. The Virginia experiment broke new ground in a new land. Mistakes were inevitable. But as the years passed, the colonists seemed to have learned little. Ten years after the first landing yet another governor, Samuel Argall, arrived to find Jamestown hardly more than a slum in the wilderness: "but five or six houses [remaining standing], the Church downe, the Palizado's [stockade fence] broken, the Bridge in pieces, the Well of fresh water spoiled; the Storehouse they used for the Church; the market-place and streets, and all other spare places planted with Tobacco." Of the 2,000 or so settlers sent since 1607, only 400 remained alive and only 200 of them, Argall complained, were either trained or fit enough to farm. Even John Rolfe, who was usually willing to put as good a face on affairs as possible, could not help taking away with the left hand the praises he bestowed with the right. "Wee found the Colony (God be thanked) in good estate," he wrote home hopefully, "however in buildings, fortyfications, and of boats, much ruyned and greate want." All in all, it was not much of a progress report after ten years.

   In England, Sir Edwin Sandys was one of the adventurers who watched with distress as the company's efforts came to naught. Sandys lacked the financial means of bigger investors like Thomas Smith, who had often presided as the company's treasurer. But that was precisely the point. Smith and the other big investors considered the Virginia enterprise just one venture among many: the East India Company, trading in the Levant, the Muscovy Company. If Virginia did not pay immediate dividends, they could afford to wait. Sandys and his followers, with less capital and less margin for error, pressed for immediate reform. By 1618 Smith had agreed to introduce significant changes into the colony's organization; the following year Sandys was elected treasurer of the company. With real power in his hands for the first time, he set out to reconstruct the failing colony from the bottom up.

BLUEPRINT FOR A VIRGINIA UTOPIA

Sandys knew that if his schemes for reform were to succeed, he would have to attract both new investors to the company and new settlers to the colony. Yet the Virginia Company was deeply in debt and the colony was literally falling apart. In order to entice both settlers and investors, Sandys offered the only commodity the company possessed in abundance —land.

   In the first years of the colony, Virginia land had remained company land. Settlers who worked it might own shares in the company, but even so, they did not profit directly from their labor, since all proceeds went into the treasury to be divided only if there were any profits. There never were. In 1617 the company formally changed its policy. "Old Planters," those settlers who had arrived in Virginia before the spring of 1616, were each granted 100 acres of land. Freemen received their allotment immediately, while those settlers who were still company servants received their land when their terms of service expired.

Sandys lured new investors with the promise of property too. For every share they purchased, the company granted them 100 acres. More important, Sandys encouraged immigration to the colony by giving investors additional land if they would pay the ship passage of tenant laborers. For every new tenant an investor imported to Virginia, he received fifty additional acres. Such land grants were known as "headrights," since the land was apportioned per each "head" imported. Of course, if Old Planters wished to invest in the company, they too would receive 100 acres plus additional 50-acre headrights for every tenant whose passage they paid. Such incentives, Sandys believed, would attract needed funds to the company while also promoting immigration.

And so private property came to Virginia. This was the much-heralded event that every school child is called upon to recite as the salvation of the colony. "When our people were fed out of the common store and labored jointly together, glad was he could slip away from his labour, or slumber over his taske," noted Ralph Hamor. But "now for themselves they will doe in a day" what before they "would hardly take so much true paines in a weeke." It is important to understand, however, that the company still had its own common land and stock from which it hoped to profit. Thus a company shareholder had the prospect of making money in two ways: from any goods marketed by company servants working company lands, or directly from his newly granted private lands, also known as "Particular Plantations."

Sandys's administration provided still other openings for private investment. By 1616 the company had already granted certain merchants a four-year monopoly on providing supplies for the colony. The "Magazine," as it was called, sent supply ships to Virginia. There its agent, a man known as the Cape Merchant, sold the goods in return for produce. In 1620 the company removed the Magazine's monopoly and allowed other investors to send over supply ships.

Sandys and his friends also worked to make the colony a more pleasant place to live. Instead of being governed by martial law, as the colony had since 1609, the company instructed the new governor, George Yeardly, to create an assembly with the power to make laws. The laws would be binding so long as the company subsequently approved them. Inhabitants of the various company settlements as well as of the particular plantations were to choose two members each as their burgesses, or representatives. When the assembly convened in 1619 it became the first representative body in the English colonies.

Historians have emphasized the significance of this first step in the evolution of American democracy, and significant it was. But the colony's settlers may have considered it equally important that the company had figured out a way to avoid saddling them with high taxes to pay for their government. Once again, the answer was land, which the company used to pay officials' salaries. Thus the governor received a parcel of 3,000 acres plus 100 tenants to work it, the treasurer of the colony received 1,500 acres and 50 tenants, and so on. Everybody won, or so it seemed. The officers got their salaries without having to "prey upon the people"; the settlers were relieved "of all taxes and public burthens as much as may be"; and the sharecropping tenants, after splitting the profits with company officials for seven years, got to keep the land they worked. If the company carried out its policy, John Rolfe observed enthusiastically, "then we may truly say in Virginia, we are the most happy people in the world."

In 1619, with the reforms in place and Sandys in the treasurer's seat, the company moved into high gear. New investors sent scores of tenants over to work the particular plantations; the company sent servants to tend officers' lands; and lotteries throughout England provided income to recruit ironmongers, vine-tenders, and glassblowers for the New World. The records of the Virginia Company tell a story of immigration on a larger scale than ever before: over a thousand settlers in 1619, Sandys's first year, and equal numbers in the following three years. Historians who do a little searching and counting in company records will find that some 3,570 settlers were sent to join a population that stood, at the beginning of Sandys's program, around 700.

It would have been an impressive record, except that in 1622, three years later, the colony's population still totalled only about 700 people.

The figures are in the records; you can check the addition yourself. What it amounts to is that in 1622, there are 3,500 Virginians missing. No significant number returned to England; most, after all, could hardly afford passage over, let alone back. No significant number migrated to other colonies. We can account for the deaths of 347 colonists, slain in an Indian attack of 1622. But that leaves over 3,000 settlers and there seems to be only one way to do the accounting. Those immigrants died.

Who—or what—was responsible for the deaths of 3,000 Virginians? Something had gone terribly wrong with Sandys's plans. The magnitude of the failure was so great that the leaders of the company did not care to announce it openly. When the king got word of it, only after the company had virtually bankrupted itself in 1624, he revoked its charter. The historian who confronts the statistical outlines of this horror is forced to ask a few questions. Just what conditions would produce a society in which the death rate was in the neighborhood of 75 to 80 percent? A figure that high is simply staggering; for comparison, the death rate during the first (and worst) year at the Pilgrims' Plymouth colony stayed a little below 50 percent. During the severe plague epidemics that swept Britain in the fourteenth century, the death rate probably ranged from 20 to 45 or 50 percent.

Obvious answers suggest themselves. The colony could not sustain such an influx of new settlers, especially since Sandys, in his eagerness to increase the population, sent so many men unprepared. Immigrants often arrived with little or no food to tide them over until they could begin raising their own crops. Housing was inadequate; indeed, the records are replete with letters from the company in London begging the colony's governors to build temporary "guest houses" for the newcomers, while the governors' letters in return begged the company to send more adequate provisions with their recruits.

Disease took its toll. Colonists had discovered early on that Virginia was an unhealthy place to live. For newcomers, the first summer proved particularly deadly, so much so that it was called the "seasoning time." Those who survived the first summer significantly raised their chances of prospering. But dangers remained year round, especially for those weakened by the voyage or living on a poor diet. Contaminated wells most likely contributed to outbreaks of typhoid fever, and malaria claimed victims.

The obvious answers do much to explain the devastating death rates, but anomalies remain. Even granting the seriousness of typhoid and other diseases, why a death rate higher than the worst plague years? Virginia's population was made up of younger men primarily and lacked the older men and women who would have been most weakened by these conditions. Even healthy men, of course, may be affected by malnutrition and semistarvation, but that brings the problem right back to the question of why, after more than ten years, the Jamestown colony was not yet self-sufficient.

To be self-sufficient required that colonists raise their own food. And the principal food raised in the area was corn. So the historian asks a simple question. How much work did it take to grow corn? A quick look at the records confirms what might be suspected—that no Virginian in those first years bothered to leave behind a treatise on agriculture. But a closer search of letters and company records provides bits of data here and there. The Indians, Virginians discovered, spent only a few days out of the year tending corn, and they often produced surpluses that they traded to the Virginians. A minister in the colony reported that "in the idle hours of one week," he and three other men had planted enough corn to last for four months. Other estimates suggested that forty-eight hours' work would suffice to plant enough corn to last a whole year. Even allowing for exaggeration, it seems clear that comparatively little effort was needed to grow corn.

Yet if corn can be grown easily, and if it is needed to keep the colonists alive, what possible sense is the historian to make of a document we encountered earlier—Governor Argall's proclamation of 1618, requiring "Every man to sett 2 acres corn (Except Tradesmen following their trades). . . ." That year is not the last time the law appears on the books. It was re-entered in the 1620s and periodically up through the 1650s.

It is a puzzle. A law *requiring* Virginians to plant corn? The colony is continually running out of corn, people are starving, and planting and reaping take only a few weeks out of the year. Under these circumstances, the government has to *order* settlers to plant corn?

Yet the conclusion is backed up by other company records. Virginians had to be forced to grow corn. The reason becomes clearer if we re-examine Governor Argall's gloomy description of Jamestown when he stepped off the boat in 1617. The church is down, the palisades pulled apart, the bridge in pieces, the fresh water spoiled. Everything in the description indicates the colony is decrepit, falling apart, except for one paradoxical feature—the weeds in the street. The stockades and buildings may have languished from neglect, but it was not neglect that caused "the market-place and streets, and all other spare places" to be "planted with Tobacco." Unlike corn, tobacco required a great deal of attention to cultivate. It did not spring up in the streets by accident. Thus Governor Argall's description indicates that at the same time that settlers were willing to let the colony fall apart, they were energetically planting tobacco in all the "spare places" they could find.

Settlers had discovered as early as 1613 that tobacco was marketable, and they sent small quantities to England the following year. Soon shipments increased dramatically, from 2,500 pounds in 1616 to 18,839 pounds in 1617 and 49,518 pounds in 1618. Some English buyers thought that tobacco could be used as a medicine, but most purchased it simply for the pleasure of smoking it. Sandys and many other gentlemen looked upon the "noxious weed" as a vice and did everything to discourage its planting. There had been "often letters from the Counsell" in London, he complained, "sent lately to the Governour for restraint of that immoderate following of Tobacco and to cause the people to apply themselves to other and better commodities." But his entreaties, as well as the corn laws, met with little success. Tobacco was in Virginia to stay.

VIRGINIA BOOM COUNTRY

The Virginia records are full of statistics like the tobacco export figures given in the last paragraph. Number of pounds shipped, price of the "better sort" of tobacco for the year 1619, number of settlers arriving on the *Bona Nova.* This is the sort of "linescore" evidence, recorded by pedestrian clerks for pedestrian reasons, that we noted earlier. Yet once the historian strips the facts of their pedestrian perspective and uses them for his own purposes, they begin to flesh out an astonishing picture of Virginia. Historian Edmund Morgan, in his own reconstruction of the situation, aptly labelled Virginia "the first American boom country."

For Virginia had indeed become a boom country. The commodity in demand—tobacco—was not as glamorous as gold or silver, but the social dynamics operated in similar fashion. The lure of making a fortune created a volatile society where wealth changed hands quickly, where an unbalanced economy centered on one get-rich-quick commodity, and where the values of stability and human dignity counted for little.

The implications of this boom-country society become clearer if we ask the same basic questions about tobacco that we asked about corn. Given the fact that Virginians seemed to be growing tobacco, just how much could one person grow in a year? If tobacco was being grown for profit, could Virginians expect to get rich doing it?

Spanish tobacco grown in the West Indies fetched 18 shillings a pound on the English market. Even the highest quality Virginia product was markedly inferior and sold for only 3 shillings. And that price fluctuated throughout the 1620s, dropping as low as 1 shilling. What that price range meant in terms of profits depended, naturally, on how much tobacco a planter could grow in a year. As with corn, the few available estimates are widely scattered. John Rolfe suggested 1,000 plants in one year. William Capps, another seasoned settler, estimated 2,000 and also noted that three of his boys, whose labor he equated with one and a half men, produced 3,000 plants. Fortunately Capps also noted that 2,000 plants made up about 500 "weight" (or pounds) of tobacco, which allows us to convert number of plants into number of pounds.

By comparing these figures with other estimates, it is possible to calculate roughly how much money a planter might receive for his crop. The chart below summarizes how many plants or pounds of tobacco one or more workers might harvest in a year. Extrapolating, the numbers in parentheses show the number of pounds harvested per worker and the income such a harvest would yield if tobacco were selling at either one or three shillings a pound.

TOBACCO PRODUCTION AND INCOME ESTIMATES*

Number of workers . . .	In one year produce. . . number of plants	number of lbs.	One man lbs/yr	Income, @ 1s	3s
1 (Rolfe)	1,000		(250)	£12	£37.5
1 (Capps)	2,000	500	(500)	25	75
3 boys (1½ men)	3,000		(500)	25	75
4 men		2,800	(930)	46.5	139.5
6–7 men	3,000–4,000		(540)	27	81

*Based on data presented in Morgan, *American Slavery, American Freedom* (New York, 1975)

These estimates indicate that the amount of tobacco one man could produce ranged from 250 to 930 pounds a year, an understandable variation given that some planters undoubtedly worked harder than others, some years provided better growing weather, and that, as time passed, Virginians developed ways to turn out bigger crops. Even by John Rolfe's estimate, made fairly early and therefore somewhat low, a man selling 250 pounds at 1 shilling a pound would receive £12 sterling for the year. On the high side, the estimates show a gross of £140 sterling, given good prices. Indeed, one letter tells of a settler who made £200 sterling after the good harvest of 1619. Such windfalls were rare, but considering that an average agricultural worker in England made from 30 to 50 shillings a year (less than £3), even the lower estimates look good.

They look particularly good for another reason—namely, because they indicate what a planter might do working *alone.* In a society where servants, tenants, and apprentices were commonplace, Virginians quickly discovered that if they could get other people to work for them, there were handsome profits to be made.

Back to the basic questions. How did an Englishman get others to work for him? In effect, he simply hired them and made an agreement, a bond indicating what he gave in return for their service and for how long the agreement was to run. The terms varied from servant to servant but fell into several general classes. Most favorable, from the worker's point of view, was the position of tenant. A landowner had fields that needed working; the tenant agreed to work them for a certain period of time, usually from four to seven years. In return, the tenant kept half of what he produced. From the master's point of view, a servant served the purpose better, since he was paid only room and board, plus his passage from England. In return he gave his master everything he produced. And then there were the apprentices, usually called "Duty boys" in Virginia, since the ship *Duty* brought many of them over. Apprentices served for seven years, then another seven as tenants. Again the master's cost was only transportation over and maintenance once in Virginia.

Little in the way of higher mathematics is required to discover that if it cost a master about £10 to £12 sterling to bring over a servant—as it did—and that if that master obtained the labor of several such servants for seven years, or even for two or three, he stood fair to make a tidy fortune. In the good harvest of 1619 one master with six servants managed a profit of £1,000 sterling. That was unusual perhaps, but by no means impossible. And Sandys's headright policies unwittingly played into the hands of the fortune-makers: every servant imported meant another fifty acres of land that could be used for tobacco.

The opportunities were too much to resist. Virginians began bending every resource in the colony toward growing tobacco. The historian can now appreciate the significance of the governor's proclamation (page 8) that no hay should be used to "sweat" or cure tobacco: obviously, colonists were diverting hay from livestock that desperately needed it ("it robs the poor beasts of their fodder"), thus upsetting Virginia's economy. The scramble for profits extended even to the artisans whom Sandys sent over to diversify the colony's exports. The ironmongers deserted in short order, having "turned good honest Tobaccoemongers"; and of similar well-intentioned projects, the report came back to London that "nothinge is done in anie of them but all is vanished into smoke (that is to say into Tobaccoe)." The boom in Virginia was on.

Planters were not the only people trying to make a fortune. The settler who raised tobacco had to get it to market in Europe somehow, had to buy corn if he neglected to raise any himself, and looked to supply himself with as many of the comforts of life as could be had. Other men stood ready to deal with such planters, and they had a sharp eye to their own profit.

The company, of course, sought to provide supplies through the maga-

zine run by the Cape Merchant, Abraham Peirsey. And if we now return
to the Virginia assembly's order, quoted earlier, requiring Peirsey to
accept 3 shillings per pound for the "better sort" of tobacco, we can
begin to understand why the assembly was upset enough to pass the
regulation. Peirsey was charging exorbitant prices for his supplies. He
collected his fees in tobacco because there was virtually no currency in
Virginia. Tobacco had become the economic medium of exchange. If
Peirsey counted a pound of the better sort of tobacco as worth only 2
shillings instead of 3, that was as good as raising his prices by fifty
percent. As it happened, Peirsey charged two or three times the prices
set by the investors in London. Further, he compounded injury with
insult by failing to reimburse the company for their supplies that he sold.
Sandys and the other investors never saw a cent of the magazine's profits.

   Another hunt through the records indicates what Peirsey was doing
with his ill-gotten gain: he ploughed it back into the most attractive
investment of all, servants. We learn this not because Peirsey comes out
and says so, but because the census of 1625 lists him as keeping thirty-
nine servants, more than anyone else in the colony. At his death in 1628
he left behind him "the best Estate that was ever yett knowen in Virginia." When the company finally broke the magazine's monopoly in
1620, other investors moved in. They soon discovered that they could
make more money selling alcohol than the necessities of life. So the
Virginia boom enriched the merchants of "rotten Wynes" as well as the
planters of tobacco, and settlers went hungry, in part, because liquor
fetched a better return than food.

   Given these conditions in Virginia—given the basic social and economic structures deduced from the historical record—put yourself in the
place of an average tenant or servant. What would life be like for him
under these conditions? What were his chances for success?

   For servants, the prospect is bad indeed. First, they face the fierce
mortality rate. Chances are they will not survive the first seasoning
summer. Even if they do, their master is out to make a fortune by their
labor. Any servant, poor as he is to begin with, is in no position to protect
himself from abuse. In England the situation was different. Agricultural
workers usually offered their services once a year at hiring fairs. Since
their contracts lasted only a year, servants could switch to other employers if they became dissatisfied. But going to Virginia required the expense of a long voyage; masters would hire a person only if he signed
on for four to seven years. Once in Virginia, what could a servant do
if he became disillusioned? Go home? He had little enough money for
the voyage over, and likely even less to get back.

Duty boys, the children, were least in a position to improve their lot. The orphans Sandys hoped to favor by taking them off the London streets faced a hard life in Virginia. They were additionally threatened by a law the Virginia labor barons put through the assembly declaring that an apprentice who committed a crime during his service had to begin his term all over again. What constituted a crime, of course, was left up to the governor's council. One Duty boy, Richard Hatch, appeared before the council because he had commented, in a private house, on the recent execution of a settler, one Richard Cornish, for sodomy. Hatch had remarked "that in his consyence he thought that the said Cornishe was put to death wrongfully." For this offense he was to be "whipt from the forte to the gallows and from thence be whipt back againe, and be sett uppon the Pillory and there to loose one of his eares." Although Hatch had nearly completed his term of service—to Governor George Yeardly, who also sat on the council—he was ordered to begin his term anew.

Tenants would seem to have been better off, but they too were subject to the demand for labor. If an immigrant could pay his passage over but was unable to feed himself upon arrival, he had little choice but to hire himself out as a servant. And if his master died before his term was up, there was virtually always another master ready to jump in and claim him, legally or not, either as a personal servant or as a company tenant due in payment of a salary. When George Sandys, Sir Edwin's brother, finished his term as colony treasurer, he dragged his tenants with him even though they had become free men. "He maketh us serve him whether wee will or noe," complained one, "and how to helpe it we doe not knowe for hee beareth all the sway."

Even independent small planters faced the threat of servitude if their crops failed or if Indian attacks made owning a small, isolated plantation too dangerous. William Capps, the small planter who recorded one of the tobacco production estimates, described his own precarious situation vividly. His plantation threatened by Indians, Capps proposed that the governor's council outfit him with an expedition against the neighboring tribes. The council refused, and the indignant Capps angrily suggested what was going through the wealthy planters' minds. "Take away one of my men," he imagines them saying,

there's 2000 Plantes gone, thates 500 waight of Tobacco, yea and what shall this man doe, runne after the Indians? soft, I have perhaps 10, perhaps 15, perhaps 20 men and am able to secure my owne Plantacion; how will they doe that are fewer? let them first be crusht alitle, and then perhaps they will themselves make up the Nomber for their owne safetie. Theis I doubt are the Cogitacions of some of our worthier men.

AND SLAVERY?

This reconstruction of Virginia society, from the Duty boy at the bottom to the richer planters at the top, indicates that all along the line labor had become a valuable and desperately sought commodity. Settlers who were not in a position to protect themselves found that the economy put constant pressure on them. Their status as free men was always in danger of debasement: planters bought, sold, and traded servants without their consent, and on occasion they even used them as stakes in gambling games. There had been "many complaints," acknowledged John Rolfe, "against the Governors, Captaines, and Officers in Virginia: for buying and selling men and boies," something that "was held in England a thing most intolerable." One Englishman put the indignity quite succinctly: "My Master Atkins hath sold me for a £150 sterling like a damnd slave."

Indeed, quite a few of the ingredients of slavery are there: the feverish economic boom that sparked an insatiable demand for human labor, the mortality rate that encouraged survivors to become callous about human life, the servants who were being bought and sold, treated as property; treated, almost, as slaves. If we were looking, in the abstract, to construct a society where social and economic pressures combined to encourage the development of human slavery, boom-town Virginia would fit the model neatly. Yet the actual records do not quite confirm the hypothesis.

The first record of blacks being imported to Virginia was John Rolfe's offhand report in 1619 that "About the last of August came in a dutch man of warre that sold us twenty Negars." Sold, yes. But sold as slaves or as servants? Rolfe doesn't say. Historians have combed the sparse records of early Virginia, looking at court records, inventories, letters, wills, church records—anything that might shed light on the way blacks were treated. Before 1640, there is virtually nothing in the surviving records; before 1660, bits and pieces of evidence do indicate that some blacks were held as slaves for life, but some definitely as servants. Other blacks either were given their freedom or were able to purchase it. Only during the 1660s did the Virginia assembly begin to pass legislation that separated blacks from whites, that defined slavery, legally, as an institution. Blacks, in other words, lived with white Virginians for over forty

"**About the last of August** came in a dutch man of warre that sold us twenty Negars." So wrote John Rolfe in 1619. Yet the status of these and other early blacks remains unclear. Court records indicate that in the 1640s at least some blacks had been freed and were purchasing their own land. One black, Anthony Johnson, even owned his own slave. The illustration is by Howard Pyle, a popular nineteenth-century artist whose meticulous research made his scenes accurate in terms of costume and setting.

years before their status had become fully and legally debased. The facts in the records force us to turn the initial question around. If the 1620s with its boom economy was such an appropriate time for slavery to have developed, why *didn't* it?

Here, the talents of historians are stretched to their limits. They can expect no obvious explanations from contemporaries like John Rolfe, Captain Smith, or William Capps. The development of slavery was something that snuck up on Virginians. It was part of the "inner dynamic" of the society, as sociologists would say—hidden from the awareness of the social actors in the situation. Even the records left by the clerks of society are scant help. The best that can be done is intelligent conjecture, based on the kind of society that has been reconstructed.

Was it a matter of the simple availability of slaves? Perhaps. The African slave trade was still in its infancy, and even if Virginians wanted slaves, they may have found them hard to come by. During the time that Virginia was experiencing its boom of the 1620s, the West Indian islands like Barbadoes and St. Kitts were being settled. There, where the cultivation of sugar demanded even more intensive labor than tobacco, the demand for slaves was extremely high, and slavery developed more rapidly. If traders sailing from Africa could carry only so many slaves, and if the market for them were better in the Barbadoes than in Virginia, why sail all the way up to Chesapeake Bay? The slave traders may not have found the effort worth it. That is the conjecture of one historian, Richard Dunn.

Edmund Morgan has suggested another possibility, based on the continuing mortality rate in Virginia. Put yourself in the place of the planter searching for labor. You can buy either servants or slaves. Servants come cheaper than slaves, of course, but you only get to work them for seven years before they receive their freedom. Slaves are more expensive, but you get their labor for the rest of their lives, as well as the labor of any offspring. In the long run, the more expensive slave would have been the better buy. But in Virginia? Everyone is dying anyway. What are the chances that either servants or slaves are going to live for more than seven, five, even three years? The chances are not particularly good. Wouldn't it make more sense to pay less and buy servants, on the assumption that whoever is bought may die shortly anyway?

It is an ingenious conjecture, but it must remain that—for the present at least. No plantation records or letters have been found indicating that planters actually thought that way. Available evidence does suggest that the high death rate in Virginia began to drop only in the 1650s. If that were the case, it makes sense that only then, when slaves became a profitable commodity, would laws come to be passed formally establishing their chattel status. Whatever the reasons may have been, one thing seems clear: Slavery did not flourish markedly along with the boom of 1620.

Sometime between 1629 and 1630, the economic bubble popped. The price of tobacco plummeted from 3 shillings to 1 penny a pound. Virginians tried desperately to prop it up again, either by limiting production or by simple edict, but they did not succeed. Tobacco prices in the 1630s occasionally floated as high as sixpence, but more often they stayed at three. That meant planters still could make money, but the chance for a quick fortune had vanished—"into smoke," as Sandys or one of his disillusioned investors would no doubt have remarked. The Virginia Company's experiment in social reconstruction had failed, but the records of their investments, their wranglings, and the fortune-hunting survived them. Not all the records survived, by any means. Many of them were lost, many more burned with the capture of Richmond during the Civil War. But enough survived in Richmond, in London, in the estates of English lords and gentry to piece together the story of the early Virginians, rich and poor, and the social structure that bound them together. It is much to the credit of historians that the feverish world of the Chesapeake has not, like its cash crop, entirely vanished into smoke.

Additional Reading

The works of Captain John Smith make a delightful introduction to Virginia. Smith is one of those Elizabethans whose prose struts, bounces, jars, and jounces from one page to the next. His writings are conveniently gathered in Edward Arber and A. G. Bradley, eds., *The Travels and Works of Captain John Smith*, 2 vols. (Edinburgh, 1910). Although caution is necessary in reading Smith, much within these pages provides excellent source material for learning about early encounters between Europeans and native Americans. Henry Adams's attack on the Pocahontas story can be found in Charles Francis Adams, *Chapters of Erie and Other Essays* (Boston, 1871), while the best modern defense of the captain's veracity is Philip Barbour, *The Three Worlds of Captain John Smith* (London, 1964). A recent interpretation of white-Indian contact in the New World is Francis Jennings, *The Invasion of America* (Chapel Hill, N.C., 1975), a book that is deliberately provocative yet often convincing.

The reconstruction of boom-country Virginia described in this chapter depends heavily on the research presented in Edmund S. Morgan's *American Slavery, American Freedom* (New York, 1975). Morgan's account combines a lucid and engaging prose style with the imaginative and thorough research that is a model for the discipline. His book makes an excellent starting place for those wishing to learn more about seventeenth-century Virginia. It is only the high point, however, in a resurgence of interest by historians in the whole Chesapeake Bay region. A useful starting point for sorting out these materials is Thad W. Tate and David L. Ammerman, eds., *The Chesapeake in the Seventeenth Century: Essays on Anglo-American Society* (Chapel Hill, N.C., 1979), in particular the bibliographical essay by Tate. Darrett B. and Anita Rutman, *A Place in Time: Middlesex County, Virginia, 1650–1750* (New York, 1984) continues Virginia's social history, using the kind of microcosmic techniques we will be examining, for New England, in the following chapter.

Those readers wishing to explore primary source material on early Virginia will probably find that contemporary narratives like Smith's provide the best introduction. Many are available in Philip Barbour, ed., *The Jamestown Voyages Under the First Charter, 1606–1609*, 2 vols. (Cambridge, 1969) and in the older but more complete Alexander Brown, *The Genesis of the United States* (Boston, 1890). Additional details about the starving time of 1609–1610 can be found in George Percy, "A Trewe Relacyon of the Procedinges and Occurentes of Momente . . ." in *Tyler's Quarterly Historical and Genealogical Magazine*, II (1922),

260–282. Much rougher going than these collections are the official records of the Virginia Company and the colony. As we have seen, however, they provide vital evidence. Interested readers will most profit if they bring to their reading a definite idea of the sorts of facts and the specific questions they wish to answer. For the early years, see Alexander Brown's collection; the period from 1619–1624 is covered in Susan Kingsbury, ed., *The Records of the Virginia Company of London*, 4 vols. (Washington, D.C., 1906–1935). For the later period, surviving records can be found in H. R. McIlwaine, ed., *Minutes of the Council and General Court of Colonial Virginia* (Richmond, Va., 1924) and William W. Hening, *The Statutes at Large: Being a Collection of All the Laws of Virginia* (Richmond, Va., 1809–1823).

The question of why slavery did not develop during the first tobacco boom is discussed in Morgan's *American Slavery, American Freedom.* A more wide-ranging treatment of the slavery question is available in Winthrop Jordan's excellent *White Over Black: American Attitudes Toward the Negro, 1550–1812* (Chapel Hill, N.C., 1968). For more detailed though opposing discussions of how the institution of slavery evolved in Virginia, see Oscar and Mary F. Handlin, "Origins of the Southern Labor System," in *William and Mary Quarterly*, 3rd Series, VII (1950), 199–222; Carl N. Degler, "Slavery and the Genesis of American Race Prejudice," *Comparative Studies in Society and History,* II (1959), 49–66; and Paul C. Palmer, "Servant Into Slave: The Evolution of the Legal Status of the Negro Laborer in Colonial Virginia," *South Atlantic Quarterly,* LXV (1966), 355–370.

The Visible and Invisible Worlds of Salem

Historians, we have seen, are in the business of reconstruction. Seventeenth-century Virginia, with its world of slaves, indentured servants, small planters, and tobacco barons, had to be built anew, not just lifted intact from the record. It follows, then, that if historians are builders, they must decide at the outset on the scale of their projects. How much ground should be covered? A year? Fifty years? Several centuries? How will the subject matter be defined or limited? The story of slavery's arrival in Virginia might be ranked as a moderately large topic. It spans some sixty years, involves thousands of immigrants and an entire colony. Furthermore, it is large as much because of its content as its reach over time and space. The genesis of slavery surely ranks as a central strand of the American experience; to understand it adequately requires more research and discipline than, for instance, the history of American hats over a similar time span. The lure of topics both broad and significant is undeniable, and there have always been historians willing to pull on their seven-league boots, from Edward Gibbon and his *Decline and Fall of the Roman Empire,* to Ariel and Will Durant with their *Story of Civilization.*

The great equalizer of such grand plans is the twenty-four hour day. Historians have only a limited amount of time, and the hours, they sadly discover, are not expandable. Obviously, the more years that are covered, the less time there is available to research the events in each one.

Conversely, the narrower the area of research, the more it is possible to become immersed in the details of a period. Relationships and connections can be explored that would have gone unnoticed without the benefit of a microscopic focus. Of course, small-scale history continually runs the risk of becoming obscure and pedantic. But a keen mind working on a small area will yield results whose implications go beyond the subject matter's original boundaries. By understanding what has taken place on a small patch of ground, the historian can begin to see more clearly the structure and dynamics of the larger world around it.

Salem Village in 1692 is a microcosm familiar to most students of American history. That was the place and the time witchcraft came to New England with a vengeance, dominating the life of the village for ten months. Because the witchcraft episode exhibited well-defined boundaries in both time and space, it provides an excellent illustration of the way a traditional and oft-told story may be transformed by the intensive research techniques of small-scale history. Traditionally, the outbreak of witchcraft at Salem has been viewed as an incident divorced from the cause-and-effect sequences of everyday village life. Even to label the events as an "outbreak" suggests that they are best viewed as an epidemic, alien to the normal functions of the community. The "germs" of bewitchment break out suddenly and inexplicably—imposed, as it were, by some invading disease pool. Only a few townspeople are first afflicted; then the contagion spreads through the village and runs its destructive course before subsiding.

Recently, however, historians have studied the traumatic experiences of 1692 in greater detail. In so doing they have created a more sophisticated model of the mental world behind the Salem outbreaks. They have also suggested ways in which the witchcraft episode was integrally connected with the more mundane events of village life. The techniques of small-scale history, in other words, have provided a compelling psychological and social context for the events of 1692.

BEWITCHMENT AT SALEM VILLAGE

Most accounts of the trouble at Salem begin with the kitchen of the village's minister, Samuel Parris. There in the early months of 1692, a group of adolescent girls gathered to attempt a bit of crystal-ball reading. The young women sought to discover what sort of men their future husbands might be, a subject of natural enough interest to them. Lacking a crystal ball, they used the next available substitute, the white of a raw egg suspended in a glass of water. The young women were aided in their efforts by a West Indian slave then living with the Parrises, a woman named Tituba. At some point during the seances, things went sour. One of the women thought she detected "a specter in the likeness of a coffin" in the crystal ball—hardly an auspicious omen—and soon the more susceptible among them began behaving in a strange manner.

Detailed accounts of the earliest fits are scarce, but the "strange and unusual" actions noted did include "getting into Holes, and creeping under Chairs and Stools, [using] sundry odd Postures and Antick Gestures, uttering foolish ridiculous Speeches, which neither they themselves nor any others could make sense of." The Reverend Parris was at a loss to understand the afflictions, but not so Tituba. She and her husband John Indian baked a "witch cake" made of rye meal and urine given them by the possessed women. The cake was fed to a dog on the supposition that the charm would reveal whether any bewitchment was taking place (the theory confirmed, presumably, if the dog suffered torments similar to those of the afflicted women).

The charm never had a chance to achieve its result because Samuel Parris got wind of the experiment and at last discovered what had been going on for so long in his kitchen. He and other adults in the community had been greatly puzzled by the young women's strange behavior; now they began viewing the illnesses not as the result of disease, but of crime. For seventeenth-century New Englanders, witchcraft was conceived in criminal terms. If the adolescents were being tormented, it was necessary to discover who was responsible. The hunt for witches began.

The afflicted women were the keys to determining who was a witch. Although some of their behavior seemed merely eccentric (Abigail Williams came running through the house yelling "Whish! Whish! Whish!" arms apart as if she were flying), other incidents were more sinister. The possessed claimed to see specters, invisible to others, who pinched, kicked, and choked them. Victims writhed on the floor, screamed piteously, or carried on arguments with their invisible tormentors. Deodat Lawson, a former minister of the village who visited Salem during the crisis, was horrified to observe Mary Walcott convulsed before him— being bitten, she claimed, by a specter. Lawson could not see the specter but noted with mounting astonishment the teethmarks that appeared on Mary Walcott's arm.

After village leaders pressed the tormented women to identify the specters, they at last provided three names: Sarah Good and Sarah Osbourne, two old women unpopular in the village, and Tituba herself. Village officials arrested all three for examination, and during the questioning Tituba confessed. There were four women and a man, she said, who were causing the trouble. Good and Osbourne were among them. "They hurt the children," she testified. "And they lay all upon me and they tell me if I will not hurt the children, they will hurt me." The tale continued, complete with apparitions of black and red rats, a yellow dog with a head like a woman, "a thing all over hairy, all the face hairy, and a long nose," and midnight rides to witches' meetings where plans were being laid to attack Salem.

If a witch confessed, the matter of identification was simple enough. If he or she refused to admit guilt, as many of the accused did, magistrates had to look for corroborating proof. Physical evidence, such as voodoo dolls and pins found among the suspect's possessions, was the most convincing. There might be other signs, too. If the devil made a pact with someone, he supposedly required a physical mark of allegiance, and thus created a "witch's tit," where either he or his "familiar," a likeness in animal form, might suck.* Prisoners in the Salem trials were often examined to see if they had any abnormal marks on their bodies.

Aside from physical signs, villagers looked for evidence of a cause-and-effect relationship between a witch's act of malice and consequent suffering on the part of the victim. Sarah Gadge, for instance, testified that two years earlier she had refused Sarah Good lodging for the night. According to Gadge, Good "fell to muttering and scolding extreamly and so told said Gadge if she would not let her in she should give her something . . . and the next morning after to said Deponents best remembrance one of the said Gadges Cowes Died in a Sudden terrible and Strange unusuall maner. . . ." In an attempt to confirm the connection between malice and torment, the magistrates kept the afflicted women in the courtroom to observe their behavior. Sure enough, when an accused witch shifted position while on the witness stand, the young women would often be afflicted in the same way, as if tormented by the action. Rebecca Nurse, another accused witch, "held her neck on one side and Eliz. Hubbard (one of the sufferers) had her neck set in that posture whereupon another patient Abigail Williams, cryed out, set up Goody Nursis head, the maid's neck will be broke. And when some set up Nurse's head Aaron Way observed that Betty Hubbards was immediately righted."**

*Hence the expression still used today, "Cold as a witch's tit." Tradition had it that the mark, formed of unnatural flesh, would be cold and lifeless.
**"Goody" was short for "Goodwife," a term used for most married women. Husbands were addressed as Goodman. The terms *Mr.* and *Mrs.* were reserved for those of higher social standing.

The magistrates also considered what they called "spectral evidence," at once the most damning and dangerous kind of proof. Spectral evidence involved the visions of specters—likenesses of the witches —that victims reported seeing during their torments. The problem was that spectral evidence could not be corroborated by others; generally only the victim saw the shape of her tormentor. Furthermore, some people argued that the devil might assume the shape of an innocent person. What better way for him to spread confusion among the faithful? All the same, the magistrates were inclined to believe that Satan could not use a shape without that person's permission—not very often, at any rate—so they tended to accept spectral evidence in their pretrial examinations.

During the first seventy years of settlement in New England, few witchcraft cases had come before the courts. Those that had were dispatched quickly, and calm soon returned. Salem proved different. In the first place, Tituba had described several other witches and a wizard, though she claimed she was unable to identify them personally. The villagers felt they could not rest while other witches remained at large. Furthermore, the young women continued to name names—and now not just outcasts but respectable church members from the community. The new suspects joined Tituba, Sarah Gadge, and Sarah Osbourne in jail. By the end of April the hunt had led to no less a personage than the Reverend George Burroughs, a former minister of the village living in Maine. Constables marched to Maine, fetched him back, and threw him in jail.

Throughout the spring of 1692, no trials of the accused had been held, for the simple reason that Massachusetts was without legal government. In 1684 the Crown had revoked the colony's original charter and set up his own arbitrary government, but in 1689, William of Orange forced James to flee England. In the years following, Massachusetts continually attempted to have its original charter restored. Until it succeeded, however, court cases had been brought to a standstill. Finally in May 1692 the new governor, Sir William Phips, arrived with a charter and promptly established a special court of Oyer and Terminer to deal with the witchcraft cases.

On June 2 the court heard its first case, that of tavernkeeper Bridget Bishop. Bishop was quickly convicted and eight days later, hung from a scaffold on a hill just outside Salem Town. The site came to be known as Witch's Hill—with good reason, since on June 29 the court again met and convicted five more women. One of them, Rebecca Nurse, had been found innocent, but the court's Chief Justice, William Stoughton, disapproved the verdict and convinced the jurors to change their minds. On July 19 Goody Nurse joined the other four women on the scaffold, staunch churchwoman that she was, praying for the judges' souls as well as her own. Sarah Good remained defiant to the end. "I am no more a witch than you are a wizard," she told the attending minister, "and if you take away my life, God will give you blood to drink."

Still the accusations continued; still the court sat. As the net was cast wider, more and more accused were forced to work out their response to the crisis. A few, most of them wealthy, went into hiding until the furor subsided. Giles Cory, a farmer whose wife Martha was executed as a witch, refused even to plead innocent or guilty, in effect denying the court's right to try him. The penalty for such a refusal was the *peine fort et dure,* in which the victim was placed between two boards and heavy stones placed on him until he agreed to plead. On September 19, Cory was slowly crushed to death, stubborn to the end. His last words were said to be, "More weight."

Some of the accused admitted guilt, the most satisfactory solution for the magistrates. Puritans could be a remarkably forgiving people. They were not interested in punishment for its own sake. If a lawbreaker gave evidence of sincere regret for his misdeeds, Puritan courts would often reduce or suspend his sentence. So it was in the witchcraft trials at Salem, but the policy had unforeseen consequences. Those who were wrongly accused quickly realized that if they did *not* confess, they were likely to be hanged. If they did confess, they could escape death, but would have to demonstrate their sincerity by providing details of their misdeeds and names of other participants. The temptation must have been great to confess and, in so doing, to implicate other innocent people.

Given such pressures, the web of accusations continued to grow. August produced six more trials and five hangings. Elizabeth Proctor, the wife of another tavernkeeper, received a reprieve because she was pregnant, the court being unwilling to sacrifice the life of an innocent child. Her husband John was not spared. September saw another eight victims hung with no end in sight. Over a hundred suspected witches remained in jail.

Pressure to stop the trials had been building, however. One member of the court, Nathaniel Saltonstall, resigned in protest after the first execution. More important, the ministers of the province were becoming uneasy. They had supported the trials publicly but in private had written letters cautioning the magistrates in their use of evidence. Finally in early October Increase Mather, one of the most respected divines in the province, published a sermon signed by fourteen other pastors which strongly condemned the use of spectral evidence. Mather argued that to convict on the basis of a specter, which everyone agreed was the devil's creation, in effect took Satan at his own word. That, in Mather's view, risked disaster. "It were better that ten suspected witches should escape, than that one innocent person should be condemned," he concluded.

Mather's sermon convinced Governor Phips that the trials had gone too far. He forbade any more arrests and dismissed the court of Oyer and Terminer. The following January a new court met to dispose of the remaining cases, but this time the great majority of defendants were acquitted. Phips immediately granted a reprieve to the three women who were convicted and in April released the remaining prisoners. Satan's controversy with Salem was finished.

That, in outline, is the witchcraft story as it has come down to us for so many years. Rightly or wrongly, it is a story that has become an indelible part of American history. The startling fits of possession, the drama of the court examinations, the eloquent pleas of the innocent condemned—all these make for a superb drama that casts into shadow the rest of Salem's more pedestrian history.

Indeed, the episode is unrepresentative. Witchcraft epidemics were not a serious problem in New England; even less of one in other American colonies. Such persecutions were much more common in old England and Europe, where they had reached frightening proportions. The death of 20 people at Salem is sobering, but the magnitude of the event diminishes considerably alongside the 900 witches burned in the city of Bamberg during the first half of the seventeenth century or the 5,000 over a similar period in the province of Alsace. Furthermore, it can be safely said that the witchcraft affair had no lasting effect on the political or religious history of America, or even of Massachusetts.

Now, a curious thing has resulted from this illumination of a single, isolated episode. Again and again, the story of Salem Village has been told, quite naturally, as a drama complete unto itself. The workaday history that preceded and followed the trials—the petty town bickerings, the arguments over land and ministers, the village's economic patterns —all this has been largely passed over. Yet the disturbances at Salem did not occur in a vacuum. They may indeed have constituted an epidemic but not the sort caused by some mysterious germ pool brought into the village over the rutted roads from Boston. So the historian's first task is to take the major strands of the witchcraft affair and see how they are woven into the larger fabric of Salem society. Salem Village is small enough so that virtually every one of its residents can be identified. We can find out who owned what land, the amount of taxes each resident paid, what sermons people listened to on Sundays. In so doing, a richer, far more intriguing picture of Salem Village life begins to emerge.

THE INVISIBLE SALEM

Paradoxically, the most obvious facet of Salem life that the historian must recreate is also the most insubstantial: what ministers of the period would have called the "invisible world." Demons, familiars, and witches all shaped the world of seventeenth-century New England, just as they shaped the worlds of Britain and Europe. For Salem Villagers, Satan was a living, supernatural being who could and did appear to people, either in his own form or that of another. He could converse with mortals, bargain with them, even enter into agreements with them. The witches who submitted to such devilish compacts bargained their souls in return for special powers or favors: money and good fortune, perhaps, or the ability to revenge themselves on others.

The outlines of such beliefs are easily enough sketched, but they convey the emotions of witchcraft about as successfully as a recital of the Apostle's Creed conveys the fire of the Christian faith. Historians who do not believe in a personal, witch-covenanting devil are entering a psychological world in which they are outsiders. They may think it a simple matter to understand how a Salem Villager would behave, but people who hold beliefs foreign to our own do not often act the way that we think they should. Over the years, historians of the Salem incident have insufficiently appreciated that fact.

One of the first people to review Salem's troubles was Thomas Hutchinson, who in 1750 published a history of New England's early days. Hutchinson did not believe in witchcraft; fewer and fewer educated people did as the eighteenth century progressed. Therefore he faced an obvious historical question. If the devil was not behind the Salem witch trials, who or what was? The question centered on motivation. The possessed women claimed they were being afflicted by witches, as the historical record made clear. Yet, reasoned Hutchinson, if the devil never actually covenanted with anyone, how were the young women's actions to be explained? Some of Hutchinson's contemporaries argued that the bewitched were suffering from "bodily disorders which affected their imaginations." He disagreed. "A little attention must force conviction that the whole was a scene of fraud and imposture, begun by young girls, who at first perhaps thought of nothing more than being pitied and indulged, and continued by adult persons who were afraid of being accused themselves." Charles Upham, a minister who published a two-volume study of the episode in 1867, was equally hard on the young women. "There has seldom been better acting in a theatre than displayed in the presence of the astonished and horror-stricken rulers," he concluded tartly.

The view that the possessed were shamming has persisted well into the twentieth century, and indeed, the historical record does supply some evidence to substantiate this hypothesis. Several defenders of the accused witches reported that on occasion the accusers seemed to be caught in their own jesting. One adolescent who cried out that she saw the specter of Elizabeth Proctor was immediately challenged by several spectators. The woman replied, "She [Elizabeth Proctor] did it for sport; they must have sport." Then in April Mary Warren, another of the young women, recovered from her fits and began to claim "that the afflicted persons did but dissemble"—that is, they were shamming. For the first time, the possessed began seeing Mary's specter, and the court quickly summoned her on suspicion of witchcraft. The tables had been turned.

On the witness stand, Mary again fell into a fit "that she did neither see nor hear nor speak." The examination record continues:

> Afterwards she started up, and said I will speak and cryed out, Oh! I am sorry for it, I am sorry for it, and wringed her hands, and fell a little while into a fit again and then came to speak, but immediately her teeth were set, and then she fell into a violent fit and cryed out, oh Lord help me! Oh Good Lord Save me!
>
> And then afterwards cryed again, I will tell I will tell and then fell into a dead fit againe.
>
> And afterwards cryed I will tell, they did, they did they did and then fell into a violent fit again.
>
> After a little recovery she cryed I will tell they brought me to it and then fell into a fit again which fits continueing she was ordered to be had out. . . .

The scene is tantalizing. It appears as if Mary Warren is about to confess, when pressure from the other girls forces her back to her former role as one of the afflicted. In the following months the magistrates questioned Mary repeatedly, with the result that her fits returned and she again joined in the accusations. Such evidence suggests that the girls may well have been acting.

Yet such a theory leaves certain points unexplained. If the girls were only acting, what are we to make of the many other witnesses who testified to deviltry? One nearby villager, Richard Comans, reported seeing Bridget Bishop's specter in his bedroom. Bishop lay upon his breast, he reported, and "so oppressed" him that "he could not speak nor stur, noe not so much as to awake his wife" sleeping next to him. Comans and others who testified were not close friends of the girls; they were obviously not conspiring with each other. How does the historian explain their actions?

Even some of the afflicted women's behavior is difficult to explain as conscious fraud. It is easy enough to imagine counterfeiting certain fits: being flown through the room crying "whish, whish"; being struck dumb. Yet other behavior was truly sobering. Being pinched, pummeled, nearly choked to death; bodies being twisted into unnatural postures for long periods of time; tongues thrust upward until they almost touched the nose; fits so violent several grown men were required to restrain the victims. Is it conceivable that all this could be counterfeited—convincingly, realistically—day after day for five or six months?

Even innocent victims of the accusations were astounded by such behavior. Rebecca Nurse on the witness stand could only look in astonishment at the "lamentable fits" she was accused of causing. "Do you think these [women] suffer voluntary or involuntary?" asked John Hathorne, one of the examining magistrates. "I cannot tell," replied Goody Nurse hesitantly. Hathorne pressed his advantage. He knew the fits looked as genuine to Nurse as they did to everyone else. "That is strange," he replied. "Everyone can judge."

> NURSE: I must be silent.
> HATHORNE: They accuse you of hurting them, and if you think it is not unwillingly but by designe, you must look upon them as murderers.
> NURSE: I cannot tell what to think of it.

Hathorne pressed others who were accused with similar results. What ails the girls, if not your torments? "I do not know." Do you think they are bewitched? "I cannot tell." What do you think *does* ail them? "There is more than ordinary. . . ."

More than ordinary. Modern historians may accept that supposition without necessarily supposing, with Hathorne, the presence of the preternatural. Psychiatric research has long established what we now take almost for granted: that people may act for reasons they themselves do not fully understand, from motives buried deep within the unconscious. Even more: that emotional problems may be the subconscious cause of apparently physical disorders. The rationalistic psychologies of Thomas

Hutchinson and Charles Upham led them to reject any middle-ground explanations of motivation. The Salem women had not really been tormented by witches, Hutchinson and Upham reasoned; therefore they must have been acting voluntarily, consciously. But if we fully appreciate the mental attitudes that accompanied the belief in devils and witches, it is possible to understand the Salem episode, not as a game of fraud gone out of control, but as a study in abnormal psychology on a community-wide scale.

To understand why, turn to the testimony taken by the magistrates in their preliminary hearings. Here are the affidavits, the warrants for arrest, the cross-examinations—all the alleged incidents of witchcraft. Significantly, the incidents are not clustered around the pivotal year of 1692; they range over a broad period of time. "About four years agoe," an affadavit will begin; or "about six or seven years past"; "about five years sence"; "about twenty fower years ago. . . ." The record book, in other words, has acted as a magnet, drawing out for the historian stories that normally would never have been included in the record. It demonstrates just how deeply superstition ran in Salem, not just in 1692, but day in, day out. People were always taking note of strange incidents, wondering at remarkable coincidences, and seeing ominous signs.

To modern eyes, the signs often seem inconsequential. Mary Easty complains to Sam Smith that his conversation is "rude" and that he may "rue it here after." As Smith is going home that night he receives "a little blow on my shoulder with I know not what and the stone wall rattled very much." Easty at work, he suspects. Martha Carrier argues with Benjamin Abbott about land he has bought, telling him he "should Repent of it afore seven years come to an end." Abbott is soon afflicted with an infected foot and running sores. His wife notes that some cattle die strangely, others "come out of the woods with their tongues hanging out of their mouthes in a strange and affrighting manner . . . which we can give noe account of the reason of, unless it should be the effects of Martha Carrier threatenings." There are the bedside visions like Richard Comans's ("sometime about eight years since") or demon dogs, black and white, chasing men along the road, then disappearing into the ground. Lights in the night. Unaccountable illnesses. The New England villager's world was filled with what he called "remarkable providences." Most of them, to be sure, were the workings of a just and almighty God, but some were accomplished at the behest of Satan.

Follow the consequences of this attitude a step further. If Salem villagers believed that the devil's magic really could bestow power, might not a few people try to make use of it? Such is the suggestion of historian

Chadwick Hansen, who argues that some villagers did practice witchcraft. We have already seen one instance of magical practice, the witch
cake. Tituba, who baked it, confessed to being a witch. Even if her
dramatic tales of supernatural meetings were embellishments to please
the magistrates, her habitual sessions with the girls and her acquaintance
with West Indian voodoo demonstrate a definite involvement with
magic. The examination records also place Bridget Bishop under suspicion. As early as 1680 she had been unsuccessfully taken to court on the
charge of witchcraft. Ever since she carried that reputation. In 1692 her
own husband accused her of using the black arts, and even more damning, two laborers testified that when they dismantled a basement wall in
her old house they found several rag puppets with headless pins stuck
in them, telltales of a witch at work.

Other villagers appear to have toyed with witchcraft even if they did
not embrace it outright. Questioning of George Burroughs, the village's
former minister, revealed some unusual and disturbing facts. When
pressed, Burroughs admitted that only one of his children was baptized,
despite the common Puritan custom of having children baptized as soon
as was practicable after birth. When asked for the date of the last time
he had taken communion, Burroughs said it "was so long since he could
not tell."

Burroughs was short, compact, and extremely strong for his size. So
strong, in fact, that he was reputed to have hefted large barrels of
molasses and held a heavy rifle at arm's length by inserting his fingers
in the barrel. Since witches were said to possess preternatural strength,
this was damning evidence indeed. The historian who examines the
affidavits will quickly notice that virtually all of them report what Burroughs *said* he could do, not what witnesses actually saw. Yet the testimony suggests a good deal. Burroughs, being quite short, may have
been sensitive about his height and used his reputation for strength to
impress acquaintances. So too he may have used magic. Testimony reveals that the minister bragged of his uncanny mind-reading abilities,
often startling his wife by telling her "he knew what [she and her
friends] said when he was abroad"—that is, away from the house. Perhaps Burroughs was innocent of witchcraft. But in a world where people readily believed such claims, boasting of uncommon powers was a
dangerous business. It apparently cost Burroughs his life.

If the climate of superstition encouraged some villagers to take up
witchcraft, it affected the supposed victims of bewitchment in equally
palpable ways. The fear that gripped susceptible subjects certainly must
have been extraordinary. Here were specters of the devil, intent on

torment or even murder, and locked doors were no protection. One gauge of the magnitude of such fear may be found in cross-cultural comparisions. Anthropologists who have examined witchcraft in entirely different contexts note that bewitchment can be traumatic enough to lead to death. An Australian aborigine who discovers himself bewitched will

> stand aghast. . . . His cheeks blanch and his eyes become glassy. . . . He attempts to shriek but usually the sound chokes in his throat, and all that one might see is froth at his mouth. His body begins to tremble and the muscles twist involuntarily. He sways backwards and falls to the ground, and after a short time appears to be in a swoon; but soon after he writhes as if in mortal agony. . . .

Afterwards the victim refuses to eat, loses all interest in life, and dies. As might be expected, attitude plays a paramount role in the bewitchment. One physician found that he could save similar victims of sorcery in Hawaii by giving them methylene blue tablets. The tablets colored the victims' urine and thus convinced them that a successful counter-charm had been administered. Although there are no well-documented cases of bewitchment death in Salem, the anthropological studies indicate the remarkable depth of reaction possible in a community that believes in its own magic.*

It is even more enlightening to compare the behavior of the bewitched with the neurotic syndrome psychologists refer to as conversion hysteria. A neurosis is a disorder of behavior that functions to avoid or deflect intolerable anxiety. Normally, an anxious person deals with his or her emotion through conscious action or thought. If the ordinary means of coping fail, however, the unconscious takes over. Hysterical patients will convert their mental worries into physical symptoms such as blindness, paralysis of various parts of the body, choking, fainting, or attacks of pain. These symptoms, it should be stressed, cannot be traced to organic causes. There is nothing wrong with the nervous system during an attack of paralysis, or with the optic nerve in a case of blindness. Physical disabilities are mentally induced. Such hysterical attacks often occur in patterns that bear striking resemblance to some of the Salem afflictions.

---

*The records hint that a few bewitchment deaths may have occurred, however. Daniel Wilkins apparently believed that John Willard was a witch and meant him no good. Wilkins sickened and some of the afflicted girls were summoned to his bedside where they claimed that they saw Willard's specter afflicting him. The doctor would not touch the case, claiming it "preternatural." Shortly after, Wilkins died.

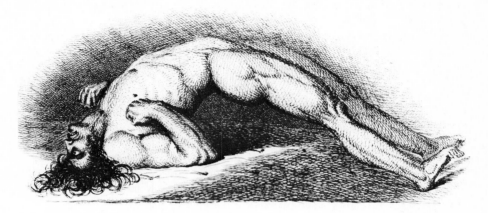

A classical hysterical convulsion, the *arc de cercle,* took the form shown in this nineteenth-century drawing.

Pierre Janet, the French physician who wrote the classic *Major Symptoms of Hysteria* (1907), reported that a characteristic hysterical fit begins with a pain or strange sensation in some part of the body, often the lower abdomen. From there, he explained, it

> seems to ascend and to spread to other organs. For instance, it often spreads to the epigastrium [the region lying over the stomach], to the breasts, then to the throat. There it assumes rather an interesting form, which was for a very long time considered as quite characteristic of hysteria. The patient has the sensation of too big an object as it were, a ball rising in her throat and choking her.

Most of us have probably experienced a mild form of the last symptom —a proverbial "lump in the throat" that comes in times of stress. The hysteric's lump, or *globus hystericus,* is more extreme, as are the accompanying convulsions: "the head is agitated in one direction or another, the eyes closed, or open with an expression of terror, the mouth distorted." Often the patient will form what was known as the *arc de cercle,* head thrown back, abdomen raised up, body arched in a backward arc.

Compare those symptoms with the ones manifested by the witching victims. Samuel Willard, a Boston minister, described with particular care the fit of Elizabeth Knapp, an adolescent who had come under his care in 1671:

In the evening, a little before she went to bed, sitting by the fire she cried out, "Oh! My legs!" and clapped her hand on them; immediately, "Oh! My breast!" and removed her hands thither; and forthwith, "Oh! I am strangled!" and put her hands on her throat.

The fits continued, Willard wrote, "violent in body motions, leapings, strainings and strange agitations, scarce to be held in bound by the strength of three or four." During the Salem trials Elizabeth Brown's fit was described in similar fashion:

When [the witch's specter] did come it was as birds pecking her legs or pricking her with the motion of thayr wings and then it would rize up into her stamak with pricking pain as nayls and pins of which she did bitterly complayn and cry out like a woman in travail and after that it would rise to her throat in a bunch like a pullets egg and then she would tern back her head and say witch you shant choak me.

Similar symptoms are reported throughout the trial records. Choking is unusually common; there are cases of *arc de cercle;* and the hysteric's ability to induce bruises or welts on the skin may well explain some of the "teeth" marks and other signs of tormentors that so astonished the Salem authorities.

The diagnosis of hysteria certainly helps resolve the historical debate over the afflicted girls' motivation. Adolescents, especially in the presence of Tituba, might very well have succumbed to the suggestion of bewitchment. The fits they experienced were very likely genuine, born of anxiety over a magic that threatened to overpower them. The diagnosis also explains many of the adult fits experienced by those who were convinced that their neighbors were conjuring against them. This is not to say that there was no acting at all; indeed, hysterics are notably suggestible, and no doubt the young women shaped their performances, at least instinctively, to the expectations of the community. "Differences between malingerers and hysterics are not absolute," notes one modern psychiatry text, "and we often find many hysterical traits in malingerers and some near-conscious play acting in the hysterical patient." We will probably never know for sure how much the behavior of the possessed was play acting, but it seems clear that in a world where witches were reputed to possess the powers of life and death and where preternatural occurrences were an everyday affair, Abigail Williams, Mary Warren, and the other girls suffered torments that were very real indeed.

THE VISIBLE SALEM

So far, our reconstruction has dealt with only one aspect of the microcosm that was Salem in 1692—its invisible world. The area is a natural one to examine because it helps answer the central question of why the actors in the drama behaved the way they did. It would be tempting, having made the diagnosis of conversion hysteria, to suppose

A hysterical convulsive attack of one of the patients in Salpêtrière Hospital during the nineteenth century. J. M. Charcot, the physician in charge of the clinic, spent much of his time studying the disorder. Note the crossed legs, similar to some of the Salem girls' fits.

that we had pretty well explained the Salem trials. There is the natural
satisfaction of placing the symptoms of the twentieth-century hysteric
next to those of the seventeenth-century bewitched and seeing them
match. Further correlations obtained from the primary sources make
the explanation a convincing one. Yet it takes only a moment's reflection to see that, by narrowing the inquiry to the motivations of the
possessed, we have left many other facets of the Salem episode unexplored.

In the first place, hysteria as a cause deals with the Salem trials on a
personal rather than a social level. Hysteria is, after all, a disorder that
affects individuals. In Salem it spread far enough to be labelled mass
hysteria, but even that is less a social explanation than a personal one
writ large. Granting for the moment that the afflicted really did make
their accusations out of hysterical delusion, there are the accused themselves to consider—some 150 of them all told. Why were those particular people singled out? A few may have been practicing witchcraft,
but the majority were innocent. Is there any common bond among the
150 that would explain why they, and not others, were accused? Only
after we have examined their social identities can we answer that question.

Another indication that we need to examine the social context of
Salem Village is the nature of hysteria itself. Hysterics are notably suggestible: sensitive to the influence of their environment. Nineteenth-
century patients who were kept in insane asylums along with epileptics,
for example, began having seizures that mimicked those suffered by
the epileptics. If hysterics, then, are especially influenced by the behavior of those around them, it seems logical to assume that the possessed
at Salem might have been influenced by the expectations of the adult
community. Scattered testimony in the court record suggests that
sometimes when the young women saw specters whom they could not
identify, adults suggested names. "Was it Goody Cloyse? Was it
Rebecca Nurse?" If such conditions were operating, they confirm the
need to move beyond strictly personal motivations to the social setting
of the community.

In doing so, a logical first step would be to look for correlations:
characteristics common to groups that might explain their behavior. Are
the accusers all church members and the accused non-church members?
Are the accusers wealthy and respectable while the accused are poor and
disreputable? The historian assembles the data, patiently shuffles them
around, and looks for match-ups.

Take the two social characteristics already mentioned, church membership and wealth. Historians can compile lists from the trial records of both the accusers and the accused. With those lists in hand, they can begin checking the church records to discover which people on each list were church members. Or they will search tax records to see whose tax rates were highest and thus which villagers were wealthiest. Records of land transactions are recorded, indicating which villagers owned the most land. Inventories of personal property are made when a member of the community dies, so at least historians have some record of an individual's assets at his death, if not in 1692. Other records may mention a trade or occupation, which will give a clue to relative wealth or social status.

If you make such calculations for the Salem region, you will quickly find yourself at a dead end, a spot altogether too familiar to practicing historians. True, the first few accused witches were not church members, but soon enough the faithful found themselves in jail along with non-church members. A similar case holds for wealth: although Tituba, Sarah Good, and Sarah Osbourne were relatively poor, merchants and wealthy farmers were accused as the epidemic spread. The correlations fail to check.

This was roughly the point that had been reached by two historians, Paul Boyer and Stephen Nissenbaum, when they were inspired, in effect, to take literally the advice about going back to the drawing board. More than a hundred years earlier Charles Upham had made a detailed map of Salem for his own study of the witchcraft episode. Upham examined the old town records, paced the actual sites of old houses, and established to the best of his knowledge the residences of a large majority of Salem Villagers. Boyer and Nissenbaum took their list of accuser and accused and noted the location of each village resident on the map.* The results were striking, as can be seen from the map, on the next page.

Of the fourteen accused witches living in the village, twelve lived in the eastern section. Of the thirty-two adult villagers who testified against the accused, thirty lived in the western section. "In other words," concluded Boyer and Nissenbaum, "the alleged witches and those who accused them resided on opposite sides of the Village." Furthermore, of

---

*Since many of the so-called witches and their accusers came from surrounding towns, only those from the village and from the area close by were included in the calculations. A few villagers' residences were also unknown.

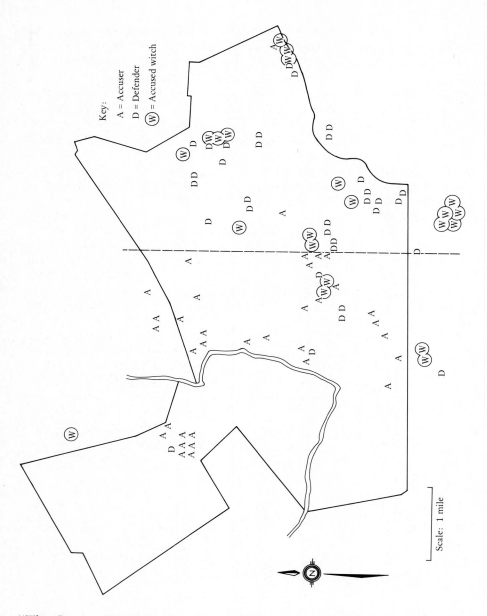

Key:

A = Accuser
D = Defender
(W) = Accused witch

Scale: 1 mile

"The Geography of Witchcraft," in Boyer and Nissenbaum, *Salem Possessed* (Harvard University Press, 1974).

twenty-nine residents who publicly defended the accused in some way (marked by a "D" on the map), twenty-four lived in the eastern half of the village. Often they were close neighbors of the accused. It is moments like these that make the historian want to behave, were it not for the staid air of research libraries, like Archimedes in his fabled bathtub.

The discovery is only the beginning of the task. The geographic chart tells us more about what the trials were *not* than what they were. We can see, at least, that the controversy did not arise out of neighborhood quarrels in the narrow sense of the word—people thinking their next-door neighbors were witches and accusing them. What seems to be at work is a larger division. What that division is, other than a general "east–west" split, the map does not say. But it does provide a clue about where to begin.

Boyer and Nissenbaum began to explore the history of the village itself, expanding their microcosm of 1692 backward in time. They investigated a condition that historians had long recognized but had never associated with the Salem witch trials. That was Salem Village's anomalous relation to its social parent, Salem Town.

Salem Town's settlement followed the pattern of most coastal New England towns. Original settlers usually set up houses around a central location and carved their farmlands out of the surrounding countryside. As a settlement prospered, the land in its immediate vicinity came to be completely taken up. In many cases, a group of settlers would then move out and start a new settlement, like bees hiving off for a new home. Other times, the process was less deliberate. Houses were erected farther and farther away from the central meeting house. When enough outlying residents found it inconvenient to come to church or attend to other civic duties, they sought recognition as a separate village, with their own church, their own taxes, and their own elected officials.

Here the trouble started. The settlers who lived toward the center of town were reluctant to let their outlying neighbors break away. Everyone paid taxes to support a minister for the town church, to maintain the roads, and to care for the poor. If a chunk of the village split off, revenue would be lost. Furthermore, outlying settlers would no longer share the common burdens, such as guarding the town at night. So the centrally located settlers usually resisted any movement for autonomy by their more distant neighbors. Such disputes were a regular feature of New England life.

Salem Town had followed this pattern. Its first settlers located on a peninsula extending into Massachusetts Bay, where they might ply a

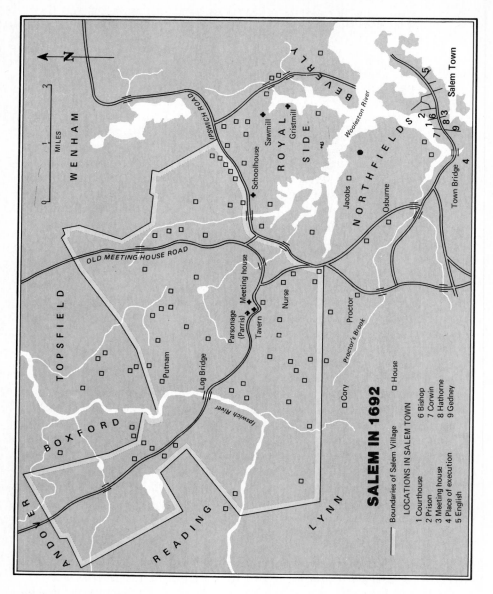

On the map:

N

WENHAM

IPSWICH ROAD

BEVERLY

Salem Town

Wooleston River

ROYAL SIDE

Sawmill
Gristmill

5
2
1 7 6
8 3
9

7

NORTHFIELDS

Town Bridge
4

Schoolhouse

Jacobs
Osburne

OLD MEETING HOUSE ROAD

TOPSFIELD

Parsonage (Parris)
Meeting house
Tavern
Nurse

Proctor's Brook
Proctor

Putnam

Log Bridge

Ipswich River

Cory

House

SALEM IN 1692

LYNN

LOCATIONS IN SALEM TOWN

— Boundaries of Salem Village
□ House

1 Courthouse   6 Bishop
2 Prison   7 Corwin
3 Meeting house   8 Hathorne
4 Place of execution 9 Gedney
5 English

BOXFORD

ANDOVER

READING

MILES

"**Salem in 1692**," from *Freedom and Crisis* by R. Jackson Wilson and Allen
Weinstein (Random House, 1974), p. 83.

prosperous colonial trade. By 1668 four outlying areas (Wenham, Man-
chester, Marblehead, and Beverly) had already become separate towns.
Now the "Salem Farmers," living directly to the west, were petitioning
for a similar settlement, and the "Townsmen" were resisting. In 1672

the General Court of Massachusetts, the colony's legislature, allowed
Salem Village to build its own meeting house instead of forcing residents
to worship in Salem Town. In other matters, however, the Court kept
the village dependent. Salem Town still collected village taxes, chose
village constables, arranged for village roads, established the prices at
which certain grains could be sold, and continued to oversee village land
grants. The General Court records include petition after petition from
villagers, submitted to no avail, complaining about tax rates, patrol duties, boundary rulings. Admittedly, the village's semi-autonomous status
was unusual. In most town disputes the General Court either allowed a
new settlement to separate or it didn't. But for whatever unknown
reasons, the Court granted autonomy only in 1752, sixty years after the
witchcraft episode.

Here, then, is one definite "east–west" split. But it is important to
remember that thus far, we have described a division between the village
and the town. The line so graphically drawn on Boyer and Nissenbaum's
map is within the village itself. What cause would the village have for
division?

Many causes, the records indicate; chief among them the choice of a
minister. Not long after the village received the right to build its own
meeting house, it settled down to arguing over who ought to preach
from its pulpit. Matters began well enough in 1673 with the selection
of James Bayley, but then complaints began to be heard. Bayley didn't
attend regularly to his private prayers. Church members had not been
fully consulted before his selection. After a flurry of petitions and
counter-petitions, Bayley left in 1680, and George Burroughs was
hired. Three years later Burroughs left in another dispute. He was
succeeded by Deodat Lawson, who lasted through four more years of
quarrels. Finally Samuel Parris occupied the pulpit after 1688. His
term was equally stormy, and in 1696 his opponents finally succeeded
in starving him out of the job by refusing to collect taxes to pay his
salary.

The maneuverings that went on during the years of bickering were
intricate enough to discourage most historians from bothering with
them. But Boyer and Nissenbaum recognized that the church records,
the petitions and counter-petitions, the minutes of the Village Committee provided an invaluable key to local divisions. At bottom, it was not
the piety of the ministers alone that was in dispute. Equally crucial was
who had power in the village—power over piety or anything else. When
the lists from the different quarrels were compared, Boyer and Nissenbaum found that the same names were being grouped together. The

people who supported James Bayley usually supported George Burroughs and then opposed the second two ministers. Conversely, the supporters of Deodat Lawson and Samuel Parris had been the people who complained about Bayley and Burroughs. And—here is the connecting link—the two lists from those disputes coincide closely with the divisions in 1692 between accusers and accused.

Suddenly the Salem witch trials take on an entirely new appearance. Instead of being a dramatic disruption that appears out of nowhere in a village kitchen and then disappears equally suddenly at the end of ten months, it becomes an elaboration of a quarrel that has gone on for nearly twenty years!

What lay behind the divisions? One reading of the evidence suggests that the larger split between Salem Town and Salem Village was reflected in the village itself, with the villagers on the east retaining enough of a common bond with the town to continue their affiliation and the westerners favoring complete separation. Boyer and Nissenbaum argue that the division also went beyond the simple geographical one to a difference in outlook and lifestyle. Salem Town was entering into its own as one of the two major commercial centers of New England. It had a growing merchant class whose wealth would soon support the building of fine mansions and an opulent living style. By contrast the farmers in the western portion of Salem Village were tied more closely to traditional agrarian life: subsistence farming, spartan daily lives, a suspicion of the commercial habits of credit extension and speculative investment. What was worse, the Salem Farmers found themselves increasingly hard-pressed economically. The land available in the village was dwindling. What land there was proved less fertile than the broad plains on the eastern side of the village and along the northern flats of Salem Town.

Once again, the statistics of the social historian substantiate this portrait. Draw a map of Salem Village indicating land holdings, and you will find the eastern faction's property tending to enclose the village on all but its western borders. Make a list of the farmers and merchants who were elected town selectmen, and you will find that before 1665, twice as many farmers as merchants were chosen, but from 1665 to 1700 the ratio was six to one in favor of the merchants.

Look, too, at the occupations of the accused witches and their defenders. Many lived along the Ipswich Road, a route that passed by the village rather than through it, a main thoroughfare for travellers and for commerce. The tradesmen who had set up shop there included a carpenter, sawmill operator, shoemaker, miller. And of course there were the taverns, mainstays of travellers, yet always slightly suspect to Puritans. The people along the Ipswich Road were not rich, most of them, but their commercial links were with Salem Town and with outsiders; they were small-scale entrepreneurs rather than farmers. Out of twenty-one villagers who lived along or near the road, only two signed petitions linking them with the western faction; thirteen signed petitions linking them with the eastern faction. Two tavernkeepers, John Proctor and Bridget Bishop, were hung as witches; Elizabeth Proctor barely escaped with her life; and Joshua Rea, another tavernkeeper on the road, signed a petition defending Goody Nurse.

Given Boyer and Nissenbaum's portrait of village factions, we can begin to suggest an alternate way of looking at the Salem trials. Traditional accounts place Samuel Parris, the examining magistrates, and their supporters as the protagonists, terrorizing innocent villagers and controlling the trials as undisputed leaders of the village. Certainly Parris's supporters had their day in 1692, but from the longer perspective they appear to have been fighting a losing battle. The Salem trials can be seen as an indirect yet anguished protest of a group of villagers whose agrarian way of life was being threatened by the rising commercialism of Salem Town. Similar conflicts were to be repeated, in different forms, throughout American history. Thomas Jefferson in his own day would contrast the corrupting influence of cities and manufacturers with the virtuous life of the independent yeoman farmer; western Populists a century later would arraign the "Money Power" of the East for its commercial sins. Salem's uniqueness lay, if Boyer and Nissenbaum's reconstruction proves correct, in the indirect means by which the conflict was expressed. Their reconstruction suggests that the Salem body politic was experiencing its own social analogue of conversion hysteria. When the political and religious institutions of town and village government were unable to resolve divisions on a conscious level, the conflict was converted into the camouflaged symptoms of an entirely different sort—a plague from the invisible world.

"WOMEN ALONE"

While Boyer and Nissenbaum have gone to ingenious lengths to tease out correlations based on the geography of witchcraft, there is another striking connection to be made. That is the link between witchcraft and gender.

By a large majority, the accused witches of Salem were women. As historian Carol Karlsen has determined, out of 178 accused witches who can be identified by name, more than three out of four were female. And if the backgrounds of accused men are examined, it turns out that nearly half of them were husbands, sons, or other relatives of accused women. The gender gap widens further when witchcraft outside Salem is examined. Of 147 additional accused witches in seventeenth-century New England, 82 percent were women. In those cases which actually came to trial (41), thirty-four involved women and only seven involved men. Of the women tried, 53 percent were convicted. Of the men only two were convicted, or 29 percent. And of those who were not only convicted but executed, women outnumbered men 15 to 2.

When Karlsen examined the trial records in more detail, she found that the authorities tended to treat accused women differently from men. Magistrates and ministers often put pressure on women to confess their guilt. In New England cases (excluding Salem), when that pressure led a woman to confess a "familiarity with Satan," she was invariably executed, in accordance with the Biblical command, "Thou shalt not suffer a witch to live." But when men were accused, pressure was seldom applied to make them confess. In fact, confessions from men were not always accepted. In 1652, one John Broadstreet of Rowley admitted having familiarity with Satan. The court ordered him whipped and fined twenty shillings "for telling a lie." In 1674, Christopher Brown confessed to "discoursing with . . . the devil," but the court rejected his statement as being "inconsistent with truth." Hugh Crotia admitted that he had "signed the Devills book and then seald it with his bloud." A Hartford grand jury refused to indict him.

Such evidence suggests that, by and large, most seventeenth-century New Englanders *expected* women to be witches, whereas men who confessed were seldom believed. But why should women be singled out for such attention?

Part of the answer, Karlsen argues, lay in the cultural position of women. Women were traditionally subordinate to men and seen as the "weaker sex." In medieval Europe, this was made abundantly clear by the reigning folklore. One of the most widely read books on witchcraft was *Malleus Maleficarum,* issued in 1486 by Heinrich Kramer and Jacob Sprenger. "More women than men are ministers of the devil," Kramer and Sprenger explained, because "all witchcraft comes from carnal lust, which is in women insatiable." On the other hand, continued Kramer and Sprenger, "Christ was willing to be born and to suffer" in his life on earth, in order to preserve "the male sex from so great a crime."

The Puritans of New England were by no means as explicit in their denunciation of women. Like Martin Luther and other Reformation theologians, they exalted the role of motherhood over the chaste life of the convent, seeing women as partners and helpmeets in marriage. For all that, though, Puritans retained a hierarchical conception of marriage. They viewed families as miniature commonwealths, with the husband as the ruler and his family willing subjects. "A true wife accounts her subjection [as] her honor and freedom," noted Governor John Winthrop of Massachusetts.

A wife's unequal status was reflected legally as well: she was known in law as a feme covert—one whose identity was "covered" by that of her husband. As such, she had no right to buy or sell property, sue or be sued, or make contracts. Similarly, the patterns of inheritance in New England were male dominated. A husband might leave his widow property—indeed, the law required him to leave her at least a third of his estate. But she was to "have and enjoy" that property only "during term of her natural life." She could not waste or squander it, for it was passed on to the family's heirs at her death. Similarly, daughters might inherit property, but if they were already married, it belonged to the husband. If a young woman had not yet married, property usually seems to have been held for her, "for improvement," until she married.

Thus the only sort of woman who held any substantial economic power was a widow who had not remarried. Such a woman was known as a feme sole, or "woman alone." She did have the right to sue, to make contracts, and to buy or sell property. Even when remarrying, a widow could sometimes protect her holdings by having her new husband sign an antenuptial contract, guaranteeing before marriage that the wife would keep certain property as her own. In male-dominated New England, these protections made the feme sole stand out as an anomaly—a "woman alone" who did not fit comfortably into the ordinary scheme of things.

Given that women in Puritan society were placed in decidedly subordinate roles, how does that help explain the preponderance of female witches? As it turns out, a significant number of accused witches were women who were *not* subordinate in some way. They did not fit accepted stereotypes of the way women were expected to behave. In refusing to conform, they threatened the traditional order of society. And standing out as they did, Karlsen argues, they were more likely to be perceived as the ultimate "subversives" of seventeenth-century society: those who joined Satan in an attempt to subvert the heavenly order itself.

One way a woman might stand out was through a contentious, argumentative nature. If it was a woman's duty to submit quietly to the rule of men and glory in "subjection," then quite a few witches refused to conform to the accepted role. We have already seen how Martha Carrier's "threatenings" and Sarah Good's "muttering and scolding extreamly" was perceived by Salem Villagers to have caused the death of cattle. Trial records are filled with similar accusations. On the other hand, the behavior of accused witches was not always the spark which started a quarrel. In some cases, a town resident seems to have tried to take possession of a widow's lands. When the widow protested, or brought a countersuit, she was accused of witchcraft. In either situation, the women at risk were those who refused to bend submissively to the will of the accuser.

More than short tempers were at stake, however. A remarkably high percentage of accused women were "women alone" in an economic sense. Of the 124 witches whose inheritance patterns can be reconstructed from surviving records, as many as 71 (57 percent) lived or had lived in families with no male heirs. Another 14 accused witches were the daughters or granddaughters of witches who did not have brothers or sons to inherit their property. This is at least twice the number one would expect, given the usual percentage of "women alone" in the New England population. Furthermore, of the women executed at Salem, over half had inherited, or stood to inherit their own property. Such statistics indeed seem to indicate why witchcraft controversies so often centered on women.

Having reconstructed the social fabric of Salem—either in terms of "women alone" or a rising tide of commercialism—must we discard our earlier theories about conversion hysteria and the motivations of accusers? Not necessarily. The witchcraft controversy may well have started innocently enough in the kitchen of Samuel Parris. Tituba, Bridget Bishop, and others may well have been practicing magic. Certainly an agrarian faction in the village did not consciously "get up" the trials to punish their commercial neighbors. Nor was the male Puritan patriarchy launching a deliberate war against women. But as the accusations spread wider and controversy engulfed the town, it was only natural that longstanding quarrels and prejudices were drawn into the debate. The interconnections between a people's religious beliefs, their habits of commerce, even their dream and fantasy lives, are intricate and fine, entwined with one another like the delicate root system of a growing plant. Historians who limit their examination to a small area of time and space are able to untangle, through persistent probing, the many strands of emotions, motivations, and social structures that provided the context for those slow processions to the gallows on Witch's Hill.

Additional Reading

Marion Starkey's *The Devil in Massachusetts* (New York, 1949) is the book most often cited as the best "lively" account of the Salem episode. It probably is, although to our way of thinking it idealizes both the accused and the Salem world in general. Giles Corey, George Burroughs, and Bridget Bishop may have been martyrs, but they were also a lot stranger and more interesting than Starkey makes them out to be. A helpful corrective is Chadwick Hansen's *Witchcraft at Salem* (New York, 1969), which catches the temper of Salem's invisible world much more accurately. For a detailed reconstruction of the seventeenth-century heritage of magic and superstition, see Keith Thomas, *Religion and the Decline of Magic* (London, 1971).

On the subject of hysteria, Pierre Janet's *Major Symptoms of Hysteria* (New York, 1907) provides instructive case histories, though it should be supplemented by a modern psychiatry text such as F. C. Redlich and D. X. Freedman, *Theory and Practice of Psychiatry* (New York, 1966). Ilza Veith, *Hysteria: The History of a Disease* (Chicago, 1965) provides background on how the disorder has been interpreted and treated over the centuries.

Paul Boyer and Stephen Nissenbaum apply the techniques of social history with unusual lucidity and grace in *Salem Possessed: The Social Origins of Witchcraft* (Cambridge, Mass., 1974). Their thesis, sketched only in outline here, is elaborated there in full. For purposes of comparison, there is Alan Macfarlane's social history of witchcraft in Essex County, England, *Witchcraft in Tudor and Stuart England* (New York, 1970). Our discussion of gender and witchcraft relies heavily on the research of Carol Karlsen, whose study will be published by. W. W. Norton as *The Devil in the Shape of a Woman.* We are indebted to her for advice and for allowing us to read her manuscript. Another approach to the gender question can be found in John Putnam Demos, *Entertaining Satan: Witchcraft and the Culture Of Early New England* (New York, 1982). Like Karlsen, Demos notes the importance of gender, but lays heavy emphasis on developmental psychology, drawing connections between the position of mothers—who appeared omnipotent to infants during their first years—and witches, who likewise seemed all-powerful. For a sociologist's view, see Richard Weisman, *Witchcraft, Magic and Religion in Seventeeth Century Massachusetts* (Amherst, Mass., 1984).

The most fascinating primary sources are the records of pretrial examinations made by the Salem magistrates. They contribute as much to a portrait of the seventeenth-century mind as they do to a history of the Salem outbreak. W. Elliott Woodward published them originally in 1864 as the *Records of Salem Witchcraft Copied from the Original Documents;* they were reprinted in 1969. More accurate and complete transcripts of the records are available in typescript at the Essex Institute, Salem. George Lincoln Burr, ed., *Narratives of the Witchcraft Cases, 1648–1706* (New York, 1914; reissued 1968) is a convenient compendium of some of the contemporary accounts. Boyer and Nissenbaum have collected their own anthology of primary documents in *Witchcraft at Salem Village* (Belmont, Calif., 1972). The collection includes Upham's map and many church records, deeds, wills, and petitions that can be used to reconstruct the social portrait of the town. With this book, Burr's collection, and Woodward's *Records,* the lay reader can make a good start at an investigation without having to trek to a major library.

Studies to date have by no means exhausted serious avenues of inquiry. For another interesting line of inquiry, see James Kences, "Some Unexplored Relationships of Essex City Withcraft to the Indian Wars of 1675 and 1689," *Essex Institute Historical Collections* 120 (July, 1984), 179–212. A number of the possessed young women of 1692 were orphans who had lost parents during Indian raids. Readers may find it interesting to compare the Salem mass hysteria to a modern outbreak described in James A. McKnight et al., "Epidemic Hysteria: A Field Study," *American Journal of Public Health,* 55 (1965), 858–865. This case occurred in 1962 in a southern Louisiana high school where some twenty-two students, all but one female, experienced hysterical fits over a period of six months. Some interesting parallels can be drawn. In the area of social reconstruction, Boyer and Nissenbaum's study deals only with the relationships between accused and accusers in Salem Village itself. Many of the accused came from Andover and other surrounding areas; thus far no historian has tied these towns' factional disputes to the witchcraft cases. Can correlations between agrarian and commercial orientations be made elsewhere? If not, how and why does the witchcraft epidemic spread to the surrounding towns? There is plenty of digging left to be done here.

THREE

Declaring
Independence

Good historians share with magicians a talent for elegant sleight of hand. In both professions, the manner of execution conceals much of the work that makes the performance possible. Like the magician's trapdoors, mirrors, and other hidden props, historians' primary sources are essential to their task. But the better historians are at their craft, the more likely they will focus their readers' attention on the historical scene itself and not on the supporting documents. The more polished the historical narrative, the less the audience will be aware of how much labor has gone into the reconstruction.

Contrary to prevailing etiquette, we have gone out of our way to call attention to the preliminary questions that historians ask, the problems of evidence to be solved before a historical narrative is presented in its final, polished form. As yet, however, we have not examined in detail the many operations a historian must perform on a single document, from the first encounter with it to its final use in a narrative. What at first seems a relatively simple job of collecting, examining, and cataloguing may become remarkably complex, especially when the document in question is of major importance.

So let us narrow our focus even more than in the previous two chapters, by concentrating not on a region (Virginia) or a town (Salem), but on one document. The document in question admittedly carries more import than most that historians encounter in their daily work. Yet it remains brief enough to be read in several minutes. It also has the merit of being one of the few primary sources which virtually every reader of this book already will have encountered: the Declaration of Independence.

The Declaration, of course, is one of the most celebrated documents in the nation's history. Drafted by Thomas Jefferson, adopted by the Second Continental Congress, published for the benefit of the world, memorialized throughout the nineteenth century in patriotic speeches, it is today respectfully hawked on authentic simulated parchment, emblazoned on restaurant placemats, and given the place of honor on basement recreation-room walls. Every schoolchild knows that Congress declared the colonies' independence by issuing the document on July 4, 1776; nearly everyone has seen the painting by John Trumbull which depicts members of Congress receiving the parchment for signing on that day.

So the starting place is familiar enough. Yet there is a good deal to establish when unpacking the facts about such a basic document. Under what circumstances did Jefferson write the Declaration? What people, events, or other documents influenced him? If changes were made in Jefferson's original draft, when were they made and why? Only when such questions are answered in more detail does it become clear that quite a few of the "facts" enumerated in the previous paragraph are either misleading or incorrect. And the confusion begins in trying to answer the most elementary questions about the Declaration.

A CONTEXT FOR INDEPENDENCE

In May 1776 Thomas Jefferson travelled to Philadelphia, as befit a proper gentleman, in a coach and four with two attending slaves. He promptly took his place on the Virginia delegation to the Second Continental Congress. This was not Jefferson's first appearance; he had represented Virginia on and off since the first Congress met in May 1775. After twelve months of fighting, he found Congress still debating whether the break with England was irreparable. Sentiment for independence ran high in many areas but by no means everywhere. The greatest reluctance lay in the middle colonies, particularly in Pennsylvania. Many of the Pennsylvania delegation, including the distinguished John Dickinson, still hoped to patch up the quarrel with England.

Such cautious sentiments infuriated the more radical members of Congress, especially John and Samuel Adams. The two Adamses had worked for independence from the opening days of Congress, but found the going slow. America, complained John, was "a great, unwieldy body. It is like a large fleet sailing under convoy. The fleetest sailers must wait for the dullest and the slowest." And so the radicals continued their patient, persistent efforts. "We have been obliged to keep ourselves out of sight," Adams wrote in a letter home, "and to feel pulses, and to sound the depths; to insinuate our sentiments, designs and desires by means of other persons."

Jefferson also favored independence, but he lacked the Adamses' taste for political infighting. While the men from Massachusetts pulled their strings in Congress, Jefferson only listened attentively and took notes. Thirty-three years old, he was the youngest delegate to Congress, and no doubt this contributed to his diffidence. Privately, he conversed more easily with friends, sprawling casually in a chair with one shoulder cocked high, the other low, and his long legs extended. He got along well with the other delegates, and performed his committee assignments dutifully.

In May of 1776, however, Jefferson hoped only to leave Philadelphia as quickly as possible and return to the convention meeting at Williamsburg, Virginia. There, in his opinion, lay the most challenging theater of action. Congress would putter interminably over the question of independence while his "country," Virginia, took the bold step of drawing a new frame of government. Jefferson had definite ideas about what ought to be incorporated in the Virginia constitution; he wanted to be on hand when it was drafted.

But it was last-minute news from Virginia that brought affairs to a head in Philadelphia. In late May, delegate Richard Henry Lee arrived from Williamsburg under instructions to force Congress to act. On Friday, June 7, Lee rose in Congress and offered the following resolutions:

> That these United Colonies are, and of right ought to be, free and independent States, that they are absolved from all allegiance to the British crown, and that all political connection between them and the state of Great Britain is, and ought to be, totally dissolved.
>
> That it is expedient forthwith to take the most effectual measures for forming foreign alliances.
>
> That a plan of confederation be prepared and transmitted to the respective colonies for their consideration and approbation.

On Saturday and again on Monday, moderates and radicals earnestly debated the propositions. They knew that a declaration of independence would make the breach with England final. The Secretary of the Congress, Charles Thomson, cautiously recorded in his minutes only that "certain resolutions" were "moved and discussed"—the certain resolutions, of course, treasonous in the extreme.

Still, sentiment appeared to be running with the radicals. Delegate James Wilson of Pennsylvania surprised the Congress by announcing that he felt ready to vote for independence. He asked only that action on the resolutions be postponed three weeks, until the Pennsylvania legislature had an opportunity to get firmly behind the movement. The radicals grudgingly agreed, but not without setting the wheels for independence in motion by appointing a five-member committee "to prepare a Declaration to the effect of the said first resolution."

The events that followed can be traced, in bare outline at least, in a modern edition of Secretary Thomson's minutes, edited by Worthington Ford. Using the Ford edition, we learn that on June 11, 1776 Congress constituted Jefferson, John Adams, Benjamin Franklin, Roger Sherman, and Robert Livingston as a Committee of Five responsible for drafting the declaration. Then, for over two weeks, Thomson's *Journal* remains silent on the subject. Only on Friday, June 28 does it note that the committee "brought in a draught" of an independence declaration.

On Monday, July first, Congress resolved itself into a Committee of the Whole "to take into consideration the resolution respecting independency." Since Thomson's official minutes did not record the activities of committees, Congress could freely debate the sensitive question of independence as a "Committee of the Whole" without leaving any record of debate or disagreement in the official minutes. On July second, the Committee of the Whole went through the motions of "reporting back" to Congress (that is, to itself). The minutes note only that Richard Lee's resolution, then "being read" in formal session, "was agreed to as follows"—printing the original resolves of June 7.

Thus the official Journal makes it clear that Congress voted for independence on July second, not the fourth. And the adopted resolution was not the five-member committee's declaration but Richard Henry Lee's original proposal of June 7. When John Adams wrote home on July third to his wife Abigail, he exulted in the actions of Congress, predicting that July second would be remembered as "the most memorable Epoca in the History of America. I am apt to believe that it will be celebrated, by succeeding Generations, as the great anniversary Festival. . . . It ought to be solemnized with Pomp and Parade, with Shews, Games, Sports, Guns, Bells, Bonfires and Illuminations from one End of this Continent to the other from this Time forward forever more."

As it turned out, Adams picked the wrong date for the fireworks. Although Congress had officially broken the colonies' ties with England, the declaration *explaining* the action to the rest of the world had not yet been approved. On July third and fourth Congress again met as a Committee of the Whole. Only then was the formal declaration reported back, accepted, and sent to the printer. Ford's edition of the *Journal* notes, "The foregoing declaration was, by order of Congress, engrossed, and signed by the following members. . . ." Here is the enactment familiar to everyone: the "engrossed" parchment (one written in large, neat letters) beginning with its bold, "IN CONGRESS, JULY 4, 1776" and concluding with the president of the Continental Congress's signature, so flourishing that we still speak of putting our John Hancock to paper. Below that, the signatures of fifty-five other delegates appear more modestly inscribed.

If mention of the Declaration in Thomson's minutes concluded with the entry on the fourth, schoolchildren might emerge with their memories reasonably intact. But it continues, confusingly. For July 19: *"Resolved,* that the Declaration passed on the 4th, be fairly engrossed in parchment, with the title and stile of 'The unanimous declaration of the thirteen United States of America,' and that the same, when engrossed, be signed by every member of Congress." This is a surprise. Hasn't the Declaration been engrossed and signed already—on the fourth? The entry of August second compounds the problem: "The declaration of independence being engrossed and compared at the table was signed by the members."

Thus the *Journal* appears to record *two* signings of the Declaration— one the fourth of July, one the second of August. Yet there is only one engrossed copy. What is the explanation?

A check of the introduction to Ford's edition reveals that, in fact, there was more than one *Journal* of Congress. Secretary Thomson made his original entries in the "rough" Journal. From these minutes Thomson and his assistants then prepared a "corrected" version, which formed the basis of the text as Congress later printed it. Ford's edition indicates that the entry which has the Declaration being "engrossed and signed" on July fourth appeared only in the corrected journal. In the rough journal, Thomson did not copy the Declaration or insert an engrossed copy; he only left a space and then pasted in a copy of the version Congress had ordered printed. This version does not include the phrase, "The unanimous declaration of the thirteen United States of America" (as the engrossed copy does), nor does it include the fifty-six signatures—only the printed names of Hancock (the president) and Thomson (the secretary).

In all likelihood, then, the Declaration was not signed on the fourth after all, but on the second of August. To muddy the waters even further, it appears that not all those who signed the Declaration did so on August second. In 1906 historian John Hazelton established that not all the signers were even in Philadelphia on August second. Some of them could not have signed the document until October or November.

So the upshot of the historian's preliminary investigation is that (1) Congress declared independence on the second of July, not the fourth; (2) most members officially signed the engrossed parchment only on the second of August; and (3) all the signers of the Declaration never met together in the same room at one time, John Trumbull's famous painting notwithstanding. In the matter of establishing the most basic facts surrounding a document, historians are all too ready to agree with John Adams's bewildered search of his recollections: "What are we to think of history? When in less than 40 years, such diversities appear in the memories of living men who were witnesses."

The Committee of Five—Adams, Sherman, Livingston, Jefferson, and Franklin—present their work to John Hancock, president of the Continental Congress, in a detail from *The Declaration of Independence,* by John Trumbull. When Hancock finally put his elaborate signature to the engrossed copy, he is reported to have said, "There! John Bull can read my name without spectacles, and may now double his reward of £500 for my head."

THE TRANSFORMATION OF A TEXT

Although the details of the Declaration's signing are at first confusing, historians can, with patience, sort them out. And they have available an authentic text—the engrossed parchment signed on August second. Yet the official document does not answer many questions about the writing of the Declaration. Although Jefferson drafted it, what did the Committee of Five contribute? What happened during the congressional debate on July third and fourth? If the delegates made changes in Jefferson's version, for what purpose? A historian will want to know which parts of the completed document were most controversial; even more, whether certain passages were so controversial, Congress eliminated them altogether. Surviving copies of earlier drafts could shed valuable light on these questions.

The search for an accurate version of the Declaration's drafting began even while the protagonists were still living. Some forty years after the signing, both Jefferson and John Adams tried to set down the sequence of events. Adams recalled the affable and diplomatic Jefferson suggesting that Adams write the first draft. "I will not," replied Adams.

"You shall do it," persisted Jefferson.

"Oh no!"

"Why will you not do it? You ought to do it."

"I will not."

"Reasons enough."

"What can be your reasons?"

Adams ticked them off. "Reason 1st. You are a Virginian and a Virginian ought to be at the head of this business. Reason 2nd. I am obnoxious, suspected and unpopular; you are very much otherwise. Reason 3rd. You can write ten times better than I can."

"Well," said Jefferson, "if you are decided, I will do as well as I can."

Jefferson, for his part, did not remember this bit of diplomatic shuttlecock. In a letter to James Madison in 1823 he asserted that

The Commitee of 5 met. . . [and] they unanimously pressed on myself alone to undertake the draught. I consented; I drew it; but before I reported it to the committee I communicated it separately to Dr. Franklin and Mr. Adams requesting their corrections; . . . and you have seen the original paper now in my hands, with the corrections of Dr. Franklin and Mr. Adams interlined in their own handwriting. Their alterations were two or three only, and merely verbal [that is, changes of phrasing, not substance]. I then wrote a fair copy, reported it to the committee, and from them, unaltered to the Congress.

So far so good. Jefferson's "original paper"—which he endorsed on the document itself as the "original Rough draught"—is preserved in the Library of Congress. But what exactly is this "original" draft? Take a look at the two reproductions on this page and the next. One of them is a section of the "original Rough draught," the other a fragment of a different copy, discovered in 1947 by Julian Boyd. Which of the two was written first?

Comparing the documents phrase by phrase, it becomes clear that Jefferson's "original" rough draft actually had a predecessor. Both documents read, "at this very time, too, they are permitting their chief magistrate to send over not only soldiers of our common blood but Scotch & foreign mercenaries. . . ." But when Jefferson wrote the fragmentary draft, he first used "at this time are permitting," before correcting it to read "at this very time too, they are permitting." Similarly he changed "our own blood" to "our common blood" and "foreign mercenaries" to "Scotch & foreign mercenaries." The "rough" draft has incorporated all these changes into its version smoothly, which indicates that it was a later copy. The rough draft also makes further changes that are *not* present on the earlier draft: mercenaries who "deluge us in blood" is replaced with the simpler "destroy us."

Fragment of a draft of the Declaration of Independence, discovered in 1947.

The same section of the Declaration in Jefferson's "Rough draught."

For these and other reasons, Julian Boyd has argued that this fragmentary draft is part of Jefferson's earliest attempt to compose the Declaration. The later "original Rough draught" appears to be the first smooth copy of his efforts. Obviously the fragmentary draft, with all its corrections, made for difficult reading. Jefferson would have wanted to put it into more legible form before showing it to Franklin and Adams.

Yet even the rough draft, as it now stands, is not a smooth copy. As historian Carl Becker pointed out,

> the inquiring student, coming to it for the first time, would be astonished, perhaps disappointed, if he expected to find in it nothing more than the 'original paper . . . with the corrections of Dr. Franklin and Mr. Adams interlined in their own handwriting.' He would find, for example, on the first page alone nineteen corrections, additions or erasures besides those in the handwriting of Adams and Franklin. It would probably seem to him at first sight a bewildering document, with many phrases crossed out, numerous interlineations, and whole paragraphs enclosed in brackets.

This makes the rough draft more difficult to read, but in the end also more rewarding. For the fact is, Jefferson continued to record on this copy successive alterations of the Declaration, not only by Adams and Franklin, but by Congress in its debates of July third and fourth. In addition, Jefferson allowed copies to be made of his rough draft at different times during those weeks.

Thus by careful comparison and reconstruction, we can accurately establish the sequence of changes made in one crucial document, from the time it was first drafted on several pieces of paper, through corrections in committee, to debate and further amendment in Congress, and finally on to the engrossed parchment familiar to history. The changes were not slight. In the end, Congress removed about one-quarter of Jefferson's original language. Eighty-six alterations were made by one person or another, including Jefferson.

To these alterations the original author behaved as might be expected of any creator proud of his work: he squirmed. As Congress debated the document, Jefferson followed his usual custom and remained silent, but the pain must have been evident on his face. Benjamin Franklin noticed, and leaned over with a few consoling words. "I have made it a rule," he said,

whenever in my power, to avoid becoming the draughtsman of papers to be reviewed by a public body. I took my lesson from an incident which I will relate to you. When I was a journeyman printer, one of my companions, an apprentice Hatter, having served out his time, was about to open shop for himself. His first concern was to have a handsome signboard, with a proper inscription. He composed it in these words: 'John Thompson, Hatter, makes and sells hats for ready money,' with the figure of a hat subjoined. But he thought he would submit it to his friends for their amendments. The first he shewed it to thought the word 'hatter' tautologous, because followed by the words 'makes hats' which shew he was a hatter. It was struck out. The next observed that the word 'makes' might as well be omitted, because his customers would not care who made the hats. If good and to their mind, they would buy, by whomsoever made. He struck it out. A third said he thought the words 'for ready money' were useless as it was not the custom of the place to sell on credit. Every one who purchased expected to pay. They were parted with, and the inscription now stood 'John Thompson sells hats.' '*Sells* hats' says his next friend? Why nobody will expect you to give them away. What then is the use of that word? It was stricken out, and 'hats' followed it, the rather, as there was one painted on the board. So his inscription was reduced ultimately to 'John Thompson' with the figure of a hat subjoined.

Most historians agree that the majority of changes made by Congress strengthened the Declaration rather than weakened it. They are grateful, however, that Jefferson retained enough pride in his creation to preserve the original drafts that now make it possible to chart the course of the document over those fateful three weeks of 1776.

THE TACTICS OF INTERPRETATION

So far, our analysis has been confined to laying groundwork: establishing the actual text of the Declaration and sketching the circumstances of its origin. Having done that, the historian must attempt the more complicated task of interpreting the document.

Here, historians' paths are most likely to diverge—and understandably so. To determine the historical significance of a document requires placing it within the larger context of events. Because that context is so varied and complex, historians quite easily find many different combinations of significant facts. There is no single proper method for approaching and analyzing a document; if there were, the historical profession would be a good deal simpler, if not a great deal duller.

The situation is not so chaotic as it appears, however. While historians consistently interpret documents differently, they do share certain common analytical tactics—general approaches that have consistently yielded profitable results. Historians will not employ all of these tactics each time they confront a document, but they will usually employ more than one, in order to approach their subject from several perspectives. Each new approach requires the historian to read the document afresh, subjecting it to different questions, searching it for previously unnoticed relationships.

What follows, then, is one set of tactical approaches to the Declaration of Independence. These are by no means the only ways of making sense of the document. But they do suggest some range of the interpretive options that historians normally call upon.

The document is read, first, to understand its surface content. This step may appear too obvious to bear mentioning, but not so. The fact is, most historians examine a document for specific reasons, from a particular and potentially limiting viewpoint. A diplomatic historian, for instance, may approach the Declaration with an eye to the role it played in cementing a formal alliance with France. A historian concerned with political theory would more likely focus on the theoretical justifications of independence. Both perspectives are legitimate, but by beginning with such specific interests, historians risk prejudging the document. They are likely to notice only the kinds of evidence they are seeking.

So it makes sense to begin by temporarily putting aside any specific questions and approaching the Declaration as a willing, even uncritical listener. Ask only the most basic questions. How is the document organized? What are its major points, briefly summarized?

THE UNANIMOUS DECLARATION OF THE THIRTEEN UNITED STATES OF AMERICA.

When in the Course of human events, it becomes necessary for one people to dissolve the political bands, which have connected them with another, and to assume among the powers of the earth, the separate and equal station to which the Laws of Nature and of Nature's God entitle them, a decent respect to the opinions of mankind requires that they should declare the causes which impel them to the separation.—We hold these truths to be self-evident, that all men are created equal, that they are endowed by their Creator with certain unalienable Rights, that among these are Life, Liberty and the pursuit of Happiness.—That to secure these rights, Governments are instituted among Men, deriving their just powers from the consent of the governed,—That whenever any Form of Government becomes destructive of these ends, it is the Right of the People to alter or to abolish it, and to institute new Government, laying its foundation on such principles and organizing its powers in such form, as to them shall seem most likely to effect their Safety and Happiness. Prudence, indeed, will dictate that Governments long established should not be changed for light and transient causes; and accordingly all experience hath shewn, that mankind are more disposed to suffer, while evils are sufferable, than to right themselves by abolishing the forms to which they are accustomed. But when a long train of abuses and usurpations, pursuing invariably the same Object evinces a design to reduce them under absolute Despotism, it is their right, it is their duty, to throw off such Government, and to provide new Guards for their future security.—Such has been the patient sufferance of these Colonies; and such is now the necessity which constrains them to alter their former Systems of Government. The history of the present King of Great Britain is a history of repeated injuries and usurpations, all having in direct object the establishment of an absolute Tyranny over these States. To prove this, let Facts be submitted to a candid world.—He has refused his Assent to Laws, the most wholesome and necessary for the public good.—He has forbidden his Governors to pass Laws of immediate and pressing importance, unless suspended in their operation till his Assent should be obtained; and when so suspended, he has utterly neglected to attend to them.—He has refused to pass other Laws for the accommodation of large districts of people, unless those people would relinquish the right of Representation in the Legislature, a right inestimable to them and formidable to tyrants only.—He has called together legislative bodies at places unusual, uncomfortable, and distant from the depository of their public Records, for the sole purpose of fatiguing them into compliance with his measures.—He has dissolved

Representative Houses repeatedly, for opposing with manly firmness his invasions on the rights of the people.—He has refused for a long time, after such dissolutions, to cause others to be elected; whereby the Legislative powers, incapable of Annihilation, have returned to the People at large for their exercise; the State remaining in the meantime exposed to all the dangers of invasion from without, and convulsions within.—He has endeavoured to prevent the population of these States; for that purpose obstructing the Laws for Naturalization of Foreigners; refusing to pass others to encourage their migrations hither, and raising the conditions of new Appropriations of Lands.—He has obstructed the Administration of Justice, by refusing his Assent to Laws for establishing Judiciary powers. —He has made Judges dependent on his Will alone, for the tenure of their offices, and the amount and payment of their salaries.—He has erected a multitude of New Offices, and sent hither swarms of Officers to harass our people, and eat out their substance.—He has kept among us, in times of peace, Standing Armies without the Consent of our legislatures.—He has affected to render the Military independent of and superior to the Civil power.—He has combined with others to subject us to a jurisdiction foreign to our constitution, and unacknowledged by our laws; giving his Assent to their Acts of pretended Legislation.—For quartering large bodies of armed troops among us:—For protecting them, by a mock Trial, from punishment for any Murders which they should commit on the Inhabitants of these States:—For cutting off our Trade with all parts of the world:—For imposing Taxes on us without our Consent:—For depriving us in many cases, of the benefits of Trial by Jury:—For transporting us beyond Seas to be tried for pretended offenses:—For abolishing the free System of English Laws in a neighboring Province, establishing therein an Arbitrary government, and enlarging its Boundaries so as to render it at once an example and fit instrument for introducing the same absolute rule into these Colonies:—For taking away our Charters, abolishing our most valuable Laws, and altering fundamentally the Forms of our Governments: —For suspending our own Legislatures, and declaring themselves invested with power to legislate for us in all cases whatsoever.—He has abdicated Government here, by declaring us out of his Protection and waging War against us.—He has plundered our seas, ravaged our Coasts, burnt our towns, and destroyed the lives of our people.—He is at this time transporting large Armies of foreign Mercenaries to compleat the works of death, desolation and tyranny, already begun with circumstances of Cruelty & perfidy scarcely paralleled in the most barbarous ages, and totally unworthy the Head of a civilized nation.—He has constrained our fellow Citizens taken Captive on the high Seas to bear Arms against their

Country, to become the executioners of their friends and Brethren, or to fall themselves by their Hands.—He has excited domestic insurrections amongst us, and has endeavoured to bring on the inhabitants of our frontiers, the merciless Indian Savages, whose known rule of warfare, is an undistinguished destruction of all ages, sexes and conditions. In every state of these Oppressions We have Petitioned for Redress in the most humble terms: Our repeated Petitions have been answered only by repeated injury. A Prince whose character is thus marked by every act which may define a Tyrant, is unfit to be the ruler of a free people. Nor have We been wanting in attentions to our Brittish brethren. We have warned them from time to time of attempts by their legislature to extend an unwarrantable jurisdiction over us. We have reminded them of the circumstances of our emigration and settlement here. We have appealed to their native justice and magnanimity, and we have conjured them by the ties of our common kindred to disavow these usurpations, which would inevitably interrupt our connections and correspondence. They too have been deaf to the voice of justice and of consanguinity. We must, therefore, acquiesce in the necessity, which denounces our Separation, and hold them, as we hold the rest of mankind, Enemies in War, in Peace Friends.—

We, therefore, the Representatives of the united States of America, in General Congress, Assembled, appealing to the Supreme Judge of the world for the rectitude of our intentions do, in the Name, and by Authority of the good People of these Colonies, solemnly publish and declare, That these United Colonies are, and of Right ought to be Free and Independent States; that they are Absolved from all Allegiance to the British Crown, and that all political connection between them and the State of Great Britain, is and ought to be totally dissolved: and that as Free and Independent States, they have full Power to levy War, conclude Peace, contract Alliances, establish Commerce, and to do all other Acts and Things which Independent States may of right do.—And for the support of this Declaration, with a firm reliance on the protection of divine Providence, we mutually pledge to each other our Lives, our Fortunes and our sacred Honor.

As befits a reasoned and lucid public document, the Declaration can be separated fairly easily into its component parts. The first sentence begins by informing the reader of the document's purpose. The colonies, having declared their independence from England, intend to announce "the causes which impel them to the separation."

The causes which follow, however, are not all of a piece. They break naturally into two sections: the first, a theoretical and general justification of revolution, and the second, a list of the specific grievances that justify this particular revolution. Because the first section deals in general, "self-evident" truths, it is the one most often remembered and quoted. "All men are created equal," "unalienable rights," "life, liberty and the pursuit of happiness," "consent of the governed"—these principles have relevance far beyond the circumstances of America in the summer of 1776.

But the Declaration devotes far greater space to a list of British actions which Congress labelled "a long train of abuses and usurpations" designed to "reduce [Americans] under absolute despotism." Since the Declaration concedes that revolution should never be undertaken lightly, the document proceeds to demonstrate that English rule has been not merely unwieldy and inconvenient, but so full of "repeated injuries" that "absolute tyranny" is the result. What threatens Americans most, the Declaration proclaims, is not the individual measures, however injurious, but the existence of a deliberate plot by the king to deprive a "free people" of their liberties. So Congress would have the candid world believe.

The final section of the Declaration turns to the colonial response. Here the Declaration incorporates Richard Lee's resolution passed on July second and ends with the signers solemnly pledging their lives, fortunes, and sacred honor to support the new government.

Having begun with this straightforward reading, the historian is less likely to wrench out of context a particular passage, magnifying its importance at the expense of the rest of the document. Yet taken by itself, the reading of "surface content" may distort a document's import. Significance, after all, depends upon the circumstances under which a statement is made as much as upon the statement itself. Thus the historian must approach a document from several perspectives in order to establish its historical context.

The context of a document may be established, in part, by asking what the document might have said but did not. When Jefferson retired to his second-floor lodgings on the outskirts of Philadelphia, placed a portable writing desk on his lap, and put pen to paper, he had many options. The Declaration in its final form was hardly a foregone conclusion. Yet the modern reader, seeing only the end result, is tempted to view the document as the logical, even inevitable result of Jefferson's deliberations. Perhaps it was, but the historian needs to ask how it might have been otherwise. What might Jefferson and the Congress have declared but did not? As

Jefferson himself remarked, "The sentiments of men are known not only by what they receive but by what they reject also." Only by identifying the range of alternatives in any historical situation can we appreciate why one path was chosen over another.

One way of reconstructing the might-have-been's in the Declaration is to locate them in earlier drafts. Here are the paths Jefferson wished to take, which Congress ultimately rejected. Perhaps most interesting is his discussion of slavery, originally included among the grievances against the king:

He has waged cruel war against human nature itself, violating it's most sacred rights of life and liberty in the persons of a distant people who never offended him, captivating & carrying them into slavery in another hemisphere or to incur miserable death in their transportation thither. This piratical warfare, the opprobrium of *infidel* powers, is the warfare of the *Christian* king of Great Britain. Determined to keep open a market where *Men* should be bought & sold, he has prostituted his negative [used his veto power] for suppressing every legislative attempt to prohibit or to restrain this execrable commerce. And that this assemblage of horrors might want no fact of distinguishing die, he is now exciting those very people to rise in arms among us, and to purchase that liberty of which he has deprived them, by murdering the people on whom he also obtruded them: thus paying off former crimes committed against the *Liberties* of one people, with crimes which he urges them to commit against the *lives* of another.

Blaming the king for slavery in America certainly was tortuous logic. Jefferson based his charge on the fact that several times during the eighteenth century, Virginia's legislature passed a tariff designed to restrict the importation of slaves. It did so not so much out of humanitarian motives, although these were occasionally mentioned, but because the slave population in Virginia was expanding rapidly. Importing too many slaves would lower the price of domestic slaves whom Virginia planters wanted to sell. It would also create an unfavorable balance of trade, drawing out of the colony funds used to pay for imported slaves. The British administration, however, consistently disallowed such laws —and thus the king had "prostituted his negative for suppressing every legislative attempt to prohibit or to restrain this execrable commerce." In part, the laws were disallowed because many Americans wished the slave trade to continue—Virginian landowners who would have benefitted from the lower prices, as well as Georgians and South Carolinians who (as Jefferson himself admitted) "had never attempted to restrain the importation of slaves, and who on the contrary still wished to continue it."

To accuse the king of enslaving colonial blacks was ridiculous enough, but Jefferson's indictment appeared even more absurd because it then turned around and hotly accused the king of *freeing* colonial blacks. In November 1775 the loyal Governor Dunmore of Virginia proclaimed that any slave who deserted his master to fight for the king would be freed. Hence Jefferson, after condemning the awful practice of slavery, called King George to account for the vile "crime" of freeing slaves who remained loyal. Congress wisely dropped the long passage and only accused the king more generally of encouraging "domestic insurrections."

Jefferson's rough draft reveals those issues he raised which Congress rejected, but it necessarily provides no clue to the alternatives which *neither* Jefferson nor Congress included in the Declaration. That there had been other alternatives can be seen by looking at a declaration made some ten years earlier by another intercolonial gathering, the Stamp Act Congress. This declaration, like Jefferson's, began by outlining general principles before proceeding to list specific grievances. In reading the first three resolves, note the difference between their premises and those of the Declaration.

> I. That his Majesty's Subjects in these Colonies, owe the same Allegiance to the Crown of *Great-Britain,* that is owing from his Subjects born within the Realm, and all due Subordination to that August Body the Parliament of *Great-Britain.*

> II. That his Majesty's Liege Subjects in these Colonies, are entitled to all the inherent Rights and Liberties of his Natural born Subjects, within the Kingdom of *Great-Britain.*

> III. That it is inseparably essential to the Freedom of a People, and the undoubted Right of *Englishmen,* that no Taxes be imposed on them, but with their own Consent, given personally, or by their Representatives.

Significantly, the rights emphasized by the Stamp Act Congress in 1765 differ from those emphasized in 1776. According to the Stamp Act resolutions, the colonists are entitled to "all the inherent Rights and Liberties" of "Subjects, within the Kingdom of *Great-Britain.*" They possess "the undoubted Right of *Englishmen.*" Nowhere in Jefferson's

Declaration are the "rights of Englishmen" once mentioned as justification for protesting the king's conduct. Instead, the Declaration magnifies what the Stamp Act only mentions in passing—natural rights inherent in the "Freedom of a People," whether they be English subjects or not.

The shift from English rights to natural rights resulted from a change in the political situation in the colonies. In the years following 1765, Americans attempted to redress their grievances within the British imperial system. Quite logically, they cited rights they felt due them as British subjects. But in 1776, the Declaration was renouncing all ties with the mother country. If the colonies were no longer a part of Great Britain, what good would it do to cite their rights as Englishmen? Thus the natural rights "endowed" all persons "by their Creator" took on paramount importance.

The Declaration makes another striking omission. Nowhere in the long list of grievances does it use that word in the first resolve of the Stamp Act Congress—"Parliament." The omission is all the more surprising because the Revolutionary quarrel had its roots in the dispute over Parliament's right to tax and regulate the colonies. The Sugar Act, the Stamp Act, the Townshend duties, the Tea Act, the Coercive Acts, the Quebec Act—Parliament is at the center of the dispute. The Declaration alludes to those legislative measures but always in the context of the king's actions, not Parliament's. Doing so admittedly required a bit of circumlocution: when Jefferson introduced the Parliamentary grievances, he wrote that the king had "combined with others [namely Parliament] to subject us to a jurisdiction foreign to our constitution and unacknowledged by our laws, giving his Assent to their Acts of pretended Legislation." Only once again did he allude to Parliament, when castigating the British people for wrongly allowing "their legislature" to extend its jurisdiction over the colonies.

Obviously, the omission came about for much the same reason that Jefferson excluded all mention of the "rights of Englishmen." At the Stamp Act Congress of 1765, virtually all Americans were willing to grant Parliament some jurisidiction over the colonies. Not the right to lay taxes without American representation, certainly, but at least the right to regulate colonial trade. Robert Livingston, who was on the committee to draft the Declaration in 1776, had also been at the Stamp Act Congress. "All agreed that we ought to obey all acts of trade [passed by Parliament] and that they should regulate our Trade," he recalled, "but many were not for making an explicit declaration of and an acknowledgment of such a Power." In the end the Congress compromised, noting only in Resolution I that Parliament deserved "all due Subordination." What exactly that meant, they left their readers to imagine; but at least they granted Parliament some sovereignty.

By 1775 the more radical colonists would not grant Parliament any authority over the colonies. They had come to recognize what an early pamphleteer had noted, that Americans could be "as effectually ruined by the powers of legislation as by those of taxation." The Boston Port Bill, which closed Boston harbor, was not a tax, nor did it violate any traditional right. Yet the radicals argued, quite correctly, that Parliament could take away Americans' freedoms by such legislation.

Although many colonists had totally rejected all Parliamentary authority in 1775, most had not yet advocated independence. How, then, were the colonies related to England if not through Parliament? The only link, radicals argued, was through the king. The colonies possessed their own sovereign legislatures, but they shared with all British subjects one monarch. It was to the king that all grievances should be addressed. Thus, when the final break with England came, the Declaration carefully laid all blame at the king's feet. Even to recognize Parliament would be tacitly to admit that it had some legitimate connection with the colonies.

What the Declaration does *not* say, then, proves to be as important as what it did say. Historians can recognize the importance of such unstated premises by continually remembering that the actors in any drama possess more alternatives than the ones they finally choose.

⟩ *A document may be understood by seeking to reconstruct the intellectual worlds behind its words.* We have already seen, in the cases of Virginia and Salem, how much history involves the task of reconstructing whole societies from fragmentary records. The same process applies to the intellectual worlds that lie behind the words of an individual document.

The need to perform this reconstruction is often hidden, however, because the English language has changed over the past two hundred years, while the words themselves remain the same. As a result, we may find ourselves reading an eighteenth-century sentence whose meaning appears perfectly clear, when in fact it had an entirely different sense for its author.

The importance of change over time in a language can be demonstrated more forcibly if we imagine how Jefferson or some other eighteenth-century American would try to make sense out of twentieth-century prose. Below are three passages taken from twentieth-century writers:

The age of widescreen began in September 1952 with the release of *This Is Cinerama.* . . . Employing stereophonic sound, Cinerama, the invention of Fred Waller, used three cameras and three projectors to cover a huge, curved screen.

The newspaper feature, the magazine article, the radio program, do not attain the dignity of being ends in themselves; they are rather means to an end: that end, of course, is to catch the reader's attention so that he will then read the advertisement or hear the commercial.

Middle-class life came to power and wealth by breaking ancient restraints; and the more successful middle classes fear new restraints upon their sometimes quite inordinate powers and privileges.*

Most likely, an eighteenth-century reader would find the first excerpt most difficult to comprehend and the third excerpt the easiest. The passage on "Cinerama," "widescreen," and "stereophonic sound" would of course be indecipherable to Jefferson. It describes a totally unfamiliar world, using a strange and unknown vocabulary. The second excerpt appears more promising, although still puzzling. Jefferson would be familiar with "newspaper" and "feature," but would not know what a "newspaper feature" was, except perhaps to guess that it might be some distinguishing mark or detail—the meaning of "feature" in his day. "Commercial" he would be accustomed to reading as an adjective, not a noun; he would be at a loss to imagine what in the world it meant to "hear" a commercial. Yet Jefferson could probably deduce the general meaning of the passage—that articles in a newspaper served only as a vehicle to get subscribers to read the advertisements.

The final passage Jefferson would comprehend easily. The general subject is political power, an area familiar to him. "Middle class" might seem a bit infelicitous on his tongue; colonists more often referred to "the middling class of people" or "the middling sort." But the meaning of the passage would appear quite clear.

Appearances, however, can be deceiving. Jefferson would surely misinterpret the last two passages, simply because he was unaware of

*The excerpts are from James Monaco, *How to Read a Film* (New York, 1977), p. 88; David Potter, *People of Plenty* (Chicago, 1954), pp. 181–182; and Reinhold Niebuhr, *The Irony of American History* (New York, 1962), p. 106.

the changed context behind the words. He would likely think foolish, for example, the idea that newspapers were printed for the benefit of advertisers rather than readers. The advertising of his day played a minor cultural role in comparison with today's multibillion-dollar industry. Similarly, Jefferson might have spoken of a "middling class of people," but the writings of Karl Marx have made it impossible today to use the word "class" without implying a whole range of meanings beyond the loose definition of the eighteenth century. To take another example, Jefferson would recognize terms such as "repression" and "unconscious," but without a knowledge of Freudian psychology, he would find their associations as shown in twentieth-century prose entirely foreign.

By the same token, eighteenth-century documents may appear deceptively lucid to twentieth-century readers. When Jefferson wrote that all men were "endowed by their Creator with certain unalienable Rights," including "Life, Liberty and the pursuit of Happiness," the meaning seems reasonably clear. But is it? Does "pursuit of Happiness," for example, have the same commonsense meaning that we attribute to it today?

Essayist and historian Garry Wills has offered his own reconstruction of the intellectual worlds behind the Declaration. Jefferson's "pursuit of Happiness," he argues, should not be interpreted merely as a vague and idealistic sentiment. Jefferson stood in the great eighteenth-century tradition of the Enlightenment; as one who had read widely in the works of European philosophes, he shared with them the belief that the study of human affairs should be conducted as precisely as study of the natural world had come to be.

During the seventeenth century, natural philosophers had increasingly relied upon mathematical equations and formulae to predict the motions of the planets, explain the principles of optics, and formulate the law of gravity. In particular, the prodigious syntheses of Isaac Newton stood as a monument to scientific progress. Alexander Pope expressed the adulation of the eighteenth century in his couplet, "Nature and Nature's laws lay hid in night: / God said, Let Newton be! and all was light." The philosophes of Pope's day hoped to extend the precision of the natural sciences to the study of man, including his psychology and his motivations.

The results of such endeavors may seem quaint today, but the philosophes took their work seriously. In 1725 Francis Hutcheson, a leader of the Scottish Enlightenment and a philosopher well known to Jefferson, attempted to quantify such elusive concepts as morality. The result was a string of equations where qualities were abbreviated by letters (B =

Benevolence, A = Ability, S = Self-love, I = Interest) and placed in their proper relations: "M = (B + S) × A = BA + SA; and therefore BA = M − SA = M − I, and B = $\dfrac{M - I}{A}$."

Jefferson possessed a similar passion for precision and quantification. He repeatedly praised the American astronomer David Rittenhouse and his orrery, a mechanical model of the solar system whose gears replicated the relative motions of the earth, moon, and planets. Jefferson also applied classification and observation as a gentleman planter. If it were possible to discover the many relationships within the natural order, he reasoned, farmers might better plant and harvest to those rhythms. For years Jefferson kept detailed notes indicating when the first dogwood blossomed, when the first whippoorwill was heard, when the first fireflies appeared, when the first asparagus came to table, when the first peaches were ripe, when the first shad arrived. Even in the White House, Jefferson kept his eye on the Washington markets and recorded the seasons' first arrivals of thirty-seven different vegetables.

Wills argues that Jefferson conceived the "pursuit of Happiness" in equally precise terms. Francis Hutcheson had suggested that a person's actions be judged by how much happiness they brought to other people. "Virtue," he argued, "is in a compound ratio of the quantity of good and number of enjoyers. . . . that action is best which accomplishes the greatest happiness for the greatest number." Such conceptions led the English deist William Wollaston to envision a balance-scale of pleasure and pain where the two opposites could be totted up metaphorically. "For nine degrees of pleasure, less by nine degrees of pain, are equal to nothing; but nine degrees of one, less by three degrees of the other, give six of the former net and true."

According to Enlightenment science, then, pleasure was a quality embedded in human nature itself, the pursuit of which governed a person's actions as surely as the laws of gravity governed walking. Further, since happiness could be quantified, a government's actions could be weighed in the balance scales to discover whether they measurably impeded a citizen's right to pursue happiness as he saw fit. When rightly apprehended, the science of government, like the science of agriculture or celestial mechanics, would take its place in the advancing progress of humankind.

Garry Wills's reconstruction of Jefferson's intellectual world, brilliant as it is, proves more speculative and uncertain than it first seems. Granted, Francis Hutcheson developed a calculus of "benevolence"; his ideas were in the air in 1776. But any number of ideas can be said to be "in the air" at a particular time. It is one thing to point out their existence, another to prove they actually influenced another person. How do we know Jefferson drew upon Hutcheson when composing the Declaration? Jefferson certainly knew of the Scottish philosopher, but had he read his works or taken them to heart? Wills has been forced to rely on circumstantial evidence, such as the presence of Hutcheson's works in Jefferson's library and Jefferson's love of precision in other fields of knowledge.

Whether or not Wills's specific case stands up to examination, his method of research is one which historians commonly employ. By understanding the intellectual world from which a document arose—by tracing, in effect, its genealogy—we understand better the document itself.

Lastly, a document may be interpreted according to the way it functions within a specific social situation. This approach relates a piece of evidence to its contemporary context rather than its genealogical past. The Declaration, after all, was written to explain and justify the circumstances of 1776. As a public document, it was addressed to a particular audience—or audiences. Who were they? What messages were being sent to those audiences and how was the Declaration designed to send them? Historians recognize that every document functions as a tool, fashioned to accomplish certain purposes within its own social situation. By studying the shape of the tool, historians can appreciate what goals the Declaration hoped to achieve and what audiences it expected to reach.

If the Declaration is to be conceived as a tool, it would be well to imagine something on the order of a fat, multibladed Swiss army knife. For the Declaration attempts to accomplish many goals and speak to several sorts of readers. True, its stated audience is a general one—the "candid world" addressed out of "a decent respect to the opinions of mankind." On the face of it, Congress seems to be appealing to a vague court of world opinion. And certainly the Declaration's preamble, grounded as it is upon the common denominator of natural rights, speaks to this general audience. It does not descend to tortuous specifics; it only outlines the general right of a people to revolt when a government becomes repressive and tyrannical. International readers need not be familiar with technical precedents of English constitutionalism to understand such arguments.

But other sections of the Declaration seem designed for specific audiences abroad. The most obvious audience is the king, his ministry, and (indirectly) Parliament, who as we have already seen, find a detailed listing of grievances laid at their door. The midsection of the Declaration reads very much like a lawyer's brief (indeed, many of the delegates were lawyers). The grievances have not been redressed, Congress concludes; therefore, it cites them one last time as the legal justification for revolution.

A second audience across the Atlantic is the British people. Once Congress disposes of the specific grievances, it looks beyond king and Parliament to the ultimate source of political power, the people. In his original rough draft, Jefferson bitterly reproached his "Brittish brethren" for permitting their elected representatives to tyrannize the colonists. Congress, aware that their English audience included those still sympathetic to the American cause, tempered Jefferson's attack, much to his displeasure. "The pusillanimous idea that we had friends in England worth keeping terms with," he complained, "still haunted the minds of many. For this reason those passages which conveyed censures on the people of England were struck out, lest they should give them offense."*

The Declaration addressed an entirely different foreign audience, but an equally crucial one, when it declared that the "United Colonies" had "full Power to levy War, conclude Peace, contract Alliances, establish Commerce, and to do all other Acts and Things which Independent States may of right do." The prime audience for this passage was France, for in July 1776 Congress wanted nothing more than to conclude a beneficial alliance. We have already followed Silas Deane, as he energetically sought aid in Paris during the summer of 1776; Congress clearly recognized that Deane would not succeed so long as France viewed America's quarrel as an internal affair of the British empire. As one delegate noted during the debate over independence, "A declaration of Independance alone could render it consistent with European delicacy for European powers to treat with us." Another influential Virginian concluded, "I am clearly of opinion that unless we declare openly for independency there is no chance for foreign aid." Thus, one of Richard Lee's June 7 resolutions directed Congress "to take the most effectual measures for forming alliances."

Although the Declaration proclaimed that its audience was the world at large, it directed its message equally to colonists at home. American sentiment for independence was by no means unanimous. Congress knew that in making the final break with England, it had moved ahead of many citizens it claimed to represent. Thus the detailed list of griev-

---

*Those censures included the rough draft passage examined earlier, condemning the British people for allowing the king to send over "Scotch & foreign mercenaries to invade and destroy us."

ances also served to remind wavering Americans of the evils wrought by king and Parliament: that the threat of tyranny was real and the patriot cause just.

In particular, some grievances appear to have been included as war propaganda designed to mobilize public opinion. The Declaration raised the spectre of the Quebec Act, which had incorporated the French territory into the British empire without providing its citizens representative government. Britain, the Declaration warned, might soon introduce "the same absolute rule into these colonies." Jefferson also called attention to alleged atrocities of war: foreign mercenaries with their "works of death, desolation and tyranny"; slaves arising against their masters; savage Indians incited to wage war against "all ages, sexes and conditions." In short, the king and his minions had "plundered our seas, ravaged our Coast, burnt our towns, and destroyed the lives of our people."

The "candid world" addressed by the Declaration was thus hardly one and indivisible. Different parts of the document addressed different audiences in order to accomplish specific goals. By analyzing the Declaration as a rhetorical tool, historians are able to delineate more clearly the ways that it functioned in the complex situation of 1776.

When the time came, on August second, to sign the document that had undergone so many revisions, alterations, and amendments, the delegates in Philadelphia perhaps came to recognize the Declaration's final audience: themselves. As president of the Congress, John Hancock was the first delegate to sign the engrossed copy. Taking pen in hand he reportedly remarked, "We must be unanimous; there must be no pulling different ways; we must all hang together." To which Ben Franklin replied, "Yes, we must indeed all hang together, or most assuredly we shall all hang separately." The conversation may only be a bit of folklore, added later to embellish the momentous occasion. Apocryphal or not, the exchange reinforces the import of Jefferson's concluding lines. "For the support of this Declaration," he wrote, "we mutually pledge to each other our Lives, our Fortunes and our sacred Honor." Many delegates took that final step only with great reluctance; even radicals like the Adamses recognized that the war was far from being won. The Declaration forced delegates to commit themselves publicly and symbolically to the Revolution, whether or not it finally succeeded. For the brief instant that each member stood in front of the table and signed, the Declaration had an audience of one. The rest of the candid world would come later.

Additional Reading

The Declaration of Independence, surely one of the most scrutinized documents in American history, stands at the center of the American Revolution, surely one of the most scrutinized events in that history. Consequently, the interested reader has plenty of material upon which to draw.

For background on the American Revolution, Edmund S. Morgan's *Birth of the Republic,* rev. ed. (Chicago, 1977) is a lively, brief, and lucid account with an up-to-date bibliography. For additional detail see John R. Alden, *A History of the American Revolution* (New York, 1969). David F. Hawke provides an engaging yet scholarly discussion of the drafting of the Declaration in *A Transaction of Free Men* (New York, 1964).

For more detailed analyses of the Declaration see Herbert Friedenwald's *The Declaration of Independence: An Interpretation and an Analysis* (New York, 1904). John H. Hazelton, *The Declaration of Independence: Its History* (New York, 1906) has much detailed material, including the investigation of who signed the Declaration and when. Perhaps the most elegant as well as most often-cited work is Carl Becker's *The Declaration of Independence: A Study in the History of Political Ideas* (New York, 1942). This volume is the best introduction both for an account of the drafting process and for the natural rights doctrines that Jefferson drew upon in summarizing the radicals' philosophy of revolution. More recently Garry Wills has provided a wide-ranging contextual analysis of the Declaration in *Inventing America: Jefferson's Declaration of Independence* (New York, 1978). Wills argues that Jefferson depended less on the ideas of John Locke (contrary to what Carl Becker had argued) and more on the philosophers of the Scottish Enlightenment. Undeniably Wills overstates his case, and he has been called to task by Ronald Hamowy in a classic cut-and-thrust maneuver entitled "Jefferson and the Scottish Enlightenment: A Critique of Garry Wills's *Inventing America,"* *William and Mary Quarterly,* third Ser., XXXVI, no. 4 (October 1979), 503–523. Devastating as Hamowy's criticisms are, they do not invalidate all of Wills's arguments. *Inventing America* is still very much worth reading.

Readers wishing to do some of their own textual analysis will find Julian P. Boyd's *The Declaration of Independence: The Evolution of the Text* (Princeton, N.J., 1945) a good starting place. Boyd's text provides facsimiles of Jefferson's "Rough Draught" of the Declaration, plus other copies Jefferson sent to friends, and Adams's copy transcribed while the document was still in committee. Until his death Boyd also edited the definitive *Papers of Thomas Jefferson*

(Princeton, N.J., 1950–); Volume I contains a facsimile of the earliest fragment of the Declaration, as well as excellent discussions by Boyd of textual matters. All in all, it is a textbook case on editing texts.

As a starting point for the role of the Continental Congress, see Worthington C. Ford, ed., *Journals of the Continental Congress: 1774–1789* (Washington, D.C., 1904–1937). The reader will soon find, however, that Charles Thomson's minutes are tantalizingly brief and only hint at the issues on the delegates' minds. To supplement this, Edmund C. Burnett published a collection of the *Letters of Members of the Continental Congress* (Washington, D.C., 1921–1936), which provides much more material. Since Burnett's collection was by no means complete, however, the Library of Congress has sponsored a new edition of letters as a bicentennial project, Paul H. Smith, ed., *Letters of Delegates to Congress, 1774–1789* (Washington, D.C., 1976–). At this writing, ten volumes are available, providing much fuller coverage than Burnett (some 1,250 pages versus about 290 pages for a comparable period in Burnett).

In addition to Garry Wills's study of Jefferson's intellectual world, earlier useful works include Adrienne Koch, *The Philosophy of Thomas Jefferson* (New York, 1943) and Daniel Boorstin, *The Lost World of Thomas Jefferson* (New York, 1948), as well as Dumas Malone's biography, *Jefferson and His Time,* 6 vols. (Boston, 1948–1981). Perhaps the most indispensible aid to tracing the change of a word's meaning over time is the *Oxford English Dictionary.* This thirteen-volume work provides short natural histories of words, complete with examples taken from published works to demonstrate usage changes over time. Once again, Wills's *Inventing America* supplies abundant examples of this sort of word detective-work.

Finally, readers interested in further exercises in establishing the context of a document may wish to consult Philip S. Foner's collection of subsequent declarations of independence, *We, the Other People* (New York, 1976). The excerpts range from the "Workingman's Declaration of Independence" issued in 1829 to one put out by the "People's Bicentennial Commission" in 1975.

CHAPTER

FOUR

❖

Jackson's Frontier – and Turner's

Ceremony, merriment, and ballyhoo came to Chicago in the summer of 1893, and predictably, the crowds swelled the fairgrounds to get a taste of it. Buffalo Bill's Wild West Show went through its usual bronco-busting, war-whooping routines. Visitors gawked at a giant map of the United States, fashioned entirely from pickles. Also on display were a huge telescope, destined for Yerkes Observatory; a long-distance telephone, connected with New York City; and oil paintings and porcelains by the thousands. A splendid time was guaranteed for all.

The excuse for the fuss was Chicago's "World's Columbian Exposition," held ostensibly to salute the four-hundredth anniversary of the discovery of America. More plausibly, the fair allowed proud Chicagoans to prove that they were more than hog-butchers to the world and that they could out-exposition any metropolis on the globe. Given the total attendance of 27 million people over six months, the city made its case.

As an adjunct to the fair, and to add further glory and respectability, the exposition convened several scholarly congresses, including a World's Congress of Historians and Historical Students. And so on July 12, the curious tourist had the opportunity (or misfortune) of straying away from the booming cannibal drums of the Midway Plaisance and into the Art Institute, where five eager historians waited to present the fruits of their labors.

Now, historical conferences are not the sort of events to be entered upon lightly under any circumstances, but the audience on this hot evening had to endure a particularly heavy bombardment from the podium. Five papers were read back-to-back without respite, ranging from a discussion of "English Popular Uprisings in the Middle Ages," to "Early Lead Mining in Illinois and Wisconsin." The hardy souls who weathered the first four presentations saw a young man in starched collar rise to present yet another set of conclusions, this time on "The Significance of the Frontier in American History."

The young man was Frederick Jackson Turner, a historian from the University of Wisconsin. Although none in the audience could have suspected it, his essay on the frontier eventually sparked four generations of scholarship and historical debate. The novelty of Turner's essay resulted not from his discovery of any previously unknown facts, but because he proposed a new theory, one that took old facts and placed them in an entirely different light. Known popularly as Turner's "frontier hypothesis," it is a theory that even today attracts staunch defenders.

THE SIGNIFICANCE OF THEORY

Turner's hypothesis is only one of many theoretical concepts that historians have advanced in order to unify and make sense of the chaotic past. Yet thus far, this book has avoided a direct discussion of the term *theory*. It has done so partly because many historians work with theory more intuitively than explicitly. Even those practitioners who attempt a certain theoretical consistency, such as Marxist or Freudian theorists, often argue among themselves over who is most accurately following in the master's footsteps. Yet despite theory's generally low profile and nebulous character, it remains an essential, inseparable part of the discipline.

At one level, theory can be defined simply as hypothesis. In this sense, it is the analysis that explains a relationship between two or more facts. During the Salem witch trials, "afflicted" townspeople acted in certain violent but consistent ways. Before historians can conclude that these acts constituted symptoms of neurotic behavior, they must have accepted the concept of conversion hysteria as a valid theoretical explanation. Note that the Salem records do not provide this interpretation; theory is indispensable to the explanation.

In a broader sense, theory can be defined as a body of theorems presenting a systematic view of an entire subject. We use the term this way when speaking of the "theory of wave mechanics" or a "germ theory of disease." Often, small-scale theoretical constructs are a part of a larger theoretical framework. Conversion hysteria is only one of many behavioral syndromes classified as neuroses; in turn, the concept of neurosis is only one part of the larger body of theory accepted by modern psychology. Physicists, chemists, and other natural scientists often use mathematic formulae to summarize their general theories, but among social scientists and humanists, theorems become less mathematic and more elastic. Even so, when historians discuss a "theory of democracy" or a "theory of economic growth," they are applying a set of coherent principles to the study of a particular situation.

Because historians study an event or period in its entirety, historical narrative usually incorporates many theories rather than just one. The historian of early Virginia will draw on theories of economic behavior (the development of joint stock companies as a means of capital formation), sociology (the rise of slavery as an institution of color), psychology (the causes of friction between white and black laboring classes), and so on. In this broadest sense historical theory encompasses the entire range of a historian's training, from competence in statistics to opinions on politics and philosophies of human nature. It is derived from formal education, reading, even from informal discussions with academic colleagues and friends.

It follows that theory in this wider sense—"grand theory," as it might be called—plays a crucial role in historical reconstruction. While small-scale theory is called on to explain specific puzzles (why didn't slavery become entrenched in Virginia before 1660?), grand theory is usually part of a historian's mental baggage *before* he immerses himself in a particular topic. It encourages historians to ask certain questions, and not to ask others; it tends to single out particular areas of investigation as worthy of testing, and to dismiss other areas of inquiry as either irrelevant or uninteresting. Thus anyone who ventures into the field of history —the lay reader as well as the professional researcher—needs to be aware of how grand theory exerts its pervasive influence. Nowhere in American history is this influence better illustrated than in Frederick Jackson Turner's venerable frontier hypothesis.

Turner began his Chicago lecture with a simple yet startling fact he had culled from the 1890 census. "Up to and including 1880, the country had a frontier of settlement," the census reported, "but at present the unsettled area has been so broken into by isolated bodies of settlement that there can hardly be said to be a frontier line." Turner seized upon this "event"—the passing of the frontier—as a "great historic moment." The reason for its importance seemed clear: "Up to our own day, American history has been in a large degree the history of the colonization of the Great West. The existence of an area of free land, its continuous recession, and the advance of American settlement westward, explain American development."

Turner's broad assertion—a manifesto, really—challenged on several counts the prevailing historical wisdom. Scholars of Turner's day had approached their subject with an Atlantic-coast bias. They viewed the East, and especially New England, as the true bearer of American culture; developments in the mid- and far-west were either ignored or treated sketchily. Turner, who had grown up in the rural setting of Portage, Wisconsin, and taken his undergraduate degree at the University of Wisconsin, resented that attitude.

In addition, the reigning scholarship focused almost exclusively on political and constitutional developments. "History is past Politics and Politics present History" ran the slogan on the wall of the Johns Hopkins seminar room where Turner had taken his Ph.D. In contrast, young

Turner in 1893, the year he presented his thesis at the Columbian World Exposition; and the Johns Hopkins University seminar room for history students. At the head of the table is Professor Herbert Baxter Adams, who argued that American democratic institutions could be traced to British and European roots. "It is just as improbable that free local institutions should spring up without a germ along American shores as that English wheat should have grown there without planting," he wrote. Turner resented the lack of interest in the West at Hopkins. "Not a man I know here," he commented, "is either studying, or is hardly aware of the country behind the Alleghenies."

Turner strongly believed that this narrow political perspective neglected the broader contours of social, cultural, and economic history. Historians who took the trouble to examine those areas, he felt, would discover that the unique physical and cultural conditions of the frontier, and not eastern cities, had shaped American character.

The frontier's effect on American character had been recognized in a casual way by earlier observers, but Turner attempted a more systematic analysis. In doing so, he drew upon the scientific "grand theory" most prominent in his own day, Charles Darwin's theory of evolution. Where Darwin had proposed an explanation for evolution in the natural world, Turner suggested that America was an ideal laboratory for the study of cultural evolution. The American frontier, he argued, returned man to a primitive state of nature. With the trappings of civilization stripped away, the upward process of evolution was re-enacted. Dramatically, Turner recreated the sequence for his audience:

> The wilderness masters the colonist. It finds him a European in dress, industries, tools, modes of travel, and thought. It takes him from the railroad car and puts him in the birch canoe. It strips off the garments of civilization and arrays him in the hunting shirt and the moccasin. It puts him in the log cabin of the Cherokee and Iroquois and runs an Indian palisade around him. Before long he has gone to planting Indian corn and plowing with a sharp stick; he shouts the war cry and takes the scalp in orthodox Indian fashion. In short, at the frontier the environment is at first too strong for the man. He must accept the conditions which it furnishes, or perish, and so he fits himself into the Indian clearings and follows the Indian trails. Little by little he transforms the wilderness, but the outcome is not the old Europe. . . . The fact is that here is a new product that is American.

Turner suggested that the evolution from frontier primitive to civilized townsman occurred not just once but time and time again, as the frontier moved west. Each time, settlers shed a bit more of their European ways, each time a more distinctively American culture emerged. That was why the perspective of Eastern historians was so warped: they stubbornly traced American roots to English political institutions, or even worse, the medieval organization of the Germanic town. "The true point of view in the history of this nation is not the Atlantic coast," Turner insisted, "it is the Great West."

From this general formulation of the frontier's effects, Turner de-

duced several specific traits that the recurring evolutionary process produced. Chief among them were nationalism, independence, and democracy.

Nationalism, Turner argued, arose as the frontier broke down the
geographic and cultural identities of the Atlantic coast: New England
with its Yankees and the tidewater South with its aristocratic planters.
The mixing and amalgamation of sections was most clearly demonstrated
in the middle states, where both Yankees and Southerners migrated over
the mountains, where Germans and other northern Europeans joined
Englishmen in seeking free land. There a new culture developed, pos-
sessing "a solidarity of its own with national tendencies. . . . Interstate
migration went steadily on—a process of cross-fertilization of ideas and
institutions."*

The frontier also promoted independence, according to Turner. The
first English settlements had depended on the mother country for their
material goods, but as settlers pressed farther west, England found it
difficult to supply the backcountry. Frontier towns became self-sufficient,
and Eastern merchants increasingly provided westerners with American
rather than English products. The economic system became more American, more independent.

Most important, suggested Turner, the individualism of the frontier
promoted democracy and democratic institutions. "Complex society is
precipitated by the wilderness into a kind of primitive organization based
on the family," Turner argued. "The tendency is anti-social. It produces
antipathy to control, and particularly to any direct control." Thus Westerners resented being taxed without being represented, whether by
England and Parliament or by the Carolina coastal planters whom the
backcountry Regulators fought. The frontier also broke down social
distinctions that were so much a part of the East and Europe. Given the
fluid society of the frontier, poor farmers or traders could and did
become rich almost overnight. Social distinctions disappeared when
placed against the greater necessity of simple survival.

Turner even argued that the West, with its vast supply of free land,
encouraged democracy in the East. The frontier acted as a safety valve,
he suggested, draining off potential sources of discontent before they
disrupted society. "Whenever social conditions tended to crystallize in
the East, whenever capital tended to press upon labor or political restraints to impede the freedom of the mass, there was this gate of escape

*Once again, note the Darwinian metaphor.

to the free conditions of the frontier. . . . Men would not accept inferior wages and a permanent position of social subordination when this promised land of freedom and equality was theirs for the taking."

The upshot of this levelling process was nothing less than a new American character. Turner waxed eloquent in his description of frontier traits:

> That coarseness and strength combined with acuteness and inquisitiveness; that practical, inventive turn of mind, quick to find expedients; that masterful grasp of material things, lacking in the artistic but powerful to effect great ends; that restless, nervous energy; that dominant individualism, working for good and for evil, and withal that buoyancy and exuberance which comes with freedom—these are the traits of the frontier, or traits called out elsewhere because of the existence of the frontier.

This was what Turner offered his Chicago listeners—not only "the American, this new man," as Hector St. John de Crevecoeur had called him in 1778—but also a systematic explanation of *how* the new American had come to be.

It would be proper etiquette here to scold Turner's Chicago audience for failing to recognize a masterpiece when they were read one. But in some ways it is easier to explain his listeners' inattention than account for the phenomenal acceptance of the frontier thesis by later historians. Undeniably, Turner's synthesis was fresh and creative. But as he himself admitted, the essay was a hypothesis in need of research and testing. Of this, Turner proved constitutionally incapable. Although he loved to burrow in the archives for days on end, he found writing an unbearable chore, especially when attempting a book-length effort.

Consequently, Turner published only magazine articles in the influential *Atlantic Monthly* and other journals; for the most part, they merely reiterated his thesis. The articles, along with numerous lectures and a flock of enthusiastic students, proved sufficient to make Turner's reputation, but they also made trouble. Publishers flocked to Wisconsin seeking books by the celebrated historian. Turner, with hopelessly misplaced optimism, signed contracts with four publishers to produce eight separate manuscripts. None ever saw the light of day. The single full-length book he completed appeared only through the frantic efforts of yet another editor, Albert Bushnell Hart, who was driven to wheedling, cajoling, and threatening in order to obtain the desired results. "It ought to be carved on my tombstone," Hart later remarked, "that I was the only man in the world that secured what might be classed an adequate volume from Turner."*

Why Turner's remarkable success? Certainly not because of his detailed research, which remained unpublished. Success was due to the attraction of his grand theory. Later critics have taken Turner to task for imprecision and vagueness, but these defects are compensated by an eloquence and magnificence of scale. "The United States lies like a huge page in the history of society," Turner would declaim, and then proceed to lay out history with a continental sweep. The lure of his hypothesis for historians was much like the lure of a unified field theory for natural scientists—a set of equations, as physicist Freeman Dyson has remarked, that would "account for everything that happens in nature. . . . a unifying principle that would either explain everything or explain nothing." In similar (though less galactic) fashion, Turner's theory captured historians' imaginations. "The existence of an area of free land, its continuous recession, and the advance of American settlement westward, explain American development." That is about as all-encompassing a proposal as a historian could desire!

The theory seemed encompassing, too, in its methods. Using the techniques of social science in historical research is so familiar today, we forget the novelty and brilliance of Turner's insistence on "unifying" the tools of research. Go beyond politics, he argued; relate geography, climate, economics, and social factors to the political story. Not only did he propose this, Turner also provided a key focus—the frontier—as the laboratory in which these variables could be studied. The fresh breeze of Turner's theory succeeded in overturning the traditional approaches of Eastern historians.

By the time Turner died in 1932, a tide of reaction had set in. Some critics pointed out that the frontier thesis severely minimized the democratic and cultural contributions of the English heritage. Others attacked Turner's vague definition of the "frontier." (Was it a geographical place? A type of population, such as trappers, herders, and pioneers? Or a process, wherein European traits were stripped off and American ones formed?) Other critics disputed the notion of the frontier as a "safety valve" for the East. Few European immigrants actually settled on the frontier; if anything, population statistics showed more farmers moving to the cities.

*Turner also reprinted some of his essays in *The Frontier in American History* (New York, 1920). The book Hart edited was *The Rise of the New West,* which appeared in 1906.

For our own purposes, however, it would be misleading to focus on these battles. Whether or not Turner was right, his theory dramatically influenced the investigations of other historians. To understand how, we need to take Turner's general propositions and see how he and others applied them to a specific topic.

An ideal subject for this task is the man whose name Turner himself shared—Andrew Jackson.* Jackson is one of those figures in history who, like Captain John Smith, seems always to be strutting about the stage just a bit larger than life. Furthermore, Jackson's wanderings took him straight into the most central themes of American history. "Old Hickory" led land-hungry pioneers into the southeastern United States, displacing Native Americans from their lands east of the Mississippi, expelling the Spanish from Florida, and repelling the English from New Orleans. As President, he launched the war against the "monster" Bank of the United States, placing himself at the center of the perennial American debate over the role of economic power in a democracy. Above all, he came to be seen as the political champion of the common people, his backwoods origins and forceful personality epitomizing the style of the new American democracy. Here is a man whose career makes it impossible to avoid dealing with the large questions grand theory will suggest.

How, then, did Turner's frontier hypothesis shape historians' perception of Jackson? What features of his career did it encourage them to examine?

JACKSON: A FRONTIER DEMOCRAT (TARNISHED)

For Frederick Turner, Andrew Jackson was not merely "one of the favorites of the west," he was "the west itself." Turner meant by that rhetorical proclamation that Jackson not only spoke for the West, his whole life followed precisely that pattern of frontier evolution wherein eastern culture was stripped bare and replaced by the "contentious, nationalistic democracy of the interior."

Jackson's Scotch-Irish parents had joined the stream of eighteenth-century immigrants who landed in Pennsylvania, pushed westward until they bumped up against the Appalachians, and then filtered southwest

*The bond of names is more than coincidental. Frederick Jackson Turner's father, Andrew Jackson Turner, was born in 1832 and named in honor of the President re-elected that year.

into the Carolina backcountry. This was the process of "mixing and amalgamation" that Turner outlined in his essay. Turner had also shown how the frontier stripped away higher social organizations, leaving only the family as a sustaining bond. Andrew Jackson was denied even that society. His father died before Jackson's birth, his only two brothers and his mother died during the Revolution. At the age of seventeen, Andrew left Waxhaw, his boyhood home, never to return again. In effect, he was a man without a family—but not, as Turner saw it, a man without a backcountry.

Jackson first moved to the town of Salisbury, North Carolina, reading law by day and, with the help of similarly high-spirited young friends, raising hell by night. Brawling in barrooms, sporting with young ladies, moving outhouses in the hours well past midnight—such activities gave Jackson a reputation as "the most roaring, game-cocking, horse-racing, card-playing, mischievous fellow that ever lived in Salisbury," according to one resident.

In 1788 the footloose Jackson grabbed the opportunity to become public prosecutor for the Western district of North Carolina, a region that then stretched all the way to the Mississippi. There, in the frontier lands that now comprise Tennessee, Jackson hoped to make his reputation. It was still primitive land. Two hundred miles of wilderness separated eastern Tennessee settlements around Jonesborough from the western Cumberland Valley and Nashville. Travel between the two areas invited clashes with Indians. Into this life Jackson plunged with ambitious enthusiasm. Once settled in Nashville, he handled between a quarter and a half of all court cases in his home county during the first few years of his arrival. On top of that, he made the hazardous journey to Jonesborough three times a year to pursue cases there.

Jackson dispensed justice with the kind of "coarseness and strength" Turner associated with the frontier personality. When one enraged defendant stepped on prosecutor Jackson's toe to indicate his displeasure, Jackson calmly cold-cocked the offender with a stick of wood. On another occasion, when Jackson had been appointed superior court judge in the newly created state of Tennessee, he stalked off the bench to summon a defendant before the court when no one else dared, including the sheriff and posse. The man in question, one Russell Bean, had threatened to shoot the "first skunk that came within ten feet," but when Jackson came roaring out of the courthouse, Bean pulled in his horns. "I looked him in the eye, and I saw shoot," said Bean, "and there wasn't shoot in nary other eye in the crowd; and so I says to myself, says I, hoss, it's about time to sing small, and so I did."

Jackson the frontiersman: Russell Bean surrenders to Justice Jackson, as depicted in an 1817 biography. Wrote Turner, "If Henry Clay was one of the favorites of the West, Andrew Jackson was the West itself. . . . the very personification of the contentious, nationalistic democracy of the interior. . . ."

All in all, Jackson seemed a perfect fit for frontier democrat—a man who indeed "was the west itself." Turner described in characteristic terms Jackson's election to the House of Representatives in 1796:

The appearance of this frontiersman on the floor of Congress was an omen full of significance. He reached Philadelphia at the close of Washington's administration, having ridden on horseback nearly eight hundred miles to his destination. Gallatin (himself a western Pennsylvanian) afterwards graphically described Jackson, as he entered the halls of Congress, as "a tall, lank, uncouth-looking personage, with long locks of hair hanging over his face, and a cue down his back tied in an eel-skin; his dress singular, his manners and deportment those of a rough backwoodsman." Jefferson afterwards testified to Webster: "His passions are terrible. When I was President of the Senate, he was a Senator, and he could never speak, on account of the rashness of his feelings. I have seen him attempt it repeatedly, and as often choke with rage." At length the frontier, in the person of its leader, had found a place in the government. This six-foot back-woodsman, angular, lantern-jawed, and thin, with blue eyes that blazed on occasion; this choleric, impetuous, Scotch-Irish leader of men; this expert duellist and ready fighter; this embodiment of the contentious, vehement, personal west, was in politics to stay.

This was Turner at his rhetorical best, marshalling all the striking personal details that supported his theory. But he was not writing a full-length biography and so confined his discussion of Jackson either to a few paragraphs of detail or to the traditional rousing generalities.

One of Turner's graduate students went further. Thomas Perkins Abernethy studied at Harvard during the period when the university had lured Turner east from his home ground at the University of Wisconsin. Abernethy believed that to test the frontier hypothesis adequately, it ought to be examined on a local level, in more detail. In this respect, he felt, previous historians had not been scientific enough. "Science is studied by the examination of specimens, and general truths are discovered through the investigations of typical forms," he asserted. In contrast, "history has been studied mainly by national units, and the field is too broad to allow of minute examination." But Tennessee provided a perfect "specimen" of the western state. It broke away from its parent, North Carolina, during its frontier days; it was the first area of the nation to undergo territorial status; and from its backwoods settlements came Andrew Jackson himself, the embodiment of western democracy. Why not trace the leavening effects of the frontier within this narrower compass? Abernethy set out to do just that in his book, *From Frontier to Plantation in Tennessee*.

Obviously, he had learned his mentor's techniques well. Turner encouraged students to trace the effects of geography and environment on politics. Abernethy perceived that Tennessee's geography divided it into three distinct agricultural regions, providing a "rare opportunity to study the political effects of these several types of agricultural economy." Turner emphasized the role of free land as a crucial factor in the west. Abernethy agreed that land was "the chief form of wealth in the United States in its early years" and paid particular attention to the political controversies over Tennessee's vast tracts of land. Always, he was determined to look beyond the surface of the political arena to the underlying economic and geographic considerations.

These were Turner's techniques, all right, but the results produced anything but Turner's conclusions. *From Frontier to Plantation* is dedicated to Frederick Jackson Turner, but the book directly refutes Turner's optimistic version of western history.

As Abernethy began unravelling the tangled web of Carolina-Tennessee politics, he discovered that Americans interested in western free land included more than pioneer squatters and yeoman farmers of the "interior democracy." Prosperous speculators who preferred the comforts of the civilized east perceived equally well that land which stood forested and uncultivated would skyrocket in value once settlers poured over the Appalachians in search of homesteads.

The scramble for land revealed itself in the strange and contradictory doings of the North Carolina legislature. During the Revolutionary War, inflation had plagued the state, largely because the legislature had continuously issued its own paper money when short of funds. The value of this paper money plummeted to a fraction of its original face value. After the war, the legislature retrenched by proclaiming that all debtors would have to repay their debts in specie (i.e., gold or silver coins) or its equivalent in paper. If a person owed £10 and the going rate set £400 in paper notes as equal to £1 in actual silver, debtors who repaid using paper money would owe £4000. In effect, the legislature was repudiating its paper currency and saying that only specie would be an acceptable medium of exchange.

This made sense if the legislature was trying to put the state's finances on a stable footing. But Abernethy noticed that in the same session, the legislature turned around and issued a *new* run of paper money—printing up a hundred thousand dollars. Why issue more paper money when you've just done your best to get rid of the older stuff?

Abernethy also noticed that during the same legislative session, land offices were opened up to sell some of North Carolina's western lands. The state sold these lands only under certain conditions. The claimant had to go out into the woods and mark the preliminary boundaries of his claim. Then he had to come back and enter the claim at a designated land office. Finally, a government surveyor would survey the lot, submit his report to the Secretary of State for the governor's authentication, and enter it in the county register.

And how were these lands to be paid for? Well, gold or silver was permissible, of course, but so was *the state's paper money*—at rates specified by the legislature.

The situation hardly confirmed Turner's conception of the frontier, Abernethy concluded. First, who ended up being able to buy the new land? Not the squatter or yeoman farmer, certainly—few of them could fulfill the requirements of marking out land, returning east to register it, having it officially surveyed, and entering it. Instead, land speculators in the east, including state legislators, stepped in to make a killing. The career of William Blount, one of the most successful of speculators, illustrated the process at work. As a state legislator, Blount had led in passing the land legislation; at the same time, he paid James Robertson, a Tennessee pioneer, to go west and mark out vast tracts of land. Blount, for his part, registered the claim and paid for the land.

Sometimes the money that paid for the land was the old paper currency, bought up for a fraction of its original price from poorer folk who had no means of claiming their own land. The new paper money could also be used at face value to pay for the lands. Was it coincidence only that Blount had been the legislator proposing the new issue of paper money? Abernethy thought not.

Instead of confirming Turner's version of a hardy democracy, then, Abernethy painted a picture of "free" Tennessee lands providing fortunes for already-powerful men. Blount used "the entire Southwest [as] his hunting ground and he stuffed his pockets with the profits of his speculations in land. In the maw of his incredible ambition—or greed— there originated land grabs involving thousands of choice acres." And Blount was only one of many across the country. "In those days," Abernethy concluded, "America was run largely by speculators in real estate."

It was into this free-for-all country that Andrew Jackson marched in 1788, but Abernethy's new frame of reference placed his career in a different light. Compare Turner's description of Jackson's "pioneer" ride to Philadelphia with Abernethy's version of Jackson's horseback arrival in Tennessee. "Tradition has it," reported Abernethy, that Jackson

> arrived at Jonesboro . . . riding a fine horse and leading another mount, with saddle-bags, gun, pistols, and fox-hounds. This was elaborate equipment for a struggling young lawyer, and within the year he increased it by the purchase of a slave girl. . . . Jackson still found time to engage in his favorite sport of horse-racing, and he fought a bloodless duel with Waightstill Avery, then the most famous lawyer in western North Carolina. All this makes it clear that the young man had set himself up in the world as a "gentleman." Frontiersmen normally fought with their fists rather than with pistols, and prided themselves more upon physical prowess, than upon manners. Though commonly looked upon as a typical Westerner, Jackson was ever an aristocrat at heart.

Jackson cemented his ties with the upper layers of society in more substantial ways. Turner had noted Jackson's practice as a "public prosecutor—an office that called for nerve and decision, rather than legal

Jackson the gentleman: Thomas Abernethy argued that the history of Jackson's Tennessee demonstrated how "the wealthy rose to the top of affairs even on the frontier, and combined through their influence and common interests to control economic legislation. From time to time they found it necessary to make some obvious concession to democracy, such as broadening the suffrage or lowering the qualifications for office. But, while throwing out such sops with one hand, they managed to keep well in the other the more obscure field of economic legislation." The portrait of Jackson is by Thomas Sully.

acumen, in that turbulent country." What frontier lawyering also called for, which Turner neglected to mention, was a knack for collecting debts, since Jackson most often represented creditors intent on recovering loans. During his first month of legal practice, he issued some seventy writs to delinquent debtors. This energetic career soon came to the notice of none other than William Blount, who had by this time gotten himself appointed governor of the newly created Tennessee territory. He and Jackson became close political allies.

Jackson too had an eye for speculating, and it almost ruined him. Like Blount, he had cashed in on Tennessee's lands, buying 50,000 acres on the site of the future city of Memphis. In 1795 Jackson took his first horseback ride to Philadelphia, a year before the one Turner eloquently described, in order to sell the Memphis land at a profit. Few Philadelphians wanted to buy, but Jackson finally closed a deal with David Allison, another of Blount's cronies. Allison couldn't pay in cash, so he gave Jackson promissory notes. Jackson, in turn, used the notes to pay for goods to stock a trading post he wanted to open in Tennessee.

Scant months after Jackson returned home, he learned that David Allison had gone bankrupt. Even worse, since Jackson had signed Allison's promissory notes, Allison's creditors were now after Jackson. "We take this early opportunity to make known to you that *we* have little or no expectations of getting paid from him," they wrote, "and that we shall have to get our money from you." Suddenly Jackson found himself in the middle of a financial nightmare. He was, he admitted, "placed in the Dam'st situation ever a man was placed in."

To get himself out, he was forced to speculate even more heavily. Buy a parcel of land here, sell it there. Cash in his trading post, make a small profit, invest it in more land. Exchange the new land for another buyer's promissory note. And so on. Not until 1824 did he settle the final claims in the tangle. Abernethy sketched these financial transactions in a chapter entitled "Andrew Jackson as a Land Speculator." Clearly, he believed that Jackson's horseback rides on behalf of real estate deserved more emphasis than any romantic notions of a galloping frontier democrat.

Despite such a devastating attack on the frontier thesis, Abernethy's admiration for Turner was genuine, no doubt because he recognized how much the thesis had guided his research. It is easy to conclude that the value of a theory rests solely on its truth. Yet even if Turner's hypothesis erred on many points, it provided a focus that prodded Abernethy to investigate important historical questions—the implications of western land policy, the effect of environment on character, the social and geographical foundations of democracy. All these topics had been slighted by historians.

Theory, in other words, is often as important for the questions it raises as for the answers it provides. In this sense it performs the same function in the natural sciences. Thomas Kuhn, a historian of science, has demonstrated just how indispensable an older scientific theory is in pointing the way to the theory that replaces it. As the old theory is tested, attention is naturally focused on problem areas—places where the results are not what the old theory predicts. The new theory emerges, Kuhn pointed out, "only for the man who, knowing *with precision* what he should expect, is able to recognize that something has gone wrong." Abernethy was able to discern that something had "gone wrong" in Tennessee politics, but only because Turner's hypothesis had shown him what questions needed to be asked and where to look for answers.

JACKSON: WORKINGMAN'S FRIEND

Theory, then, can actually sharpen a historian's vision by limiting it— aiding the process of selection by zeroing in on important issues and data. It stands to reason, however, that trade-offs are made in this game. If a theory focuses attention on certain questions, it necessarily also causes a historian to ignore other facts, trends, or themes. Theory can limit in a negative as well as a positive sense.

Abernethy's disagreement with Turner illustrates this problem. Although the two historians reached diametrically opposed conclusions about Andrew Jackson, they carried on the whole debate within the framework of Turner's thesis. Did Jackson embody the democratic, individualistic West? Yes, argued Turner. No, countered Abernethy. Yet both men accepted the premise suggested by Turner's thesis, that the influence of the West was the crucial issue to examine.

That might serve well enough for a study limited to Tennessee politics, but Jackson went on to achieve national fame at New Orleans and was elected to the Presidency in 1828. He triumphed in all the southern coastal states, in Pennsylvania, and also received a majority of New York's electoral votes. In New York too he cemented an alliance with Martin Van Buren, the sophisticated eastern leader of the "Albany Regency" political faction.

Such facts call attention to something that Turner's frame of reference overlooked. As a national president, Jackson made friends in the East as well as the West, in cities as well as in the country. Historian Arthur Schlesinger, Jr., believing that Abernethy as well as Turner overemphasized the importance of Jackson's western roots, determined to examine the eastern sources of Jackson's democratic coalition. "A judgment on the character of Jackson's democracy must be founded on an examination of what Jackson did as President," he argued, "and on nothing else; certainly not on an extrapolation made on the basis of his career before he became President." The result of Schlesinger's research was *The Age of Jackson* (1945), a sweeping study that highlighted the influence of eastern, urban laboring classes on Jacksonian democracy.

In part, Schlesinger's theoretical approach had been the natural consequence of his upbringing. He spent his childhood within the civilized environs of Cambridge, Massachusetts, where his father, Arthur Meier Schlesinger, Sr., held a chair in history at Harvard. Like Turner, Schlesinger Sr. preferred the wider horizons of social and cultural history over traditional political history. Unlike Turner, he emphasized the role of urban society and culture in American life. His article, "The City in American History," sparked a generation of scholarship on peculiarly urban problems such as industrial labor and immigration. The article, Schlesinger later suggested generously, "did not seek to destroy the frontier theory but to substitute a balanced view: an appreciation of both country and city in the rise of American civilization." Nevertheless, Schlesinger Sr.'s interest clearly lay with the cities.

The younger Schlesinger admired his father—so much so that at the age of fifteen he changed his name from Arthur Bancroft Schlesinger to Arthur Meier Schlesinger, Jr. More significant, the son shared the same scholarly dispositions. After schooling at the prestigious Phillips Exeter Academy, Arthur completed a brilliant undergraduate and graduate career at Harvard.* It was out of this intellectual training that Schlesinger wrote his book.

The Age of Jackson also reflected a set of attitudes and emphases popular in the 1930s that distanced Schlesinger from the Progressive outlook Turner had shared at the turn of the century. The thirties saw the country plunged into a depression so severe that it shook many Americans' faith in the traditional economic system. Theories of class struggle, of conflict between capital and labor, became popular in scholarly circles. As an avid supporter of Franklin Roosevelt, Schlesinger by no means accepted the doctrines of the communist left, but he did believe that class conflict played a greater role in American history than the sectional disputes that Turner had emphasized. Significantly, Schlesinger used a quotation from George Bancroft, a radical Jacksonian from New England, as the super-

---

*Like many midwesterners, Schlesinger Sr. believed wholeheartedly in the virtues of public education. But he felt compelled to send Arthur Jr. to Exeter after discovering that his tenth-grade public school teacher taught that "the inhabitants of Albania were called Albinos because of their white hair and pink eyes."

scription for his book. It affirmed the importance of class struggle but still embraced the liberal's hope for a nonviolent resolution of conflict:

> The feud between the capitalist and laborer, the house of Have and the house of Want, is as old as social union, and can never be entirely quieted; but he who will act with moderation, prefer fact to theory, and remember that every thing in this world is relative and not absolute, will see that the violence of the contest may be stilled.

Given Schlesinger's background and temperament, his research focused on substantially different aspects of Jackson's career. It portrayed Old Hickory as a natural leader who, though he came from the West, championed the cause of laborers in all walks of life—city "mechanicks" as well as yeoman farmers. Jackson's chief political task, argued Schlesinger, was "to control the power of the capitalist groups, mainly Eastern, for the benefit of the noncapitalist groups, farmers and laboring men, East, West, and South." Schlesinger made his opposition to Turner abundantly clear:

> The basic Jacksonian ideas came naturally enough from the East, which best understood the nature of business power and reacted most sharply against it. The legend that Jacksonian democracy was the explosion of the frontier, lifting into the government some violent men filled with rustic prejudices against big business does not explain the facts, which were somewhat more complex. Jacksonian democracy was rather a second American phase of that enduring struggle between the business community and the rest of society which is the guarantee of freedom in a liberal capitalist state.

Consequently, much of *The Age of Jackson* is devoted to people the Turner school neglected entirely: the leaders of workingmen's parties, the broader labor movement, and the efforts of Democratic politicians to bring them within the orbit of Jackson's party. Abernethy's treatment of Jackson as land speculator is replaced by attention to Jackson's vigorous war on the Second Bank of the United States, where Democratic leaders are shown forging an alliance with labor. "During the Bank War," Schlesinger concluded, "laboring men began slowly to turn to Jackson as their leader, and his party as their party."
Like Turner, Schlesinger came under critical fire. Other historians have argued that much of Jackson's so-called labor support was actually middle- or even upper-class leaders who hoped to channel worker senti-

Jackson, champion of the working people: "The specific problem was to control the power of the capitalistic groups, mainly Eastern, for the benefit of the noncapitalist groups, farmers and laboring men, East, West and South," wrote Arthur Schlesinger, Jr. "The legend that Jacksonian democracy was the explosion of the frontier, lifting into the government some violent men filled with rustic prejudices against big business, does not explain the facts. . . ." Here, "King Mob" goes to work on a giant cheese at a White House celebration in 1837. The odor of the cheese lingered for months.

ments for their own purposes. At the same time, many in the real laboring classes refused to support Jackson. But again—what is important for our present purposes is to notice how Schlesinger's general concerns shaped his research. It is not coincidental that Jackson's celebrated kitchen cabinet, in Schlesinger's retelling, bears a marked resemblance to Franklin Roosevelt's "brain trusters." It is not coincidental that Jackson attacks the "monster Bank" for wreaking economic havoc much the way that FDR inveighed against the "economic royalists" of the Depression era. Nor is it coincidental that *The Age of Jackson* was followed, in 1957, by *The Age of Roosevelt*. Schlesinger may have displayed his political and economic philosophy more conspicuously than most historians, but no scholar can escape bringing some theoretical framework to his or her research. One way or another, theory inevitably limits and focuses the historian's perspective.

JACKSON: THE GREAT WHITE FATHER

Schlesinger's urban orientation encouraged him to shift focus away from the "old facts" that Turner's theory emphasized, instead dealing with an entirely different area of research. But theory can produce new results simply by providing a means of viewing the "old facts" in a new light. Historian Michael Rogin's biography of Andrew Jackson, *Fathers and Children,* illustrates this process at work. Rogin's research covered ground already well-examined by Turner and other historians. In fact, *Fathers and Children* reiterated some of Turner's major assumptions and metaphors. It acknowledged that the conditions of the frontier gave American culture its unique stamp. "The new American world undermined the authority provided by history, tradition, family connection, and the other ties of old European existence," Rogin agreed. He also accepted Turner's metaphor of evolutionary development, that "America was continually beginning again on the frontier." Such assertions, he pointed out, were commonplace even during the period of westward expansion.

Yet Rogin drew radically different conclusions from Turner's postulates, primarily because his own theoretical training was so much at variance with Turner's progressive philosophy. For one, Rogin did his research during the late 1960s and early 1970s, when American society had become increasingly conscious of minority groups and cross-cultural conflict. Turner's original frontier thesis largely ignored Native American cultures, by implicitly denying that any significant "culture" existed. For Turner, Indian society was no society, the bottom rung on the cultural ladder, where the frontiersman at first found himself pitched. ("Before long . . . he shouts the war cry and takes the scalp in orthodox Indian fashion. . . .")

This lack of interest in the Indian led to a curious result, Rogin noted. Undeniably, the growth of the United States from thirteen Atlantic colonies to a continental empire constituted a major theme in American history. Yet historians largely ignored the policies of Indian removal needed to accomplish that goal—policies which Andrew Jackson supported and vigorously executed. Historians, he argued, "have failed to place Indians at the center of Jackson's life. They have interpreted the Age of Jackson from every perspective but Indian destruction, the one from which it actually developed historically."

Rogin wished not only to tell the story of Indian removal but also to probe the psychological motives that impelled Americans to destroy Indian culture so thoroughly. To do so, he relied on Freudian psychological theory, a second theoretical perspective that distanced him from Turner. Rogin admitted that many readers would consider Freudian analysis unnecessary. "The sources of white expansion onto Indian land . . . seem straightforward," he granted. "Surely land hunger and the building of a national empire provided the thrust." But Rogin argued that the psychological dimensions of Indian removal were too significant to be ignored.

Indeed, the language with which nineteenth-century Americans described Indians and white–Indian relationships has remarkable psychological overtones. Paternal and familial metaphors were used often. Treaty negotiators constantly urged Indians to make peace with their "white father," the President of the United States. If friendly tribes did not conclude treaties, Jackson once warned, "We may then be under the necessity of raising the hatchet against our own friends and brothers. Your father the President wishes to avoid this unnatural state of things."* White American leaders were seen as the "fathers" of civilization, Indians as "untutored children of the forest." Remarked editor Horace Greeley, "The Indians are children. . . . Any band of schoolboys from ten to fifteen years of age, are quite as capable of ruling their appetites. . . ." Historian Francis Parkman, who journeyed westward along the Oregon Trail in 1846, referred to the Indian as an "irreclaimable son of the wilderness, the child who will not be weaned from the breast of his rugged mother."

Why had historians remained "systematically deaf" to such familial rhetoric, with its imagery of children "weaned from the breast" and talk of an "unnatural state of things" among white–Indian "family" relations? Rogin believed that such deafness resulted from a theoretical block. "Lacking a theory which sensitized them to such a vocabulary and helped them interpret it, they could not hear what was being said. Let

---

*At the time, in 1818, Jackson was negotiating the cession of land from the Choctaw Indians on behalf of the Monroe administration.

us, to begin with, take seriously the words of those who made our Indian policy."

Because Jackson was so prominent in shaping Indian policy, and because he embodied "in extreme form the central cultural tensions of his time," Rogin began with a close examination of Andrew's childhood development. Like Turner, he made much of the independence forced on the young boy by his early loss of family. But Rogin doubted whether the loss fostered a genuine psychological maturity. Psychoanalytic theory has stressed the rage and resentment an infant feels when being separated from his mother and from the comfort and security of suckling at her breast. Later childhood or even adult shocks, it suggests, may sometimes revive the fears and rages arising from maternal separation. Although no clinical evidence survived to connect Jackson's mature temperamental outbursts with his childhood experiences, Rogin noted certain suggestive facts: "Jackson was a posthumous child; did his father's death affect his mother during his infancy? Problems in infancy, involving feeding, weaning, or holding the child, often intensify infantile rage and accentuate later difficulties in the struggle of the child to break securely free of the mother." Like Turner, Rogin quoted Jefferson's description of Jackson "choking with rage" on the Senate floor, and noted that according to eyewitnesses, Jackson often slobbered and spoke incoherently when excited or angry. "Jackson's slobbering," argued Rogin, "suggests early problems with speech, mouth, and aggression. Speech difficulties often indicate a problematic oral relationship."

Even if Jackson's adult rages reflected the resentment he felt at childhood separation experiences, he certainly did not allow childhood fantasies to dominate his adult life. Indeed, Jackson's political success came from mastering his rages and using them for his own political purposes. He successfully "externalized inner enemies, and battled them in the world." In doing so, Rogin argued, Jackson reflected American culture of the period. For Jackson's "externalized" enemies were also the enemies of other Americans of the backcountry: the native "untutored children of the forest."

Indian society and behavior contrasted strikingly with "civilized" lifestyles, as Americans repeatedly perceived. To European-Americans, Rogin argued, Indians appeared playful, violent, improvident, wild, and in harmony with nature. American society exalted contrasting virtues: discipline, work, the acquisition of private property. Such ascetic values "generated a forbidden nostalgia for childhood," Rogin believed, "—for the nurturing, blissful, primitively violent connection to nature that white Americans had to leave behind." The result was envy and rage;

But Jackson didn't start this

envy that Indian "children" were so apparently free to indulge every childish whim; and rage, in an attempt to prove white independence from childhood by mastering and destroying any evidence of such infantile behavior. Thus white Americans were impelled to break the Indian's tie with nature, "literally by uprooting him, figuratively by civilizing him, finally by killing him."

For Rogin, Jackson's career demonstrated that such conflicting feelings were resolved by developing a paternalistic attitude toward "childlike" adversaries. He argued that since Jackson had grown up without a father, he compensated in adult life by stressing his own role as "father" to Indians. Perhaps equally significant, Jackson was denied the pleasure of becoming a natural father in adult life; he and his wife Rachael had no children. Here too, the couple compensated, raising a dozen infants, most of them orphaned relatives of the Jacksons' families.

Among the adopted children was a three-year-old Indian boy, Lincoya, encountered during the Creek war. The boy had been found "pressed to the bosom of its lifeless mother," explained one of Jackson's friends, and because the rest of the baby's family were dead, the Creek women meant to kill Lincoya. But Jackson intervened, in part because he recognized the similarity to his own childhood: "he[,] as to his relations—is so much like myself I feel an unusual sympathy to him. . . ." Both fatherless and childless, then, Jackson adopted a particularly strong paternal outlook. By demanding that Indian "children" obey their "white fathers" in their own best interests, he and similarly minded Americans "indulged primitive longings to wield total power," concluded Rogin. "They sought to regain the primal infant–mother connection from a position of domination instead of dependence."

For Jackson, this paternalism extended beyond Indians. Rogin argued that as president, Jackson applied the same emotional relationship to his conception of democracy. "Jackson had successfully asserted paternity . . . over Indians. Might not fatherhood now also extend its protecting arm to the generality of poor, weak, and virtuous? Might it not reform the civilian world?" Jackson approached the presidency acutely aware of the burden imposed on him by political paternity—the heritage of the Founding Fathers. He recognized that his generation lived in the shadow, to use his own words, "of the illustrious actions of their fathers in the war of the revolution." The younger generation had to demonstrate that they were not "a degenerate race . . . unworthy of the blessings which the blood of so many thousand heroes has purchased for them." Thus Jackson strove to identify himself with the "Fathers"—

indeed, adopted them as his own—while identifying nearly everyone else as his children. He became champion of the downtrodden because his primary relation to the electorate was as a father to his sons.

Viewed through Rogin's theoretical framework, many of Jackson's well-known actions as President took on new significance. When South Carolina attempted to nullify the tariff law passed by Congress, Jackson demanded obedience—just as a stern father might command his unruly children. In a draft of his nullification speech, he addressed South Carolinians in distinctly paternal tones: "Seduced as you have been my

Jackson, the "effectionate parent": "Pressed with mutiny and sedition of the volunteer infantry—To suppress it, having been compelled to arrange my artillery, against them, whom I once loved like a father loves his children. . . . I felt the pangs of an effectionate parent, compelled from duty to chastise his child —to prevent him from destruction & disgrace and it being his duty he Shrunk not from it—even when he knew death might ensue." So Jackson wrote to his wife, describing how he singlehandedly quelled a mutiny of Tennessee troops during his campaign against the Creek nation.

fellow Countrymen by the delusive theories and misrepresentation of ambitious, deluded and designing men, I call upon you, in the language of truth and with the feelings of a father to retrace your steps."

Similarly, when making war on the Bank of the United States, Jackson viewed himself paternally. "It is the natural instinct of wealth and power to reach after new acquisitions," he lectured his Cabinet. "It was to arrest them that our Fathers perilled their lives." As heir to "the Fathers," Jackson clearly implied, he too might peril his life. "The bank, Mr. Van Buren, is trying to kill me," he once told his ally, *but I will kill it.*" As one of his contemporaries acutely observed, Old Hickory was much like George Washington: "Providence denied him children, that he might be the father of his country."

Rogin freely admitted that for many readers his psychoanalytical approach to Jackson, Indian removal, and the new Democracy "must seem bizarre." Indeed, many professional historians, let alone lay readers, find the use of such analytical concepts as "infant rage" and "problematic oral relationships" inappropriate or even ludicrous. The use of psychiatric theory by historians certainly deserves closer scrutiny, and we will return to the topic in a later chapter. For the present, however, the merits of the case concern us less than the undeniable effect theory has had in shaping historical research. Rogin's sensitivity to familial language and his interest in the psychological dynamics of childhood have led him to evaluate old evidence in a new light. However debatable his conclusions, he has rightly perceived that once sensitized to familial language, inquiring historians will find in nineteenth-century sources far more references than they expected to "white fathers," Revolutionary "fathers," Indian "sons," the "mother country" England—even "Mother Bank," as one pro-Jacksonian cartoon noted. Once again, theory has helped to focus on a previously unperceived problem.

After such a procession of grand historical theories, what may be said of the "real" Andrew Jackson? Skeptics may be tempted to conclude that there was not one, but four Old Hickories roaming the landscape of Jacksonian America—Jackson the frontier democrat; Jackson the aristocratic planter and speculator; Jackson, friend of labor; and Jackson, paternal ruler of both Indians and common folk. The use of historical theory seems to have led the reader into a kind of boggy historical relativism, where there is no real Jackson, only men conjured up to fit the formula of particular historical theories.

But that viewpoint is overly pessimistic. It arises from the necessary emphasis of this chapter, where our concern has been to point out the

2   hypotheses

general effects of grand theory rather than to evaluate the merits of each case. Theory, we have stressed, provides a vantage point which directs a researcher's attention to significant areas of inquiry. But the initial theorizing is only the beginning. Theories can be and are continually tested. Sometimes old theories are thrown out, replaced by new ones. In such fashion did Copernicus replace Ptolemy. But some theories stand up to testing, or are merely refined to fit the facts more closely. In yet other instances, old theories are incorporated into more-encompassing frameworks. Newtonian mechanics are still as valid as ever for the everyday world, but they have been found to be only a special case of the broader theories of relativity proposed by Einstein. And of course, Einstein continued to search for ways to incorporate his special theories of relativity into a more general, unified field theory.

Similarly we may argue that, far from having four different Jacksons roaming the historical landscape, we are seeing various aspects of Jackson's personality and career which need to be incorporated into a more comprehensive framework. It is the old tale of the blind men describing the different parts of an elephant: the elephant is real enough, but the descriptions are partial and fragmentary. Frederick Jackson Turner was writing about a nebulous Jacksonian style—indeed, one may as well come out with it—"democracy" and "individualism" were, for Turner, little more than styles. Abernethy, on the other hand, was looking at the concrete material interests and class alliances that Jackson developed during his Tennessee career, with almost no attention to the presidential years. Schlesinger did precisely the opposite: picked up Jackson's story only after 1824, and in the end was more concerned with the Jacksonian movement than with its nominal leader. Finally, enter Rogin, who examined Jackson's career from childhood to old age, in Tennessee and in Washington, but whose real subject was the peculiar psychological intensity, even ferocity, that Jackson brought to his experience.

Would it be possible to incorporate these various viewpoints within a larger framework? One can imagine the outlines of such a general construct. Fatherless, poor boys in a highly mobile frontier setting are driven by the potential "democracy" and "individualism" inherent in such settings to identify themselves as much as possible with elites—to set themselves apart from the common masses. But given the pervasive rhetoric of equality and democracy, they do so in a way that is uneasy, and always vulnerable to some sudden exposure of their rootless, lower-class origins. Their attitudes toward wealth and authority are ambivalent. They will seek both. But they will need constantly to have their status and power ratified by the common consent of all—their neighbors, at first, but if their careers take a political shape, by every possible constituency: farmers, soldiers, eastern workingmen—even those "children of the forest," Indians.

A unified field theory for Jacksonian America? Perhaps the outlines are there, but the task must be left to some future Turner of the discipline. What remains clear is that, however much particular theories will continue to be revised or rejected, theory itself will accompany historians always. Without it, researchers cannot begin to select from among an infinite number of facts; they cannot separate the important from the incidental; they cannot focus on a manageable problem. Albert Einstein put the proposition succinctly. "It is the theory," he concluded, "which decides what we can observe."

Additional Reading

The reader who doubts our assertion that the theories of Turner, Schlesinger, and others have been evaluated and analyzed, need only spend an afternoon in the card catalog of any major library. A recent bibliographical essay on Jacksonian America, listing only the "more important" books and articles, ran to over 700 entries.

Andrew Jackson himself may be most easily approached through several of many biographies (most of which are rather unimaginatively titled, *The Life of Andrew Jackson*). Earliest is John Reid and John Henry Eaton, *The Life of Andrew Jackson* (Philadelphia, 1817; reissued, 1974). The volume has much authentic material for Jackson's early years, but beware later "campaign" editions of 1824 and 1828, to which chunks of political puffery were added. One of the more critical biographies was done by James Parton, *The Life of Andrew Jackson*, 3 vols. (Boston, 1866); it includes the recollections of Jackson's boyhood neighbors, whom Parton interviewed many years later. Marquis James, *The Life of Andrew Jackson*, 2 vols. (Indianapolis, Ind., 1938) is a modern and extremely flattering portrait. Robert Remini has completed a three-volume study which incorporates the most recent scholarship yet remains eminently readable: *Andrew Jackson and the Course of American Empire; 1767–1821; Andrew Jackson and the Course of American Democracy, 1822–1832;* and *Andrew Jackson and the Course of American Freedom, 1833–1845* (New York, 1977–84).

Primary sources are less conveniently available. John Spencer Bassett has edited the *Correspondence of Andrew Jackson,* 6 vols. (Washington, D.C., 1926–1933). Many of Jackson's papers are in the Library of Congress and are also available on microfilm in some university libraries. Jackson's backwoods spelling and punctuation can be slow going.

To understand the role of theory, in both science and history, readers will profit from Thomas Kuhn, *The Structure of Scientific Revolutions* (Chicago, 1962). The revised edition (1970) contains a few remarks by Kuhn on the applicability of his theory to social science disciplines. Further background on the major interpretations of Jackson and Jacksonian America is available in Charles G. Sellers, "Andrew Jackson Versus the Historians," *Mississippi Valley Historical Review* (currently issued as the *Journal of American History*), XLIV (March, 1958), 615–634 and Edward Pessen, *Jacksonian America,* rev. ed., (Homewood, Ill., 1978).

Frederick Jackson Turner's major works are *The Frontier in American History*

(New York, 1920), *The Rise of the New West* (New York, 1906), and *The Significance of Sections in American History* (New York, 1932). The best accounts of Turner's life and work are by Ray Billington, who probably set to print more words on Turner than Turner himself ever got to press on American history. *Frederick Jackson Turner: Historian, Scholar, Teacher* (New York, 1973) is a full and entertaining biography, while *The Genesis of the Frontier Thesis* (San Marino, Calif., 1971) describes just that. A contrasting view may be found in Richard Hofstadter, *The Progressive Historians: Turner, Beard, Parrington* (New York, 1968). David Potter, *People of Plenty* (Chicago, 1954) has an excellent discussion of Turner and the concept of national character.

In addition to Thomas Abernethy's *From Frontier to Plantation in Tennessee* (Chapel Hill, N.C., 1932), see his views in "Andrew Jackson and the Rise of Southwestern Democracy," *American Historical Review*, XXXIII (October, 1927), 64–77 and his biography of Andrew Jackson in the *Dictionary of American Biography*. A few remarks on Abernethy's career may be found in Darett Rutman, ed., *The Old Dominion: Essays for Thomas Perkins Abernethy* (Charlottesville, Va., 1964). Arthur Schlesinger, Jr.'s *Age of Jackson* (Boston, 1945) has generated much discussion among historians, summarized well in Edward Pessen's bibliographical essay, cited above. Information on Schlesinger's career may be gained from his father's autobiography, *In Retrospect* (New York, 1963) and from the essay on Schlesinger, Jr., in Marcus Cunliffe and Robin Winks, eds., *Pastmasters: Some Essays on American Historians* (New York, 1969).

Michael Rogin's *Fathers and Children: Andrew Jackson and the Subjugation of the American Indian* (New York, 1975) has appeared too recently to have attracted much systematic examination. Remini's biography, cited above, carries on a polite but firm running war in the footnotes. Of the major reviews by historians, the most interesting includes one by Lewis Parry in *History and Theory*, XVI, no. 2 (1977), 174–195 which, among other things, points out that Jackson's drooling in adult life might have been caused by mercury poisoning that Jackson sustained from medication that he often took—a potion of gin, sugar of lead, and calomel. Elizabeth Fox Genovese bitterly attacks Rogin's grand theorizing in *Reviews in American History*, III (December, 1975), 407–417. Genovese is a Marxist and she accuses Rogin of mating a fraudulent Marxism with an improperly conceived Freudianism. The result, she claims, is a mule of dubious pedigree. Readers will quickly discover that Andrew Jackson and his generation are not the only ones who argue over their legitimate paternity.

CHAPTER

FIVE

❖

The Invisible Pioneers

Sometime in the early 1700s, somewhere along the rolling foothills of
Montana, a man named Shaved Head lay in hiding, staring into the
distance at a group of very big dogs.

To the west lay the peaks of the Rockies and the continental divide;
to the east, the short-grass plains stretching for hundreds of miles.
Shaved Head's usual haunts were some distance to the north, in what is
now Saskatchewan. But together with a group of Blackfeet comrades, he
had run and walked south for several days, leading a war party in search
of the people who came from across the mountains to hunt buffalo—
probably the Snake Indians. At last he had discovered one of their camps.

And in it stood a number of these strange big dogs.

The Blackfeet had dogs, of course. They used them to haul skin
lodges, cooking pots, and utensils whenever they moved camp. But these
dogs were different from any Shaved Head had ever seen. They were
tall as a man and more the size of elk, except they seemed to have lost
their horns. Still, they couldn't be elk, for they were obviously slaves to
the Snake people, just as dogs were slaves to the Blackfeet.

Shaved Head managed to steal a few of the animals. But when his
warriors tried to mount them, the creatures began walking and the
men quickly jumped off. Cautiously they led the animals home, where
everyone in the band gathered around and marveled. At first, people
tried putting robes on the animals' backs, but that made them jump.
After a time a woman said, "Let's put a travois on one of them, just
like we do on our small dogs." So they made a travois and attached it

115

to one of the gentler animals. He didn't kick or jump. Then the people led him around with the travois attached. Finally a woman mounted the animal and rode it. In years after, they called these creatures *ponokamita,* or elk dogs.

The elk dogs, so strange to the Blackfeet, were actually horses. Such creatures had been extinct in North America for 10,000 years, until the Spanish reintroduced them in the sixteenth century. From Spanish outposts they gradually spread north and east, finally reaching the Blackfeet early in the eighteenth century. Shaved Head's account of their arrival is noteworthy for several reasons. In the first place, it rests on a remarkable oral tradition. Anthropologist John Ewers heard the story in the 1940s from an eighty-year-old Blackfoot named Weasel Tail who, in turn, had heard it growing up as a boy, in the 1860s and '70s, from an elderly member of the tribe named Two Strikes Woman. She was passing along accounts that her great-grandfather had given her father. Thus the tradition passed through at least four generations. To be sure, such oral evidence lacks the authority of written or eyewitness accounts, especially since the events in question took place more than 200 years earlier. (In Chapter 7, we will have occasion to examine in more detail the problems of oral evidence.) Still, other available records suggest that, however the details fell out, the Blackfeet first gained the use of horses sometime in the early 1700s, well before they were ever visited by whites.

Weasel Tail's story is useful for another reason. It suggests a markedly different way to understand the process of westward expansion along the American frontier. For if the frontier marked the boundary between white settlements and the lands that lay beyond, then historians have most often concentrated on what happened on the eastern side of the line. Even Turner, that staunch defender of a "western" point of view, was in this sense an easterner. By "the west," Turner meant that portion of European settlement abutting the frontier—not the Indian cultures lying beyond. He examined how the political institutions of the East were shaped by the frontier experience; how democracy flourished when Americans transformed a "wilderness" that threatened to overpower them.

In doing so, Turner only mirrored the preconceptions of his forebears. Most Americans heading west in the 1840s did not envision the land beyond as one filled with competing cultures. For them, the frontier was a line between settled land and unsettled—between populated communities and virtually empty wilderness. Lansford Hastings, who crossed the continent in 1842, expressed the idea clearly in his *Emigrants' Guide to Oregon and California.* The territory west of the Missouri, he proclaimed, was full of "wild forests, trackless plains, untrodden valleys. . . ." An Illinois congressman of the day painted a similar picture:

> Only think of it: men, women, and children, forsaking their homes, bidding farewell to all the endearments of society, setting out on a journey of over two thousand miles, upon a route where they have to make their own roads, construct their own bridges, hew out their own boats, and kill their own meat. . . . [where they are] exposed to every variety of weather, and the naked earth their only resting-place! In sickness they have no physician; in death there is no one to perform the last sad offices. Their bodies are buried by the wayside, to be exhumed and defiled by the Indians, or devoured by the wolves.

Thus the far side of the frontier was seen as totally wild, existing in a natural state, with the Indians little different from nomadic wolves. Such descriptions were commonplace in the nineteenth century; indeed, they can be traced all the way back to William Bradford's famous account of the Pilgrim's frontier of 1620: "they had now no friends to welcome them nor inns to entertain or refresh their weatherbeaten bodies; no houses or much less towns to repair to. . . . Besides, what could they see but a hideous and desolate wilderness, full of wild beasts and wild men. . . ."

In contrast, Weasel Tail's story reminds us that the frontier was a two-sided boundary, not simply a line between the "civilized" and the "wild." Indian societies, some remarkably populous and complex, lay on the far side of the frontier. Just as Europeans were discovering and adapting to conditions in their "New" World, Native Americans were discovering and adapting to the culture that came to them from across the oceans. Even more to the point, the crucial adaptations along the frontier cannot be described in terms of human contact alone. As Weasel Tail's story indicates, horses from European culture interacted with Blackfoot society years before whites themselves appeared. There was not only a human frontier line but also a "horse frontier" as well as myriad other plant and animal frontiers—not the least of them a critical frontier of microorganisms.

The boundaries that must be drawn, then, are not simply between differing cultures but between differing ecological systems. And although such lines may at first seem unimportant, they had a profound impact on the settlement of North America. Europeans and Indians had developed different ways of exploiting the plants and animals of their environments. When these competing methods met, they were all too often disastrously incompatible. A full understanding of the expansion of the United States to the Pacific must take account of these ecological conflicts. In many ways, European flora and fauna were the invisible yet indispensable pioneers of the advancing frontier.

To watch these larger frontiers in action, our approach in this chapter must be nearly the opposite of the microcosmic focus used to examine the witchcraft outbreak at Salem. Instead of looking at a small patch of ground in detail, we must pull on the proverbial seven-league boots and seek out trends at work over centuries and across an entire continent. The center of the story will remain the westward-moving frontier of the nineteenth century. But it is important to look first at North America before there was a frontier line—when the Atlantic Ocean remained the boundary between European and American cultures. What were some of the features of this precontact era? How did the new frontier affect not only European cultures and ecologies but also those of Native Americans?

A LAND OF ABUNDANCE

If modern Americans were somehow able to return to the North America of 1450 and trek across it, they would most likely be struck by the sheer abundance of wildlife. Certainly, many of the first European colonists remarked on the profusion of birds, beasts, and fish.

Francis Higginson, an early settler at Salem, Massachusetts, knew that his friends in England would be skeptical of the reports he was sending. "The aboundance of Sea-Fish are almost beyond beleeving," he noted, "and sure I should scarce have beleeved it except I had seene it with mine owne eyes." Another New Englander reported that "I myself at the turning of the tyde have seen such multitudes of sea bass that it seemed to me that one might goe over their backs dri-shod." In Virginia, settlers fording streams on horseback sometimes found that the hooves of their mounts killed fish, the rivers were so thick with them. Governor Thomas Dale, in one setting of his seine, hauled in 5,000 sturgeon. Even in the early eighteenth century, salmon were so abundant in the Connecticut River that farm laborers there would not accept such low-class food more than once a week from their masters.

And size! Some of the sturgeon in Governor Dale's nets were twelve feet long, while Virginia crabs ran to a foot in length. A Dutch visitor to Brooklyn reported being treated to a pail of "Gowanes oysters which are the best in the country . . . large and full, some of them not less than a foot long." As for the lobsters coming out of New York Bay, another traveler reported that "those a foot long are better for serving at table." He meant in comparison to the five and six-footers that were being taken. Such granddaddy lobsters continued to be trapped from time to time through much of the eighteenth century.

As with fish, so with wildfowl. Governor Berkeley of Virginia spoke of massive flocks of ducks, geese, brant, and teal, whose beating wings sounded "like a great storm coming over the water." Two centuries later, Lewis and Clark marveled at the same abundance along the shores of the Pacific. Clark "could not sleep for the noise" kept up by the "White & black brants Duck &c. . . . they were emencly numerous and their cries horrid." And the number of passenger pigeons—a bird that had been hunted into extinction by 1914—astounded everyone, including naturalist John James Audubon. In 1813, along the banks of the Ohio River, Audubon watched flocks pass that darkened the sun with their numbers. In "almost solid masses, they darted forward in undulating and angular lines, descended and swept close over the earth with inconceivable velocity, mounted perpendicularly so as to resemble a vast column, and, when high, were seen wheeling and twisting within their continued lines, which then resembled the coils of a gigantic serpent." At night when they arrived at their roosting place, Audubon was waiting, along with hunters who had come with poles to knock them down.

> As the birds . . . passed over me, I felt a current of air that surprised me. . . . The fires were lighted [by the hunters], and a magnificent as well as wonderful and almost terrifying sight presented itself. The pigeons, arriving by thousands, alighted everywhere, one above another, until solid masses, as large as hogsheads, were formed on the branches all round. . . . It was a scene of uproar and confusion. I found it quite useless to speak or even to shout to those persons who were nearest to me.

Similar tales were told of mammals. Red and fallow deer congregated along the Virginia coasts in the hundreds. Gray and black squirrels ate so much of the colonists' grain that bounties for squirrels were offered. In Pennsylvania, over 600,000 were killed in one year alone. When settlers crossed the Great Plains in the 1840s and '50s, they were amazed by the villages and even whole "cities" of prairie dogs. "There is no end seemingly," wrote one pioneer. In some cases, even "city" was a misnomer. In 1905 a scientist from the U.S. Biological Survey reported finding the remnants of a Texas prairie dog colony whose underground passages stretched for nearly 25,000 square miles, an area the size of West Virginia. The colony's estimated population had been 400 million.

Above ground, bison roamed the prairies in herds estimated to number 50 million, and not only on the prairies and plains. Herds had moved east as far as Pennsylvania, Kentucky, and a few even into Virginia along the Potomac River. To the west, their range extended past the Rockies. Pronghorn antelope roamed in huge numbers and may have even outnumbered buffalo. Beaver swelled the streams of eastern forests as well as those of the Rockies, and Meriwether Lewis praised the headwaters of the Missouri as being "richer in beaver and otter than any country on earth." Grizzly bears "were everywhere," reported one mountain man, "—upon the plains, in the valleys, and on the mountains, so that I have often killed as many as five or six in one day, and it is not unusual to see fifty or sixty within the twenty-four hours." Another trapper, James Ohio Pattie, claimed to have sighted 220 in one day.

It is possible, then, to assemble a picture of the North American continent as a sort of natural Eden teeming with life. Yet while this picture is accurate in many details, it presents certain problems. The accounts from which it is drawn were written by a wide variety of people. Some, like Audubon, possessed well-deserved reputations for accuracy; a few, like the scientists from the U.S. Biological Survey, were even conducting systematic research. On the other hand, when we hear James Ohio Pattie's report of seeing 220 grizzlies in one day, how seriously are we to take it? (In ten hours of wandering, that would mean sighting an average of twenty-two bears every hour, or about one every three minutes.) Pattie, a rough and ready mountain man, was never known to let the truth stand in the way of a good story. Was 220 based on an actual count, or was it merely his rough translation for "a hell of a lot more bears than I saw *most* days"? Even if we believe Pattie, we cannot assume that such densities applied equally throughout the Rockies or even in that particular region at all times. (Grizzlies, for example, are more likely to congregate during mating season than other times of the year.) Individual observations, in other words, must be evaluated as critically in ecology as in history.

There is a second reason for proceeding cautiously. We must be critical not only of data provided by observers but also of ecological theory itself. Ecologists, like historians, need coherent hypotheses to organize their information; and as with historians, theory shapes the way facts are analyzed. In describing the ecological systems of precontact America, it is easy to assume not only that existing plants and animals were abundant but that they lived together in a kind of mutually adjusting, harmonious balance. Indeed, ecologists of the early twentieth century encouraged this notion. The influential Frederic Clements argued that, while natural systems went through certain stages of growth, eventually they reached a "climax," or mature phase. At that point, the animals and plants within the system remained in dynamic balance. Under such conditions, stability was the norm.

More recently, ecologists have suggested that this model idealizes too much the notion of stability. Few ecosystems settle into a long-term equilibrium without experiencing disruptions. Such changes ought not to be seen as aberrations but as something to be expected. Even without human intervention, instability is normal. As a case in point, the abundant beaver of the Rockies were subject to cycles of disruption. As populations built up along streams, closer contact allowed disease to spread from one colony to another. At such times epizootics (epidemics in animal populations) wiped out large numbers of beaver. A dry year, too, lowered stream levels, making the spread of disease easier.

Epizootics are only one example of dramatic change. The abundance —or rather overabundance—of a particular species often altered other parts of an ecosystem. Audubon saw quite clearly the destructive effects of passenger pigeons: "Many trees, two feet in diameter . . . were broken off at no great distance from the ground; and the branches of many of the largest had given way, as if the forest had been swept by a tornado." Similarly, when large herds of buffalo cropped the grasses of the plains too closely, the old vegetation was driven out by faster-growing, hardier weeds. When Lewis and Clark complained that their moccasins were constantly pierced by spikes of the prickly pear cactus along the upper Missouri, they were not describing vegetation that had grown there since time immemorial but relatively new growth, taking advantage of the conditions of overgrazing.

It would be equally misleading to assume that Native Americans before 1492 harmonized so well with their world that they were a "natural" part of the system's ecology, unlike the white invaders of 1492. The idea that Indians were protoecologists of some sort is only a more sophisticated version of the pioneers' belief that the Indians were "children of nature" and the land still virgin wilderness. In truth, Native Americans were quite active in altering and controlling their environment.

SHAPERS OF THE ENVIRONMENT

To begin with, horticulture played a crucial role in many Native American cultures. In the Southwest, the Anasazi devised a sophisticated system of dikes and dams to flood their fields, while the Hohokam dug canals, some of them thirty miles long. The peoples east of the Mississippi, whom popular literature tends to portray primarily as hunters, in fact regularly raised "vast quantities of pease, beans, potatoes, cabbages, Indian corn, pumpions [pumpkins], melons" to supply the greater part of their food needs. Both men and women worked to clear fields, plow, sow, and weed. And it was Indian surplus corn that kept the English alive so often in the early years of the Virginia colony. Even in the plains region, horticulture was important to many tribes.

Indian fields did not usually resemble those of Europe. In the Northeast, for example, they were multicrop, with beans planted right along with squash and corn. The cornstalks thus served as beanpoles while the tendrils of squash plants spread between plants, helping to keep the weed population down. But these were fields nonetheless, and horticulture had changed the natural face of North America in many areas.

The most widespread way in which Native Americans altered their environment was through fire. All across the continent, Indians regularly burned large tracts of land. Cabeza de Vaca, the Spanish explorer who crossed much of the Southeast during the 1530s, noted that the Ignaces Indians of Texas went about

> with a firebrand, setting fire to the plains and timber so as to drive off the mosquitoes, and also to get lizards and similar things which they eat, to come out of the soil. In the same manner they kill deer, encircling them with fires, and they do it also to deprive the animals of pasture, compelling them to go for food where the Indians want.

Plains Indians used fires for communication: to report a herd of buffalo or warn of danger, as well as to drive off enemies in war. In California, where grass seeds were an important food, Indians burned fields annually to remove old stocks and increase the yield. In fact, in 1602 the Spanish explorer Vizcaino reported that near San Diego the Indians "made so many columns of smoke on the mainland that at night it looked like a procession and in the daytime the sky was overcast."

Along the Atlantic coast, Indians regularly set fires to to keep down the scrub brush. As William Wood observed in New England, fire consumed "all the underwood and rubbish which otherwise would overgrow the country, making it unpassable, and spoil their much affected hunting." The resulting forest was almost parklike, with large, widely spaced trees, few shrubs, and plenty of succulent grasses. In Virginia the first English found the open woods "all flowing over with fair flowers

Fires could spread quickly through parched prairie grass, and in such cases Indians of the plains used fire defensively as well as offensively, as artist Alfred Jacob Miller recorded in this watercolor painted in 1837. The approach of a prairie fire was "insidious enough," Miller noted; "at first a slight haze is seen near the horizon, but the experienced eye of the Trapper or Indian immediately detects the nature of the visitor, and all hands in the camp are immediately busy in setting fire to the long grass about them;—not suffering it to make much headway, but beating it down with cloths & blankets. In this manner large spaces are cleared, horses, mules, and tents are secured in the burnt areas, which are enlarged as time permits, and escape from certain death is thus averted. . . . The fire sweeps round with the speed of a race horse, licking up every thing that it touches with its fiery tongue,—leaving nothing in its train but a blackened heath."

of sundry colors and kinds, as though it had been in any garden or orchard in England." As historian William Cronon has pointed out, such tended forests

> not merely attracted game but helped create much larger populations of it. Indian burning promoted the increase of exactly those species whose abundance so impressed English colonists: elk, deer, beaver, hare, por-

cupine, turkey, quail, ruffed grouse, and so on. When these populations increased, so did the carnivorous eagles, hawks, lynxes, foxes, and wolves. In short, Indians who hunted game animals were not just taking the "unplanted bounties of nature"; in an important sense, they were harvesting a foodstuff which they had consciously been instrumental in creating.

Such carefully nurtured abundance did not mean that Native Americans lived free from want, in a land of milk and honey. In fact, scarcity was an equally crucial element of their ecology. For abundance was above all seasonal, a fact many enthusiastic European explorers failed to take into account. "When I remember the high commendations some have given of the place," wrote one New Englander, "I have thought the reason thereof to be this, that they wrote surely in strawberry time." Governor Thomas Dale's 5,000 sturgeon were caught in spring or summer, when the fish were running, not during the sluggish days of February. Furthermore, animal populations fluctuated from season to season, and herds of antelope, bison, and caribou migrated along unpredictable routes. To survive, Indians had to take advantage of different seasons of abundance at different locations as well as get through the lean winter. Ecologists summarize these constraints in what is known as Liebig's law: that biological populations are limited not by the total resources available but by the minimum amount of food that can be found during the scarcest times of the year.

Often the conditions of scarcity led Indians to extract every conceivable benefit from available resources. The buffalo, for example, provided not only meat but also hides for teepees and clothing, sinew for thread and bowstrings, bones for tools, and horns for eating utensils. Even the dung was burned as fuel. On the other hand, a "feast or famine" attitude also developed, encouraging practices of questionable ecological value. Before the coming of horses, Plains Indians most often caught buffalo by stampeding them over cliffs or, when cliffs were unavailable, into rude corrals. Such stampedes could kill many more buffalo than were needed. "Today we passed . . . the remains of a vast many mangled carcases of Buffalow," wrote Lewis in 1804, "which had been driven over a precipice of 120 feet by the Indians & perished; the water appeared to have washed away a part of this immence pile of slaughter and still there remained the fragments of at least a hundred carcases, they created a most horrid stench." Over 120 years earlier, Father Louis Hennepin noted that in times of plenty, Indians "sometimes kill'd forty or fifty [buffalo], but took only the Tongues, and some other of the best Pieces. . . ."

"The riders now urge their horses at full speed, yelling like so many demons, the unsuspecting animals rushing headlong towards the rift (being packed close together) have no means of escape, but as they reach the ledge, topple down one after another, until they form a huge compound hecatomb at the bottom." Alfred Jacob Miller's watercolor, "Hunting Buffalo," portrays the stampede. By Miller's time, the plains Indians had obtained horses, whose mobility made such herding much easier.

From the Indian point of view, some of these practices were quite defensible. While a successful hunt might lead to much waste, success itself was never certain. A herd might easily flee if it scented its pursuers. On other occasions, only a small number of animals might be killed while the rest broke through the ranks of Indian herders. Yet for all that, Indians ought not to be portrayed merely as the spiritual forerunners of today's environmentalists. They had developed many ways of controlling and altering their surroundings—some remarkably ingenious in terms of husbanding resources, others relatively wasteful.

In addition to the way Native Americans altered their environment, it is equally important to know how many of them were at work and how densely settled their populations. Unfortunately, the question of population is an immensely difficult one. Hundreds of separate cultures spread across North America in the precontact era, with, of course, no surviving census to enumerate them. To the south, Aztec and other Indian cultures were known to have kept detailed records, but the vast majority of these materials were destroyed by the Spanish. How can historians even begin to calculate a precontact population?

One method that has been used was simply to collect and combine any available statistics from early white explorers and settlers. Based on this technique, most historians assumed that about a million Indians lived north of Mexico at the time of first contact. Yet this figure was based on surprisingly little systematic research. Its principal source was James Mooney, a respected ethnologist who assembled his figures in the early twentieth century. In trying not to exaggerate, Mooney used numbers that had already undergone a process of shrinkage over the years.

For example, in 1674 Daniel Gookin, a New Englander in charge of Indian missions, attempted to calculate the size of the native population before whites arrived in the region. Talking to Indian elders, he obtained estimates of the number of warriors each nation had been able to field. Based on a count of 18,000, it was possible to calculate a total precontact population of anywhere from 72,000 to 90,000 people, assuming that for every warrior there would be an average of three to four additional women and children. In the nineteenth century, historian John Palfrey noted Gookin's estimate but, for reasons he left unstated, preferred a lower number of 50,000. Mooney took that figure and conservatively cut it to "about 25,000 or about one half what the historian Palfrey makes it."

Furthermore, Mooney's totals for North America were not published until after his death. In assembling them for the press, his editor lowered estimates yet another notch, to about 1.15 million. Even this was discounted another 10 percent by anthropologist Alfred Kroeber, down to a million even or less. Kroeber reasoned that Indian societies in general were characterized by "insane, unending, continuously attritional" warfare and that Native Americans had scant abilities at organizing politically complex societies. Hence, it seemed unlikely to him that such peoples could ever have supported truly large populations.

It is evident, even from this brief summary, that the task of "compiling" figures is more complicated than it first might appear. Why should a compiler be "conservative" and cut numbers in half rather than "liberal" and double them? A researcher who believes that complex societies could hardly be created by people engaging in "insane, unending" warfare is more likely to try to explain away figures that indicate the contrary.* Certainly, a similar bias has affected population

*One might point out that the highest casualty figures from "insane" warfare have always been produced by societies with highly organized political systems, which

estimates for Central and South America. More than one Spanish source from the sixteenth century placed the Indian population as high as 40 to 60 million. But historians and anthropologists of the early twentieth century found it difficult to believe such counts and assumed their sources were inflated. "All parties were equally interested in exaggerating the flourishing state of the recently discovered nations," noted one scholar, while another observed that "to count is a modern practice; the ancient method was to guess; and when numbers are guessed they are always magnified." These, of course, are legitimate hypotheses, but the scholars who made them did not offer any concrete evidence of exaggeration.

By the mid 1970s, many anthropologists had come to believe that the conservative population estimates were seriously flawed. In arriving at new ones, especially in Mexico and Spanish California, they developed a number of useful techniques. One, known as *projection,* focused on the detailed study of one small region, where population could be determined more accurately. Having established a density for that limited area, anthropologists could then project the result over larger regions, making allowances for varying conditions and climates. Anthropologists also used the technique of *cross-checking* to compare the results of several different methods of calculation. For example, some Spanish churches recorded the number of Indian children brought to be baptized during their "age of innocence"—that is, age four or younger. By drawing on other population studies to determine what percentage of Indians would have been four or under (about 10 percent), it is possible to calculate a rough total population. At the same time, suppose the records supply a conquistador's estimate of the number of warriors from the same village. Using the kind of technique we saw applied to Daniel Gookin's figures, a second estimate might be derived. Archaeological studies might supply the number of houses in the village, from which we can make a third calculation. By cross-checking these different estimates, it is possible to see whether the results reinforce each other, improving reliability.

Finally, it is crucial to try to project population trends over time. If the records provide two estimates, a number of years apart, from one area, a ratio either of population growth or of depopulation may be established. If tax records show, for example, that in some villages the Indian population dropped by 50 percent over forty years, it is possi-

---

can mechanize and carry out slaughter on a truly grand scale. Sixteenth-century Europeans and Native Americans could both be remarkably barbarous, but alongside the combatants of recent world wars, they look like mere greenhorns.

ble, using that depopulation ratio, to project earlier populations for regions that have figures only for the later period. All these methods, while admittedly still inexact, are at least less subject to bias than the older calculations, which took for granted "that the Spaniards counted or estimated excessively." (As more recent research has revealed, Spanish landowners actually had incentive to underreport native population, for they had to pay taxes based on the number of workers they controlled.)

The results using these new methods are astonishing. Where earlier estimates had set total population in North and South America at no more than 8 to 14 million, more recent studies suggest a total as high as 100 million, 10 million of which lived north of Mexico. The figures go a long way toward shattering the stereotype of precontact America as virgin, untamed wilderness. If they are correct, when Columbus landed in 1492 at Hispaniola, that island alone was inhabited by as many as 8 million people, compared with about 7 million for all of Spain, an area seven times as large. (England's population at the time was only about 3 million.) The Aztec capital of Tenochtitlán, estimated to have held 250,000 inhabitants, was double the size of the largest European cities of the day: Constantinople, Naples, Venice, Milan, and Paris. In fact, there may have been more people living in the New World in 1492 than in western Europe.

CONTACT: THE VIRULENT PIONEERS

It would be natural to expect that figures compiled from existing records might be inaccurate to a certain degree. But why were such estimates as much as ten times too low? The main reason was that historians failed to take into account the catastrophic effect of Eurasian and African diseases in America. In 1492, Native Americans had never been exposed to smallpox, measles, malaria, or yellow fever. When their ancestors came to America tens of thousands of years earlier, the process of migration cut them off from the major disease pools of the world. In order to survive, disease-carrying microorganisms need a host population large and dense enough to prevent the disease from gradually running out of new victims. Thus, large cities or any large groups of people (armies, schools) are prime disease pools. The pools need not be human: domestic animals such as cattle and horses are often hosts for infections that periodically spread to their caretakers.

But the first hunters who made their way over the Asian land bridge to America migrated in sparsely populated bands. They did not bring herds of domestic animals. And the cold climates through which they passed served as a barrier to many disease-carrying microorganisms. As a result, Native Americans were not subjected to cycles of epidemics like those that drastically reduced populations in Europe and Asia. Even in the dense urban areas of the Aztec and Inca empires, major epidemics seem to have been largely unknown.

Of course, the relative freedom from disease made for a better life. But it entailed long-term risks. European and Asian populations exposed to disease were at first decimated, but after five or six generations, they built up resistance to the invading microorganisms. Diseases that had once been life-threatening became mere "childhood diseases," which children routinely picked up and recovered from because of an immunity passed to them through their parents (or, today, through vaccination). Current childhood diseases include measles, mumps, whooping cough, smallpox, and chicken pox.

For virgin populations, however, such diseases were deadly. Much has been written, for example, about how conquistadors under Cortés were able to conquer the Aztec empire because of their superior armor and weapons as well as the terror inspired by their horses, which were new to the Aztecs. Under closer scrutiny, however, those explanations seem hardly sufficient. After all, horses or no, Cortés had brought only about 400 soldiers to throw against Tenochtitlán's population of a quarter of a million; and after a tense six months of diplomatic cat-and-mouse, he was driven from the city. But before the Aztecs could mount a counterattack, Spanish reinforcements arrived—along with, as it happened, a few cases of smallpox. The disease soon "spread over the people as great destruction . . ." one Indian recalled. "They could not walk; they only lay in their resting places and beds. They could not move; they could not stir; they could not change position. . . . And if they stirred, much did they cry out." When the Spanish finally entered the conquered city, "the streets, squares, houses, and courts were filled with bodies, so that it was almost impossible to pass. Even Cortés was sick from the stench in his nostrils." Elsewhere in Mexico, Indians "died in heaps, like bedbugs." Recent estimates suggest that in the decade following Cortés's arrival, the population of Mexico dropped from 25 to about 16.8 million. Measles, new smallpox epidemics, and other diseases also took their toll. By 1568, only 3 million Indians were left, a mere 12 percent of the population of 1500. As nineteenth-century historian Hubert Howe Bancroft rather smugly concluded, "thus bravely worked the smallpox for Cortez and the superior civilization."

The Kiowa Indians kept pictorial calendars recording important events in their history. The winter of 1839-40 was characterized as *Ta dalkop Sai,* "Smallpox winter," as the figure at left indicates. The Kiowa were also decimated in 1849 by cholera, represented at right by a man with his limbs drawn up by the painful cramps of the disease. Cholera spread all along the westward trails in 1849; Indians caught the disease not only from visiting infected camps but also from digging up the graves of cholera victims to obtain clothing. (After a drawing by James Mooney, 1898)

In North America, depopulation estimates are harder to come by, but available evidence suggests a catastrophe of similar dimensions. The Pilgrims arriving at Cape Cod found a land that was cleared and had been cultivated but was now empty because of a recent epidemic. Devoutly, they thanked God for "sweeping away great multitudes of natives . . . that he might make room for us there." The epidemic, most likely chicken pox, had been brought by fishermen to American shores around 1616 and subsequently raged for three years from Maine to Cape Cod. Many villages experienced mortality rates as high as 95 percent, and the first European colonists were astonished to find pile after pile of unburied bones, picked clean by the wolves and bleached by the sun. In 1633 the smallpox struck, as William Bradford so graphically recorded:

The condition of this people was so lamentable and they fell down so generally of this disease as they were in the end not able to help one another, no not to make a fire nor to fetch a little water to drink, nor any to bury the dead. But would strive as long as they could, and when they could procure no other means to make fire, they would burn the wooden trays and dishes they ate their meat in, and their very bows and arrows. And some would crawl out on all fours to get a little water, and sometimes die by the way and not be able to get in again.

Similar epidemics struck down Native Americans along the Great Lakes, where French trappers and priests penetrated, while in the southern colonies, smallpox "destroy'd whole Towns, without leaving one *Indian* alive in the Village." Along the Pacific coast, similar epidemics reduced the populations by as much as 90 percent.

As nineteenth-century Americans pushed westward, the invisible pioneers preceded them, spreading from one Indian village to the next. We can perhaps sense the magnitude of the problem by following the course of only one epidemic. In 1837 the American Fur Company steamer, the *St. Peter,* left St. Louis carrying supplies and passengers for the trading posts along the upper Missouri. When the boat stopped near Fort Clark on June 18, all seemed well. But by a week later, when it pulled into Fort Union, at least one person on board had broken out with smallpox. The traders, well aware of the disease's effect, tried to protect the Indians at the fort by inoculating them with smallpox pus.* Unfortunately, the attempt miscarried and most of the Indians died. At the same time, a band of forty Indians arrived at the fort, eager to barter. The trader in charge refused to admit them, but they kept pounding at the gate, until finally he opened it briefly to exhibit a boy whose face was covered with a mass of smallpox scabs. The Indians retreated, but they took the disease with them. Over half the party died.

Traders tried to keep smallpox from Fort McKenzie, the next stop upstream, by unloading their cargo halfway and sending word to the fort not to come for it until the risk of catching the disease had passed. But the Indians, eager for goods and suspicious of white motives, pressed the chief trader to bring the boat up, and again the epidemic spread.

The accompanying map shows the depressing progress of the disease.

*The technique of variolation, or transferring pus from a smallpox victim to a healthy subject, was often used before vaccination with cowpox became common. Although riskier, variolation often reduced mortality rates significantly.

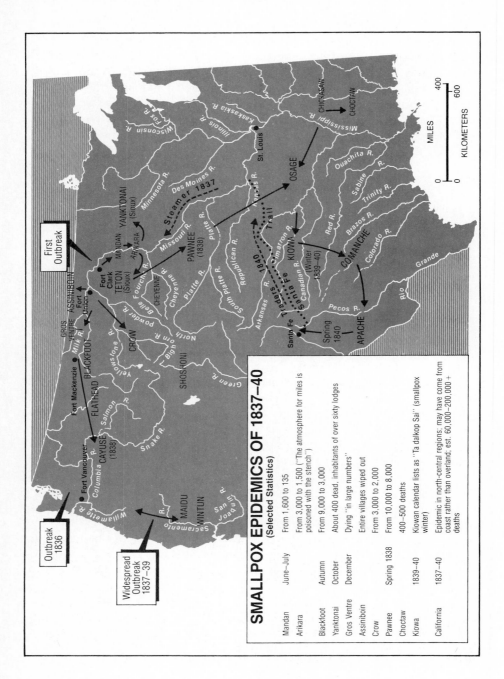

SMALLPOX EPIDEMICS OF 1837–40
(Selected Statistics)

Mandan	June–July	From 1,600 to 135
Arikara		From 3,000 to 1,500 ("The atmosphere for miles is poisoned with the stench")
Blackfoot	Autumn	From 9,000 to 3,000
Yanktonai	October	About 400 dead, inhabitants of over sixty lodges
Gros Ventre	December	Dying "in large numbers"
Assiniboin		Entire villages wiped out
Crow		From 3,000 to 2,000
Pawnee	Spring 1838	From 10,000 to 8,000
Choctaw		400–500 deaths
Kiowa	1839–40	Kiowan calendar lists as "Ta dalkop Sai" (smallpox winter)
California	1837–40	Epidemic in north-central regions; may have come from coast rather than overland; est. 60,000–200,000 + deaths

Near Fort Clark, smallpox appeared among the Mandan a month after the *St. Peter* passed through. From there it spread to the Arikara during the summer and to the Sioux by October. The Assiniboin picked up the disease, probably from Fort Union, and soon after, the Crow got it. The Gros Ventres were infected by December. Since the disease often spread far from white posts, its route was not always easy to trace; but by 1838 it had apparently crossed the Rockies to the Cayuse, who blamed missionary Marcus Whitman and attacked his settlement. In 1838 it also moved south, reaching the Pawnee by way of several Sioux prisoners taken that spring. From the Pawnee it spread to the Osage and thence to the Kiowa and other Texas tribes, killing many Apache and Comanche. Moving west into New Mexico, it reached Santa Fe, and from there white traders carried it full circle, back to the frontiers of the United States.

Loss of life ran anywhere from 50 to 95 percent of the populations affected. But horrifying as these numbers are, they fail to tell the whole tale. At stake were not only lives but the viability of entire cultures. The dislocations caused by disease were economic, social, and spiritual.

Economically, many Indian peoples could not carry out even their basic day-to-day work. In part, this was because the epidemics proved most deadly to those between the ages of fifteen and forty. (Scientists are still not sure why, in unexposed populations, this age group seems to be the hardest hit.) Healthy, in the prime of life, these victims were precisely those members of the community who contributed the most economically, as hunters, farmers, or food gatherers. Furthermore, the survivors of an epidemic often fled in terror from their traditional homelands. Resettling, they were obliged to discover anew the best hunting spots, places to gather nuts or berries, or sites with rich soils.

Socially, the disruptions were equally severe. Since male warriors were among those hit hardest, hostile neighbors, either white or Indian, were more difficult to resist. The plague-stricken Indians of New England had "their courage much abated," reported one colonist; "their countenance is dejected, and they seem as a people affrighted." Near Charleston, South Carolina, an Indian told a settler they had "forgotten most of their traditions since the Establishment of this Colony, they keep their Festivals and can tell but little of the reasons: their Old Men are dead." Farther west, Lewis and Clark traveled up the Missouri only a few years after the smallpox epidemic of 1801–02. Clark reported that the remnant of the Omaha nation, "haveing no houses no Corn or anything more than the graves of their ansesters to attach them to the old Village," led a much more nomadic existence. "I am told when this fatal malady [smallpox] was among them they Carried their franzey to verry extraordinary length, not only of burning their Village, but they put their *wives* and children to *Death* with a view of their all going together to some better Countrey."

George Catlin, an artist who traveled in the West shortly after the epidemic of 1837, reported a similar despair among the Mandans. When the disease struck, he noted, they were surrounded by hostile Sioux and unable to disperse from their village onto the plains. The smallpox

> in a few days became so very malignant that death ensued in a few hours after its attacks; and so slight were their hopes when they were attacked, that nearly half of them destroyed themselves with their knives, with their guns, and by dashing their brains out by leaping head-foremost from a thirty foot ledge of rocks in front of their village. . . .

Even when despair did not lead to suicide, Native Americans were severely challenged by what seemed to be the Europeans' superior gods. Both Indians and whites read supernatural meaning into the epidemics, attributing such outbreaks to divine anger. Yet because the new diseases singled out nonimmune Native Americans and spared Europeans, both peoples tended to credit the superiority of the European deity. When Francis Drake's sailors brought illness to Florida in 1585, "the wilde people . . . died verie fast and said amongst themselves, it was the Inglisshe God that made them die so fast." More cynical whites were not above capitalizing on this dread. In 1812 James McDougall warned the Chinook Indians of the Columbia River not to carry out an attack against the whites:

> You imagine that because we are few you can easily kill us, but it is not so; or if you do you will only bring the greater evils upon yourselves. The medicine of the white man dead is mightier than that of the red man living. . . . You know the smallpox. Listen: I am the smallpox chief. In this bottle I have it confined. All I have to do is to pull the cork, send it forth among you, and you are dead men. But this is for my enemies and not for my friends.

Given that disease did strike Indians more severely than whites, it is no wonder many believed such exhortations. In any case, the result was to severely strain Native Americans' traditional beliefs.

FULL CONTACT: COMPETING ECOLOGICAL SYSTEMS

Undoubtedly, the spread of European microorganisms had an immense effect on the cultural balances of North America. But other ecological pioneers played important roles. Colonists imported plants and animals that were new to America, and the ways settlers made use of them differed markedly from the way Native Americans used their own natural resources. In large part, the Old World meeting the New became a clash between competing ecological systems. In the ensuing struggle, the European ecologies eventually prevailed.

Many of the European plants that came to America spread for the same reasons European diseases did. More than a few American plants, having been relatively isolated from competition for thousands of years, yielded quickly to hardier European stocks. Some plants spread so widely that today they are commonly taken to be native. "Kentucky" blue grass originated in Europe. So did the dandelion, the daisy, white clover, ragweed, and plantain. (The last was called "the Englishman's foot" by New England Indians, for it seemed to sprout wherever the new settlers wandered.)

Many of these plants were introduced purely by accident. Seeds might arrive in chests of folded clothes or in clods of mud or dung. But settlers also deliberately imported many plants. On the Oregon trail, several overlanders made a business of carrying trees and fruits across the country. The most successful was an Iowa Quaker, Henderson Luelling, who in 1847 hauled 700 trees, vines, and shrubs in his wagons, including such varieties as apple, cherry, pear, plum, black walnut, and quince. His imports helped launch a multimillion-dollar orchard business in California and Oregon.*

As for the animal frontier, we have already seen that the horse outran Europeans in crossing the continent. Most Indian peoples took to the

---

*Limitations of space make it impossible to discuss an equally important topic, the migration of American flora and fauna to the Old World. Perhaps the most influential Native American contributions to world civilization were agricultural products. Maize corn, unknown in Europe, had been developed by Indians over thousands of years, from ears that were originally the size of a finger. The tomato, now so closely linked with Italian cuisine, was an American product; so too was the potato, before it ever reached Ireland. These imports may have contributed significantly to the rise of population in Europe, which began an upward trend in the sixteenth century.

horse rapidly; in performance they soon outstripped the Spaniards, who were a horse-loving people to begin with. Plains Indians learned to ride bareback, controlling their mounts with a gentle pressure of the knees instead of using reins. This left a rider's hands free to use a bow and arrow. A good hunter-warrior could travel at full gallop, drop to one side of his pony for cover, and launch a continuous stream of arrows with such force that a shaft might bury itself entirely in a buffalo. The Comanche were such accomplished riders that a unit of the U.S. Cavalry was in one contest disgusted to find its finest Kentucky mare beaten by a "miserable sheep of a pony" upon which a Comanche rider was mounted backward, so he could mockingly wave (with "hideous grimaces") for his American rival to "come on a little faster!"

Above all, horses gave those Indians who possessed them immensely greater mobility. Previously, all hunting had to be done on foot; mounted, Indians searched out the buffalo with comparative ease. In addition, mounted nations were able to drive rivals from long-held territories. By 1826, according to an early fur trader, the Klamath Indians along the California–Oregon border had been raided so often by their well-mounted enemies that one village was forced in desperation to relocate on land surrounded by marsh and water, "approachable only by canoes."

While the supply of horses diffused toward the north and east, another frontier—that of guns—moved in the opposite direction, west and south. The Spanish possessed firearms, but their laws forbade selling any to Indians. English and French fur traders of the Northeast, however, operated under no such restraints. The gun and horse frontiers met along the upper Missouri during the first half of the eighteenth century and, in crossing, touched off an extremely unsettled period for Indians of the West. In the late 1700s, the Cree, Assiniboin, and Ojibwa, with their guns, forced the Teton Sioux, Cheyenne, Arapaho, and Crow south across the Missouri River. Agricultural peoples, such as the Mandan and Arikara, found themselves more frequently attacked, while tribes that were originally nomadic became even more so.

Women of nomadic tribes were also affected by the coming of the horse. With mounts available as beasts of burden, they were required to do much less hauling when camps were moved. In some tribes, women were even allowed to own their own horses. Homes, too, became more spacious: in "dog days," teepees had been constructed of five or six skins, small enough to be carried on the dog travois. With horses to carry them, the teepees grew to fifteen or twenty skins. A fur trader in 1805 summed

While Indian men often rode bareback, women such as this Sioux used a saddle with high ends fore and aft, to help keep from being pitched off. Decorations include brightly colored cloth bordered by porcupine quills and beads. Even the horse has pendants dangling from his ears! Wrote Miller, "To have a good horse and full equipment is the realization of heaven on earth to an Indian girl, never having heard of the Poet's 'Beauty unadorned,' she goes to the other extreme, and piles it on as thick as possible, in the way of ornament; and what with hawk's bells innumerable, and tags of tin fastened to her fringes, the movements of her horse create abundance of noise as she gallops over the prairie."

the situation up by noting that while Crow women did "most of the work," they were "not so wretchedly situated as those nations who live in the forests. . . . [and] are indebted solely to their having horses for the ease they enjoy more than their neighbors." Older people may well have benefited too, for nomadic tribes sometimes abandoned or killed those who were too feeble to travel. With horses to carry the infirm, such practices seem to have lessened.

While the horse changed the lives of Plains Indians, it did not radically alter their cultures. It was as "an intensifier of original Plains traits" that the horse presented its strongest claim, noted anthropologist Clark Wissler. The situation was far different once whites themselves reached

Native American lands. Their coming set in motion a train of events that fundamentally changed the relationships between the land and the Indians who used it.

Underlying this change was the apparently simple fact that, from the very first, European explorers came to America in search of resources that were scarce in Europe. Invariably, they returned home praising the many precious "commodities" that were available. Spain reaped vast profits from the gold and silver of Central and South America, and the French and English hoped to follow suit. In the end, though, they discovered that the most easily extractable commodities of North America were the animals of the forest: beaver, fox, marten, muskrat, otter.

Native Americans had hunted such animals time out of mind; Europeans merely encouraged them to trap a larger surplus. But the act of creating this surplus, and then linking it to a worldwide economy, meant that trading took on a different aspect for Indians. As William Cronon has pointed out, the fur trade was

> far more complicated than a simple exchange of European metal goods for Indian beaver skins. . . . Trade linked these groups with an abstract set of equivalent values measured in pelts, bushels of corn, fathoms of wampum, and price movements in sterling on London markets. The essential lesson for the Indians was that certain things began to have *prices* that had not had them before. In particular, one could buy personal prestige by killing animals and exchanging their skins for wampum or high-status European goods.

Even by the 1640s, the demand for furs had depleted beaver near the New England coast. By the end of the century, most of the region's streams and forests were trapped out. And the pattern repeated itself as the frontier moved westward. Lewis and Clark's Rocky Mountains, which in 1804 were "richer in beaver and otter than any country on earth," by 1840 were so poor, according to one trapper, "that one would stand a right good chance of starving, if he were obliged to hang up here for seven days. The game is all driven out."

The pressure on resources became even keener once pioneers began to cross the plains. The case of timber provides a good example. Wood is a resource not usually associated with the vast plains and open prairies. Yet precisely because trees were so scarce, they were highly valued by the Indians and played an important part in their ecology. Cottonwood, clustered along the richer bottomlands of plains rivers, offered crucial protection during winter blizzards as well as concealing a village's smoke from its enemies. In lean seasons, horses fed on its bark, which was surprisingly nourishing. And during spring breakup along rivers, men, women, and children could be seen leaping onto the ice floes as they swirled downstream, tying cords to floating deadwood and hauling it ashore. Timber was worth taking big risks to obtain.

The overland migrations of the 1840s and '50s created severe wood shortages in many areas along the trails. Although most settlers were only passing through, fully a quarter of a million whites made the trip before the Civil War, and the pressure of such numbers soon showed itself. "The road, from morning till night, is crowded like Pearl Street or Broadway," wrote a traveler in 1850. It was not uncommon for several thousand people to pass Fort Laramie in a single day. Such hordes inevitably destroyed many of the best timber stands. "By the Mormon guide we here expected to find the last timber," wrote A. W. Harlan, along the Platte, "but all had been used up by others ahead of us so we must go about 200 miles without any provisions cooked up. . . ." A few weeks later, with the Black Hills in sight, he wrote, "we have passed many cottonwood stumps but no timber. . . . we have I might say no grass to night."

Faced by this constant procession of wagon trains, many Indian nations responded by demanding payment, usually in provisions, for the privilege of passing through their homelands. Some bands even erected bridges and attempted to collect tolls at strategic stream crossings. In either case, they made it clear that they regarded such fees as compensation for the use of their homelands, for the rights to timber, grazing, and the animals shot in their hunting territories. Some emigrants grudgingly paid the fees, but others took matters into their own hands. "When we got to the bridge there was a lot of Indians standing there," wrote one overlander, "and my Partner made a motion to the right & Left but the Indians did not move he made a dive for the nearest one and with his fist knocked him spralling and with his left fist sent another one down and he had 3 of them down in half the time I have been writing it. . . . the[y] got out of the way and we had no further trouble."

The loss of timber or grazing areas was bad enough, but Native Americans had an even more serious complaint—that "the buffalo are wantonly killed and scared off, which renders their only means of subsistence every year more precarious." This was especially grave not only because the bison, like the beaver, became an important commodity in the trading economy but also because white settlers were replacing such wildlife with their own livestock. A large part of Indian life revolved around the hunting of wild creatures: deer, moose, buffalo, antelope.

"A Chief Forbidding the Passage of a Train through His Country." Government Indian agents recognized that Native Americans had a right to ask compensation for white use of hunting grounds and grazing lands, but such official support usually only enraged frontier settlers. "The whole is a gross imposition," noted overlander Isaac Lord; "the 'idea' that an old Indian should lay claim to a tract of land as large as all the New England States, and levy black mail on all passers, is sufficiently absurd; but when it is done by the connivance of the U. S. government. . . . language becomes useless, and men had better think."

Over time, the land occupied by these animals came to be seen by whites as desirable for cattle, sheep, or pigs. The resulting competition for grazing lands spelled the death knell for Native American ways. Next to the invisible pioneers of disease, the "emigrants" that most threatened Indian cultures were European domestic animals.

In the precontact era, Native Americans had only a few domesticated animals—in North America, primarily the dog. Wild animals, on the other hand, were viewed as property only after they had been killed. This differed from the European notion that one might raise and own animals as a source of food. Even if such stock was allowed to roam free, it was still owned by individuals, as the brand on a cow's flank or the cut on a sheep's ear signified. Domestic animals like oxen also allowed Europeans to use plows on a widespread scale, which meant more fields could be cultivated and their surpluses sold in an expanding capitalist economy. All these customs—central to the way Europeans managed their resources—were foreign to Native Americans.

New Englanders created conflicts almost immediately when they let their cattle or swine roam through the nearby meadows, forests, and seashores. As Roger Williams noted, English hogs were in the habit of digging and rooting for clams "wheresoever they come, and [they] watch the low water (as the Indian women do). . . . Of all English Cattell, the Swine (as also because of their filthy dispositions) are most hateful to all Natives, and they call them filthy cut throats." When Indians shot roaming livestock, irate New Englanders fined them and passed laws to protect their animal property. The Indians eventually accepted this custom and even turned the situation to their advantage on occasion, taking New Englanders to court when hogs or cattle uprooted Indian corn-fields.

In Mexico, agriculture played an even more important role in feeding large native populations. There, the Spanish ranchers who turned corn and bean fields into grazing lands upset a pivotal Indian resource. The first viceroy of New Spain, Antonio de Mendoza, recognized the problem and wrote the king, warning "May your Lordship realize that if cattle are allowed, the Indians will be destroyed." Spanish pigs also spread quickly, both as domestic animals and wild. To cite only one example, Hernando DeSoto brought 13 pigs to Florida in 1539; these multiplied in only three years to over 700.

On the Great Plains, domestic cattle and sheep replaced bison and antelope, just as cattle, swine, and sheep had replaced deer in the East. Although the cowboy came into his own only after the Civil War, live-stock drives were common along the overland trails in the 1850s. Perhaps a half million cattle and another half million sheep made the trek. At first, such drives did not destroy the traditional plains ecology. In California, early ranching even seemed to help some wildlife temporarily, like the grizzly, who gorged on the corpses of stock skinned for their hides. Sheep, too, fell as easy prey to coyotes. But hunting pressure on the bison steadily increased. In the 1850s a traveler was already writing that "the valley of the Platte for 200 miles presents the aspect of the vicinity of a slaughter yard; dotted all over with skeletons of buffa-los. . . ." By the 1860s wagon trains could no longer count on hunting food on the way across; grocery stores had sprung up instead, including one advertising itself as "The American Ranche, a Home for the Weary."

Once the transcontinental railroad was completed, the slaughter of the herds began in earnest. "Buffalo Bill" Cody gained prominence as a hunter for the train crews of the Kansas Pacific. Sportsmen riding the rails took potshots from the passing cars or, seeking better yields, tracked down the big herds and opened fire with such abandon that their gun barrels overheated after a time. A single hunter could kill over a hundred animals in an hour. By the early 1870s the demand for buffalo robes had risen sharply in the East, so commercial companies hauled out thousands upon thousands of hides each year. A decade later the herds were nearly gone, their lands being swiftly occupied by cattle, sheep, cowpunchers, and sodbusters.

America had been transformed. The land of 1890 was vastly different from the precontact world of 1490, in large part because of the series of ecological frontiers that had crossed the continent. Beyond doubt, the most important was the frontier of disease, which provided Europeans with nothing less than the opportunity to remake the Americas in their own image. Today, having lived so long with the outcome, we tend to take the results as a foregone conclusion. We assume that European success in America was due to superior technology and efficient social and economic organization. No doubt these elements played a role. But during the same era Spain, England, France, and Portugal were also expanding eastward, with markedly different results. In China and India, where diseases did not decimate the local populations, Asian cultural and political traditions remained strong, regardless of "superior" European technology. European merchants and settlers were confined to trading stations and coastal enclaves. Even where Western elites came to rule a country, as the British did in India, they remained only the upper stratum of a colonial system. In the twentieth century, when nationalist movements ejected the colonial powers, Asian cultures played a renewed and revitalized role.

But in the Americas? The Aztecs and Incas had complex civilizations and, if they had not been decimated by disease, they too might have kept the Spanish pinned down along the coast. Farther north, the English found it difficult enough as it was to establish colonies. They might have been even less successful if the full complement of Native Americans had survived to resist them. But with 50 to 90 percent of the population wiped out within a century, not only peoples but cultures effectively perished. And hard upon the heels of disease came a host of other

European "pioneers"—horses, pigs, and cattle—led by masters who employed these new beasts to organize society in foreign ways.

Even after the frontier passed into history, ecological constraints continued to influence American development. Newcomers to the plains soon found that natural limits forced them to change their ways. Barbed wire and sod huts replaced the wood traditionally used for fences and homes. Dry farming techniques were needed to make the land yield adequate harvests. Windmills used the ample resource of the wind to secure the much scarcer resource of water. But these stories belong to a later era—even in this chapter, seven-league boots have their limits. What remains clear is that, on both sides of the frontier, American history has been shaped and altered by ecological factors that historians have too often lightly passed over.

Additional Reading

The subject of this chapter (not to mention its chronological span) is so vast that we can only make the briefest attempt at a bibliography. Almost every topic discussed—the effect of the horse on Native American cultures, of human-caused fires on the environment, of epidemic disease on native populations—has produced a sizable literature.

For an introduction to ecology, especially as it relates to history, see John W. Bennett, *The Ecological Transition: Cultural Anthropology and Human Adaptation* (New York, 1976). William L. Thomas, ed., *Man's Role in Changing the Face of the Earth* (Chicago, 1956), is a wide-ranging collection of papers, including some on the Indians' use of fire and the effect of domestic livestock on the grasslands of the plains. For information on the history of ecology itself, see Donald Worster, *Nature's Economy* (San Francisco, 1977) and Ronald C. Tobey, *Saving the Prairies: The Life Cycle of the Founding School of American Plant Ecology, 1895–1955* (Berkeley, Calif., 1981). Alfred W. Crosby, Jr., provides an excellent overview of American ecological frontiers in *The Columbian Exchange: Biological and Cultural Consequences of 1492* (Westport, Conn., 1972). For a model of how ecology and history may be united in the study of one region, it would be hard to surpass William Cronon's *Changes in the Land: Indians, Colonists, and the Ecology of New England* (New York, 1983), a work that has been most helpful to us.

The abundance of flora and fauna of precontact North America may be inferred from the descriptions left by early white visitors. Alice Morse Earle gives a concrete sense of nature's bounties along the Atlantic coast in *Home Life in Colonial Days* (New York, 1899). Travelers' accounts are another source; among the many worth consulting, Peter Kalm's *Travels in North America* (New York, 1964) provides material for the mid-eighteenth century. For the early nineteenth, Lewis and Clark's journals, available in a number of editions, are informative, as is Paul Cutright's *Lewis and Clark: Pioneering Naturalists* (Urbana, Ill., 1969).

For a sense of how complicated the area of population estimates can be, see Henry F. Dobyns, "Estimating Aboriginal Population: An Appraisal of Techniques with a New Hemispheric Estimate," *Current Anthropology,* VII (1966), 395–416. This article was one of the most influential in revising upward the older estimates of precontact population. More recently Dobyns has published

Their Number Become Thinned: Native American Population Dynamics in Eastern North America (Knoxville, Tenn., 1983), which raises his earlier estimate of 10 million in North America to 18 million. But many scholars are highly skeptical of this latest claim. For a survey of other studies, see William M. Denevan, ed., *The Native Population of the Americas in 1492* (Madison, Wis., 1976), which includes a discussion of James Mooney's estimates. The most sophisticated work on population is probably Sherburne Cook and Woodrow Borah, *The Aboriginal Population of Central Mexico on the Eve of the Spanish Conquest,* Ibero-Americana, 45 (Berkeley, 1963).

William McNeill's superb *Plagues and Peoples* (Garden City, N.Y., 1976) is the starting point for anyone seeking to understand the effects of disease in history. When it comes to seven league boots, no one strides farther than McNeill, and few can match his abilities. Alfred Crosby discusses "Virgin Soil Epidemics as a Factor in the Aboriginal Depopulation in America" in *William and Mary Quarterly,* 33 (April 1976), 289–299; see also Wilbur R. Jacobs, "The Tip of an Iceberg: Pre-Columbian Indian Demography and Some Implications for Revisionism," *William and Mary Quarterly,* 31 (January 1974), 123–132. For smallpox, see E. Wagner Stearn and Allen E. Stearn, *The Effect of Smallpox on the Destiny of the Amerindian* (Boston, 1945).

Of the innumerable works on Indian-white relations, we can list here only a few whose ecological perspective we have found helpful. Cronon, cited above, covers early New England, while the southeastern frontier is discussed in James Merrill, "The Indians' New World: The Catawba Experience," *William and Mary Quarterly,* 41 (October 1984), 537–565. The work of John Ewers, always lively and astute, can be sampled in *Indian Life of the Upper Missouri* (Norman, Okla., 1968); he is the source of Weasel Tail's account of how the Blackfeet discovered horses. Francis Jennings, *The Invasion of America* (Chapel Hill, N.C., 1975) demolishes the conception of Native America as a "virgin land."

For animal frontiers, see the exhaustive (and sometimes exhausting) Frank Gilbert Roe, *The North American Buffalo: A Critical Study of the Species in Its Wild State* (Toronto, 1970). With equal pertinacity, Roe has surveyed *The Indian and the Horse* (Norman, Okla., 1955). Frank R. Secoy traces how the horse and gun frontiers affected Indian life in *Changing Military Patterns on the Great Plains: 17th Century through Early 19th Century* (Locust Valley, N.Y., 1953). Our own chaper has been able to give only scant attention to the important effects of the fur trade on Native American life. For one ecologically sensitive introduction, see David J. Wishart, *The Fur Trade of the American West, 1807–1840: A Geographical Synthesis* (Lincoln, Nebr., 1979). Calvin Martin's *Keepers of the Game* (Berkeley, Calif., 1978) is a controversial attempt to see Indian overtrapping as a consequence of the newly introduced epidemics; for a response, see Shepard Krech III, ed.,

Indians, Animals and the Fur Trade (Athens, Ga., 1981). Eric Wolf adopts a global perspective in *Europe and the People Without History* (Berkeley, Calif., 1982).

For the traditional frontier of the overland trail, John D. Unruh, *The Plains Across: Overland Emigrants and the Trans-Mississippi West, 1840–60* (Urbana, Ill., 1982) dispels the myth of the lonely trail. While not focused on ecological aspects of the frontier, Unruh is sensitive to the movement of livestock and the effect of whites' grazing and hunting on Indian lands. The demise of the bison is covered in E. Douglas Branch, *The Hunting of the Buffalo* (New York, 1929), as well as in Roe, cited above. And for an introduction to the adaptations that cowboys and sodbusters were forced to make to the drier conditions on the plains, see Walter Prescott Webb's classic *The Great Plains* (New York, 1931).

The Madness of John Brown

For over two months the twenty-one men had hidden in the cramped attic. They were mostly idealistic young men in their twenties, bound together during the tedious waiting by a common hatred of slavery. Now, on October 16, 1859, their leader, Old John Brown, revealed to them his final battle plan. The group comprised five blacks and sixteen whites, including three of the old man's sons, Owen, Oliver, and Watson. For years Brown had nurtured the idea of striking a blow against the southern citadel of slavery. Tomorrow, he explained, they would move into Harpers Ferry, Virginia, and capture the town and its federal arsenal. As they gathered arms, slaves would pour in from the surrounding countryside to join their army. Before the local militia organized, they would escape to the nearby hills. From there, they would fight a guerilla war until the curse of slavery had been exorcised and all slaves freed from bondage. No one among them questioned Brown or his plan.

An autumn chill filled the air, and a light rain fell as the war party made its way down the dark road toward Harpers Ferry. Three men had remained behind to handle supplies and arm slaves who took up the fight. A sleepy stillness covered the small town nestled in the hills where the Shenandoah joined the Potomac sixty miles from Washington, D.C. It was a region of small farms and relatively few slaves. Most likely, the presence of the arsenal and an armory explain why Brown chose to begin his campaign there.

The attack began without a hitch. Two raiders cut telegraph lines running east and west from the town. The others seized a rifle works, the armory, and three hostages, including a local planter descended from the Washington family. Soon the sounds of gunfire drew the townspeople from their beds. Amid the confusion, the church bell pealed the alarm dreaded throughout the South—slave insurrection! By late morning the hastily joined militia and armed farmers had trapped Brown and his men in the engine house of the Baltimore and Ohio Railroad. One son had been killed and another lay dying at his father's side. Drunken crowds thronged the streets crying for blood and revenge. When news of the raid reached Washington, President Buchanan dispatched federal troops under Colonel Robert E. Lee to put down the insurrection.

Thirty-six hours after the first shot, John Brown's war on slavery had ended. By any calculation the raid had been a total failure. Not a single slave had risen to join Brown's army. Ten of the raiders lay dead or dying; the rest had been scattered or captured. Though himself

John Brown, man of action: After the Pottawatomie Massacre, Brown grew a beard to disguise his appearance. His eastern backers were impressed with the aura he radiated as a western man of action. The image was not hurt by the fact that Brown hinted darkly of vigorous actions soon to be taken, or that he carried a bowie knife in his boot and regularly barricaded himself nights in his hotel rooms as a precaution against proslavery agents.

wounded, Brown had miraculously escaped death. The commander of the assault force had tried to kill him with his dress sword, but it merely bent double from the force of the blow. Seven other people had been killed and nine more wounded during the raid.

Most historians would agree that the Harpers Ferry raid was to the Civil War what the Boston Massacre had been to the American Revolution: an incendiary event. In an atmosphere of aroused passions, profound suspicions, and irreconcilable differences, Brown and his men put a match to the fuse. Once their deed had been done and blood shed, there seemed to be no drawing back for either North or South. The shouts of angry men overwhelmed the voices of compromise.

From pulpits and public platforms across the North leading abolitionists leapt to Brown's defense. No less a spokesman than Ralph Waldo Emerson pronounced the raider a "saint. . . . whose martyrdom, if it shall be perfected, will make the gallows as glorious as the cross." Newspaper editor Horace Greeley, who directed a generation of young men to the West, called the raid "the work of a madman" for which he had nothing but the highest admiration. At the same time the defenders of national union and of law and order generally condemned Brown and his violent tactics. Such northern political leaders as Abraham Lincoln, Stephen Douglas, and William Seward spoke out against Brown. The Republican party in 1860 went so far as to adopt a platform censuring the Harpers Ferry raid.

Reasoned northern voices were lost, however, on southern hotheads, to whom all abolitionists and Republicans were potential John Browns. Across the South angry mobs attacked northerners regardless of their views on the slave question. Everywhere the specter of slave insurrection fed irrational fears and the uproar strengthened the hand of secessionists who argued that the South's salvation lay in expunging all traces of northern influence.

THE MOTIVES OF A FANATIC

And what of the man who triggered all those passions? Had John Brown foreseen that his quixotic crusade would reap such a whirlwind of violence? On that issue both his contemporaries and historians have been sharply divided. Brown himself left a confusing and often contradictory record of his objectives. To his men, and to Frederick Douglass, the former slave and black abolitionist, Brown made clear he intended nothing less than to provoke a general slave insurrection. His preparations all pointed to that goal. He went to Harpers Ferry armed for such a task, and the choice of the armory as the raid's target left little doubt he intended to equip a slave army. But throughout the months of preparation, Brown had consistently warned the co-conspirators financing his scheme that the raid might fail. In that event, he told them, he still hoped the gesture would so divide the nation that a sectional crisis would ensue, leading to the destruction of slavery.

From his jail cell and at his trial Brown offered a decidedly contradictory explanation. Ignoring the weapons he had accumulated, he suggested that the raid was intended as an extension of the underground railroad work he had previously done. He repeatedly denied any intention to commit violence or instigate a slave rebellion. "I claim to be here in carrying out a measure I believe perfectly justifiable," he told a skeptical newspaper reporter, "and not to act the part of an incendiary or ruffian, but to aid those [slaves] suffering great wrong." To Congressman Clement Vallandigham of Ohio who asked Brown if he expected a slave uprising, the old man replied, "No, sir; nor did I wish it. I expected to gather them up from time to time and set them free." In court with his life hanging in the balance, Brown once again denied any violent intent. He sought only to expand his campaign for the liberation of slaves.

Brown's contradictory testimony has provoked much speculation over the man and his motives. Was he being quite rational and calculating in abruptly changing his story after capture? Certainly Brown knew how much his martyrdom would enhance the abolitionist movement. His execution, he wrote his wife, would "do vastly more toward advancing the cause I have earnestly endeavored to promote, than all I have done in my life before." On the other hand, perhaps Brown was so imbued with his own righteousness that he deceived himself into believing he had not acted the part of "incendiary or ruffian," but only meant to aid those slaves "suffering great wrong." "Poor old man!" commented Republican presidential hopeful Salmon Chase. "How sadly misled by his own imaginations!"

Yet for every American who saw Brown as either a calculating insurrectionist or a genuine if somewhat self-deluded martyr, there were those who thought him insane. How else could they explain the hopeless assault of eighteen men against a federal arsenal and the state of Virginia —where slaves were "not abundant" and where "no Abolitionists were ever known to peep"? Who but a "madman" (to quote Greeley) could have concocted, much less attempted, such a wild scheme?

Nor was the issue of John Brown's sanity laid to rest by his execution on December 2, 1859. Brown had become a symbol, for both North and South, of the dimensions of the sectional struggle, condensing the issues

John Brown, the impractical idealist: "The old idiot—the quicker they hang him and get him out of the way, the better." So wrote the editor of a Chicago paper to Abraham Lincoln. Many contemporaries shared the view of the cartoon reprinted here, that Brown was a foolish dreamer. Yet Brown had other ideas. "I think you are fanatical!" exclaimed one southern bystander after Brown had been captured. "And I think you are fanatical," Brown retorted. " 'Whom the Gods would destroy they first made mad,' and you are mad."

of the larger conflict in his own actions. Inevitably, the question of personal motivation becomes inextricably bound to historians' interpretations of the root causes of sectional and social conflict. Was Brown a heroic martyr— a white man in a racist society with the courage to lay

John Brown, martyr of freedom:
  John Brown of Ossawatomie, they led him out to die;
  And lo! a poor slave-mother with her little child pressed nigh,
  Then the bold, blue eye grew tender, and the harsh face grew mild,
  And he stooped between the jeering ranks and kissed the Negro's child!
John Greenleaf Whittier based this incident in his poem, "Brown of Ossawatomie" (December 1859), on an erroneous newspaper report. Apparently Brown
did kiss the child of a white jailer he had befriended. Brown also remarked to
the same jailer that "he would prefer to be surrounded in his last moments by
a poor weeping slave mother with her children," noting that this "would make
the picture at the gallows complete."

down his life on behalf of his black brothers and the principles of the Declaration? Or was he an emotionally unbalanced fanatic whose propensity for wanton violence propelled the nation toward avoidable tragedy?

During the middle years of the twentieth century the view of Brown as an emotional fanatic gained ground. John Garraty, in a currently popular college text, describes Brown as so "deranged" that rather than hang him for his "dreadful act. . . . It would have been far wiser and more just to have committed him to an asylum. . . ." Allen Nevins defined a middle ground when he argued that on all questions except slavery, Brown could act coherently and rationally. "But on this special question of the readiness of slavery to crumble at a blow," Nevins thought, "his monomania . . . or his paranoia as a modern alienist [psychoanalyst] would define it, rendered him irresponsible."

Brown's most recent academic biographer, Stephen Oates, while recognizing in Brown much that was in no sense "normal," rejected the idea that insanity could either be adequately demonstrated or used in any substantive way to explain Brown's actions. That Brown had an "excitable temperament" and a single-minded obsession with slavery Oates conceded. He concluded, too, that Brown was egotistical, an overbearing father, an often inept man worn down by disease and suffering, and a revolutionary who believed himself called to his mission by God.

But having said all that, Oates demanded that before they dismissed Brown as insane, historians must consider the context of Brown's actions. To call him insane, Oates argued, "is to ignore the tremendous sympathy he felt for the black man in America. . . ." And, he added, "to label him a 'maniac' out of touch with 'reality' is to ignore the piercing insight he had into what his raid—whether it succeeded or whether it failed—would do to sectional tensions. . . ."

Given such conflicting views on the question of John Brown's sanity, it makes sense to examine more closely the evidence of his mental state. The most readily available material, and the most promising at first glance, was presented after the original trial by Brown's attorney, George Hoyt. As a last-minute stratagem, Hoyt submitted nineteen affidavits from Brown's friends and acquaintances, purporting to demonstrate Brown's instability.

Two major themes appear in those affidavits. First, a number of people testified to a pronounced pattern of insanity in the Brown family, particularly on his mother's side. In addition to his maternal grandmother and numerous uncles, aunts, and cousins, Brown's sister, his brother Salmon, his first wife Dianthe, and his sons Frederick and John Jr. were all said to have shown evidence of mental disorders. Second, some respondents described certain patterns of instability they saw in Brown himself. Almost everyone agreed he was profoundly religious and that he became agitated over the slavery question. A few traced Brown's insanity back through his years of repeated business failures. The "wild and desperate" nature of those business schemes and the rigidity with which he pursued them persuaded several friends of his "unsound" mind and "monomania."

Many old acquaintances thought that Brown's controversial experiences in Kansas had unhinged the man. There, in May 1856, proslavery forces had attacked the antislavery town of Lawrence. In retaliation, Brown led a band of seven men (including four of his sons) in a midnight raid on some of his proslavery neighbors at Pottawatomie Creek. Although the Pottawatomie residents had taken no part in the attack on faraway Lawrence, Brown's men, under his orders, took their broadswords and hacked to death five neighbors. That grisly act horrified free state and proslavery advocates alike. John Jr., one of Brown's sons who had not participated in the raid, suffered a nervous breakdown from his

John Brown, the terrorist:
Mahala Doyle, the wife of James P. Doyle, one of those Brown killed at Pottawatomie, testified of Brown, "He said if a man stood between him and what he considered right, he would take his life as cooly as he would eat his breakfast. His actions show what he is. Always restless, he seems never to sleep. With an eye like a snake, he looks like a demon."

own personal torment and from the abuse he received after being thrown into prison. Another of Brown's sons, Frederick, had been murdered a few months later in the civil war that swiftly erupted in Kansas.

Thus a number of acquaintances testified in 1859 that from the time of the Pottawatomie killings onward, Brown had been mentally deranged. E. N. Sill, an acquaintance of both Brown and his father, admitted that he had once had considerable sympathy for Brown's plan to defend antislavery families in Kansas. "But from his peculiarities," Sill recalled, "I thought Brown an unsafe man to be commissioned with such a matter. . . ." It was Sill who suggested the idea, which Allen Nevins later adopted, that on the slavery question alone Brown was insane. "I have no confidence in his judgment in matters appertaining to slavery," he asserted. "I have no doubt that, upon this subject . . . he is surely as monomaniac as any inmate in any lunatic asylum in the country." David King, who talked to Brown after his Kansas experience, observed that "on the subject of slavery he was crazy" and that Brown saw himself as "an instrument in the hands of God to free slaves."

Such testimony seems to support the view that Harpers Ferry was the outcome of insanity. Yet even then and ever since many people have rejected that conclusion. Confronted with the affidavits, Governor Henry Wise of Virginia thought to have Brown examined by the head of the state's insane asylums. Upon reflection he changed his mind. Wise believed Brown perfectly sane and had even come to admire begrudgingly the old man's "indomitable" spirit. Wise once described Brown as "the gamest man I ever saw."

For what it is worth, Brown himself rejected any intimation that he was anything but sane. He refused to plead insanity at his trial and instead adopted the posture of the self-sacrificing revolutionary idealist. For him, slavery constituted an unethical and unconstitutional assault of one class of citizens against another. Under that assault acts which society deemed unlawful—dishonesty, murder, theft, or treason—could be justified in the name of a higher morality.

Furthermore, Oates and other historians have attacked the affidavits presented by Hoyt as patently unreliable. Many people had good reason to have Brown declared insane. Among those signing the affidavits were friends and relatives who hoped Governor Wise would spare Brown's life. Might they not have exaggerated the instances of mental disorders in his family to make their case more convincing? Most had not taken Brown's fanaticism seriously until his raid on Harpers Ferry. That event, as much as earlier observation, had shaped their opinions. Just as important, none of them had any medical training or experience that would qualify them to determine with any expertise whether Brown or any member of his family could be judged insane. Only one affidavit came from a doctor, and, like most physicians of the day, he had no particular competence in psychological observation.

Though it would be foolish to suggest that we in the twentieth century are better judges of character than our forefathers, it is fair to say that at least we have a better clinical understanding of mental disorders. Many symptoms which the nineteenth century lumped together under the term insanity have been since identified as a variety of very different diseases, each with its own distinct causes. Among those "crazy" Brown relatives were those who, based on the descriptions in the affidavits, may have suffered from senility, epilepsy, Addison's disease, or brain tumors. Thus the "preponderance" of insanity in Brown's family could well have been a series of unrelated disorders. Even if the disorders were related, psychologists today still hotly debate the extent to which psychological disorders are inheritable.

The insanity defense also had considerable appeal to political leaders. Moderates from both North and South, seeking to preserve the Union, needed an argument to soften the divisive impact of Harpers Ferry. Were Brown declared insane, northern abolitionists could not so easily portray him as a martyr. Southern secessionists could not treat Brown as typical of all northern abolitionists. As a result, their argument that the South would be safe only outside the Union would have far less force. Historian C. Vann Woodward has pointed out that the Republicans were eager to dissociate their abolitionist rhetoric from Brown's more radical tactics. During the 1859 Congressional elections, the Democrats tried to persuade voters that Harpers Ferry resulted inevitably from the Republicans' appeal to the doctrine of "irresistible conflict" and "higher law" abolitionism. To blunt such attacks, leading Republicans regularly attributed the raid to Brown's insanity.

Clearly, the affidavits provide only the flimsiest basis for judging the condition of Brown's mental health. But some historians have argued that the larger pattern of Brown's life demonstrated his imbalance. Indeed, even the most generous biographers must admit that Brown botched miserably much that he attempted to do. In the years before moving to Kansas, Brown had tried his hand at tanning, sheepherding, surveying, cattle-driving, and wool-merchandising—all with disastrous results. By 1852 he had suffered fifteen business failures in four different states. Creditors were continually hounding him. "Over the years before his Kansas escapade," John Garraty concluded, "Brown had been a drifter, horse thief and swindler, several times a bankrupt, a failure in everything he attempted."

But this evidence, too, must be considered with circumspection. During the period Brown applied himself in business, the American economy went through repeated cycles of boom and bust. Many hardworking entrepreneurs lost their shirts in business despite their best efforts. Brown's failures over the years may only suggest that he did not have an aptitude for business. His schemes were usually ill-conceived, and he was too inflexible to adapt to the rapidly changing business climate. But to show that Brown was a poor businessman and that much of his life he pursued the wrong career hardly proves him insane. Under those terms, much of the adult population in the United States would belong in asylums.

To call Brown a drifter is once again to condemn most Americans. Physical mobility has been such a salient trait of this nation that one respected historian has used it to distinguish the national character. During some periods of American history as much as twenty percent of the population has moved *each year!* In the 1840s and 1850s, a whole generation of Americans shared Brown's dream of remaking their fortunes in a new place. Many like him found the lure of new frontiers irresistible. And just as many failed along the way, only to pack up and try again.

The accusation that Brown was a swindler and horse thief, while containing a measure of truth, convicts him on arbitrary evidence. After several of his many business disasters, creditors hounded him in the courts. A few accused him of fraud. Yet Simon Perkins, an Ohio businessman who lost more money to Brown and who was more familiar with his business practices than anyone else, never accused Brown of swindling, even when the two dissolved their partnership in 1854. Again, it was poor business sense rather than a desire to swindle that led Brown into his difficulties.

The horse thievery charge hinges on the observer's point of view. During the years of fighting in Kansas, Brown occasionally "confiscated" horses from proslavery forces. Those who supported his cause treated the thefts as legitimate acts of war. Brown's enemies never believed he was sincere in his convictions. They accused him of exploiting the tensions in Kansas to act like a brigand. But in any case, it is far from clear that Brown ever stole for personal gain. Whatever money he raised, save for small sums he sent his wife, went toward organizing his crusade against slavery. Besides, it is one thing to establish Brown's behavior as antisocial and quite another to find him insane.

From the point of view of the "facts of the case," the question of insanity cannot be easily resolved. The issue becomes further muddled when we consider its theoretical aspects. Theory, as we saw when examining Andrew Jackson, will inevitably affect any judgment in the case. The question, "Was John Brown insane?" frames our inquiry and determines the kind of evidence being sought. And in this case, the question is particularly controversial because it remains unclear just exactly what we are asking. What does it mean, after all, to be "insane"?

Modern psychologists and psychiatrists have given up using the concept of insanity diagnostically because it is a catch-all term and too unspecific to have definite meaning. The only major attempt to define the concept more precisely has been in the legal world. In civil law insanity refers to the inability of individuals to maintain contractual or other legal obligations. Thus, to void a will, an injured party might try to demonstrate at the time of composition its author was not "of sound mind"—that is, not responsible for his or her actions. Insanity is considered sufficient grounds to commit an individual to a mental hospital. But since it involves such a curtailment of rights and freedom, it is extremely difficult to prove and generally requires the corroboration of several disinterested professionals.

Insanity has been widely used as a defense in criminal cases. By demonstrating that at the time of the crime a client could not distinguish right from wrong or was incapable of determining the nature of the act committed, a lawyer can protect the accused from some of the legal consequences of the act. To find Brown insane, as attorney Hoyt attempted to have the court do, would have been to assert Brown's inability to understand the consequences of his actions at Harpers Ferry. The raid would represent the irrational anger of a deranged man, deserving pity rather than hatred or admiration.

In the legal sense, then, Brown would have to be considered fit to stand trial. He may have been unrealistic in estimating his chance of success at Harpers Ferry, but he repeatedly demonstrated that he knew the consequences of his actions: that he would be arrested and punished if caught; that large portions of American society would condemn him; that, nevertheless, he believed himself in the right. In the legal sense, Brown was quite sane and clear-headed about his actions.

THE MOTIVES OF A SON—AND A FATHER

Yet the court's judgment, accurate as it may have been, is likely to leave us uneasy. To have Brown pronounced "sane" or "insane," in addition to "guilty" or "not guilty," does little to explain, deep down, why the man acted as he did. The verdict leaves us with the same emptiness that impelled psychologists to reject the whole concept of insanity. What drove John Brown to crusade against slavery? to execute in cold blood five men along a Kansas creek? to lead twenty-one men to Harpers Ferry? Many other northerners abhorred the institution of slavery. Yet only John Brown acted with such vehemence. In that sense he was far from being a normal American; far, even, from being a normal abolitionist. How can we begin to understand the intensity of his deeds?

Here we approach the limits of explanations based upon rational motives. To describe John Brown simply by referring to his professed —and undoubtedly sincere—antislavery ideology; or to explain his actions in terms of consciously held plans, is to leave unexplored the fire in the man. It focuses too much on rationalistic explanations of behavior, assuming that consciously expressed motivations can be taken largely at face value. Yet we have already seen, in the cases of the bewitched at Salem and the strong-willed Andrew Jackson, that unconscious motivations play a crucial role in human behavior. If it is not possible even for ostensibly "normal" people fully to explain or understand their behavior, how much less satisfying such rational explanations must seem in explaining people like Brown.

The discipline of psychoanalysis, pioneered by Sigmund Freud, offers the historian one way of understanding and discussing unconscious motivations. Freud assumed that everybody inevitably experiences intensely personal conflicts in life, which are extremely difficult to deal with. When a person resists coming to terms with such situations in an open and direct manner, he represses the conflict; that is, he is *unable* to think about it consciously. At this level, the conflict comes to be expressed unconsciously and indirectly—perhaps disguised in dreams or fantasies, or else resolved in actions which have significance beyond the apparent, or manifest, reasons for being performed.

Freud called special attention to two areas of life he thought were the source of much tension and conflict: instinctual sexual drives and the formative experiences of infancy and childhood. By exploring a patient's life history through a process of free association, the psychoanalyst takes the fragments of evidence presented by the patient and guides him toward a recognition of the unconscious forces that have shaped the personality. Thus the analyst seeks to explore the territory of the unconscious much as the historian seeks to make sense out of the jumble of documentary evidence.

In order to gain some concrete sense of how psychoanalytic theory might be used to understand a historical figure like John Brown, we will do well to concentrate on just one of Freud's concepts—what he called the oedipal stage of a child's development. The concept draws its name from Sophocles' *Oedipus Rex,* a Greek tragedy in which Oedipus unknowingly commits incest with his mother. For this "crime" he suffers blindness and exile. Psychoanalysis contends that somewhere between the ages of three and six, boys normally pass through the oedipal phase. As their demand for erotic gratification intensifies, it is directed toward the mother. Strong attraction for a forbidden love object is fraught with psychic peril. It invites in the child's fears his father's jealous and destructive wrath.

Resolution of the oedipal conflict occurs when the child relinquishes his erotic impulses toward the mother and identifies with the father as the adult role model. The prohibitions against sexual gratification become internalized in normal individuals as the superego. The superego in turn acts as an ethical monitor controlling instinctual impulses as the child matures. Successful resolution of oedipal conflicts leads to increased self-control, improved capacity to test external reality, and reduced dependence on maternal response.

Failure to resolve the intense guilt, fears, and ambivalence associated with the oedipal phase can block formation of an integrated adult personality. Symptoms of unresolved conflict may take physical forms such as nervous twitches, tics, impaired bodily functions, or stammering. Phobias and compulsive rituals are neurotic symptoms linked to oedipal conflict. Some socially unacceptable behaviors may also result—sadistic cruelty or masochistic submission, stealing, lying, insatiable demanding, and excessive selfishness. Sexual intimacy in adulthood may become difficult or impossible. Some people go through life with intense feelings of guilt or inferiority. Other people assume personality traits that are mutually incompatible or even self-destructive. So we sometimes find people who are simultaneously conceited and desperate for positive reinforcement.

John Brown is, of course, more than a hundred years out of reach of the analyst's couch. Yet even if it is impossible to obtain further evidence from the man himself, psychoanalytic theory provides historians with a new perspective that can be used to reinterpret long-familiar records. Because Freudian insight depends so much on the experiences of infancy and childhood, one document of Brown's deserves especially close examination, a long letter written by him at the age of fifty-seven. The letter was addressed to thirteen-year-old Harry Stearns, the son of one of Brown's wealthy financial supporters. In it, Brown told the story of "a certain boy of my acquaintance" who, "for convenience," he called John. This was especially convenient since the boy was none other than

Brown himself. This letter, a revealing portrait of Brown's early years, is one of the few surviving sources of information about his childhood.

And yet, even before we begin to approach the letter from a psychoanalytic perspective, it is important to understand the limits of such an exercise. No matter how much this story of childhood is analytically dissected, it cannot provide a full explanation of why John Brown became an abolitionist. Another person with an essentially similar psychic profile but a different career might become—no doubt did become—a southern fire-eater. Nor can psychoanalytic theory provide a sufficient explanation of how John Brown came to attack Harpers Ferry in October 1859. To do so would be to ignore specific and crucial historical events that affected Brown over the years and that had nothing to do with his early childhood experiences.

But if psychoanalytic theory cannot explain *what* John Brown did, it can at least suggest *why* he did things the *way* he did them. It can do so by exploring some of the early emotional currents in his personality and by examining how these forces affected his behavior in later life. Such an exploration is particularly useful in John Brown's case because, as we have seen, Brown's "mad" behavior at Harpers Ferry seems to be grounded in several seemingly contradictory elements of his personality. On the one hand, Brown identified himself with black slaves—the most helpless and weak members of American society. On the other hand, he claimed for himself a mission and a power that was really vast: the God-given right to defy the laws of the United States, free and arm the slaves, and lead a rebellion designed to spread chaos throughout the South. How can we account for this peculiar combination of humility and arrogance, submission and aggression, murder and martyrdom?

At first, Brown's tale of simple boyhood recollections would seem to be of little help. The letter is reprinted here with only a few omissions of routine biographical data:

> I can not tell you of anything in the first Four years of John's life worth mentioning save that at that *early age* he was tempted by Three large Brass Pins belonging to a girl who lived in the family & *stole them.* In this he was detected by his Mother; & after having a full day to think of the wrong; received from her a thorough whipping. When he was Five years old his Father moved to Ohio; then a wilderness filled with wild beasts, & Indians. During the long journey, which was performed in part or mostly with an *ox-team;* he was called on by turns to assist a boy Five years older (who had been adopted by his Father & Mother) & learned to think he could accomplish *smart things* by driving the Cows; & riding the horses. Some-

times he met with Rattle Snakes which were very large; & which some of the company generally managed to kill. After getting to Ohio in 1805 he was for some time rather afraid of the Indians, & of their Rifles; but this soon wore off: & he used to hang about them quite as much as was consistent with good manners; & learned a trifle of their talk. His father learned to dress Deer Skins, & at 6 years old John was installed a young Buck Skin. He was perhaps rather observing as he ever after remembered the entire process of Deer Skin *dressing;* so that he could at any time dress his own leather such as Squirel, Raccoon, Cat, Wolf and Dog Skins, and also learned to make Whip Lashes, which brought him some change at times, & was of considerable service in many ways. At Six years old he began to be a rambler in the wild new country finding birds and squirrels and sometimes a wild Turkey's nest. But about this period he was placed in the school of *adversity;* which my young friend was a most necessary part of his early training. You may *laugh* when you come to read about it; but these were *sore trials* to John: whose earthly treasures were very *few & small.* These were the beginning of a severe but *much needed course* of discipline which he afterwards was to pass through; & which it is to be hoped has learned him before this time that the Heavenly Father sees it best to take all the little things out of his hands which he has ever placed in them. When John was in his Sixth year a poor *Indian boy* gave him a Yellow Marble the first he had ever seen. This he thought a great deal of; & kept it a good while; but at last *he lost it* beyond recovery. *It took years to heal the wound* & I *think* he cried at times about it. About Five months after this he caught a young Squirrel tearing off his tail in doing it; & getting severely bitten at the same time himself. He however held on *to the little bob tail Squirrel;* & finally got him perfectly tamed, so that he almost idolized his pet. *This too he lost;* by its wandering away; or by getting killed; & for a year or two John was *in mourning;* and looking at all the Squirrels he could see to try & discover Bobtail, *if possible.* I must not neglect to tell you of a verry *bad and foolish* habbit to which John was somewhat addicted. I mean *telling lies;* generally to screen himself from blame; or from punishment. He could not well endure to be reproached; & I now think had he been oftener encouraged to be entirely frank; *by making frankness a kind of atonement* for some of his faults; he would not have been so often guilty of this fault; nor have been (in after life) obliged to struggle *so long* with *so mean* a habit.

John was never *quarelsome;* but was *excessively* fond of the *hardest & roughest* kind of plays; & could *never get enough* [of] them. Indeed when for a short time he was sometimes sent to School the opportunity it afforded to wrestle & Snow ball & run & jump & knock off old seedy Wool hats;

offered to him almost the only compensation for the confinement, & restraints of school. I need not tell you that with such a feeling & but little chance of going to school *at all:* he did not become much of a schollar. He would always choose to stay at home & work hard rather than be sent to school; & during the warm season might generally be seen *barefooted & bareheaded:* with Buck skin Breeches suspended often with one leather strap over his shoulder but sometimes with Two. To be sent off through the wilderness alone to very considerable distances was particularly his delight; & in this he was often indulged so that by the time he was Twelve years old he was sent off more than a Hundred Miles with companies of cattle; & he would have thought his character much injured had he been obliged to be helped in any such job. This was a boyish kind of feeling but characteristic however.

At Eight years old, John was left a Motherless boy which loss was complete and pearmanent for notwithstanding his Father again married to a sensible, intelligent, and on many accounts a very estimable woman; yet he never *adopted her in feeling;* but continued to pine after his own Mother for years. This opperated very unfavourably upon him; as he was both naturally fond of females; &, withall, extremely diffident; & deprived him of a suitable connecting link between the different sexes; the want of which might under some circumstances, have proved his ruin. . . .

During the war with England [in 1812] a circumstance occured that in the end made him a most *determined Abolitionist:* & led him to declare, or *Swear: Eternal war* with Slavery. He was staying for a short time with a very gentlemanly landlord since a United States Marshall who held a slave boy near his own age very active, inteligent and good feeling; & to whom John was under considerable obligation for numerous little acts of kindness. *The master* made a great pet of John: brought him to table with his first company; & friends; called their attention to every little smart thing he *said or did:* & to the fact of his being more than a hundred miles from home with a company of cattle alone; while the *negro boy* (who was fully if not more than his equal) was badly clothed, poorly fed; *& lodged in cold weather;* & beaten before his eyes with Iron Shovels or any other thing that came first to hand. This brought John to reflect on the wretched, hopeless condition, of *Fatherless & Motherless* slave *children:* for such children have neither Fathers or Mothers to protect, & provide for them. He sometimes would raise the question *is God their Father?* . . .

I had like to have forgotten to tell you of one of John's misfortunes which set rather hard on him while a young boy. He had by some means *perhaps* by gift of his father become the owner of a little Ewe Lamb which did finely till it was about Two Thirds grown; & then sickened & died. This brought another protracted *mourning season:* not that he felt the pecuniary loss so much: for that was never his disposition; but so strong & earnest were his attachments.

John had been taught from earliest childhood to "fear God and keep his commandments;" & though quite skeptical he had always by turns felt much serious doubt as to his future well being; & about this time became to some extent a convert to Christianity & ever after a firm believer in the divine authenticity of the Bible. With this book he became very familiar, & possessed a most unusual memory of its entire contents.

Now some of the things I have been *telling of;* were just such as I would recommend to you: & I would like to know that you had selected these out; & adopted them as part of your own plan of life; & I wish you to have some *deffinite plan.* Many seem to have none; & others never stick to any that they do form. This was not the case with John. He followed up with *tenacity* whatever he set about so long as it answered his general purpose; & hence he rarely failed in some good degree to effect the things he undertook. This was so much the case that he *habitually expected to succeed* in his undertakings. With this feeling *should be coupled;* the consciousness that our plans are right in themselves.

During the period I have named, John had acquired a kind of ownership to certain animals of some little value but as he had come to understand that the *title of minors* might be a little imperfect: he had recourse to various means in order to secure a more *independent;* & perfect right of property. One of those means was to exchange with his Father for something of far less value. Another was by trading with others persons for something his Father had never owned. Older persons have some times found difficulty with *titles.*

From Fifteen to Twenty years old, he spent most of his time working at the Tanner & Currier's trade keeping Bachelors hall; & he officiating as Cook; & for most of the time as foreman of the establishment under his Father. During this period he found much trouble with some of the bad habits I have mentioned & with some that I have not told you off: his conscience urging him forward with great power in this matter: but his close attention to *business;* & success in its management; together with the way he got along with a company of men, & boys; made him quite a favorite with the serious & more inteligent portion of older persons. This was so much the case; & secured for him so many little notices from those he esteemed; that his vanity was very much fed by it: & he came forward to manhood quite full of self-conceit; & self-confident; notwithstanding his *extreme* bashfulness. A younger brother used sometimes to remind him of this: & to repeat to him *this expression* which you may somewhere find, "A

King against whom there is no rising up." The habit so early formed of being obeyed rendered him in after life too much disposed to speak in an imperious or dictating way. From Fifteen years & upward he felt a good deal of anxiety to learn; but could only read & studdy a little; both for want of time; & on account of inflammation of the eyes. He however managed by the help of books to make himself tolerably well acquainted with common arithmetic; & Surveying; which he practiced more or less after he was Twenty years old. . . .

Before exploring the letter's significance in psychoanalytic terms, it may be worth reminding ourselves what a straightforward reading of the document provides. Attention would naturally center on Brown's striking tale of how, as a twelve-year-old, he was first roused to oppose slavery. Shocked by the cruel treatment of his young black friend, John was further incensed by the unfair and contrasting treatment he benefited from simply because he was white. Here is a vivid, emotional experience that seems to go a good way toward explaining why the evil of slavery weighed so heavily on Brown's mind. In writing an article on the motivations behind the raid at Harpers Ferry, this anecdote is quite clearly the one piece of evidence worth extracting from the long letter. The additional material on Brown's childhood, which often seems to ramble incoherently, might be included in a book-length biography of Brown, but hardly seems relevant to an article which must quickly get to the heart of the man's involvement with abolition.

Yet when we look more closely, Brown's story of the mistreated young slave does not go very far toward explaining Brown's motives. In a land where slavery was central to the culture, hundreds, even thousands of young white boys must have had similar experiences, where black playmates were unfairly whipped, degraded, and treated as inferiors. Nonetheless, many of those boys went on to become slaveholders. Furthermore, although some undoubtedly developed a strong dislike of slavery (Abraham Lincoln among them*), none felt compelled to mount the kind of campaigns Brown did in Kansas and at Harpers Ferry. Why did Brown's rather commonplace experience make such a strong impression on him?

Psychoanalytic theory suggests that the answer to that question may be learned if we do not dismiss the other portions of Brown's childhood experiences as irrelevant but instead examine them for clues to his psy-

---

*As a young man, Lincoln was reputed to have been strongly moved by the sight of slaves being auctioned in New Orleans.

chological development. So let us turn, for a moment, from a direct examination of Brown's abolitionism to the other elements of the letter to Harry Stearns. In doing so we must consider each of Brown's stories, illustrations, and comments with care, keeping in mind Freud's stress on unconscious motivations. In previous chapters we have seen that historians must always treat primary sources skeptically, identifying the personal perspectives and biases which may influence the writer. Psychoanalytic theory requires us to take that skepticism one step further, assuming not only that the evidence may be influenced by unstated motivations (such as Brown's wishing to impress Harry Stearns's father with his virtue) but also that some, even the most powerful of Brown's motivations, may be unconscious—hidden even from Brown himself.

At first glance the narrative appears to recount fairly ordinary events in a child's life. Who, after all, has not cried one time or another at the loss of a pet, or has not been proud of accomplishments like driving cows and riding horses? Yet we must remember that these are only a few events selected from among thousands in Brown's childhood; events meaningful enough to him that he has remembered and related them over fifty years later. Why did Brown retain these memories rather than others? What suggestive images and themes recur? Because psychoanalytic theory emphasizes the importance of parental relationships, we may begin by examining Brown's relationship with his mother and father.

Of the two parents, John's mother is the most visible of the two in this letter, and it is clear that Brown loved her dearly. Notice the language describing his mother's death. John "was left a Motherless boy," he writes—not the simpler and less revealing, "John's mother died," which places the emphasis on the mother rather than on the loss incurred by the "Motherless boy." Furthermore, the loss was "complete & pearmanent." Brown never grew to love his new mother and "continued to pine after his own Mother for years." The phrase, "pine after" (which the Oxford English Dictionary defines as being "consumed with longing," or languishing "with intense desire") has erotic overtones, which are made even more manifest by the sentence that follows. Brown moves directly from his love for his mother to the erotic temptations young women had for him, implicitly linking the two: "This opperated very unfavourably uppon him; as he was both naturally fond of females; & withall extremely diffident; & deprived him of a suitable connecting link between the different sexes; the want of which might under some circumstances have proved his ruin."

John's father, at first glance, appears to have taken a less prominent role in the letter, either positively or negatively. True, Owen Brown does teach John the art of dressing skins (and also, John takes care to note, of making "Whip lashes"); but the attention centers not on the father's devoted teaching so much as John's remarkable ability to learn by watching his father only once. Perhaps most revealing, however, is an ambiguous passage in which Brown's father does *not* appear, yet plays a substantial, hidden role. The relevant paragraph begins by noting that John had "acquired a kind of ownership to certain animals of some little value. . . ." From earlier parts of the letter, we are aware how much these pets meant to him—the loss of the squirrel "Bob tail" (which he "almost idolized") and later the ewe lamb (which he had *"perhaps"* by gift of his father become the owner). Now, Brown indicates that he had owned other animals, but apparently not completely. He is curiously circum-spect about explaining why: the ownership, he says, was incomplete because "the *title of minors"* was "a little imperfect." Apparently, animals which he thought he owned were taken away from him, on the grounds that he did not have "title" to them as a minor. So John, being extremely strong-willed despite his bashfulness, determinedly set out to "secure a more independent; & perfect right of property." Significantly, this ques-tion of ownership appears to have occurred more than once, for Brown noted that he devised "various means" to deal with it.

What is happening here? Brown's evasive language makes the situa-tion difficult to reconstruct, but certain outlines emerge. The only logical person who might repeatedly prevent John from obtaining full "title" to his pets was his father Owen. Why Owen objected is never stated, but several ideas suggest themselves. Conceivably the elder Brown needed one of John's "pet" sheep or cows to feed the family or to sell for income. Furthermore, in a frontier settlement where unfenced wood-lands merged with small farms, wild or stray domestic animals might have roamed onto the Brown farm from time to time. If young John Brown found them, he would likely have claimed them as pets, only to discover that the animal was on father Owen's land—and duly appro-priated for food or income.

Whatever the specific situations, young Brown repeatedly attempted to secure his property through one of two means. "One of those means was to exchange with his Father for something of far less value." The implication is that in some cases Owen Brown allowed John to treat animals as pets if they were formally "purchased" from his father for a token fee ("something of far less value"). In such cases, Owen Brown acted kindly toward his son, though rigorously insisting that the formali-ties of "property" and "title" be observed. But on other occasions John apparently could not convince his father to spare such pets, for the letter indicates that another means of obtaining them "was by trading with others persons for something his Father had never owned." If Owen would not give him pets, John would be able to get them from more willing neighbors.

The conflict of ownership between father and son obviously left a strong imprint. More than forty years later, Brown still vividly remembered how Owen confiscated his pets, as well as the means he worked out to satisfy, or in some cases, actually to evade his father's authority. Even more important, the evasive language in the passage demonstrates that Brown still remained unable to acknowledge his anger openly. In effect, the paragraph reveals a concealed hostility which Brown was still carrying toward his father. The last sentence amounts to a condemnation, but the son could only express his anger indirectly, through use of a generality: "Older persons have some times found difficulty with titles."

Unconsciously, Brown may have been applying the last phrase to himself as well. For the crucial message of the passage is not Brown's hostility toward his father, but the issues through which the hostility is

John Brown, the kindly father: Brown's daughter Ruth remembered the following incident from her childhood: "When I first began to go to school, I found a piece of calico one day behind one of the benches,—it was not large, but seemed quite a treasure to me, and I did not show it to any one until I got home. Father heard me then telling about it, and said, 'Don't you know what girl lost it?' I told him I did not. 'Well, when you go to school to-morrow take it with you, and find out if you can who lost it. It is a trifling thing, but always remember that if you should lose anything *you* valued, no matter how small, you would want the person that found it to give it back to you.'"

expressed: that is to say, title and ownership. Indeed, a psychoanalytic interpretation of Brown's childhood suggests that throughout his life, Brown never fully resolved the question of "titles" of his own identity. The more the letter is probed, the more it reveals a patterned obsession with property and title. Brown continually describes himself as finding some piece of "property," forming strong attachments to it, and then losing it and severely mourning the loss.

What, after all, is the very first experience in Brown's life which he can recall? Before the age of four, John steals three brass pins, discovers that his title to them is imperfect, has them taken away, and is severely whipped. At six, John receives a treasured yellow marble, loses it, and mourns for "years." Soon afterwards, John catches a squirrel, pulling its tail out in the process; then tames and idolizes it; then loses it and mourns another year or two. At eight, John loses another precious possession— his mother—and pines after her for years. Then comes the story of the lamb; and later, his conflicts with his father over the ownership of other pets. The religious moral drawn from these lessons ("a severe but *much needed course* of discipline,") was that "the Heavenly Father sees it best to take all the little things out of his hands which he has ever placed in them." Clearly, the process of becoming an independent adult was for John Brown a continuing effort to reconcile his guilt and anger over losing property with his fierce desire to become truly independent, to possess clear title to his own pets, to become a "propertied" father like Owen and—dare we say it? even like God the father himself. Paradoxically, only when Brown internalized and accepted the authority of his "fathers" could he then act the part of a stern loving parent himself. Submission to his father's authority made it possible for him to accept as legitimate his own authority over his own "pets."

The pattern of Brown's struggle for autonomy is reflected in the role he played as father to his own children. Owen Brown had been a stern disciplinarian, in part because he had felt the lack of a strong hand in his own childhood. John internalized and emulated this severe approach early on. When his younger brother, Salmon, had been pardoned for some misdeed by a boarding-school teacher, John went to the teacher and told him that "if Salmon had done this thing at home, father would have punished him. I know he would expect you to punish him now for doing this—and if you don't, I shall." When the schoolmaster persisted in his lenience, John was reported to have given Salmon a "severe flogging." As a parent, Brown's discipline was equally harsh. When his three-year-old son Jason claimed that a certain dream actually had occurred, Brown felt obliged to whip the boy for lying. The father's immense ambivalence in such a situation was evidenced by the tears that welled up in his eyes as he performed the whipping.

For Brown, even sins took on an aspect of property. The father kept a detailed account book of his son John Jr.'s transgressions, along with the number of whiplashes each sin deserved. Recalled the son:

> On a certain Sunday morning he invited me to accompany him from the house to the tannery, saying that he had concluded it was time for a settlement. We went into the upper or finishing room, and after a long and tearful talk over my faults, he again showed me my account, which exhibited a fearful footing up of *debits.* . . . I then paid about one-third of the debt, reckoned in strokes from a nicely-prepared blue-beech switch, laid on 'masterly.' Then, to my utter astonishment, father stripped off his shirt, and, seating himself on a block, gave me the whip and bade me 'lay it on' to his bare back. I dared not refuse to obey, but at first I did not strike hard. 'Harder!' he said; 'harder, harder!' until he received the *balance of the account.* Small drops of blood showed on his back where the tip end of the tingling beech cut through. Thus ended the account and settlement, which was also my first practical illustration of the Doctrine of Atonement.

In this astonishing tableau, Brown's personal conflicts are vividly reflected. The father punishes the son as justice demands; yet Brown also plays the wayward son himself. And as John Brown, Jr., recognized only later, his father was consciously assuming the mantle of Christ, whom the heavenly father had permitted mankind to crucify and punish, in order that his other children's sins would be forgiven.

The upshot of such discipline was that Brown's sons harbored a similar ambivalence toward their father—an intense feeling of loyalty and submission countered by a strong desire for independence. The contradiction of such training became apparent to one of Brown's sons, Watson, during the raid on Harpers Ferry. "The trouble is," Watson remarked to his father, "you want your boys to be brave as tigers, and still afraid of you." "And that was perfectly true," agreed Salmon Brown, another son.

Psychoanalytic insight has thus helped to reveal some of John Brown's most intense personal conflicts: his ambivalence toward his father's strict discipline; the paradox of his struggle to internalize and accept his father's authority in order to become independent himself; and his excessive concern with property and "pets" as a means of defining his independence. Having exposed these themes, let us now return to the

John Brown, the stern father: Brown was influenced in his harsh discipline by his father Owen (left) and in turn influenced his own son, John, Jr. (right). The father kept a detailed account book of John, Jr.'s sinful acts, along with the number of whiplashes each sin deserved. Even sins, it seemed, were carefully enumerated as property.

starting point of our original analysis of the letter—the anecdote about Brown and the young slave. Suddenly, what had seemed a straightforward tale is filled with immensely suggestive vocabulary, whose overtones reveal a great deal. The passage is worth reading once again:

During the war with England a circumstance occurred that in the end made him a most *determined Abolitionist:* & led him to declare, or *Swear: Eternal war* with Slavery. He was staying for a short time with a very gentlemanly landlord since a United States Marshall who held a slave boy near his own age very active, inteligent and good feeling; & to whom John was under considerable obligation for numerous little acts of kindness. *The master* made a great pet of John: brought him to table with his first company; & friends; called their attention to every little smart thing he *said or did:* & to the fact of his being more than a hundred miles from home with a company of cattle alone; while the *negro boy* (who was fully if not more than his equal) was badly clothed, poorly fed; & *lodged in cold weather;*

& beaten before his eyes with Iron Shovels or any other thing that came
first to hand. This brought John to reflect on the wretched, hopeless
condition, of *Fatherless & Motherless* slave *children:* for such children have
neither Fathers or Mothers to protect, & provide for them. He sometimes
would raise the question *is God their Father?*

Upon this second reading, it becomes evident that Brown's language
and metaphors here are full of references to parental relationships, dependence, and authority. John stayed with a "very gentlemanly landlord"
who "made a great pet of John," treating the boy just as John treated his
own pets. At the same time, however, this gentlemanly father acted like
no father at all to the negro boy, beating him unmercifully. This led John
to reflect "on the wretched, hopeless condition, of *Fatherless & Motherless*
slave *children. . . .*" "*Is God their Father?*" he asked himself.

The situation confronted young Brown with two starkly contrasting
models of a father, corresponding with the boy's own ambivalent feelings toward Owen. Naturally, John wanted his own father to discipline
him less harshly. He wanted to be treated as a "pet;" as his own animals
were treated; as this gentleman treated him. Similarly, he identified with
the negro boy, an innocent lad who was being punished just as Owen
Brown punished John. Yet like all boys, he also identified with his own
father. He desired as well as hated the power Owen wielded over him,
and that this gentleman wielded over the negro boy. He thus felt the tug
of two conflicting loyalties. To use the religious imagery so familiar to
that age, John Brown wanted to grow up and act both as God the
merciful Father and as God the righteous Judge.

This ambivalent father–son relationship suggests that Brown's intense
lifelong identification with black slaves might well have sprung from the
struggle he experienced with paternal discipline. Helping slaves was
ultimately a means of helping himself without consciously recognizing
the source of his emotions and convictions. He could channel the re-
pressed hostility toward his father into a more acceptable form—hatred
of the slaveholders, another class of paternalistic oppressors who cruelly
whipped their charges. In attacking the planters, Brown relieved the
sense of guilt he harbored for secretly wishing to destroy his father. After
all, God the implacable Father and Judge was using Brown as his instrument for bringing justice to the world. At the same time, by protecting
and defending the helpless slaves, Brown carried out God's will as a
merciful father. In liberating the black nation, he could free himself. In
some indirect yet significant way, the raid at Harpers Ferry involved the
working out of psychological turmoil that had troubled Brown since
childhood.

Does all this speculation lead us then to assume that childhood neuroses rather than moral conviction dictated Brown's actions? No responsible historian or psychoanalyst would jump to such a conclusion. To do so would be to take a reductionist view of history, explaining major events by tracing them to infantile conflicts. Such an approach assumes that the explanation for what has happened in the past lies in the psychic turmoil of great men. We might then conclude that had John Brown not been abused by his father, the raid on Harpers Ferry would never have occurred. Since Harpers Ferry led directly to the Civil War, even the war might have been avoided. How much more peaceful history would be in a world where all boys and girls enjoyed a childhood free of trauma!

No, a full explanation of any person's actions and beliefs must, in the end, be multicausal if it is to reflect the complexity of real life. We cannot minimize the sincerity—nor the nobility—of Brown's belief in the brotherhood of blacks and whites. Yet the stirrings of deeply rooted unconscious forces can no more be neglected than the more rational components of behavior.

This psychoanalytic interpretation, then, is not offered as a definitive or an exclusive one. And our brief exposition of one letter constitutes only one small part of what should properly be a much larger analysis of Brown's personality and career. But the exposition is ample enough to suggest how fruitful a psychoanalytical approach can be. As Michael Rogin suggested in the case of Andrew Jackson, it provides historians with a theory which sensitizes them to profitable themes, motifs, and vocabularies. An awareness of recurring tensions stemming from Brown's childhood makes it possible to appreciate how his personal sufferings incorporated the larger events of the period. Erik Erikson, the psychologist who has done the most to introduce psychoanalytic insight into history, has at the same time stressed the need to root psychology firmly in contemporary historical context. What Erikson said of such great men as Martin Luther or Mahatma Gandhi could easily be said of Brown. All three shared a "grim willingness to do the dirty work of their ages." They achieved a spiritual breakthrough by translating their inner conflicts into behaviors that spoke to the consciousness of their generations. Or as Erikson said of Luther, Brown had to strike his blow against slavery "to lift his individual patienthood to the level of a universal one, and to try to solve for all what he could not solve for himself alone."

At the moment Brown transcended his life of failure, he forced his generation to identify either positively or negatively with the action he took to liberate black Americans. His act of violence was appropriate to what Oates described as "the violent, irrational, and paradoxical times in which he lived." Given his profoundly religious nature and commitment to human liberty and equality, Brown could not be at peace until his society recognized the contradiction between its religious and political ideals and the existence of slavery. Within Erikson's historical scheme Brown's angry messianism on the slave question intersected with the collective history of the racist, slave society in which he lived.

In the end, John Brown turned the tables on society. His raid on Harpers Ferry pressed his fellow Americans to consider whether it was not actually their values, and society's, which were immoral and "abnormal." The outbreak of civil war, after all, demonstrated that American society was so maladjusted and so divided that it could not remain a "normal," integrated whole without violently purging itself. If Brown's raid was an isolated act of a disturbed man, why did it drive an entire generation to the brink of war? Why did Brown's generation find it impossible to agree about the meaning of Harpers Ferry? As C. Vann Woodward concluded, the importance lay not so much in the man or event, but in the use made of them by northern and southern hotheads. For every Emerson or Thoreau who pronounced the raid the work of a saint, a southern fire-eater condemned the venture as the villainy of all northerners.

None of these partisans paid much attention to evidence. A crisis mentality thwarted any attempts at understanding or reconciliation. In the fury of mutual recrimination, both sides lost sight of the man who had provoked the public outcry and propelled the nation toward war. In such times it will always be, as abolitionist Wendell Phillips remarked, "hard to tell who's mad."

Additional Reading

John Brown's truth goes marching on, and so do the books about him. In the 1970s, four full-scale biographies were issued, the best of which is Stephen Oates, *To Purge This Land with Blood* (New York, 1970). Oates's treatment is even-handed, scholarly, and stirring in its narrative. (Other biographies available are by Jules C. Abels, Truman Nelson, and Richard O. Boyer.) Oswald Garrison Villard, *John Brown, 1800–1859: A Biography Fifty Years After* (Boston, 1910) is an older work worth reading. It draws upon and excerpts many primary sources. C. Vann Woodward, "John Brown's Private War," is one of the best short interpretive essays available on the raid and can be found in his *Burden of Southern History* (Baton Rouge, La., 1968). For a detailed account of Brown's earlier doings in Kansas, see James C. Malin, *John Brown and the Legacy of Fifty-six* (Philadelphia, 1942).

Readers wishing to see for themselves the evidence and conflicting interpretations of Brown will do well to begin with Jonathan Fanton and Richard Warch, eds., *John Brown* (Englewood Cliffs, N.J., 1973). This well-edited collection of primary and secondary materials concentrates on documenting the Harpers Ferry raid and its preparations. It also provides evidence relating to Brown's personality and previous career. Franklin B. Sanborn, *The Life and Letters of John Brown* (Boston, 1891), unabashedly sympathetic to Brown, contains many valuable personal letters for those wishing to pursue psychoanalytic (or other) interpretations. The fullest collection of materials on the raid and trial is *The Life, Trial and Execution of John Brown* (New York, 1859).

The field of psychohistory is broad and diverse. Not only is applying psychiatric theory to historical situations a delicate task, psychology and psychoanalysis are fields undergoing continuous revision. With so little space available in this chapter, we chose to avoid the intricacies of debate over the validity of psychoanalytic methods and have concentrated on giving readers a taste of the kinds of evidence that psychohistorians habitually examine and the kinds of deductions they make. Psychoanalysis can be an arcane discipline, and it harbors more than its share of dogmatists and true-believers. We would argue, as critic Frederick Crews once noted, that it is possible to "dissent" from the rigid orthodoxy of psychoanalytic theory "without forsaking the most promising aspects of psychoanalysis—its attentiveness to signs of conflict, its hospitality to multiple significance, its ideas of ambivalence, identification, repression, and projection." Those readers who wish further introduction to psychoanalytic theory may consult Franz Alexander and Helen Ross, *The Impact of Freudian Psychiatry* (Chicago, 1961) and J. A. C. Brown, *Freud and the Post-Freudians* (London, 1960).

The promise of psychoanalytic techniques for doing history received widespread attention when William L. Langer used his presidential address to the American Historical Association to call for further efforts in the genre. Langer's address, "The Next Assignment," is reprinted in the *American Historical Review,* LXIII (January 1958), 283–304. A more recent "state of the art" evaluation is Robert J. Lifton, ed., *Explorations in Psychohistory* (New York, 1974), which includes essays by eminent practitioners of the craft such as Lifton himself, Erik Erikson, Bruce Mazlish, Philip Rieff, and Robert Coles. Also useful is George M. Kren and Leon H. Rappoport, eds., *Varieties of Psychohistory* (New York, 1976) and Bruce Mazlish, *Psychoanalysis and History,* rev. ed. (New York, 1971).

For an example of responsible psychohistory, see Erik Erikson's excellent biographies, *Young Man Luther* (New York, 1958) and *Gandhi's Truth* (New York, 1969). On John Brown himself, Alan Nevins provides a psychological interpretation in *The Emergence of Lincoln,* vol. 2 (New York, 1950) 5–27 and 70–97. On the other hand, the excesses of the trade are lamentably demonstrated in a book co-authored by Sigmund Freud himself and William Bullitt, *Thomas Woodrow Wilson* (Boston, reprinted 1968). Skeptics who believe that psychohistory is by its very nature flawed will find comforting reinforcement in *Shrinking History* (New York, 1980), an incisive critique of the discipline by a friend and colleague of ours, David Stannard, who most emphatically had nothing to do with the present chapter.

Finally, as professed amateurs in the psychoanalytic field, we would like to thank Dr. David Musto, able psychiatrist and historian, whose graduate seminar at Yale provided a fine introduction to the territory. Our specific evaluation of John Brown's motives was substantially guided by consultation with two practicing psychiatrists, both aware of the possibilities and limitations of their discipline. Dr. Geoff Linburn of the M.I.T. mental health staff outlined the interpretive limits of what our evidence might sustain. Dr. Eric Berger of Yale's psychiatric faculty unlocked many of the possible meanings to be found in John Brown's autobiographical letter. In addition, our friend Dr. John Rugge brought into clear focus Brown's striking concern for property and ownership. None of these gentlemen, we should stress, is responsible for the final results exhibited here. It is we who wrestled Brown to the couch and, perforce, we take full responsibility for the consequences.

CHAPTER
SEVEN
❖

The View from the Bottom Rail

Thunder. From across the swamps and salt marshes of the Carolina coast came the distant, repetitive pounding. Thunder out of a clear blue sky. Down at the slave quarters, young Sam Mitchell heard the noise and wondered. In Beaufort, the nearby village, planter John Chaplin heard too, and dashed for his carriage. The drive back to his plantation was as quick as Chaplin could make it. Once home, he ordered his wife and children to pack; then looked for his slaves. The flatboat must be made ready, he told them; the family was going to Charleston. He needed eight men at the oars. One of the slaves, Sam Mitchell's father, brought the news to his wife and son at the slave quarters. "You ain't gonna row no boat to Charleston," the wife snapped, "you go out dat back door and keep a-going." Young Sam was mystified by all the commotion. How could it thunder without a cloud in the sky? "Son, dat ain't no t'under," explained the mother, "dat Yankee come to gib you freedom."

The pounding of the guns came relatively quickly to Beaufort—November of 1861, only seven months after the first hostilities at Fort Sumter. Yet it was only a matter of time before the thunder of freedom rolled across the rest of the south, from the bayous and deltas of Louisiana in 1862 to the farms around Richmond in 1865. And as the guns of the Union spoke, thousands of Sam Mitchells experienced their own unforgettable moments. Freedom was coming to a nation of four million slaves.

To most slaves, the men in the blue coats were foreigners. As foreigners, they were sometimes suspect. Many southern masters painted the

JDR

prospect of Northern invasion in deliberately lurid colors. Union soldiers, one Tennessee slave was told, "got long horns on their heads, and
tushes in their mouths, and eyes sticking out like a cow! They're mean
old things." A terrified Mississippi slave refused to come down out of
a tree until the Union soldier below her took off his cap and demonstrated he had no horns. Many slaves, however, took such tales with
more than a grain of salt. "We all hear 'bout dem Yankees," a Carolina
slave told his overseer. "Folks tell we they has horns and a tail . . . W'en
I see dem coming I shall run like all possess." But as soon as the overseer
fled, leaving the plantation in the slaves' care, the tune changed: "Good-
by, ole man, good-by. That's right. Skedaddle as fast as you kin. . . . We's

This slave family lived on a plantation at Beaufort, South Carolina, not far
from the plantation where Sam Mitchell heard the thunder of northern guns in
1861. The photograph was taken after northern forces had occupied the Sea
Island area.

gwine to run sure enough; but we knows the Yankees, an' we runs that way."

For some slaves, the habit of long years, the bond of loyalty, or the fear of alternatives led them to side with their masters. Faithful slaves hid valuable silver, persuaded Yankees that their departed masters were actually Union sympathizers, or feigned contagious illness in order to scare off marauding soldiers. One pert slave even led Yankees right to the plantation beehives. "De Yankees forgot all about de meat an' things dey done stole," she noted with satisfaction; "they took off down de road at a run." But in many cases, the conflict between loyalty and freedom caused confusion and anguish. An old Georgia couple, both over sixty, greeted the advance of Sherman's soldiers calmly and with apparent lack of interest. They seemed entirely content to remain under the care of their master instead of joining the mass of slaves flocking along behind Sherman's troops. As the soldiers prepared to leave, however, the old woman suddenly stood up, a "fierce, almost devilish" look in her eyes, and turned to her husband. "What you sit dar for?" she asked vehemently. "You s'pose I wait sixty years for nutten? Don't yer see de door open? I'se follow my child; I not stay. Yes, anudder day I goes 'long wid dese people; yes, sar, I walks till I drop in my tracks."

Other slaves felt no hesitation about choosing freedom; indeed, they found it difficult to contain the joy within them. One woman, who overheard the news of emancipation just before she was to serve her master's dinner, asked to be excused because she had to get water from a nearby spring. Once she had reached the seclusion of the spring, she allowed her feelings free rein.

> I jump up and scream, "Glory, glory hallelujah to Jesus! I'se free! I'se free! Glory to God, you come down an' free us; no big man could do it." An' I got sort o' scared, afeared somebody hear me, an' I takes another good look, an' fall on de groun' an' roll over, an' kiss de groun' fo' de Lord's sake, I's so full o' praise to Masser Jesus.

To the newly freed slaves, it seemed as if the world had been turned upside down. Rich and powerful masters were fleeing before Yankees, while freed slaves were left with the run of the plantation. The situation was summed up succinctly by one black soldier who was surprised—and delighted—to find that his former master was among the prisoners he was guarding. "Hello, massa!" he said cheerfully, "bottom rail top dis time!"

IN SEARCH OF THE FREEDMEN'S POINT OF VIEW

The freeing of four million blacks surely ranks as one of the major events in American history. Yet the story has not been an easy one to tell. To understand the personal trials and triumphs of the newly liberated slaves, or freedmen as they came to be called, historians must draw upon the personal experiences of those at the center of the drama. They must recreate the freedman's point of view. But slaves had occupied the lowest level of America's social and economic scale. They sat, as the black soldier correctly noted, on the bottom rail of the fence. For several reasons, that debased position has made it unusually difficult for historians to recover the freedman's point of view.

In the first place, most histories suffer from a natural "top-rail" bias. They tend to take as their subjects members of the higher social classes. Histories cannot be written without the aid of documentary raw material, left in the historical record by participants. The more detailed the records, the easier it is to write a history. By and large, those on the top rails of society produce the best and most voluminous records. Having been privileged to receive an education, they are more apt to publish memoirs, keep diaries, or write letters. As leaders of society who make decisions, they are the subjects of official minutes and records. They are more often written about and commented on by their contemporaries.

At the other end of the social spectrum, "bottom-rail" people lead lives that are commonly repetitious. While a political leader involves himself in what appears to be one momentous issue after another, a farmer most often plants the same crop and follows the ritual of the seasons year after year. Furthermore, the individual actions of the anonymous majority seem to have little effect on the course of history. Biographical details of such people appear both uninspiring and unavailable, at first glance anyway, when compared to the bustling lives of the powerful. Thus the elites of any society have long been the natural subjects of historians.

The decade of the 1970s saw an increasing interest by historians in the writing of social histories that would shed greater light on the activities and feelings of bottom rail people. We saw, for example, that a knowledge of the social and economic position of the serving class was essential to understanding the volatile society of early Virginia. Similarly, we turned to the social tensions of ordinary farmers in order to explain the alliances behind the witchcraft controversy at Salem. Often enough, social historians have found it difficult to piece together the lives of any anonymous class of Americans; yet reconstructing the perspective of the black slave or freedman has proved particularly challenging, simply because few written source materials are available. Black slaves were not only discouraged from learning to read and write, southern legislatures passed slave codes which flatly forbade whites to teach them.

The laws were not entirely effective; a few blacks employed as drivers on large plantations learned to read and correspond so that their absent masters might send them instructions. Some black preachers were also literate. Still, most reading remained a clandestine affair, done out of sight of the master or other whites. During the war, a literate slave named Squires Jackson was eagerly scanning a newspaper for word of northern victories when his master unexpectedly entered the room and demanded to know what the slave was doing. The surprised reader deftly turned the newspaper upside down, put on a foolish grin, and said, "Confederates done won the war!" The master laughed and went about his business.

Even though most slaves never wrote letters, kept diaries, or left any other written records, it might at first seem easy enough to learn about slave life from accounts written by white contemporaries. Slavery, after all, was an institution whose faults and alleged virtues were hotly debated by nineteenth-century Americans. Any number of letters, books, travellers' accounts, and diaries survive, full of descriptions of life under slavery and of the experiences of freedmen after the war. Yet here too, the question of perspective raises serious problems. The vantage point of white Americans observing slavery was emphatically not that of slaves who lived under the "peculiar institution," nor of those freedmen forced to cope with their dramatically changed circumstances. The marked differences between the social and psychological positions of blacks and whites make it extremely difficult to reconstruct the black point of view solely from white accounts.

Consider, first, the observations of whites who associated most often and most closely with black slaves: their masters. The relation between master and slave was inherently unequal. Blacks were at the mercy of their owners' whims. Slaves could be whipped for trifling offenses; they could be sold or separated from their families and closest friends; even under "kind" masters, they were bound to labor as ordered if they wanted their ration of food and clothing. With slaves so dependent on the master's authority, they were hardly likely to reveal their true feelings; the dangerous consequences of such indiscretion were too great.

In fact, we have already encountered an example where a black was forced to deceive his master, the case of Squires Jackson and his newspaper. A moment's reflection will indicate that we narrated that story from Jackson's point of view, not the master's. Our impression of the slave's conduct would have been remarkably different if we had access only to a diary kept by Jackson's master. "A humorous incident occurred today," the entry might have read.

> While entering the woodshed to attend some business, I came upon my slave Squires. His large eyes were fixed with intense interest upon an old copy of a newspaper he had come upon, which alarmed me some until I discovered the rascal was reading its contents upside down. "Why Squires," I said innocently. "What is the latest news?" He looked up at me with a big grin and said, "Massa, de 'Federates jes' won de war!" It made me laugh to see the darkey's simple confidence. I wish I could share his optimism.

This entry is fictional, but having Jackson's version of the story serves to cast suspicion on similar entries in real planter diaries. One Louisiana slaveowner, for instance, marvelled that his field hands went on with their Christmas party apparently unaware that Yankee raiding parties had pillaged a nearby town. "We have been watching the negroes dancing for the last two hours. . . . They are having a merry time, thoughtless creatures, they think not of the morrow." It apparently never occurred to the planter that the "thoughtless" merriment may have been especially great because of the Northern troops nearby.*

The harsh realities of the war brought many southerners to realize for the first time just how little they really knew about their slaves. In areas where Union troops were near, slaves ran for freedom—often the very servants masters had deemed most loyal. Mary Chesnut, whose house was not far from Fort Sumter, sought in vain to penetrate the blank expressions of her slaves. "Not by one word or look can we detect any

*Readers who review the opening narrative of this chapter will discover that they have already encountered quite a few other examples of blacks concealing their true feelings. In fact, except for the black soldier's comment about the bottom rail being top, every example of white–black relations cited in the opening section has some element of concealment or deception, either by blacks toward whites, or by whites toward blacks. It may be worth noting that we did not select the opening incidents with that fact in mind. The preponderance of deception was noted only when we reviewed the draft several days after it had been written.

"They are having a merry time, thoughtless creatures, they think not of the morrow." This scene of a Christmas party, similar to the one described by the Louisiana planter, appeared with an article written by a northern correspondent for *Frank Leslie's Illustrated Newspaper* in 1857. The picture, reflecting the popular stereotype of slaves as cheerful and ignorantly content with their lot, suggests that the social constraints of the times made it as difficult for southern blacks to be completely candid with their northern liberators as it had been to be candid with their southern masters.

change in the demeanor of these Negro servants. . . . You could not tell that they even hear the awful noise that is going on in the bay [at Fort Sumter], though it is dinning in their ears night and day. . . . Are they stolidly stupid, or wiser than we are, silent and strong, biding their time?"

It is tempting to suppose that northerners, as liberators of the slaves, might provide more sympathetic or accurate accounts of freedmen's attitudes. But that is a dangerous assumption to make. Although virtually all northern slaves had been freed by 1820, race prejudice remained overwhelmingly evident. Antislavery forces often combined a vehement dislike of slavery with an equally vehement desire to keep blacks out of the North. For blacks who did live there, most housing and transportation facilities were segregated. Whites and blacks had much less contact than afforded by the easy, if unequal, familiarity common in the South.

Consequently, while some Union soldiers went out of their way to be kind to the slaves they encountered, many more looked upon blacks with distaste and open hostility. Many Yankees strongly believed that they were fighting a war to save the Union, not to free the "cursed Nigger," as one recruit put it. Even white officers who commanded black regiments could be remarkably unsympathetic. "Any one listening to your shouting and singing can see how grotesquely ignorant you are," one officer lectured his troops, when they refused to accept less than the pay promised them upon enlistment. Missionaries and other sympathetic northerners who came to occupied territory understood the slaves better, but even they had preconceptions to overcome. "I saw some very low-looking women who answered very intelligently, contrary to my expectations," noted Philadelphia missionary Laura Towne. Where she was serving, in the Carolina sea-islands near Beaufort, she observed that "some, indeed most of [the slaves], were the real bullet-headed negroes." Another female missionary, much less sympathetic than Laura Towne, bridled when a black child greeted her with too much familiarity. "I say good-mornin' to my young missus," recounted the child to a friend, "and she say, 'I slap your mouth for your impudence, you nigger.'" Such callousness underlines the need for caution when dealing with northern accounts.

Indeed, the more perceptive northern observers recognized that blacks would continue to be circumspect around whites. Just as the slave had been dependent on his southern masters, so the freedman found himself similarly vulnerable to the new class of conquerors. Blacks often responded to questions with answers carefully designed to please. "One of these blacks, fresh from slavery, will most adroitly tell you precisely what you want to hear," noted northerner Charles Nordhoff.

> To cross-examine such a creature is a task of the most delicate nature; if you chance to put a leading question he will answer to its spirit as closely as the compass needle answers to the magnetic pole. Ask if the enemy had fifty thousand men, and he will be sure that they had at least that many; express your belief that they had not five thousand, and he will laugh at the idea of their having more than forty-five hundred.

Samuel Gridley Howe, a wartime commissioner investigating the freedmen's condition, saw the situation clearly. "The negro, like other men, naturally desires to live in the light of truth," he argued, "but he hides in the shadow of falsehood, more or less deeply, according as his safety or welfare seems to require it. Other things equal, the freer a people, the more truthful; and only the perfectly free and fearless are perfectly truthful."

Even sympathetic northerners were at a disadvantage in recounting the freedmen's point of view, simply because black culture was so foreign to them. The world of the southern field hand, black religious culture, surviving African folk customs and songs—all these were unfamiliar to northern observers. Black dialect too created problems. Charles Nordhoff noted that often he had the feeling that he was "speaking with foreigners." The slaves' phrase "I go shum" puzzled him until he discovered it to be a contraction of "I'll go see about it." Another missionary was "teaching the little darkies gymnastics and what various things were for, eyes, etc. He asked what ears were made for, and when they said, 'To yer with,' he could not understand them at all."

If black dialect was difficult to understand, black culture and religion could appear even more unfathomable. Although most slaves nominally shared with northerners a belief in Christianity, black methods of worship shocked more than one staid Unitarian. After church meetings, slaves often participated in a singing and dancing session known as a "shout," where the leader would sing out a line of song and the chorus respond, dancing in rhythm to the music. As the night proceeded, the music became more vocal and the dancing more vigorous. "Tonight I have been to a 'shout,' " reported Laura Towne, "which seems to me certainly the remains of some old idol worship . . . I never saw anything so savage." Another missionary noted, "It was the most hideous and at the same time the most pitiful sight I ever witnessed."

Thus, as sympathetic as many northerners wished to be, significant obstacles prevented them from fully appreciating the freedman's point of view. With race prejudice so prevalent, with blacks in such a vulnerable position, with black culture so much at odds with white, it is not surprising that perceptive observers like Nordhoff felt as if they were speaking with "foreigners." The nature of slave society and the persistence of race prejudice made it virtually impossible for blacks and whites to deal with one another in open, candid ways.

THE FREEDMEN SPEAK

Given the scarcity of first-person black accounts, how can we fully recover the freedman's point of view? From the very beginning, some observers recognized the value that black testimony would have and worked to collect it. If few blacks could write, their stories could be written down by others and made public. Oral testimony, transcribed by literate editors, would allow blacks to speak out on issues that affected them most closely.

The tradition of oral evidence began even before the slaves were freed. Abolitionists recognized the value of firsthand evidence against the slave system. They took down the stories of fugitive slaves who had safely made their way North, and published the accounts. During the war, Congress also established the Freedman's Inquiry Commission, which collected information about blacks that might aid the government in formulating policies toward the newly freed slaves.

In the half-century following Reconstruction, however, interest in preserving black history generally languished. An occasional journalist or historian travelled through the South to interview former slaves. Educators at black schools, such as the Hampton Institute, published a few recollections. But a relatively small number of subjects were interviewed. Often the interviews were published in daily newspapers whose standards of accuracy were not high and where limitations of space required that the interviews be severely edited.

Furthermore, the vast majority of professional historians writing about Reconstruction ignored these interviews, as well as the freedmen's perspective in general. They most often relied on white accounts which, not unexpectedly, painted a rather partial picture. William A. Dunning, a historian at Columbia University, was perhaps the most influential scholar in setting forth the prevalent viewpoint. He painted the freedmen as childish, happy-go-lucky creatures who failed to appreciate the responsibilities of their new status. "As the full meaning of [emancipation] was grasped by the freedmen," Dunning wrote, "great numbers of them abandoned their old homes, and, regardless of crops to be cultivated, stock to be cared for, or food to be provided, gave themselves up to testing their freedom. They wandered aimless but happy through the country. . . ." At the same time Dunning asserted that Confederate soldiers and other southern whites had "devoted themselves with desperate energy to the procurement of what must sustain the life of both themselves and their former slaves." Such were the conclusions deduced without the aid of the freedmen's perspectives.

Only in the twentieth century were systematic efforts made to question blacks about their experiences as slaves and freedmen. Interest in the black heritage rose markedly during the 1920s, in great part spurred by the efforts of black scholars like W. E. B. DuBois, Charles Johnson, and Carter Woodson, the editor and founder of the *Journal of Negro History.* Those scholars labored diligently to overturn the Reconstruction stereotypes promoted by the Dunning school. Moreover, the growth of both sociology and anthropology departments at American universities encouraged scholars to analyze Southern culture using the tools of the new social sciences. By the beginning of the 1930s historians at Fisk and Southern universities had instituted projects to collect oral evidence.

Ironically, it was the economic adversity of the Depression that sparked the greatest single effort to gather oral testimony from the freedmen. One of the many alphabet-soup agencies chartered by the Roosevelt administration was the Federal Writers' Project (FWP). Primarily, the project sought to compile cultural guides to each of the forty-eight states, using unemployed writers and journalists to collect and edit the information. But under the direction of folklorist John Lomax, the FWP also organized staffs in many states to interview former slaves.

Although Lomax's project placed greatest emphasis on collecting *Lomax* black folklore and songs, the FWP's directive to interviewers included a long list of historical questions that interviewers were encouraged to ask. The following sampling gives an indication of the project's interests:

> What work did you do in slavery days? Did you ever earn any money?
> What did you eat and how was it cooked? Any possums? Rabbits? Fish?
> Was there a jail for slaves? Did you ever see any slaves sold or auctioned
>   off? How and for what causes were the slaves punished? Tell what you
>   saw.
> What do you remember about the war that brought you your freedom?
>   When the Yankees came what did they do or say?
> What did the slaves do after the war? What did they receive generally?
>   What do they think about the reconstruction period?

The results of these interviews are remarkable, if only in terms of sheer bulk. More than 2,300 were recorded and edited in state FWP offices and then sent to Washington, assembled in 1941, and published in typescript. A facsimile edition, issued during the 1970s, takes up nineteen volumes. Supplementary materials, including hundreds of interviews never forwarded to Washington during the project's life, comprise another twelve volumes, with additional materials forthcoming. Benjamin Botkin, the series' original editor, recognized the collection's importance:

> These life histories, taken down as far as possible in the narrator's words, constitute an invaluable body of unconscious evidence or indirect source material, which scholars and writers dealing with the South, especially,

social psychologists and cultural anthropolgists, cannot afford to reckon without. For the first and last time, a large number of surviving slaves (many of whom have since died) have been permitted to tell their own story, in their own way.

At first glance, the slave narrative collection would appear to fulfill admirably the need for a guide to the freedmen's point of view. But even Botkin, for all his enthusiasm, recognized that the narratives could not simply be taken at face value. Like other primary source materials, they need to be viewed in terms of the context in which they originated.

To begin with, no matter how massive the nineteen volumes of interviews may appear on the library shelf, they still constitute a small sampling of the original four million freedmen. What sort of selection bias might exist? Geographic imbalance comes quickly to mind. Are the slave interviews drawn from a broad cross-section of southern states? Counting the number of slaves interviewed from each state, we discover that there are only 155 interviews from blacks living in Virginia, Missouri, Maryland, Delaware, and Kentucky—about 6 percent of the total number of interviews published. Yet in 1860, 23 percent of the southern slave population lived in those states. Thus the upper South is underrepresented in the collection. For researchers who wished to investigate whether conditions varied from the border states to the deep south, this geographic bias would have to be taken into account.*

What about age? Since the interviews took place primarily between 1936 and 1938, ex-slaves were fairly old: fully two-thirds of them were over 80. The predominance of elderly interviewees raises several questions. Most obviously, the Civil War was already seventy years in the past. How sharp were the informants' memories? Ability to recall accurately varies from person to person, but common sense suggests that the further away from an event, the less detailed one's memory is likely to be. In addition, age may have biased the *type* of recollections as well as their accuracy. Historian John Blassingame has noted that the average life-expectancy of a slave in 1850 was less than 50 years. Those who lived to a ripe old age might well have survived because they were treated better than the average slave. If so, their accounts would reflect some of the milder experiences of slaves.

Secondly, if those interviewed were predominantly old in 1936, they

---

*Statistics quoted are for the original slave narrative interviews only. They do not include materials issued in the supplementary volumes, which are helping to rectify the imbalance.

were predominantly young during the Civil War. Almost half (43 percent) were less than ten years old in 1865. Sixty-seven percent were under fifteen years old, and 83 percent were under twenty. Thus, many remembered slavery as it would have been experienced by a child. Since the conditions of bondage were relatively less harsh for a child than for an adult slave, once again the FWP narratives may be somewhat skewed toward an optimistic view of slavery. (On the other hand, it might be argued that since children are so impressionable, memories both good and bad might have been vividly magnified.)

Other possible sampling biases come to mind—the sex of the subjects or the kinds of labor they performed as slaves. But distortions may be introduced into the slave narratives in ways more serious than sample bias. Interviewers, simply by choosing their questions, define the kinds of information a subject will volunteer. We have already seen that sensitive observers, such as Charles Nordhoff, recognized how important it was not to ask leading questions. But even Nordhoff may not have realized how many unconscious cues the most innocent questions carry.

Social scientists specializing in interviewing have pointed out that even the grammatical form of a question will influence a subject's response. Take, for example, the following questions:

Where did you hear about this job opening?
How did you hear about this job opening?
So you saw our want ad for this job?

Each question is directed at the same information, yet each suggests to the subject a different response. The first version (*"Where* did you hear . . ."*) implies that the interviewer wants a specific, limited answer. ("Down at the employment center.") The second question, by substituting *how* for *where,* invites the subject to offer a longer response. ("Well, I'd been looking around for a job for several weeks, and I was over at the employment office when. . . .") The final question signals that the interviewer wants only a yes or no confirmation to a question whose answer he believes he already knows.

Interviewers, in other words, constantly communicate to their subjects the kinds of evidence they want, the length of the answers, and even the manner in which answers ought to be offered. If such interviewing "cues" influence routine conversations, they prove even more crucial when a subject as controversial as slavery is involved, and where relations between blacks and whites continue to be strained. In fact, the most important cue an interviewer was likely to have given was one presented before any conversation took place. Was the interviewer white or black? William Ferris, a sociologist obtaining oral folklore in the Mississippi Delta region in 1968, discussed the problem. "It was not possible to maintain rapport with both Whites and Blacks in the same community," he noted,

> for the confidence and cooperation of each was based on their belief that I was "with them" in my convictions about racial taboos of Delta society. Thus when I was "presented" to Blacks by a white member of the community, the informants regarded me as a member of the white caste and therefore limited their lore to noncontroversial topics. . . .

Such tensions were even more prevalent throughout the South during the 1930s. In hundreds of ways, blacks were made aware that they were still considered inferior to whites, and that they were to remain within strictly segregated and subordinate bounds. From 1931 to 1935, more than 70 blacks were lynched in the South, often for minor or nonexistent crimes. Blacks in prison found themselves forced to negotiate grossly unfavorable labor contracts if they wished to be released. Many sharecroppers and other poor farmers were constantly in debt to white property owners.

Smaller matters of etiquette reflected the larger state of affairs. A southern white would commonly address adult blacks by their first names, or as "boy," "auntie," "uncle," regardless of the black person's status and even if the white knew the black's full name. Blacks were required to address whites as "ma'am" or "mister." Such distinctions were maintained even on the telephone. If a black placed a long-distance call for "Mr. Smith" in a neighboring town, the white operator would ask, "Is he colored?" The answer being yes, her reply would be, "Don't you say 'Mister' to me. He ain't 'Mister' to me." Conversely, an operator would refuse to place a call by a black who did not address her as "Ma'am."

In such circumstances, most blacks were naturally reticent about volunteering information to white FWP interviewers. "Lots of old slaves closes the door before they tell the truth about their days of slavery," noted one Texas black to an interviewer. "When the door is open, they tell how kind their masters was and how rosy it all was. . . ." Samuel S. Taylor, a skilled black interviewer in Arkansas, found that he had to reassure informants that the information they were giving would not be used against them. "I've told you too much," one subject concluded. "How come they want all this stuff from the colored people anyway. Do you take any stories from the white people? They know all about it. They know more about it than I do. They dont need me to tell it to them."

Often the whites who interviewed blacks lived in the same town and were long acquaintances. "I 'members when you was barefoot at de bottom," one black told his white (and balding) interviewer; "now I see you a settin' dere, gittin' bare at de top, as bare as de palm of my hand." Another black revealed an even closer relationship when he noted that his wife Ellen " 'joy herself, have a good time nussin' [nursing] white folks chillun. Nussed you; she tell me 'bout it many time." In such circumstances blacks could hardly be expected to speak frankly. One older woman summed up the situation quite cheerfully. "Oh, I know your father en your granfather en all of dem. Bless Mercy, child, I don't want to tell you nothin' but what to please you."

Although such statements put a researcher on guard, readers who are new to this field may still find it difficult to appreciate the varying responses that different interviewers might elicit. In order to bring home the point more forcibly, it may be helpful to analyze an interview that we came across during our own research in the slave narrative collection. The interview is with Susan Hamlin, a black who lived in Charleston, and we reprint it below exactly as it appears in typescript.

Interview With Ex-Slave

On July 6th, I interviewed Susan Hamlin, ex-slave, at 17 Henrietta street, Charleston, S. C. She was sitting just inside of the front door, on a step leading up to the porch, and upon hearing me inquire for her she assumed that I was from the Welfare office, from which she had received aid prior to its closing. I did not correct this impression, and at no time did she suspect that the object of my visit was to get the story of her experience as a slave. During our conversation she mentioned her age. "Why that's very interesting, Susan," I told her, "If you are that old you probably remember the Civil War and slavery days." "Yes, Ma'am, I been a slave myself," she said, and told me the following story:

"I kin remember some things like it was yesterday, but I is 104 years old now, and age is starting to get me, I can't remember everything like I use to. I getting old, old. You know I is old when I been a grown woman when the Civil War broke out. I was hired out then, to a Mr. McDonald, who lived on Atlantic Street, and I remembers when de first shot was fired, and the shells went right over de city. I got seven dollars a month for looking after children, not taking them out, you understand, just minding them. I did not got the money, Mausa got it." "Don't you think that was fair?" I asked. "If you were fed and clothed by him, shouldn't he be paid

"I've told you too much. How come they want all this stuff from the colored people anyway? Do you take any stories from the white people? . . . They don't need me to tell it to them." This Georgia woman, like many of the subjects interviewed for the Federal Writers' Project, was still living in the 1930s on the plantation where she had grown up as a slave child. The plantation was still owned by descendants of her former master. Under such conditions suspicion toward Project interviewers was a predictable reaction, even if the interviewer was black; doubly so if he or she was white and a resident of the community.

for your work?" "Course it been fair," she answered, "I belong to him and he got to get something to take care of me."

"My name before I was married was Susan Calder, but I married a man name Hamlin. I belonged to Mr. Edward Fuller, he was president of the First National Bank. He was a good man to his people till de Lord took him. Mr. Fuller got his slaves by marriage. He married Miss Mikell, a lady what lived on Edisto Island, who was a slave owner, and we lived on Edisto on a plantation. I don't remember de name cause when Mr. Fuller got to be president of de bank we come to Charleston to live. He sell out the plantation and say them (the slaves) that want to come to Charleston with him could come and them what wants to stay can stay on the island with his wife's people. We had our choice. Some is come and some is stay, but my ma and us children come with Mr. Fuller.

We lived on St. Philip street. The house still there, good as ever. I go 'round there to see it all de time; the cistern still there too, where we used to sit 'round and drink the cold water, and eat, and talk and laugh. Mr. Fuller have lots of servants and the ones he didn't need hisself he hired out. The slaves had rooms in the back, the ones with children had two rooms and them that didn't have any children had one room, not to cook in but to sleep in. They all cooked and ate downstairs in the hall that they had for the colored people. I don't know about slavery but I know all the slavery I know about, the people was good to me. Mr. Fuller was a good man and his wife's people been grand people, all good to their slaves. Seem like Mr. Fuller just git his slaves so he could be good to dem. He made all the little colored chillen love him. If you don't believe they loved him what they all cry, and scream, and holler for when dey hear he dead? 'Oh, Mausa dead my Mausa dead, what I going to do, my Mausa dead.' Dey tell dem t'aint no use to cry, dat can't bring him back, but de chillen keep on crying. We used to call him Mausa Eddie but he named Mr. Edward Fuller, and he sure was a good man.

"A man come here about a month ago, say he from de Government, and dey send him to find out 'bout slavery. I give him most a book, and what give me? A dime. He ask me all kind of questions. He ask me dis and he ask me dat, didn't de white people do dis and did dey do dat but Mr. Fuller was a good man, he was sure good to me and all his people, dey all like him, God bless him, he in de ground now but I ain't going to let nobody lie on him. You know he good when even the little chillen cry and holler when he dead. I tell you dey couldn't just fix us up any kind of way when we going to Sunday School. We had to be dressed nice, if you pass him and you ain't dress to suit him he send you right back and say tell your ma to see dat you dress right. Dey couldn't send you out in de cold barefoot neither. I 'member one day my ma want to send me wid some milk for her sister-in-law what live 'round de corner. I fuss cause it cold and say 'how you going to send me out wid no shoe, and it cold?' Mausa hear how I talkin and turn he back and laugh, den he call to my ma to gone in de house and find shoe to put on my feet and don't let him see me barefoot again in cold weather.

When de war start going good and de shell fly over Charleston he take all us up to Aiken for protection. Talk 'bout marching through Georgia, dey sure march through Aiken, soldiers was everywhere.

"My ma had six children, three boys and three girls, but I de only one left, all my white people and all de colored people gone, not a soul left but me. I ain't been sick in 25 years. I is near my church and I don't miss service any Sunday, night or morning. I kin walk wherever I please, I kin walk to de Battery if I want to. The Welfare use to help me but dey shut down now, I can't find out if dey going to open again or not. Miss (Mrs.) Buist and Miss Pringle, dey help me when I can go there but all my own dead."

"Were most of the masters kind?" I asked. "Well you know," she answered, "times den was just like dey is now, some was kind and some was mean; heaps of wickedness went on just de same as now. All my people was good people. I see some wickedness and I hear 'bout all kinds of t'ings but you don't know whether it was lie or not. Mr. Fuller been a Christian man."

"Do you think it would have been better if the Negroes had never left Africa?" was the next question I asked. "No Ma'am," (emphatically) dem heathen didn't have no religion. I tell you how I t'ink it is. The Lord made t'ree nations, the white, the red and the black, and put dem in different places on de earth where dey was to stay. Dose black ignoramuses in Africa forgot God, and didn't have no religion and God blessed and prospered the white people dat did remember Him and sent dem to teach de black people even if dey have to grab dem and bring dem into bondage till dey learned some sense. The Indians forgot God and dey had to be taught better so dey land was taken away from dem. God sure bless and prosper de white people and He put de red and de black people under dem so dey could teach dem and bring dem into sense wid God. Dey had to get dere brains right, and honor God, and learn uprightness wid God cause ain't He make you, and ain't His Son redeem you and save you wid His precious blood. You kin plan all de wickedness you want and pull hard as you choose but when the Lord mek up His mind you is to change, He can change you dat quick (snapping her fingers) and easy. You got to believe on Him if it tek bondage to bring you to your knees.

You know I is got converted. I been in Big Bethel (church) on my knees praying under one of de preachers. I see a great, big, dark pack on my back, and it had me all bent over and my shoulders drawn down, all hunch up. I look up and I see de glory, I see a big beautiful light, a great light, and in de middle is de Sabior, hanging so (extending her arms) just like He died. Den I gone to praying good, and I can feel de sheckles (shackles) loose up and moving and de pack fall off. I don't know where it went to, I see de angels in de Heaven, and hear dem say 'Your sins are forgiven.' I scream and fell off so. (Swoon.) When I come to dey has laid me out straight and I know I is converted cause you can't see no such sight and go on like you is before. I know I is still a sinner but I believe in de power of God and I trust his Holy name. Den dey put me wid de seekers but I know I is already saved."

"Did they take good care of the slaves when their babies were born?" she was asked. "If you want chickens for fat (to fatten) you got to feed dem," she said with a smile, "and if you want people to work dey got to be strong, you got to feed dem and take care of dem too. If dey can't work it come out of your pocket. Lots of wickedness gone on in dem days, just as it do now, some good, some mean, black and white, it just dere nature, if dey good dey going to be kind to everybody, if dey mean dey going to be mean to everybody. Sometimes chillen was sold away from dey parents. De Mausa would come and say "Where Jennie," tell um to put clothes on dat baby, I want um. He sell de baby and de ma scream and holler, you know how dey carry on. Geneally (generally) dey sold it when de ma wasn't dere. Mr. Fuller didn't sell none of us, we stay wid our ma's till we grown. I stay wid my ma till she dead.

"You know I is mix blood, my grandfather bin a white man and my grandmother a mulatto. She been marry to a black so dat how I get fix like I is. I got both blood, so how I going to quarrel wid either side?"

SOURCE: Interview with Susan Hamlin, 17 Henrietta Street.

NOTE * Susan lives with a mulatto family of the better type. The name is Hamlin not Hamilton, and her name prior to her marriage was Calder not Collins. I paid particular attention to this and had them spell the names for me. I would judge Susan to be in the late nineties but she is wonderfully well preserved. She now claims to be 104 years old.

From the beginning, the circumstances of this conversation arouse suspicion. The white interviewer, Jessie Butler, mentions that she allowed Hamlin to think she was from the welfare office. Evidently, Butler thought Hamlin would speak more freely if the real purpose of the visit was hidden. But surely the deception had the opposite effect. Hamlin, like most of the blacks interviewed, was elderly, unable to work, and dependent on charity. If Butler appeared to be from the welfare office, Hamlin would likely have done whatever she could to ingratiate herself. Many blacks consistently assumed that their white interviewers had influence with the welfare office. "You through wid me now, boss? I sho' is glad of dat," concluded one subject. "Help all you kin to git me dat pension befo' I die and de Lord will bless you, honey. . . . Has you got a dime to give dis old nigger, boss?"

Furthermore, Butler's questioning was hardly subtle. When Hamlin noted that she had to give her master the money she made from looking after children, Butler asked, "Don't you think that was fair?" "Course it been fair," came the quick response. Hamlin knew very well what was expected, especially since Butler had already answered the question herself: "If you were fed and clothed by him, shouldn't he be paid for your work?"

Not surprisingly, then, the interview paints slavery in relatively mild colors. Hamlin describes in great detail how good her master was and how she had shoes in the winter. When asked whether most masters were kind, Hamlin appears eminently "fair"—"some was kind and some was mean." She admits hearing "all kinds of t'ings but you don't know whether it was lie or not." She does note that slave children could be sold away from parents and that black mothers protested; but she talks as if that were only to be expected. ("De ma scream and holler, you know how dey carry on.")

Equally flattering is the picture Hamlin paints of relations between the races. "Black ignoramuses" in Africa had forgotten about God, she explains, just as the Indians had; but "God sure bless and prosper de white people." So blacks and the Indians are placed under white supervision, "to get dere brains right, and honor God, and learn uprightness." Those were not exactly the words proslavery apologists would have used to describe the situation, but they were the same sentiments. Defenders of slavery constantly stressed that whites served as benevolent models ("parents," Andrew Jackson might have said) leading blacks and Indians on the slow upward road to civilization.

All these aspects of the interview led us to be suspicious about its content. Moreover, there were several additional clues in the document that puzzled us. Hamlin had mentioned a man who visited her "about a month ago, say he from de Government, and dey send him to find out 'bout slavery." Apparently her interview with Jessie Butler was the second she had given. Butler, for her part, made a fuss at the end of the

transcript over the spelling of Hamlin's name. ("I paid particular attention to this.") It was "Hamlin not Hamilton" and her maiden name was
"Calder not Collins." The phrasing indicates that somewhere else Butler
had seen Hamlin referred to as "Susan Hamilton." If someone had
interviewed Hamlin earlier, we wondered, could Hamilton have been
the name on that original report?

We found the answer when we continued on through the narrative
collection. The interview following Butler's was conducted by a man
named Augustus Ladson, with a slave named "Susan Hamilton." When
compared with Jessie Butler's interview, Augustus Ladson's makes ab-
sorbing reading. Here it is, printed exactly as it appears in the collection:

Ex-Slave 101 Years of Age

Has Never Shaken Hands Since 1863
Was on Knees Scrubbing when Freedom Gun Fired

I'm a hund'ed an' one years old now, son. De only one livin' in my
crowd frum de days I wuz a slave. Mr. Fuller, my master, who was
president of the Firs' National Bank, owned the fambly of us except my
father. There were eight men an' women with five girls an' six boys
workin' for him. Most o' them wus hired out. De house in which we stayed
is still dere with de sisterns an' slave quarters. I always go to see de old
home which is on St. Phillip Street.

My ma had t'ree boys an' t'ree girls who did well at their work. Hope
Mikell, my eldest brodder, an' James wus de shoemaker. William Fuller,
son of our Master, wus de bricklayer. Margurite an' Catharine wus de
maids an' look as de children.

My pa b'long to a man on Edisto Island. Frum what he said, his master
was very mean. Pa real name wus Adam Collins but he took his master'
name; he wus de coachman. Pa did supin one day en his master whipped
him. De next day which wus Monday, pa carry him 'bout four miles frum
home in de woods an' give him de same 'mount of lickin' he wus given
on Sunday. He tied him to a tree an' unhitched de horse so it couldn't git
tie-up an' kill e self. Pa den gone to de landin' an' cetch a boat dat wus
comin' to Charleston wood fa'm products. He (was) permitted by his
master to go to town on errands, which helped him to go on de boat
without bein' question'. W'en he got here he gone on de water-front an'

ax for a job on a ship so he could git to de North. He got de job an' sail'
wood de ship. Dey search de island up an' down for him wood houndogs
en w'en it wus t'ought he wus drowned, 'cause dey track him to de river,
did dey give up. One of his master' friend gone to New York en went
in a store w'ere pas wus employed as a clerk. he reconize' pa is easy is pa
reconize' him. He gone back home an' tell pa master who know den dat
pa wusn't comin' back an' before he died he sign' papers dat pa wus free.
Pa' ma wus dead an' he come down to bury her by de permission of his
master' son who had promised no ha'm would come to him, but dey wus'
fixin' plans to keep him, so he went to de Work House an' ax to be sold
'cause any slave could sell e self if e could git to de Work House. But it
wus on record down dere so dey couldn't sell 'im an' told him his master'
people couldn't hold him a slave.

People den use to do de same t'ings dey do now. Some marry an' some
live together jus' like now. One t'ing, no minister nebber say in readin'
de matrimony "let no man put asounder" 'cause a couple would be
married tonight an' tomorrow one would be taken away en be sold. All
slaves wus married in dere master house, in de livin' room where slaves
an' dere missus an' mossa wus to witness de ceremony. Brides use to wear
some of de finest dress an' if dey could afford it, have de best kind of
furniture. Your master nor your missus objected to good t'ings.

I'll always 'member Clory, de washer. She wus very high-tempered. She
was a mulatto with beautiful hair she could sit on; Clory didn't take
foolishness frum anybody. One day our missus gone in de laundry an' find
fault with de clothes. Clory didn't do a t'ing but pick her up bodily an'
throw 'er out de door. Dey had to sen' fur a doctor 'cause she pregnant
an' less than two hours de baby wus bo'n. Afta dat she begged to be sold
fur she didn't [want] to kill missus, but our master ain't nebber want to
sell his slaves. But dat didn't keep Clory frum gittin' a brutal whippin'.
Dey whip' 'er until dere wusn't a white spot on her body. Dat wus de
worst I ebber see a human bein' got such a beatin'. I t'ought she wus goin'
to die, but she got well an' didn't get any better but meaner until our
master decide it wus bes' to rent her out. She willingly agree' since she
wusn't 'round missus. She hated an' detest' both of them an' all de fambly.

W'en any slave wus whipped all de other slaves wus made to watch. I
see women hung frum de ceilin' of buildin's an' whipped with only supin
tied 'round her lower part of de body, until w'en dey wus taken down,
dere wusn't breath in de body. I had some terribly bad experiences.

Yankees use to come t'rough de streets, especially de Big Market,
huntin' those who want to go to de "free country" as dey call' it. Men an'
women wus always missin' an' nobody could give 'count of dere disap-
pearance. De men wus train' up North fur sojus.

De white race is so brazen. Dey come here an' run de Indians frum dere own lan', but dey couldn't make dem slaves 'cause dey wouldn't stan' for it. Indians use to git up in trees an' shoot dem with poison arrow. W'en dey couldn't make dem slaves den dey gone to Africa an' bring dere black brother an' sister. Dey say 'mong themselves, "we gwine mix dem up en make ourselves king. Dats d only way we'd git even with de Indians."

All time, night an' day, you could hear men an' women screamin' to de tip of dere voices as either ma, pa, sister, or brother wus take without any warnin' an' sell. Some time mother who had only one chile wus separated fur life. People wus always dyin' frum a broken heart.

One night a couple married an' de next mornin' de boss sell de wife. De gal ma got in in de street an' cursed de white woman fur all she could find. She said: "dat damn white, pale-face bastard sell my daughter who jus' married las' night," an' other t'ings. The white man tresten' her to call de police if she didn't stop, but de collud woman said: "hit me or call de police. I redder die dan to stan' dis any longer." De police took her to de Work House by de white woman orders an' what became of 'er, I never hear.

W'en de war began we wus taken to Aiken, South Ca'lina w'ere we stay' until de Yankees come t'rough. We could see balls sailin' t'rough de air w'en Sherman wus comin'. Bumbs hit trees in our yard. W'en de freedom gun wus fired, I wus on my 'nees scrubbin'. Dey tell me I wus free but I didn't b'lieve it.

In de days of slavory woman wus jus' given time 'nough to deliver dere babies. Dey deliver de baby 'bout eight in de mornin' an' twelve had to be back to work.

I wus a member of Emmanuel African Methodist Episcopal Church for 67 years. Big Zion, across de street wus my church before den an' before Old Bethel w'en I lived on de other end of town.

Sence Lincoln shook hands with his assasin who at de same time shoot him, frum dat day I stop shakin' hands, even in de church, an' you know how long dat wus. I don't b'lieve in kissin' neider fur all carry dere meannesses. De Master wus betrayed by one of his bosom frien' with a kiss.

SOURCE Interview with (Mrs.) Susan Hamilton, 17 Henrietta Street, who claims to be 101 years of age. She has never been sick for twenty years and walks as though just 40. She was hired out by her master for seven dollars a month which had to be given her master.

Susan Hamlin and Susan "Hamilton" are obviously one and the same; yet by the end of Ladson's interview, we are wondering if we

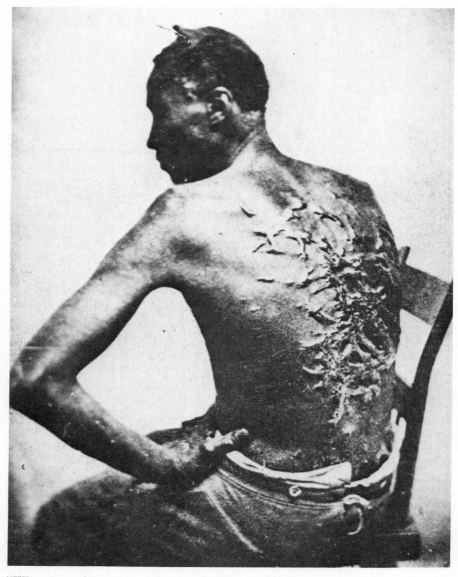

"W'en any slave wus whipped all de other slaves was made to watch. . . . I had some terribly bad experiences." The scars from whippings on this slave's back were recorded in 1863 by an unknown photographer travelling with the Union army.

have been listening to the same person! Kindness of the masters? We hear no tales about old Mr. Fuller; only vivid recollections of whippings so harsh "dere wusn't a white spot on her body." To Butler, Hamlin had mentioned only cruelties that she had heard about second-hand ("you don't know whether it was lie or not"); to Ladson, she recounts firsthand experiences ("I see women hung from de ceilin' of buildin's an' whipped with only supin tied 'round her lower part of de body.")

Discussions of happy family relations? Instead of tales about shoes in the winter, we hear of Hamlin's father, whipped so severely, he rebels and flees. We hear of family separations, not downplayed with a "you know how dey carry on," but with all the bitterness of mothers whose children had been taken "without any warnin'." We hear of a couple married one night, then callously separated and sold the next day. In the Butler account, slave babies are fed well, treated nicely; in the Ladson account, the recollection is of mothers who were given only a few hours away from the fields in order to deliver their children.

Benevolent white paternalism? This time Hamlin's tale of three races draws a different moral. The white race is "brazen," running the Indians off their land. With a touch of admiration, she notes that the Indians "wouldn't stan' for" being made slaves. White motives are seen not as religious but exploitative and vengeful: "Dey say 'mong themselves, 'we gwine mix dem up and make ourselves king. Dats de only way we'll git even with de Indians.'" The difference between the two interviews, both in tone and substance, is astonishing.

How do we account for this? Nowhere in the South Carolina narratives is the race of Augustus Ladson mentioned, but internal evidence would indicate he is black. In a culture where blacks usually addressed whites respectfully with a "Sir," "Ma'am," or "Boss," it seems doubtful that Susan Hamlin would address a white man as "son." ("I'm a hund'ed an' one years old now, son.") Furthermore, the content of the interview is just too consistently anti-white. Hamlin would never have remarked, "De white race is so brazen," if Ladson had been white, especially given the reticence demonstrated in her interview with Butler. Nor would she have been so specific about the angry mother's curses ("damn white, pale-face bastard"). It would be difficult to conceive of a more strikingly dramatic demonstration of how an interviewer can affect the responses of a subject.

FREEDOM AND DECEPTION

The slave narrative collection, then, is not the direct, unfiltered perspective that it first appears to be. In fact, interviews like the ones with Susan Hamlin seem to suggest that the search for the "true" freedmen's perspective is bound to end in failure and frustration. We have seen, first, that information from planters and other white sources must be treated with extreme skepticism; second, that northern white sources deserve similar caution. Finally, it appears that even the oral testimony of blacks themselves must be questioned, given the circumstances under which much of it was gathered. It is as if a detective discovered that all the clues he had carefully pieced together were hopelessly biased, leading his investigation down the wrong path.

The seriousness of the problem should not be underestimated. It is fundamental. We can try to ease out of the dilemma by noting that there are doubtless differing degrees of bias—that some accounts, relatively speaking, are likely to be less deceptive than others. It can be argued, for instance, that Susan Hamlin's interview with Ladson is a more accurate portrayal of her feelings than the interview with Butler. In large measure that is probably true. But does that mean we must reject all of the Butler interview? Presumably, Susan Hamlin's master did give her a pair of shoes one cold winter day. Are we to assume, because of Ladson's interview, that the young child felt no gratitude or obligation to "kind old" Mr. Fuller? Or that the old woman did not look back on those years with some ambivalence? For all her life, both slave and free, Susan Hamlin lived in a world where she was required to "feel" one set of emotions when dealing with some people and a different set when dealing with other people. Can we rest completely confident in concluding that the emotions she expressed to Ladson were her "real" feelings, while the ones to Jessie Butler were her "false" feelings? How can we possibly arrive at an objective conclusion about "real" feelings in any social situation where such severe strains existed?

Yet putting the question in this light offers at least a partial way out of the dilemma. If so many clues in the investigation are hopelessly "biased"—that is, distorted by the social situation in which they are set—then the very pervasiveness of the distortion may serve as a key to understanding the situation. The evidence in the case is warped precisely because it accurately reflects a distortion in the society itself. The elements of racism and slavery determined a culture where personal relations were necessarily grounded in mistrust and deception; where slaves could survive only if they remained acutely conscious of the need to adapt their feelings to the situation. The distortion in the evidence, in other words, speaks eloquently of the hurt inflicted in a society where personal behavior routinely operated under an economy of deception.

The deception was mutual—practiced by both sides upon each other. Susan Hamlin was adapting the story of her past to the needs of the moment, at the same time that Jessie Butler was letting Hamlin believe her to be a welfare agent. White masters painted lurid stories of Yankee devils with horns while slaves, playing roles they were expected to play, rolled their eyes in fear until they had the chance to run straight for Union lines. The deceptions fed upon each other and were compounded, becoming an inextricable part of daily life.

It would be tempting, given our awareness of this situation, simply to turn previous historical interpretations on their heads. Where William Dunning and his disciples took most of their primary sources at face value and thus saw only cheerful, childlike Sambos, an enlightened history would read the documents upside down, so to speak, stripping away the camouflage to reveal slaves who, quite rationally, went about the daily business of "puttin' on ole massa." And of course we have already seen abundant evidence that slaves did use calculated deception in order to protect themselves.

But simply to replace one set of feelings with another is to ignore the intricate and tense relationships between them. It drastically underestimates the strains that arose out of an economy of deception. The longer and more consistently masters and slaves were compelled to live false and inauthentic lives, the easier it must have been for them to mislead themselves as well as others. Where whites and blacks alike engaged in daily dissimulation, some of the deception was inevitably directed inward, simply to preserve the fiction of living in a tolerable, normally functioning society.

When the war came, shattering that fiction, whites and blacks were exposed in concrete and vivid ways to the deception that had been so much a part of their lives. For white slaveholders, the revelation usually came when Union troops entered a region and slaves deserted the plantations in droves. Especially demoralizing was the flight of blacks whom planters had believed most loyal. "He was about my age and I had always treated him more as a companion than a slave," noted one planter, of the first defector from his ranks. Mary Chesnut, the woman near Fort Sumter who had tried to penetrate the blank expressions of her slaves, discovered how impossible the task had been. "Jonathan, whom we trusted, betrayed us," she lamented, while "Claiborne, that black rascal who was suspected by all the world," faithfully protected the plantation.

Many slaveholders, when faced with the truth, refused to recognize the role that deception had played in their lives, so deceiving themselves further. "The poor negroes don't do us any harm except when they are put up to it," concluded one Georgia woman. A Richmond newspaper editor demanded that a slave who had denounced Jefferson Davis "be whipped every day until he confesses what white man put these notions in his head." Yet the war brought painful insight to others. "We were all laboring under a delusion," confessed one South Carolina planter. "I believed that these people were content, happy, and attached to their masters. But events and reflection have caused me to change these opinions. . . . If they were content, happy and attached to their masters, why did they desert him in the moment of his need and flock to an enemy, whom they did not know . . . ?"

For black slaves, the news of emancipation brought an entirely different reaction, but still one conditioned by the old habits. We have already seen how one old Georgia slave couple remained impassive as Sherman's troops passed through, until finally the wife could restrain herself no longer. Even the servant who eloquently shouted the praises of freedom at a secluded brook instinctively remembered the need for caution: "I got sort o' scared, afeared somebody hear me, an' I takes another good look. . . ." Although emancipation promised a society founded upon equal treatment and open relations, slaves could not help wondering whether the new order would fully replace the old. That would occur only if the freedmen could forge relationships that were no longer based on the customs of deception nor rooted in the central fiction of slavery —that blacks were morally and intellectually incapable of assuming a place in free society.

No historian has more vividly conveyed the freedmen's attempts to achieve that goal than Leon Litwack. Having recognized the substantial value of the slave narrative collection, Litwack drew upon its evidence as well as the standard range of primary sources to recreate the freedmen's perspectives as they sought the real meaning of their new freedom. Certainly that meaning was by no means evident once the first excitement of liberation had passed. James Lucas, a slave of Jefferson Davis, recalled the freedmen's confusion: "Dey all had diffe'nt ways o' thinkin' 'bout it. Mos'ly though dey was jus' lak me, dey didn' know jus' zackly what it meant. It was jus' somp'n dat de white folks an' slaves all de time talk 'bout. Dat's all. Folks dat ain' never been free don' rightly know de *feel* of bein' free. Dey don' know de meanin' of it." But blacks were not long in taking their first steps toward defining freedom. On the surface, many of these seemed small. But however limited, they served to distance the freedmen in significant ways from the old habits of bondage.

The taking of new names was one such step. As slaves, blacks often had no surname, or took the name of their master. Equally demeaning, given names were often casually assigned by their owners. Cicero, Pompey, and other Latin or Biblical names were commonly bestowed in jest. And whether or not slaves had a surname, they were always addressed familiarly, by their given names. Such customs were part of the symbolic language of deception, promoting the illusion that blacks were helpless and even laughable dependents of the planter's family.

Thus many freedmen took for themselves new names, severing the symbolic tie with their old masters. "A heap of people say they was going to name their selves over," recalled one freedman. "They named their selves big names. . . . Some of the names was Abraham an' some called their selves Lincum. Any big name 'ceptin' their master's name. It was the fashion." Even blacks who remained loyal to their masters recognized the significance of the change. "When you'all had de power you was good to me," an older freedman told his master, "an I'll protect you now. No niggers nor Yankees shall touch you. If you want anything, call for Sambo. I mean, call for Mr. Samuel—that's my name now."

Just as freedmen took new names to symbolize their new status, so also many husbands and wives reaffirmed their marriages in formal ceremonies. Under slavery, many marriages and family ties had been ignored through the convenient fiction that blacks were morally inferior. Black affections, the planters argued, were dominated by impulse and the physical desires of the moment. Such self-deception eased many a master's conscience when slave families were separated and sold. Similarly, many planters married slaves only informally, with a few words sufficing to join the couple. "Don't mean nuthin' less you say, "What God done jined, cain't no man pull asunder," noted one Virginia freedman. "But dey never would say dat. Jus' say, 'Now you married.' " For obvious reasons of human dignity, blacks moved to solemnize their marriage vows. There were practical reasons for an official ceremony too: it might qualify families for military pensions, or the division of lands that were widely rumored to be coming.

Equally symbolic for most blacks was the freedom to travel where they wished. As we have seen, historian William Dunning recognized this fact, but interpreted it from the viewpoint of his southern white sources as "aimless but happy" wandering. Black accounts make abundantly

clear how travel helped freedmen to rid themselves of the role they had
been forced to play during their bondage. Richard Edwards, a preacher
in Florida, explicitly described the symbolic nature of such a move:

> You ain't, none o' you, gwinter feel rale free till you shakes de dus' ob
> de Old Plantashun offen yore feet an' goes ter a new place whey you kin
> live out o' sight o' de gret house. So long ez de shadder ob de gret house
> falls acrost you, you ain't gwine ter feel lak no free man, an' you ain't
> gwine ter feel lak no free 'oman. You mus' all move—you mus' move clar
> away from de ole places what you knows, ter de new places what you don't
> know, whey you kin raise up yore head douten no fear o' Marse Dis ur
> Marse Tudder.

And so, in the spring and summer of 1865, southern roads were filled
with blacks, hiving off "like bees trying to find a setting place," as one
ex-slave recalled. Generally freedmen preferred to remain within the
general locale of family and friends, merely leaving one plantation in
search of work at another. But a sizeable minority travelled farther, to
settle in cities, move west, or try their fortunes at new occupations.

Many ex-slaves travelled in order to reunite families separated
through previous sales. Freedmen "had a passion, not so much for wandering, as for getting together," a Freedman's Bureau agent observed;
"and every mother's son among them seemed to be in search of his
mother; every mother in search of her children." Often, relatives had
only scanty information; in other cases, so much time had passed that kin
could hardly recognize each other, especially when young children had
grown up separated from their parents.

A change of name or location, the formalization of marriages, reunion
with relatives—all these acts demonstrated that freedmen wanted no part
of the old constraints and deceptions of slavery. But as much as these acts
defined black freedom, larger issues remained. How much would emancipation broaden economic avenues open to blacks? Would freedom
provide an opportunity to rise on the social ladder? The freedmen
looked anxiously for signs of significant changes.

Perhaps the most commonly perceived avenue to success was through
education. Slavery had been rationalized, in part, through the fiction that
blacks were incapable of profiting from an education. The myth of
intellectual inferiority stood side by side with that of moral inferiority.
Especially in areas where masters had energetically prevented slaves
from acquiring skills in reading, writing, and arithmetic, the freedmen's
hunger for learning was intense. When Northerners occupied the Caro-

lina Sea Islands during the war, Yankee plantation superintendents found that the most effective way to force unwilling laborers to work was to threaten to take away their schoolbooks. "The Negroes . . . will do anything for us, if we will only teach them," noted one missionary stationed on the islands.

After the war, when the Freedman's Bureau sent hundreds of northern school teachers into the South, blacks flocked enthusiastically to the makeshift schoolhouses. Often, classes could be held only at night, but the freedmen were willing. "We work all day, but we'll come to you in the evening for learning," Georgia freedmen told their teacher, "and we want you to make us learn; we're dull, but we want you to beat it into

"My Lord, ma'am, what a great thing larning is!" a freedman exclaimed to a white teacher. Many whites were surprised by the intensity of the ex-slaves' desire for an education. To say that the freedmen were "anxious to learn" was not strong enough, one Virginia school official noted; "they are *crazy* to learn." This woodcut, drawn in 1867, depicts several youngsters studying their lessons along a village street.

us!" Some white plantation owners discovered that if they wished to keep their field hands, they would have to provide a schoolhouse and teacher.

Important as education was, the freedmen were preoccupied even more with their relation to the lands they had worked for so many years. The vast majority of slaves were field hands. The agricultural life was the one they had grown up with, and as freedmen, they wanted the chance to own and cultivate their own property. Independent ownership would lay to rest the lie that blacks were incapable of managing their own affairs; but without land, the idea of freedom would be just another deception. "Gib us our own land and we take care ourselves; but widout land, de ole massas can hire us or starve us, as dey please," noted one freedman.

In the heady enthusiasm at the close of the war, many ex-slaves were convinced that the Union would divide up confiscated Confederate plantations. Each family, so the persistent rumor went, would receive forty acres and a mule. "This was no slight error, no trifling idea," reported one white observer, "but a fixed and earnest conviction as strong as any belief a man can ever have." Slaves had worked their masters' lands for so long without significant compensation, it seemed only fair that recompense should finally be made. Further, blacks had more than hopes to rely on. Ever since southern planters had fled from invading Union troops, some blacks had been allowed to cultivate the abandoned fields.

The largest of such occupied regions was the Sea Islands along the Carolina coast, where young Sam Mitchell had first heard the northern guns. As early as March 1863, freedmen were purchasing confiscated lands from the government. Then in January 1865, after General William Sherman completed his devastating march to the sea, he extended the area which was open to confiscation. In his Special Field Order No. 15, Sherman decreed that a long strip of abandoned lands, stretching from Charleston on the north to Jacksonville on the south, would be reserved for the freedmen. The lands would be subdivided into forty-acre tracts, which could be rented for a nominal fee. After three years, the freedmen had the option to purchase the land outright.

Sherman's order was essentially a tactical maneuver, designed to deal with the overwhelming problem of refugees in his path. But blacks widely perceived this order and other promises by enthusiastic northerners as a foretaste of Reconstruction policy. Consequently, when white planters returned to their plantations, they often found blacks who no longer bowed obsequiously and tipped their hats. Thomas Pinckney of South Carolina, having called his former slaves together, asked them if they would continue to work for him. "O yes, we gwi wuk! we gwi wuk all right . . ." came the angry response. "We gwi wuk fuh ourse'ves. We ain' gwi wuk fuh no white man." Where would they go to work, Pinckney asked—seeing as they had no land? "We ain't gwine nowhar," they replied defiantly. "We gwi wuk right here on de lan' whar we wuz bo'n an' whar belongs tuh us."

Despite the defiance, Pinckney prevailed, as did the vast majority of southern planters. Redistribution of southern lands was an idea strongly supported only by more radical northerners. Thaddeus Stevens introduced a confiscation bill in Congress, but it was swamped by debate and never passed. President Johnson, whose conciliatory policies pleased southern planters, determined to settle the issue as quickly as possible. He summoned General O. O. Howard, head of the Freedman's Bureau, and instructed Howard to reach a solution "mutually satisfactory" to both blacks and planters. Howard, though sympathetic to the freedmen, could not mistake the true meaning of the President's order.

Regretfully, the general returned to the Sea Islands in October and assembled a group of freedmen on Edisto Island. The audience, suspecting the bad news, was restless and unruly. Howard tried vainly to speak, and made "no progress" until a woman in the crowd began singing, "Nobody knows the trouble I've seen." The crowd joined, then was silent while Howard told them they must give up their lands. Bitter cries of "No! No!" came from the audience. "Why, General Howard, why do you take away our lands?" called one burly man. "You take them from us who have always been true, always true to the Government! You give them to our all-time enemies! That is not right!"

Reluctantly, and sometimes only after forcible resistance, blacks lost the lands to returning planters. Whatever else freedom might mean, it was not to signify compensation for previous labor. In the years to come Reconstruction would offer freedom of another sort, through the political process. By the beginning of 1866, the radicals in Congress had charted a plan that gave blacks basic civil rights and political power. Yet even that avenue of opportunity was quickly sealed off. In the decades that followed the first thunder of emancipation, blacks would look back on their early experiences almost as if they were part of another, vanished world. The traditions of racial oppression and the daily deceptions that went with them were too strong to be thoroughly overturned by the war. It is perhaps significant that the term "freedman" uses a past participle. Despite the best efforts of blacks, American society found it impossible to define them without reference to the fictions of their past.

"I was right smart bit by de freedom bug for awhile," Charlie Davenport of Mississippi recalled.

It sounded pow'ful nice to be tol: "You don't have to chop cotton no more. You can th'ow dat hoe down an' go fishin' whensoever de notion strikes you. An' you can roam 'roun' at night an' court gals jus' as you please. Aint no marster gwine a-say to you, 'Charlie, you's got to be back when de clock strikes nine.' " I was fool 'nough to b'lieve all dat kin' o' stuff.

Both perceptions—the first flush of the "freedom bug" as well as Davenport's later disillusionment—accurately reflect the black experience. Freedom had come to a nation of four million slaves, and it changed their lives in deep and important ways. But for many years after the war put an end to human bondage, the freedmen still had to settle for the view from the bottom rail.

Additional Reading

Leon Litwack's superb *Been In the Storm So Long: the Aftermath of Slavery* (New York, 1979) serves as an excellent starting point for background on the freedmen's experience after the war. Litwack supplies an interpretive framework that moves the book from topic to topic, but the material is kaleidoscopic in detail, story after story tumbling onto the page and threatening to overwhelm the book's structure. The result is a rich and vibrant portrait. Willie Lee Rose, *Rehearsal for Reconstruction: the Port Royal Experiment* (Indianapolis, Ind., 1964), tells the story of the Union occupation of the Carolina Sea Islands, where the North first attempted to forge a coherent Reconstruction policy. Black experiences can also be traced in state histories of Reconstruction, where more attention is given to grass-roots effects of the new freedom. Joel Williamson, *After Slavery* (Chapel Hill, N.C., 1965) covers South Carolina; Peter Kolchin, *First Freedom* (Westport, Conn., 1972) treats Alabama. William McFeely's *Yankee Stepfather* (New Haven, Conn., 1968) provides good coverage of the Freedman's Bureau in his biography of its leader, General O. O. Howard.

Contemporary white accounts of the slaves' first days of freedom abound. Litwack, cited above, has a helpful bibliography. Among those sources we found useful: Rupert S. Holland, ed., *Letters and Diary of Laura M. Towne* (Cambridge, Mass., 1912); Charles Nordhoff, *The Freedmen of South-Carolina* (New York, 1863); C. Vann Woodward, ed., *Mary Chesnut's Civil War* (New Haven, 1981); and Arney R. Childs, ed., *The Private Journal of Henry William Ravenel, 1859–1887* (Columbia, S.C., 1947). James L. Roark, *Masters Without Slaves* (New York, 1977) provides an account of the postwar perceptions of the planter class. In addition to the slave narrative collection discussed below, other sources for the freedmen's perspective include Octavia V. Rogers Albert, *The House of Bondage* (New York, 1891); Orland K. Armstrong, *Old Massa's People* (Indianapolis, Ind., 1931); M. F. Armstrong and Helen W. Ludlow, *Hampton and Its Students* (New York, 1875); and Laura Haviland, *A Woman's Life Work* (Cincinnati, 1881). In addition, a massive project is in progress at the University of Maryland, under the direction of historian Ira Berlin, to publish *A Documentary History of Emancipation* based on government records by and about freedmen, now housed in the National Archives. This material should provide an unsurpassed wealth of contemporary primary sources, including testimony before Freedman's Bureau courts, petitions, letters, and military files. The first volume is out: Ira Berlin, ed., *The Black Military Experience* (Cambridge, 1982), with many more to come.

The Federal Writers' Project interviews are found in George P. Rawick, *The American Slave: A Composite Autobiography,* 19 vols. & supplements (Westport, Conn., 1972–). The collection invites use in many ways. Intriguing material is available on the relations between blacks and Indians, for example, especially in the Oklahoma narratives. Because one interviewer often submitted many interviews, readers may wish to analyze strengths and weaknesses of particular interviewers. The Library of Congress, under Benjamin Botkin's direction, began such an analysis; its records can be examined at the National Archives, catalogued under Correspondence Pertaining to Ex-Slave Studies, Records of the Federal Writers' Project, Records Group 69, Works Progress Administration.

Further information on the slave narratives may be found in Norman Yetman, "The Background of the Slave Narrative Collection," *American Quarterly,* 19 (Fall 1967), 534–553. John Blassingame has an excellent discussion of oral history and its pitfalls in "Using the Testimony of Ex-slaves: Approaches and Problems," *Journal of Southern History,* XLI (November 1975), 473–492, available in expanded form in his introduction to *Slave Testimony* (Baton Rouge, La., 1977). Paul D. Escott, *Slavery Remembered: A Record of Twentieth-Century Slave Narratives* (Chapel Hill, N.C. 1979) provides interested researchers with helpful data. Escott's quantitative analysis of the narratives includes the percentage of interviews with field hands, house servants, and artisans; the occupations they took up as freedmen, and the destinations of those who migrated. The race of many of the project's interviewers is also included (although not always accurately—see Jerrold Hirsch's review of the book in *Reviews in American History,* VIII (September 1980), 312–317).

Finally, those who wish to do their own oral history should consult Stephen A. Richardson et al., *Interviewing: Its Forms and Functions* (New York, 1965) for an introduction to that art. More specific, nuts-and-bolts information can be found in James Hoopes's excellent *Oral History: An Introduction for Students* (Chapel Hill, N.C., 1979). See also Cullom Davis et al., *Oral History: From Tape to Type* (Chicago, 1977) and Ramon I. Harris, et al., *The Practice of Oral History* (Glen Rock, N.J., 1975). The latter book has erred in at least one pertinent fact, however: in the area of libel, it blithely assures would-be publishers of oral history that truth is always a sufficient defense. Truth may suffice when it comes to history, but not invariably so in the courts of law.

CHAPTER
EIGHT
❖

The Mirror
with a Memory

At the same time that freedmen all across the South were struggling to become an integral part of a free and equal society, millions of other Americans in the urbanized North and Midwest were searching for a place in the new industrial society of the late nineteenth century. In the forty years following the Civil War over 24 million people flooded into American cities. While the population of the agricultural hinterlands doubled during these years, urban population increased by more than 700 percent. Sixteen cities could boast of populations over 50,000 in 1860; by 1910 over a hundred could make that claim. New York City alone grew by two million.

Urban areas changed not only in size but also in ethnic composition. While many of the new city-dwellers had migrated from rural America, large numbers came from abroad. Where most antebellum cities had been relatively homogeneous, with perhaps an enclave of Irish or German immigrants, the metropolises at the turn of the century had become centers for large groups of southern as well as northern European immigrants. Again, New York City provides a striking example. By 1900 it included as many Irish as Dublin, the largest Jewish population of any city in the world, and more Italians and Poles than any city outside Rome or Warsaw. Enclaves of Bohemians, Slavs, Lithuanians, Chinese, Scandinavians, and other nationalities added to the ethnic mix.

The quality of living in cities changed too. As manufacturing and commerce crowded into city centers, the wealthy and middle classes fled along newly constructed trolley and rail lines to the quiet of developing suburbs. Enterprising realtors either subdivided or replaced the mansions of the rich with tenements where a maximum number of people could be packed into a minimum of space. Crude sanitation transformed streets into breeding grounds for typhus, scarlet fever, cholera, and other epidemic diseases. Few tenement rooms had outside windows; less than ten percent of all buildings had either indoor plumbing or running water.

The story of the urban poor and their struggle against the slum's cruel waste of human beings is well-known today—as it was even at the turn of the century—because of a generation of social workers and muckrakers who studied the slums firsthand and wrote indignantly about what they found. Not only did they collect statistics to document their general observations, they compiled numerous case studies that described the collective experience in compelling stories about individuals. The pioneer in this endeavor was Jacob Riis. Few books have had as much impact on social policy as his landmark study of New York's Lower East Side, *How the Other Half Lives.* It was at once a shocking revelation of the conditions of slum life and a call for reform. As urban historian Sam Bass Warner concluded, "Before Riis there was no broad understanding of urban poverty that could lead to political action."

Riis had come to know firsthand the degrading conditions of urban life. In 1870 at the age of twenty-one he joined the growing tide of emigrants who fled the poverty of the Scandinavian countryside for the opportunities offered in America. Riis was no starving peasant; in fact his father was a respected schoolmaster and his family comfortably middle class. But Jacob had rejected professional training in order to work with his hands as a carpenter. Unable to find a job in his home town, and rejected by his local sweetheart, he set out for the United States.

Once there, Riis retraced the pattern that millions of immigrants before him had followed. For three years he wandered in search of the promise of the new land. He built workers' shacks near Pittsburgh, trapped muskrats in upstate New York, sold furniture, did odd jobs, and occasionally returned to carpentry. In none of those lines of work did he find either satisfaction or success. At one point poverty reduced him to begging for crumbs outside New York City restaurants and spending nights in a police lodging house. His health failed. He lingered near death until the Danish consul in Philadelphia took him in. At times his situation grew so desperate and his frustration so intense that he contemplated suicide.

Riis, however, had a talent for talking and the hard sell. Eventually he landed a job with a news association in New York and turned his talent to reporting. The direction of his career was determined in 1877 when he became the police reporter for the *New York Tribune.* He was well suited for the job, his earlier wanderings having made him all too familiar with the seamy side of urban life. The police beat took him to headquarters near "The Bend," what Riis referred to as the "foul core of New York's slums." Every day he observed the symptoms of urban poverty. Over the course of a year police dragnets collected some forty thousand indigents who were carted off to the workhouses and asylums. And at night Riis shadowed the police to catch a view of the neighborhood "off its guard." He began to visit immigrants in their homes, where he observed their continual struggle to preserve a measure of decency in an environment of chronic unemployment, disease, crime, and cultural dislocation.

As a *Tribune* reporter, Riis published exposé after exposé on wretched slum conditions. In so doing he followed the journalistic style of the day. Most reporters had adopted the strategies found in Charles Dickens's novels, personifying social issues through the use of graphic detail and telling vignettes. Such concrete examples involved readers most directly with the squalor of city slums. The issue of female exploitation in sweat shops became the story of an old woman Riis discovered paralyzed by a stroke on her own doorstep. The plight of working children, who had neither education nor more than passing familiarity with the English language, was dramatized by the story of Pietro, the young Italian boy who struggled to keep awake at night school. Touching stories brought home the struggles of the poor better than general statistics. They also sold newspapers.

But Riis found the newspaper life frustrating. His stories may have been vivid, but apparently not vivid enough to shock anyone to action. New York authorities had made token efforts at slum clearance, but by 1890 the conditions about which Riis had protested had grown steadily worse. The Lower East Side had a greater population density than any neighborhood in the world—335,000 people to one square mile of the tenth ward and as many as one person per square foot in the worst places.*

In frustration Riis left the *Tribune* to write *How the Other Half Lives.* He wanted to make a case for reform that even the most callous officials could not dismiss, and a full-length book was more likely to accomplish

*Those readers conjuring up a picture of slum-dwellers standing like sardines row on row, each with their own square foot, must remember that tenement space reached upward through several stories. The statistic refers to square footage of ground area, not square footage of actual floor space.

what a series of daily articles could not. The new format enabled Riis to weave his individual stories into a broader indictment of urban blight. It allowed him to buttress concrete stories with collections of statistics. And perhaps most important, it inspired him to provide documentary proof of a new sort—proof so vivid and dramatic that even the most compelling literary vignettes seemed weak by comparison. Riis sought to document urban conditions with the swiftly developing techniques of photography.

From the experience of other urban reformers, Riis had learned that photographs could be powerful weapons to arouse popular indignation. In a book on London slums, *Street Life in London* (1877), authors John Thompson and Adolph Smith had decided to include photographs because, as they explained, "The unquestionable accuracy of this testimony will enable us to present true types of the London poor and shield us from accusations of either underrating or exaggerating individual peculiarities of appearance." For Riis that was a compelling argument. If photographs accompanied *How the Other Half Lives,* no corrupt politician could dismiss its arguments as opinionated word-paintings spawned by the imagination of an overheated reformer. Photography indisputably showed life as it really was.

"REALITY" AND PHOTOGRAPHIC EVIDENCE

From the moment in 1839 when the French pioneer of photography Louis Jacques Daguerre announced his discovery of a process to fix images permanently on a copper plate, observers repeatedly remarked on the camera's capacity to record reality. More than anything else, the seeming objectivity of the new medium caught the popular imagination. The camera captured only those objects that appeared before the lens, nothing more, nothing less. So faithful was the camera that people often commented that the photographic image recorded the original with an exactness "equal to nature itself." Indeed, one of the attractions of the new medium was that it could accurately reveal the look of other parts of the United States and the world. Nineteenth-century Americans were hungry for visual images of unseen places. Few had ever seen the trans-Mississippi West, much less Europe or the South Pacific. Almost no one had access to pictures that satisfied curiosity about exotic lands or people. As a result, crowds flocked to the galleries of a painter like Alfred Bierstadt when he displayed his grand landscapes of the Rocky Mountains. Even Bierstadt's paintings, though, were colored by his romantic vision of the West, just as all artists' work reflected their own personal styles and quirks.

The new photography seemed to have no style—that was its promise. It recorded only what was before the camera. Reproductions were so faithful to the original that close observation with a magnifying glass often revealed details which had been invisible to the naked eye. The American writer and physician Oliver Wendell Holmes summed up the popular conception when he noted that the camera was even more than "the mirror of reality"; it was "the mirror with a memory."

Certainly, there was no denying the camera's unprecedented ability to record detail in a way that paintings could not. Yet, from today's vantage point, it is easier to see the limits of the camera's seeming objectivity. Any modern amateur photographer who is familiar with the features of a single-lens reflex camera will appreciate immediately how deceptive the camera's claim to mirroring reality can be. Merely to sight through the viewfinder reminds us that every photograph creates its own frame, including some objects and excluding others. The problem of selection of evidence, which is at the heart of the historian's task, remains of paramount importance in photography.

The situation becomes even more complex when we begin to make simple photographic adjustments once the frame has been selected. Far from recording every detail within the lens's reach, we immediately begin excluding details by turning the focusing ring. In choosing a close-up, background details blur; if aiming for a distant subject, it is the foreground that becomes hazy. The technical constraints of the camera thus limit what can be recorded on the negative's frame. If we close down the aperture of the camera's lens (the circular hole that allows light to pass through the lens), the camera's depth of field is increased, bringing into focus a larger area within the path of the lens. On the other hand, photographers who wish to concentrate the viewer's attention on a central subject will eliminate cluttering detail by decreasing their depth of field.

Of course, it may be argued with a good deal of justice that many if not all of these distorting capabilities of the camera are irrelevant when discussing the work of Jacob Riis. Riis worked with neither a sophisticated single-lens reflex camera nor a particularly extensive knowledge of photographic principles. His primary goals were not to record scenes aesthetically and artistically, but to capture the subject matter before his camera. The niceties of art would have to wait.

Indeed, when Riis began his photographic efforts he quickly discovered that the primitive nature of photography precluded too much attention to aesthetic details, especially in his line of work. In the 1880s, taking pictures was no simple matter. Each step in the photographic process presented formidable obstacles. First, would-be photographers

The cumbersome technology of early photography restricted its use largely to professionals. Field photographers had to take along darkrooms in which they prepared the photographic plates which went into a heavy box camera. The van pictured here was used by a photographer during the Crimean War. Matthew Brady and his assistants employed similar large wagons during the Civil War. They soon discovered, much to their chagrin, that such rolling darkrooms made uncomfortably obvious targets for enemy artillery and sharpshooters.

had to learn to prepare a light-sensitive chemical mixture and spread it evenly on the glass plates that served as photographic negatives. For work in the field, they had to take along a portable darkroom, usually a clumsy tent perched on a tripod. Here the negatives were taken from the cumbersome box camera and developed in chemical baths. Additional solutions were necessary to transfer the image from the plate to the final paper print. Such a process taxed the ingenuity and dedication of even the most avid practitioners.

Fortunately, advances in chemistry, optics, and photographic technology had given birth to a new generation of equipment, the "detective camera." To ease the burden of field photographers and make possible the "candid" shot, a number of companies had introduced small cameras about the size of a cigar box. Some carried as many as twelve photographic plates that could be used before the camera required reloading. Wily photographers took to disguising cameras as doctors' satchels, briefcases, books, revolvers, and vest buttons—hence the nickname "detective camera."

George Eastman simplified the process even further with his "Kodak" camera. Introduced to the public in 1888, the Kodak was more than an improved detective camera; it was the first model that replaced glass negatives with a photographic emulsion coated on paper rolls. For twenty-five dollars an aspiring photographer could acquire the camera loaded with 100 shots. Once the film had been exposed, the owner simply returned the camera to the dealer, who removed the spool in a darkroom and shipped it to Eastman's factory for processing. For an additional ten dollars, the dealer would reload the camera with new film. So successfully had Eastman reduced the burden on amateur photographers that his ads could boast, "You press the button, we do the rest."

But even the advances in photographic technology did not eliminate Riis's difficulties. When he began his photographic work, he knew nothing of photography. To help him he enlisted the assistance of several friends in the Health Department who also happened to be amateur photographers. Together they set out to catch their subjects unaware. That meant skulking around "the Bend" in the dead of night, with the normal photographic paraphernalia increased by bulky and primitive flash equipment. For a flash to work, a highly combustible powder was spread along a pan. The pan was then held up and Riis exploded a blank cartridge from a revolver to ignite the powder. This photographic entourage sneaking about town after hours made a remarkable sight, as the *New York Sun* reported:

> Somnolent policemen on the street, denizens of the dives in their dens, tramps and bummers in their so-called lodgings, and all the people of the wild and wonderful variety of New York night life have in turn marvelled at and been frightened by the phenomenon. What they saw was three or four figures in the gloom, a ghostly tripod, some weird and uncanny movements, the blinding flash, and then they heard the patter of retreating footsteps and their mysterious visitors were gone before they could collect their scattered thoughts.

The results from using such finicky equipment were not always predictable. Sometimes the noise would awaken unsuspecting subjects and create a disturbance. On one particularly unfortunate occasion Riis had gone to "Blind Man's Alley" to photograph five sightless men and women living in a cramped attic room. Soon after his eyes cleared from the blinding flash, he saw flames climbing up the rags covering the walls. Fear gripped him as he envisioned the blaze sweeping through twelve rickety flights of stairs between the attic and safety. Fighting the impulse to flee, he beat out the flames with his coat, then rushed to the street seeking help. The first policeman who heard his story burst out laughing. "Why, don't you know that's the Dirty Spoon?" he responded. "It caught fire six times last winter, but it wouldn't burn. The dirt was so thick on the walls it smothered the fire."

Under such precarious circumstances, it might be argued that Riis's photography more closely mirrored reality precisely because it was artless, and that what it lacked in aesthetics it gained in documentary detail. On the next page, for example, we see a picture taken on one of Riis's night expeditions, of lodgers at one of the crowded "five cents a spot" tenements. The room itself, Riis informs us in *How the Other Half Lives,* is "not thirteen feet either way," in which "slept twelve men and women, two or three in bunks in a sort of alcove, the rest on the floor." The sleepy faces and supine bodies reflect the candid nature of the picture; indeed, Riis had followed a policeman who was raiding the room in order to drive the lodgers into the street. The glare of the flash, casting distinct shadows, reveals all of the crowding, dirt, and disorder. This is no aesthetic triumph, perhaps, but it does reveal a wealth of details that prove most useful to the curious historian.

We notice, for instance, that the stove in the foreground is a traditional wood-burning model, with its fuel supply stacked underneath. Space in the apartment is so crowded that footlockers and bundles have been piled directly on top of the stove. (Have they been moved from their daytime resting places on the bunks? Or do these people carry their possessions onto the street during the day?) The dishes and kitchen utensils are piled high on shelves and next to the stove. The bedding is well-used, dirty, and makeshift. Such details are nowhere near as faithfully recorded in the line drawing originally published in *How the Other Half Lives.*

Yet no matter how "artless" the photographs of Jacob Riis may be in terms of their aesthetic control of the medium, to assume they are bias-free seriously underestimates their interpretive content. However primitive a photographer Riis may have been, he still influenced the

Lodgers in a Crowded Bayard Street Tenement—"Five Cents a Spot."

messages he presented through an appropriate selection of details. Even
the most artless photographers make such interpretive choices in every
snapshot they take.

Let us look, for example, at the most artless photographic observations
of all: the ordinary family scrapbook found in most American homes.
When George Eastman marketed his convenient pocket camera, he
clearly recognized the wide appeal of his product. At long last the
ordinary class of people, and not just the rich and well-born, would
create for themselves a permanent documentary record of their doings.
"A collection of these pictures may be made to furnish a pictorial history
of life as it is lived by the owner," proclaimed one "Kodak" advertisement.

But while family albums provide a wide-ranging "pictorial history,"
they are still shaped by conventions every bit as stylized as the romantic

In the original edition of *How the Other Half Lives,* seventeen of the photographs appeared as blurry halftones and nineteen as artists' engravings, such as this rendering of the "Five Cents a Spot" photograph. A comparison of the two pictures quickly demonstrates how much more graphically the photograph presented Riis's concerns. Riis continued to take photographs for other books he published, although it was not until well into the twentieth century that mass reproduction techniques could begin to do justice to them.

conventions of Bierstadt or other artists with equally distinct styles. The albums are very much ceremonial history—birthdays, anniversaries, vacations. Life within their covers is a succession of proud achievements, celebrations, and uncommon moments. A father's retirement party may be covered, but probably not his routine day at the office. We see the sights at Disney World, not the long waits at the airport. Arguments, rivalries, and the tedium of the commonplace are missing.

If the artless photographers of family life unconsciously shape the

"**A collection of these pictures** may be made to furnish a pictorial history of
life as it is lived by the owner." Following the dictum in the Kodak advertisement, these two men pose happily, one holding one of the new Kodak cameras,
while a friend uses another to record the scene. Like so many family album
"candids," this shot follows the tradition of ceremonial history—proud achievements, celebrations, and uncommon moments. Dressed in their best, these are
tourists from Pennsylvania enjoying spring on the White House lawn in April
1889.

records they leave behind, then we must expect those who self-consciously use photography to be even more interpretive with their materials. And this is not a matter of knowing the tricks of the trade about depth of field or shutter speed, but simply the fact that intelligent people will wish to convey a coherent message with their photographs. Civil War photographer Matthew Brady wanted to capture the horrific carnage of the war. To achieve it, he did not hesitate to drag dead bodies to a scene in order to further the composition or the effect he desired.

But to point out such literal examples of the photographer's influence almost destroys the point by caricaturing it. One need not rearrange compositions in order to be photographing for interpretive, even propagandistic purposes. The western land surveys of the 1860s and 1870s, for instance, discovered that their photographs had social uses that extended beyond the narrowly geologic. Though the surveys' missions were ostensibly scientific, they required the financial patronage of Congress. As rival surveys vied for an adequate share of the limited funds, they discovered that photographs of scenic wonders produced the desired results back East. The survey headed by F. V. Hayden in 1871 documented the tall tales, which had long circulated, rumoring natural wonders in northwest Wyoming. The photographs of spectacular vistas, towering waterfalls, Mammoth Hot Springs, Old Faithful, and the geyser basins justified survey appropriations, as well as helped persuade Congress to establish Yellowstone as the first national park safe from commercial development.

A later generation of government photographers, who worked during the Great Depression of the 1930s, also viewed photographs as vehicles to convey their social messages. Few photographers were more dedicated to the ideal of documentary realism than Walker Evans, Dorothea Lange, Ben Shahn, and others who photographed tenant farmers and sharecroppers for the Farm Security Administration. Yet these photographers too brought to their work preconceived notions about how poverty should look. As critic Susan Sontag has noted, they "would take dozens of frontal pictures of one of their sharecropper subjects until satisfied that they had gotten just the right look on film—the precise expression on the subject's face that supported their own notions about poverty, light, dignity, texture, exploitation, and geometry. In deciding how a picture should look . . . photographers are always imposing standards on their subjects."

Thus any series of photographs—including those Jacob Riis took for his books—must be analyzed in the same way a written narrative is. We can appreciate the full import of the photographs only by establishing

"**Photographing in High Places.**" Teton Range, 1872. By William Henry
Jackson. A member of John Wesley Powell's earlier expedition down the
Colorado River recalled the effort involved in handling the unwieldy photographic equipment: "The camera in its strong box was a heavy load to carry up
the rocks, but it was nothing to the chemical and plate-holder box, which in turn
was feather weight compared to the imitation hand organ which served as a
darkroom." Mishaps along the way were not uncommon. "The silver bath had
gotten out of order," reported one of Powell's party, "and the horse bearing
the camera fell off a cliff and landed on top of the camera . . . with a result that
need not be described."

their historical context. What messages are they meant to convey? What are the premises—stated or unstated—which underlie the presentation of photographs? Ironically, in order to evaluate the messages in the Riis photographs, we must supplement our knowledge of his perspectives on the city by turning to his writings.

IMAGES OF THE OTHER HALF

Jacob Riis was an immigrant to America, like so many of those he wrote about. He had tasted poverty and hardship. Yet in a curious way, Riis the social reformer might best be understood as a tourist of the slums, wandering from tenement to tenement, camera in hand. To classify him as such is to suggest that despite his immigrant background, he maintained a distance between himself and his urban subjects.

In part, that distance can be explained by Riis's own background as an immigrant. Despite his tribulations, he came from a middle-class family, which made it easy to choose journalism as a career. As a boy, in fact, Riis had helped his father prepare copy for a weekly newspaper. Once established in a job commensurate with his training, Riis found it easy to accomplish the goal of so many immigrants—to rise to middle-class dignity and prosperity and to become, in the most respectable sense, not a newcomer but an American.

Furthermore, because Riis emigrated from Denmark, his northern European background made it more difficult for him to empathize with the immigrant cultures of southern and eastern Europe, increasingly the source of new immigrants in the 1880s and 1890s. Like many native-born Americans, Riis found most of their customs distasteful and doubted whether they could successfully learn the traditional American virtues. As Sam Warner remarked, Riis ascribed a "degree of opprobrium to each group directly proportional to the distance from Denmark. . . ."

Yet for all that, Riis retained a measure of sympathy and understanding for the poor. He did not work his way out of poverty only to find a quiet house far from the turmoil of the urban scene. He was unable to ignore the squalor that so evidently needed the attention of concerned Americans. Thus an ambivalence permeated Riis's writings. On the one hand he sympathized with the plight of the poor and recognized how much they were the victims of their slum environment. "In the tenements all the elements make for evil," he wrote. He struggled to maintain a distinction between the "vicious" classes of beggars, tramps, and thieves, and the working poor who made the slum their home because they had no other choice. On the other hand, Riis could not avoid using language that continuously dismissed whole classes of immigrants as inherently unable to adapt themselves to what he considered acceptable American behavior.

When he visited "Jewtown," for example, Riis scarcely commented on the strong bonds of faith and loyalty that held families and groups together in the face of all the debilitating aspects of slum life. Instead, he dwelt on the popular "Shylock" stereotype. "Money is their God," he wrote. "Life itself is of little value compared to even the leanest bank account." Upon the Irish, of course, he bestowed a talent for politics and drink. "His genius runs to public affairs rather than domestic life," said Riis of the Irish politician; "wherever he is mustered in force the saloon is the gorgeous center of political activity."

To southern and eastern Mediterranean people, Riis was least understanding. The "happy-go-lucky" Italians he observed were "content to live in a pig sty." Not only did they "come in at the bottom," but also they managed to stay there. They sought to reproduce the worst of life in Italy by flocking to slum tenements. When an Italian found better housing, "he soon reduced what he did find to his own level, if allowed to follow his natural bent." These affable and malleable souls "learned slowly, if at all." And then there was the passion for gambling and murder: "[The Italian's] soul is in the game from the moment the cards are on the table, and very frequently his knife is in it too before the game is ended." Such observations confirm our sense of Riis as a tourist in the slums, for he seemed only to have educated his prejudices without collecting objective information.

A second quality that strikes the reader of *How the Other Half Lives* is its tone of Christian moralism. Riis blamed the condition of the urban poor on the sins of individuals—greedy landlords, petty grafters, corrupt officials, the weak character of the poor, and popular indifference. Insensitive to the economic forces that had transformed cities, he never attempted a systematic analysis of urban classes and institutional structures. Instead, he appealed to moral regeneration as the means of overcoming evil, and approvingly cited the plea of a philanthropic tenement builder: "How are these men and women to understand the love of God you speak of, when they see only the greed of men?" In his own ominous warning to his fellow New Yorkers, Riis struck an almost apocalyptic note. "When another generation shall have doubled the census of our city," he warned, "and to the vast army of workers, held captive by poverty, the very name of home shall be a bitter mockery, what will the harvest be?" If conditions worsened, the violence of labor strikes during the 1870s and 1880s might seem quite tame in comparison.

Given those predispositions, how do we interpret Riis's photographs? Like the arrangers of family albums, his personal interests dictated the kind of photographs he included in his books. And as with the family albums, by being aware of these predispositions we can both understand Riis better by consciously examining his photographic messages and at the same time transcend the original intent of the pictures.

For example, Riis's Christian moralism led him to emphasize the need for stable families as a key to ameliorating slum conditions. Many American Protestants in his audience thought of the home and family as a "haven" from the bustle of the working world, as well as a nursery of piety and good morals. Fathers could return at the end of the day to the warm, feminine environment in which their children were carefully nurtured. Thus the picture we have already examined of the "five cents

Bohemian Cigarmakers at Work in Their Tenement

a spot" lodgings takes on added significance in light of these concerns. It is not simply the lack of cleanliness or space that would make such an apartment appalling to many viewers, but the corrosive effect of such conditions on family life. Yet this was a family dwelling, for Riis heard a baby crying in the adjoining hall-room. How could a family preserve any semblance of decency, Riis asked his readers, in a room occupied by twelve single men and women?

Let us turn from that photograph to another, on page 228, which is much more obviously a family portrait. The middle-class Protestant viewer of Riis's day would have found this picture shocking for the same reasons. The home was supposed to be a haven away from the harsh workaday world, yet here the factory has invaded the home. This is the small room of an immigrant Bohemian family, crowded with the tools and supplies needed to make a living. The business is apparently a family enterprise, since the husband, wife, and at least one child assist in the work. Though the young boy cannot keep his eyes off the camera, he continues to stretch tobacco leaves from the pile on his lap.

The room speaks of a rather single-minded focus on making a living. All the furnishings are used for cigarmaking, not for creature comforts or living after work. The only light comes from a small kerosene lamp and the indirect sunlight from two windows facing out on the wall of another building. Yet Riis had a stronger message for the picture to deliver. The text stresses the exploitation of Bohemians in New York, most of whom worked at cigarmaking in apartments owned by their employers, generally Polish Jewish immigrants.

The cigar trade dominated all aspects of life: "The rank smell that awaited us on the corner of the block follows us into the hallways, penetrates every nook and cranny of the house." This particular family, he noted, turned out 4,000 cigars a week, for which it was paid fifteen dollars. Out of that amount the landlord-employer deducted $11.75 in rent for three small rooms, two of which had no windows for light or air. The father was so tied to his workbench that in six years he had learned no English and, therefore, made no attempt to assimilate into American life.

It is interesting to contrast the portrait of the Bohemian family with a different family portrait, this one taken by another reforming photographer, but still often published in reprints of How the Other Half Lives. *

*The photographer is Jessie Tarbox Beals and the picture was taken in 1910. Although not included in the original edition of How the Other Half Lives, it is among the photographs in the Riis collection held by the Museum of the City of New York.

Room in Tenement Flat, 1910

Unlike the photograph of the cigarmakers' lodgings, this is a more formal family portrait. Very much aware of the camera's presence, everyone is looking directly at the lens. Perhaps the photographer could gain consent to intrude on their privacy only by agreeing to do a formal photograph. The children have been scrubbed and dressed in what appear to be their good clothes—the oldest son in his shirt and tie, his sister in a taffeta dress, and a younger girl in a frock. Unlike the "five cents a spot" lodging, where dishes were stacked one upon the other, here the family china is proudly displayed in the cabinet. Perhaps it was a valued possession carefully guarded on the journey from Europe.

Other details in the picture suggest that this family enjoyed a more pleasant environment than seen in the previous photos. Moving from left to right, we notice first a gas stove, a relatively modern improvement in an age when coal and wood were still widely used for heating and cooking. Perhaps these people had found a room in a once-elegant home divided by the realtor into a multiple dwelling. Certain details suggest that may be the case. Few tenements would have gas, much less built-in cupboards or the finished moldings around doors and windows. The window between the kitchen/bedroom and closet/bedroom indicates that the room may have once looked out on open space.

By contrast, the picture communicates a sense of crowding. This hardly seems an accident. Had the photographer wished to take only a family portrait, she could have clustered her subjects in the center of her lens. Instead, she placed them around the room, so that the camera would catch all the details of their domestic circumstance. We see not just a family, but the conditions of their lives in an area far too small for their needs. Each space and almost all the furnishings are used for more than one purpose. The wash tub just before the window and washboard behind it indicate that the kitchen doubles as laundry room—and the tub was probably used for baths as well. The bed serves during the day as a sofa. To gain a measure of privacy the parents have crowded their bed into a closet stuffed with family possessions. Seven people seem to share a room perhaps no more than 250 square feet in total. The children appear to range in age from one to twelve. If the mother is again pregnant as the picture hints, that means every two years another person enters that cramped space.

This portrait, then, does not conform to the typical stereotype we would expect to find of urban immigrant slum dwellers. In the first place, many immigrants came to America without families. Of those, a majority were young men who hoped to stay just long enough to accumulate a small savings with which to improve their family fortunes upon returning to Europe. On the other hand, immigrant families tended to be much larger than those of middle-class native-born Americans. Rather than evoking a sympathetic response among an American audience, the picture might, instead, reinforce the widespread fear that prolific breeding among foreign elements threatened white Protestant domination of American society.

What then does the modern viewer derive from this family portrait? Over all, it seems to say that immigrants, like other Americans, prized family life. The father perches at the center almost literally holding his family together, though with a rather tenuous grip. The son with his tie appears to embody the family's hopes for a better future. His mother securely holds the baby in her arms. Each element, in fact, emphasizes the virtues of the domestic family as it was traditionally conceived in America. The picture, while sending a mixed message, conveys less a sense of terrible slum conditions than a sense of the middle-class aspirations among those forced to live in inadequate housing.

Does the fact that this picture is posed make it less useful as historical evidence? Not at all. Even when people perform for the camera, they communicate information about themselves. There is no hiding the difficulty of making a decent life for seven people in a small space. Nor can the viewer ignore the sense of pride of person and place, no matter how limited the resources. What remains uncertain, however, is what message the photographer meant to convey. The scene could serve equally well to arouse nativist prejudice or to extol the strength of family ties in the immigrant community. Both were concerns that Riis addressed in his writing and photographs.

Concern over the breakdown of family life drew Riis to children. They are among his most frequently photographed subjects. He shared the Victorian notion of childhood innocence and, therefore, understood that nothing could be more disturbing to his middle-class audience than scenes of homeless children, youth gangs, and "street arabs" sleeping in alleys, gutters, and empty stairways. At first glance, the three "street arabs" on this page appear as if they might even be dead. A closer look suggests helpless innocence—children alone and unprotected as they sleep. Their ragged clothes and bare feet advertise poverty and the

Street Arabs in Sleeping Quarters

absence of parents to care for them. In each other, though, they seem to have extracted a small measure of warmth, belonging, and comfort. It would be almost impossible for any caring person to view the picture without empathy for its subjects and anger at a society that cares so little for its innocent creatures.

Riis hints at his sympathies through the location of the camera. He did not stand over the boys to shoot the picture from above. That angle would suggest visually the superiority of the photographer to his subjects. From ground level, however, observer and subject are on the same plane. We look at the boys, not down on them. And should we dismiss as accidental his inclusion of the prison-like bars over the small window? From another angle Riis could have eliminated that poignant symbol from his frame.

Certainly, we know that Riis feared that all too soon those "innocents" would become the members of slum gangs, operating outside the law with brazen disregard for society or its values. In this second picture of lost innocence (on page 234) Riis persuaded some gang members to demonstrate how they "did the trick"—that is, robbed the pockets of a drunk lying in an alley. The mere fact that Riis had obviously arranged the content of the picture, indicating that some relationship existed between the photographer and his subjects, would have made the image even more shocking. These young men were clearly proud of their acts and so confident that they were beyond the reach of the law that they could show off for the camera. We see smiles and smug satisfaction on several faces. Other members gather around to enjoy the novelty of the situation. Riis's audience would have understood quite clearly that the slums as breeding grounds for crime drove the innocence out of childhood.

Space was not only scarce in the homes of the poor. Crowding extended into public places as well. Without parks or wide streets children were forced to play in filthy alleys and garbage heaps. Adults had no decent communal space in which to make contact with the community. The picture of a tenement yard (page 235) immediately reveals a scene of chaos and crowding. As in slum apartments, every open area had to serve more than one purpose. Women doing the wash and children playing appear to fall all over one another. The fire escape doubles as a balcony. Any readers with a small yard, separate laundry room or laundress, and nearby park surely thanked their good fortune not to be part of this confusion.

Once again, however, closer scrutiny may lead us to reconsider our initial impressions. This place seems alive with energy. We see that the

Hell's Kitchen Boys—"Showing Their Tricks"

women and children are all part of a community. They have given their common space, restricted as it may be, to shared activities. Everyone seems to have a place in the scheme of things. All that laundry symbolizes a community concern with cleanliness and decency. On the balcony some people have flower boxes to add a touch of color and freshness to the drab landscape. Our initial shock gives way to a more complex set of feelings. We come to respect the durability of spirit that allowed people to struggle for a small measure of comfort amid such harsh surroundings. The message which at first seemed obvious is not so clear after all.

Tenement-house Yard

"Bottle Alley"

In the picture of "Bottle Alley," Riis has editorialized on the same theme with more telling effect. In this dingy slum, along the infamous Bend, we are still among tenements. Laundry again hangs from the balcony. A few isolated men look upon the camera as it takes in the scene. Their presence during the day suggests they are among the army of unemployed who sit aimlessly waiting for time to pass. They seem oblivious to the filth that surrounds them. We cannot help but feel that they are as degraded as the conditions in which they live. The dilapidated buildings and rickety stairs create an overall sense of decay; nothing in the picture relieves the image of poverty and disorder Riis wanted to capture. The message is all too clear.

As the case of Jacob Riis demonstrates, photography is hardly a simple "mirror of reality." The meanings behind each image must be uncovered through careful exploration and analysis. On the surface, certainly, photographs often provide the historian with a wealth of concrete detail. In that sense they do convey the reality of a situation with some objectivity. Yet Riis's relative inexperience with a camera did not long prevent him from learning how to frame the content to create a powerful image. The photographic details communicate a stirring case for social reform, full of subjective as well as objective intent. Riis did not simply want us to see the poor or the slums; he wanted us to see them as he saw them. His view was that of a partisan, not an unbiased observer.

In that sense the photographic "mirror," is silvered on both sides: catching the reflections of its user as well as its subjects. The prints which emerge from the twilight of the darkroom must be read by historians as they do all evidence—appreciating messages that may be simple and obvious or complex and elusive. Once these evidentiary limits are appreciated and accepted, one can recognize the rueful justice in Oliver Wendell Holmes's definition of a photograph: an illusion with the "appearance of reality that cheats the senses with its seeming truth."

Additional Reading

Given the importance this chapter has placed on photographic evidence, readers wishing to examine more visual evidence of how Jacob Riis's other halves lived should consult the Dover Publications edition of his book. It has a good intro-duction by Charles Madison but, most important, includes 100 photographs and several reproductions of line illustrations included in the original version. An-other edition of *How the Other Half Lives* (Cambridge, Mass., 1970) has an excellent introduction by urban historian Sam Bass Warner, but suffers because of the limited number of photos included. Peter B. Hales, *Silver Cities: Photogra-phy of Urban America, 1839–1915* (Philadelphia, 1984) has offered a persuasive interpretation of Riis's place in the tradition of urban photography and social reform. Hales makes clear how much Riis redirected both traditions—urban photography away from the celebration of an idealized urban order, social reform away from its ignorance of slum conditions and its sentimentalized view of the poor.

Riis's own account of his life is found in *The Making of an American,* Roy Lubove, ed. (New York, 1966). An interesting but dated biography exists in Louise Ware, *Jacob A. Riis, Police Reporter* (New York, 1938); see also the more recent study by Edith P. Mayer, *"Not Charity but Justice:" The Story of Jacob A. Riis* (New York, 1974). One of America's finest photographers and critics, Ansel Adams, has also done the preface to an important book on Riis, Alexander Alland, *Jacob Riis: Photographer and Citizen* (Millerton, N.Y., 1974).

Even for those whose photographic expertise is limited to a mastery of George Eastman's injunction ("You press the button . . ."), a number of excellent books provide clear discussions of the photographic medium, its potentialities, and its limitations. Susan Sontag, *On Photography* (New York, 1977) provides many stimulating ideas, particularly in her first essay, "In Plato's Cave." All followers of photographic art owe a debt to Beaumont Newhall, *The History of Photography from 1839 to the Present Day* (New York, 1964). Besides his work as photo-historian and critic, Newhall helped to establish the photographic wing of the Museum of Modern Art. Also useful for background on the technical and aesthetic developments in photography is Robert Taft, *Photography and the American Scene* (New York, 1938; reissued in 1964). For views that contrast with Riis's scenes of New York, see the Museum of the City of New York's *Once Upon a City: New York from 1890 to 1910* (New York, 1958), which features images captured by the photographer Byron.

Many photographs of historic value are on file and readily available to the public in the Library of Congress Prints and Photographs Division and the National Archives Still Picture Branch. At quite reasonable prices, interested researchers may obtain their own 8 × 10" glossy reproductions, printed from copy negatives made of the original photographs. Of the two institutions, the Library of Congress is the easier for novices to use, although the staffs at both institutions are extremely helpful. Two books provide a sampling from their collections: from the Library of Congress, *Viewpoints* (Washington, D.C., 1975); from the National Archives, *The American Image* (New York, 1979). The latter volume contains an excellent introduction by Alan Trachtenberg, whose discussions of photographic images planted the seed for this essay. Both books provide ordering numbers for the photographs reproduced, so that interested readers may order their own prints.

Excellent discussions of immigration, urbanization, and industrialization abound; here we mention only a representative and useful sampling. Among the histories and novels of the immigration experience, few have the impact of Anzia Yezierska, *Breadgivers* (New York, 1925), recently reissued with a fine introduction by Alice Kessler Harris. Umberto Nelli, *Italians of Chicago* (New York, 1972) is worth reading as a corrective to Riis's stereotypes of Italians. To appreciate Riis's impact on other urban reformers we suggest Robert Hunter, *Poverty* (New York, 1904; reissued 1965). Two brief yet informed analyses of late nineteenth-century economic development are Stuart Bruchey, *The Growth of the American Economy* (New York, 1975) and Robert Heilbroner, *The Economic Transformation of America* (New York, 1977). For the concurrent transformation of cities, see Zane Miller, *The Urbanization of Modern America* (New York, 1973) and even more stimulating, Sam Bass Warner, *The Urban Wilderness* (New York, 1972). Nor should readers miss Ray Ginger's lively discussion of urban Chicago in *Altgeld's Illinois* (Chicago, 1958). The problems and challenges of technology are treated in Nathan Rosenberg, *Technology and American Growth* (White Plains, N.Y., 1972).

One significant pleasure in a field as untapped as photographic evidence comes from doing original research yourself. Michael Lesey, *Wisconsin Death Trip* (New York, 1973) opened up the possibilities, though not without disturbing other historians. The field remains largely unexplored. Almost all readers will have access to their own family albums, local and neighborhood collections, yearbooks, newspaper files, and other sources with which to do their own investigating.

USDA Government Inspected

All of our essays tell a story and this one is no exception. But our present tale, by its very nature, partakes in large measure of the epic and the symbolic. It is a political tale, compiled largely from the accounts of politicians and the journalists who write about politicians; which is to say, it possesses much of the charm and innocence of a good, robust fairy tale. As we shall shortly discover, there are logical reasons for such larger-than-life overtones, and they deserve serious scrutiny. But the story must come first: an exciting tale of a bold president, an earnest reformer, some evil political bosses, and a lot of pork and beef.

It begins ("once upon a time") with the president, Teddy Roosevelt, who turns out to be the hero of the tale. There was nothing ordinary about Teddy, including the fact he was ever president at all. People from the Roosevelts' social class disdained politics and would never encourage their sons to take it up as a profession. But then again Teddy was not like other members of his social class nor his fellow students at Harvard. Anything he did, he did with gusto, and if being the best meant being president, then Teddy would not stop short of the White House.

His path to success was not an easy one. As a child Teddy was sickly, asthmatic, and nearsighted. He spent long hours pummelling punching bags, swinging on parallel bars, doing push-ups, and boxing in the ring to build a body as active as his mind. When he went west in the 1880s to take up ranching, he had to overcome his image as an effete eastern "dude." He soon amazed many a grizzly cowboy by riding the Dakota badlands in spring mud, blasts of summer heat, and driving winter storms. He fought with his fists and once rounded up a band of desperados at gun point.

Back East, when Teddy played tennis, he showed the same determination, his record being 91 games in a single day. When he led the Rough Riders through Cuba in 1898, he raised troop morale by walking the sentry line whistling cheerfully while his men crouched low to avoid the bullets flying overhead. As president he advised others to speak softly and carry a big stick, though he himself more often observed only the latter half of his maxim. Teddy's favorite expressions, seldom spoken softly, were "Bully!" and *"Dee-*lighted!"—uttered because he usually got his way.

By 1906 Teddy had the White House firmly in his grasp. Just two years earlier he had engineered an impressive victory to become president in his own right. He had behind him a record of achievements to which he would soon add the Nobel Peace Prize for his role in bringing an end to the Russo-Japanese war. But Teddy could never rest on his

TR, displaying characteristic gritted teeth and holding a moderately big stick. When he spoke, Roosevelt chopped every word into neat, staccato syllables, with a rhythm that bore no resemblance to the ordinary cadences of the English language. "I always think of a man biting tenpenny nails when I think of Roosevelt making a speech," remarked one acquaintance.

laurels. In February a storm broke that challenged his skill as leader of both the nation and the Republican Party.

The thunder clap that shattered the calm was the publication of *The Jungle.* The book told a lurid tale about Chicago's meatpacking industry. Its author, Upton Sinclair, was not only a reformer but a socialist as well. Most Americans of the day believed that socialists were subversives who held extreme and impractical opinions. Despite that skepticism, readers could not ignore the grisly realities recounted in *The Jungle.* It related, in often revolting detail, the conditions under which the packers proc-essed pork and beef, adulterated it, and shipped it to millions of Ameri-can consumers.

Breakfast sausage, Sinclair revealed, was more than a tasty blend of ground meats and spices. "It was too dark in these storage spaces to see clearly," he reported,

> but a man could run his hands over the piles of meat and swap off handfulls of dry dung of rats. These rats were nuisances, and the packers would put out poisoned bread for them; they would die; and then rats, bread, and meat would go in the hoppers together. This is no fairy story and no joke; the meat would be shoveled into carts, and the man who did the shoveling did not trouble to lift out a rat even when he saw one.

Rats were but one tasty additive in the meat sent to dinner tables. Potted chicken contained no chicken at all, only beef suet, waste ends of veal, and tripe. Most shocking of all, Sinclair told of men in cook-ing rooms who fell into vats and, after being cooked for days, "all but the bones had gone out into the world as Durham's Pure Leaf Lard!"

In just one week a scandalized public had snapped up some 25,000 copies of *The Jungle.* Almost all of those readers missed the socialist message. Sinclair had hoped to draw their attention to "the conditions under which toilers get their bread." The public had responded instead to the disclosures about corrupt federal meat inspectors, unsanitary slaughter houses, tubercular cattle, and the packers' unscrupulous busi-ness practices.

One of the most outraged readers was President Theodore Roosevelt. Few politicians have ever been as well-informed as TR, who devoured books at over 1,500 words per minute, published works of history, and corresponded regularly with leading business, academic, and public figures. Roosevelt recognized immediately that the public would expect government at some level—local, state, or federal—to clean up the meat industry. He invited Sinclair for a talk at the White House, and though

Hogs being scalded preparatory to scraping at a Swift and Company plant, 1905. The packers boasted that they used every bit of the pig "except the squeal," and they were probably more than right, given some of the extraneous ingredients that went into the canned goods of the period. Although modern viewers may be taken aback at the unsanitary appearance of the plant, this photograph was a promotional shot illustrating some of the better conditions in packing facilities.

he dismissed the writer's "pathetic belief" in socialism, he promised that "the specific evils you point out shall, if their existence be proved, and if I have the power, be eradicated."

Roosevelt kept his promise. With the help of allies in Congress, he quickly brought out a new bill, along with the proverbial big stick. Only four months later, on June 30, he signed into law a Meat Inspection Act that banned the packers from using any unhealthy dyes, chemical preservatives, or adulterants. The bill provided $3 million toward a new, tougher inspection system, where government inspectors could be on hand day or night to condemn animals unfit for human consumption. Senator Albert Beveridge of Indiana, Roosevelt's progressive ally in Congress, gave the president credit for the new bill. "It is chiefly to him that we owe the fact that we will get as excellent a bill as we will have," he told reporters. Once again, Americans could put canned meats and sausages on the dinner table and eat happily ever after. Or so it would seem.

THE SYMBOLS OF POLITICS

The story you have just read is true—as far as it goes. If it has taken on a legendary, even mythic quality in the telling, that is understandable given the nature of the American political system. Politics is, after all, public business. And the tales of national politics almost inescapably take on epic proportions. In such situations, symbolic language serves to simplify highly complex realities. It makes them more comprehensible by substituting concrete and recognizable actors and objects in the place of complicated, though often banal, situations. In doing so, symbols and symbolic language serve as a means of communication between political leaders and their constituencies. Skillful politicians generally have the ability to cast their actions in dramatic terms that speak to deeply felt public concerns.

Jacksonian Democrats pioneered many of the modern uses of campaign imagery. They touted their candidate, "Old Hickory," as the symbolic embodiment of the American frontier tradition. In their hands Jackson became the uncommon "Common Man." As president, he waged war against the Second Bank of the United States, fittingly symbolized by its enemies as the "Monster Bank." His Whig opposition had quickly grasped the use of such symbols; they nominated a popular general of their own, William Henry "Tippecanoe" Harrison. Their campaign rhetoric invoked the "log cabin" motif and other appropriate frontier images, even though Harrison came from a distinguished Virginia family and lived in an elegant house. Thus along with a two-party system of politics, Americans had developed a body of symbols to make complex political issues familiar and comprehensible to the voters.

Symbols as a mode of political discourse took on a new meaning

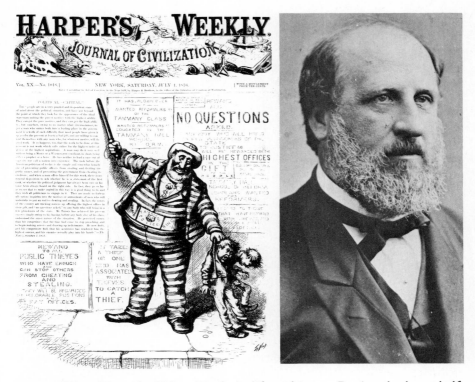

Boss William Tweed of New York, in life and in art. During the latter half of the nineteenth century, cartoons played an important part in defining the symbols of political discourse. Occasionally the representations were readily recognizable in more than a symbolic sense. When Tweed fled the United States to escape a jail term, he was arrested in an out-of-the-way Spanish village. The Spanish constables, it turned out, had recognized him from this Thomas Nast cartoon. The symbolic aspect of the drawing escaped them, however: they thought they had apprehended a notorious child kidnapper.

with an art form that reached maturity in the late nineteenth century— the political cartoon. Earlier cartoonists had portrayed Old Hickory's epic struggle with the Monster Bank, but they lacked the sophistication and draftsmanship achieved by Gilded Age caricaturists like Thomas Nast. Week after week, newspapers carried cartoons which established readily identifiable symbols. Nast conceived the elephant as a representation of the GOP (the Republicans or Grand Old Party) and the donkey for the Democrats. To Nast and his fellow cartoonists we owe our image of the political boss, decked out in his gaudy suit that assumes a striking resemblance to a convict's striped outfit. So too, we have the Monopolist or greedy capitalist, his huge, bloated waistline taking on the aspect of a bag of silver dollars. A scraggly beard, overalls, and wild, crazed eyes denoted the Populist. In place of the Monster Bank stood the Trust, vividly pictured as a grasping octopus. Such cartoons by their very nature communicated the political symbolism of their day.

The cartoonists seldom had a better subject than Teddy Roosevelt with his gleaming, oversized front teeth, bull neck, pince-nez glasses, and, of course, his big stick. Caricaturists did not have to stretch the imagination much to cast Teddy larger than life; he specialized in that department long before he reached the White House. There was the gun-toting cowboy, the New York police commissioner in his long, black cape, and the Rough Rider charging up Tea Kettle Hill. Thus it was easy during the political battles of the Progressive Era to conceive of the actors in symbolic terms. In one corner stood the reformers: Roosevelt, a policeman, clubbing the opposition with his big stick; or Sinclair, wild-eyed like all political radicals. In the other corner, during the meat inspection fight, stood the Beef Trust—Armour, Swift, and the other packers bloated by their ill-gotten gains.

Yet as we have already noted, such symbolic representations inevitably oversimplify the political process to the point of distortion. As rendered by the cartoonist, shades of gray become black and white, and political conflict becomes a Manichaean struggle between good and evil. Even more subtly, distortion arises because symbols come to personalize complex situations and processes. Inanimate institutions (trusts, political machines, Congress) appear as animate objects (a grasping octopus, predatory tigers, braying donkeys) with human motives and designs.

Consequently we tend to visualize political events as being primarily the result of individuals' actions. The story of the meat inspection law is reduced to the tale of Roosevelt, Sinclair, and their enemies. The progression, as we saw, is quite simple: (1) Sinclair's revelations scandalize the president; (2) Roosevelt determines to reform the law; (3) with his usual energy, he overwhelms the opposition and saves the consumer. Such an explanation masks the crucial truth that the actors, whether individuals, groups, or institutions, often have mixed motives and multiple objectives. The outcome of a situation may bear slight resemblance to the original design of any of the participants. As a result, symbolic explanations do not adequately portray the labyrinth of negotiations and institutional hurdles that shape the political process, sometimes to the point of determining the outcome.

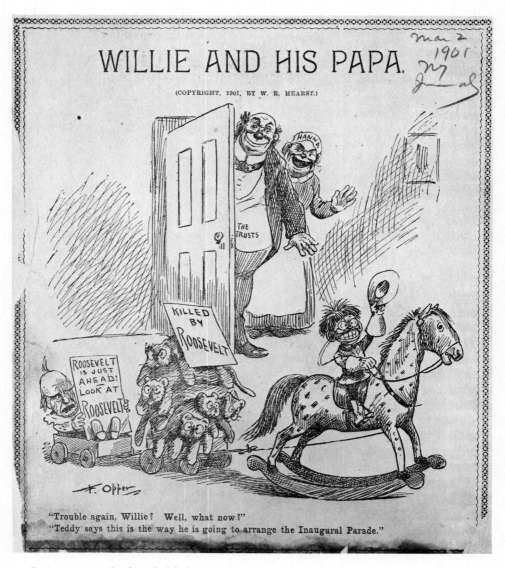

WILLIE AND HIS PAPA.

(COPYRIGHT, 1901, BY W. R. HEARST.)

"Trouble again, Willie? Well, what now?"
"Teddy says this is the way he is going to arrange the Inaugural Parade."

Caricaturists had a field day with Roosevelt's energetic and good-natured self-aggrandizement. In this cartoon by Frederick Opper, Vice-President-elect Roosevelt has rearranged the Inaugural Parade of 1901 so that President William McKinley is forced to bring up the rear. Teddy, of course, displays his teeth as well as a load of hunting trophies from western exploits, while the characteristic Trust figure looms in the background as "Willie's Papa."

Political historians, then, must handle symbolic language and explanations with caution. They cannot simply dismiss or debunk the symbolism, for it can, by influencing opinion, affect the political process. At the same time, historians cannot allow symbols to obscure the information necessary to narrate and explain political events. Granted that Roosevelt played the reformer in seeking to curb the packers' worst abuses; how successfully did he translate his intentions into an effective political instrument? Senator Beveridge, it is true, praised both the new law and the president's role in securing its passage. Yet other supporters of inspection reform did not share Beveridge's enthusiasm. "The American consumer and the ordinary American farmer have been left out of the question," Senator Knute Nelson complained shortly after the act passed. "I must say I feel disappointed. . . . When I go home I will go home like a licked dog."

In fact, prominent Republicans in the Senate led by Beveridge himself and Roosevelt's good friend, Henry Cabot Lodge of Massachusetts, had fought to defeat the law only a few days before Roosevelt signed it. They believed, as Nelson had argued, that the bill was intended "to placate the packers; next to placate the men who raise cattle; and, third to get a good market for the packers abroad." In short, many senators viewed the Meat Inspection Act as a victory for the packers and a defeat for reform. In that light Beveridge's praise has a symbolic meaning that our story thus far cannot explain.

So the historian must seek to set aside the mythic story and its symbols in order to reconstruct the institutional setting in which the real story unfolded. Individual actions must be made to square with motives. The outcome must be treated not as the inevitable triumph of good over evil but as just one of the many possible outcomes, and not necessarily the best at that. It is also the political historian's task to determine how the complex procedural tangle by which a bill becomes law limits the impact of individual actors no matter how lofty or base their motives.

THE TANGLE BEHIND THE JUNGLE

The mythic tale of the Meat Inspection Act begins with the publication of *The Jungle,* in February 1906. That, so the story goes, was the catalytic event that sparked outrage against the packers and their unscrupulous methods. Yet, while *The Jungle* certainly provoked a public outcry, we may legitimately wonder whether a single dramatic story could by itself generate such widespread controversy. For better or worse, we have no Gallup polls from 1906 to measure public response to Sinclair's lurid exposé. But if we poke around in earlier stories about the meat industry, we find that *The Jungle* was merely a final straw, albeit a weighty one, in a long train of unfavorable publicity directed against the packers.

As early as the 1870s some European governments had begun to bar importation of what they had found were unhealthy American meat products. Over the years American exports declined as the Europeans tightened their restrictions. In 1891 the worried packers persuaded Congress to pass a federal meat inspection act in order to win back their foreign customers. The federal stamp would show that all meats in

Roosevelt with his Rough Riders. TR's distrust of the packers reached as far back as the Spanish-American War, when packers had sold the American army quantities of rotten and chemically adulterated meats. Humorist Finley Peter Dunne took note of the situation—as well as the disorganized state of the regular army—when he had his fictional Irish bartender, Mr. Dooley, remark on the invincible American army of "injineers, miners, plumbers, an' lawn tinnis experts, numberin' in all four hundhred an' eighty thousand men," sent to do battle against the Spanish "ar-rmed with death-dealin' canned goods."

interstate and foreign sales had been subjected to antemortem inspection. That measure succeeded until 1897, when the "embalmed meat" scandals once again tarnished the industry's reputation. The packers who supplied American soldiers fighting in Cuba had sold the army quantities of rotten and chemically adulterated meats. As the commander of the Rough Riders, Colonel Teddy Roosevelt had seen troops die from poisonous meats as well as Spanish bullets.

Roosevelt had not forgotten what he interpreted as treachery. In 1905 he found an opportunity to punish the packers. He ordered his attorney general to bring suit against the packing house trust under the Sherman Antitrust Act. The president was particularly offended by the packers' brazen disregard for public safety. In building their industry into one of the nation's ten largest, Armour, Swift, and others boasted openly that they used every bit of the pig "except the squeal." Roosevelt was therefore beside himself when he heard that the judge had dismissed the government's suit on narrow procedural grounds. Suspicious that the packers had bribed the judge, he instructed his attorney general to release a confidential report revealing perjury in the beef trust case. Roosevelt scarcely needed to read *The Jungle* to believe that with their "public be damned" attitude the meat barons might be guilty of any manner of irresponsible behavior. *The Jungle* merely provided a new weapon for his ongoing fight.

Furthermore, the president recognized that the existing meat inspection law left much to be desired. Under it, Congress allocated money for an inspection force, but those appropriations were usually inadequate. Given the limited funds, most inspectors worked only during the day, leaving the packers free to commit their worst abuses at night. Even if inspectors did find diseased cattle at antemortem (preslaughter) inspection, they had no power to have the animals destroyed. In fact, the packers made considerable profit selling those tainted animals to other plants not under federal supervision.

The federal government actually had almost no authority over the packers. Nothing under the system forced compliance with government standards. The inspectors could only threaten to leave the premises (and take their stamps with them) if the packers ignored their rulings. And though the law did prevent the industry from exporting meat without the federal stamp of approval, there was no similar provision to protect American consumers. Once a carcass passed the inspector, the government had no further power to impose sanitary standards anywhere in the plants. Roosevelt was aware of these deficiencies and eager to see them corrected.

The public, too, had grounds for suspicion even before *The Jun-*

gle hit the bookstores. Sinclair's accusations had already been published in a popular socialist journal. In doing his research, Sinclair had received information from *The Lancet,* a distinguished British medical journal which had investigated earlier meat industry scandals. In 1905, *The Lancet* renewed its investigation of packing house filth which jeopardized both workers and consumers. At the same time, Samuel Merwyn, a well-known muckraking journalist, had written articles charging the packers with deliberately selling diseased meats.

To understand the impact of *The Jungle,* the historian must place it in the context of the popular muckraking style of journalism. Having discovered that the public possessed an almost insatiable appetite for sensational stories, leading journalists had set out to investigate corruption wherever they could find it. They had exposed the boss-dominated urban political machines, graft in government, greedy senators, Wall Street stock frauds, prostitution, quack doctors, patent medicines, women's inequality, child labor abuses, dangerous factory conditions, and a host of other social ills.

The muckrakers had much in common with the political cartoonists. Their villains made convenient, easily recognizable symbols. Evil could be personified as the Monster Trust, the Self-serving Politician, or the Avaricious Capitalist. Such an approach, while gratifying readers' love of lurid details, seldom got to the heart of social problems. In their indignant style muckrakers told Americans what was wrong with their society, but not how the problems arose nor what could be done. Somehow the exposure of the symptoms of evil was supposed to motivate reformers and an aroused public to cure the disease. In keeping with the popular style of muckraking, Sinclair had pointed an accusing finger at the packers without offering any specific suggestions for cleaning up the meat industry.

But just as *The Jungle* can be understood only within the context of the larger muckraking style, so too the Meat Inspection Act stood within the context of progressive reform. Despite Sinclair's lack of analysis, there were many Americans who had identified the sources of such corporate arrogance and who had prepared an agenda for politics. Theodore Roosevelt embodied much of the temperament of those progressive reformers. He shared their hostility to excessive concentrations of power in private hands, their approval of executive regulatory agencies, their faith in democratic forms of government, their humanitarian sensibilities, and their overriding confidence in the people's capacity to shape their future intelligently.

The progressives were actually a diverse group seeking to turn gov-

"An Alphabet of Joyous Trusts" was Frederick Opper's subject in a 1902 series of cartoons. Predictably "B" stood for the Beef Trusts. The same Trust figure is back (compare it with the one in Opper's Roosevelt cartoon), although here Opper plays on the monopolist's traditional control over market prices rather than on the unsanitary practices of the packing industry.

ernment at all levels into a weapon for social justice. They included rural reformers, good government and moral uplift advocates, economic regulators, antitrusters, and political liberals and conservatives. Roosevelt's conservative faith in traditional institutions might easily have led him to oppose the reformers, but he was never a diehard who railed against change in any form. "The only true conservative is the man who resolutely set his face to the future," he once told a progressive supporter.

It was preoccupation with morality that brought the reform movement together and which attracted Roosevelt to progressivism. "His life, he felt, was a quest for the moral," wrote one biographer, John Blum. The reformers of the early twentieth century saw themselves rooting out evil, which more often than not they defined as "corporate arrogance." Thus, when Roosevelt set out to bust a trust, he did not always pick the biggest corporations. Rather, he picked the more notorious companies like the Northern Securities railroad combination, whose reputation for stock manipulation and rate gouging against farmers and small shippers had outraged popular opinion.

Corporate misconduct would not have spurred moral outrage had the misconduct not frequently resulted in tragedy. Seeking to maximize profits, a railroad might leave a road crossing unguarded; a water company might eliminate safeguards against typhoid fever. "Such incidents made the corporation look like a killer," wrote historian David Thelen. "These specific threats united all classes; anyone's child might be careless at a railroad crossing; and typhoid fever was no respecter of social origins."

The campaign for improved meat inspection had all the ingredients that aroused progressive ire. The packing industry fit Roosevelt's definition of a "bad" trust, since its disregard for even minimum health standards threatened all classes of Americans. The problem was particularly acute because the explosive growth of cities had created a huge demand for processed foods. Other food industries had better sanitary standards than the meat packers. Milk dealers, for example, regularly increased their profits by diluting their product, using chalk, plaster, and molasses to fortify the color and taste. A popular ditty of the day expressed the widespread skepticism with processed foods:

> Things are seldom what they seem;
> Skim milk masquerades as cream;
> Lard and soap we eat for cheese;
> Butter is but axle grease.

As a result, the public was prepared to think the worst of the meat industry.

Reeling from the impact of the Sinclair scandal, the packers agreed that improved federal inspection was the best way to restore public confidence in their products. J. Ogden Armour, head of the packing house that bore his name, defended the industry in a *Saturday Evening Post* article published soon after *The Jungle* appeared. Armour confidently invited the public to visit local packing plants "to see for yourself how the hated packer takes care of your meat supply." But he frankly admitted that "no packer can do an interstate or export business without government inspection." A serious decline in both domestic and foreign meat sales confirmed Armour's estimate of the need for improved inspection. Under the shadow Sinclair had cast, millions of Americans had altered their eating habits. Many foreign countries banned American meats. An industry representative confessed that the loss of public confidence was "hurting us very, very materially."

Thus the historical context surrounding the strident confrontation between reformers and packers reveals that the dramatic appearance of *The Jungle* was only the most conspicuous—and therefore the most obviously symbolic—event among a whole series of developments. All the necessary ingredients were on hand to produce legislation for more stringent federal inspection. And on hand was Theodore Roosevelt, the master political chef who would whip all the ingredients into a dish consumers could taste with confidence.

THE LEGISLATIVE JUNGLE

In order for public outrage to find a constructive outlet, politicians must translate that anger into law. And historians, for their part, must retrace the same path through the congressional maze in order to see what compromises and deals shaped the final bill. The legislative process is so constituted that willful minorities can sometimes thwart the will of determined majorities. Skillful manipulation of parliamentary rules, the committee system, the party caucus, nuisance amendments, filibuster and other legislative procedures—all these allow senators and representatives to protect special interests, promote their own causes, or delay the legislative process until support for a bill dissolves.

It is during the legislative phase that the historian discovers that support for improved inspection was not so universal as it seemed immediately after the publication of *The Jungle*. Meat inspection, like many reforms of the progressive era, raised issues more consequential than the sanitary standards of a single industry. Many of the larger issues affected the attitudes of the individual actors. President Roosevelt, for example, had on many occasions expressed his determination "to assert the sovereignty of the National Government by affirmative action" against unchecked corporate wealth and power. When added to the Hepburn bill allowing the government to set railroad shipping rates and the Pure Food and Drug Act, a new meat inspection bill would mark a major extension of public regulatory authority over private corporations.

Many people who favored improved inspection had given no indication that they would accept Roosevelt's sweeping definition of executive authority. The popular doctrine of *caveat emptor* (let the buyer beware) placed the burden for policing the marketplace on the consumer, not the government. As recently as 1895 in the case of *E. C. Knight,* the Supreme Court had severely restricted the possible area of government regulation over commerce. The packers, for their part, had given no indication that in agreeing to inspection reform they would accept a bill that in any way impinged on their control of the meat industry. So behind a mask of general agreement many actors entered the legislative process with conflicting motives and objectives. Much of that conflict would be expressed, not as disagreement on major legal or philosophical issues, but as seemingly petty bickering over procedural questions and minutiae of the proposed law.

From the outset Roosevelt indicated that he did not expect to achieve a satisfactory bill without a struggle. He knew that Sinclair's socialist writings would not persuade conservatives in Congress to support the tough bill he wanted. Nor had the government yet taken adequate steps to investigate its own misconduct. Immediately after the furor over *The Jungle,* Agriculture Secretary James Wilson had ordered an internal investigation of the Bureau of Animal Industry (BAI) which ran the inspection system. But Wilson and Roosevelt both suspected that the investigation would not "get to the bottom of this matter." Therefore, they asked Commissioner of Labor Charles P. Neill and New York attorney James Reynolds to undertake an independent investigation. Both men had been active in "good government" causes, though neither had any familiarity with the meat industry. Once they reported back, Roosevelt would have the evidence he needed to discredit either Sinclair as a sensationalist or the meatpackers as "malefactors of wealth."

Agriculture Department investigators confirmed the president's cynicism by whitewashing the BAI. They charged Sinclair with grossly exaggerating conditions in the plants, and treating "the worst . . . which could be found in any establishment as typical of the general conditions." Although they conceded that the system could stand reforming, they argued that Sinclair's accusations against federal inspectors were "willful and deliberate misrepresentations of fact."

Neill and Reynolds suggested that, if anything, Sinclair had understated the abominable conditions. Their official report rivaled his exposé in lurid details. Slime and manure covered the walks leading into the plants. The buildings lacked adequate ventilation and lighting. All the equipment—the conveyors, meat racks, cutting tables, and tubs—rotted under a blanket of filth and blood. Meat scraps for canning or sausages sat in piles on the grimy floors. Large portions of ground rope and pigskin went into the potted ham. Just as Sinclair had charged, foul conditions in the plant proved harmful to the health of both the workers and the consumers of the products they prepared.

The Neill-Reynolds report gave Roosevelt the big stick he liked to carry into any political fight. Should the packers prove recalcitrant he could threaten to make the secret report public. "It is absolutely necessary that we shall have legislation which will prevent the recurrence of these wrongs," he warned. In Senator Albert Beveridge of Indiana he found a willing ally, already at work on a new inspection bill. Beveridge, like Roosevelt, had caught the rising tide of progressive discontent over corporate misconduct. He sensed, too, that leadership on this issue would win him the popular acclaim he craved. Assisted by Agriculture Department experts, Beveridge had a bill drafted by the middle of May 1906. He urged Roosevelt to pave the way for Senate approval by releasing the damning Neill-Reynolds report.

For the moment, the politically adept Roosevelt heeded his own admonition to speak softly. Despite his customary bluster and pugnacious temperament, the president was actually a cautious man. An unnecessary confrontation with the powerful beef trust offended his sense of political expedience. Why waste his political ammunition if he could have his way without a fight? "The matter is of such far-reaching importance," he confided to Neill, "that it is out of the question to act hastily." Besides, having once been a rancher himself, he was reluctant to injure the livestock raisers, who bore no responsibility for the packers' scandalous behavior.

The packers had indicated that they would resist efforts to regulate their business. While Neill and Reynolds were in Chicago, packing house representatives had privately admitted that all was not well in their plants. One had begged Neill to withhold his report, promising in return that the packers would carry out any "reasonable, rational, and just recommendations" within thirty days. After that Neill and Reynolds would be free to reexamine the plants. When Neill refused, packer Louis Swift rushed off to confront the president. He found Roosevelt equally unsympathetic to any scheme involving voluntary compliance. The president assured Swift that he would settle for no less than legislation to "prevent the recurrence of these wrongs."

Beveridge was now ready with his bill. On May 21, he introduced it as a Senate amendment to the House Agricultural Appropriations bill. Why, one might well ask, did such a major reform make its debut in the form of a tacked-on amendment to a House bill? Here, we begin to see how the legislative process affects political outcomes. Beveridge recognized that effective inspection required adequate funds. Previous Congresses had undermined the system by refusing to vote the money needed. Many smaller plants had no inspection at all, and the largest ones had no inspectors at night. Beveridge, therefore, had proposed to shift the funding from the small amount allotted in the House Appropriations bill to a head fee charged for each animal inspected. As the industry grew, so would the funds for the Bureau of Animal Industry. But since the Constitution requires the House to initiate all money bills, Beveridge had to amend a House bill pending before the Senate rather than introduce a separate measure.

Beveridge included two other important changes. The old law did nothing to force the packers to indicate on the label of canned meats either the date on which they were processed or the actual contents. (Neill and Reynolds, for example, discovered that the product called "potted chicken" contained no chicken at all.) The new law required dating and accurate labelling of the contents. It also invested the secretary of agriculture with broad authority to establish regulations for sanitary standards in the plants. Inspectors could then enforce those conditions as well as insure the health of animals prior to and after slaughtering. If the owners challenged an inspector's ruling, the secretary had authority to make a "final and conclusive" ruling.

Yet this comprehensive bill, which Beveridge confidently introduced in May, was hardly the same bill Roosevelt signed on June 30, 1906. The small head fee had been replaced by an annual $3 million appropriation. The secretary of agriculture no longer had "final and conclusive" authority, for the federal courts were given the right to review his rulings. And the final measure said nothing about dating canned meats. In those discrepancies undoubtedly lies the source of Senator Nelson's dismay with the outcome of the meat inspection battle. What the historian must now explain is why the reformers who entered the fray holding most of the cards in their hands had given in on so many crucial points.

The battle actually began well enough for Roosevelt and Senate re-

formers. When the packers first tried to stall Beveridge with promises
to make voluntary improvements, the senator threatened them with
more damaging disclosures. To show he meant business, he had Neill
brief lobbyists for livestock raisers and senators from western cattle states
on the contents of his report. The packers had counted on those men as
allies in their fight against overly stringent federal regulation. But faced
with the prospect of more adverse publicity, the meat and cattle interests
beat a hot retreat. The Beveridge Amendment passed in the Senate
without a single negative vote. Never known for his modesty, Beveridge
touted his measure as "the most perfect inspection bill in the world. . . ."

Roosevelt hoped that the smashing Senate victory would lead to
equally swift action by the House. The packers, however, had no intention of giving up without a fight. In the House, they had far more
substantial support, particularly on the critical Agriculture Committee.
Its chairman, James Wadsworth, a Republican from New York, was
himself a cattle breeder. He regarded *The Jungle* as a "horrid, untruthful
book" which, he claimed, had temporarily unhinged the president. To
orchestrate the opposition, Wadsworth could count on the unflagging
support of "Blond Billy" Lorimer, a senior committee member, a notorious grafter, and the Republican representative from Chicago's packing
house district. The Beveridge bill aroused Lorimer like a red flag waved
before a bull: "This bill will never be reported by my committee—not
if little Willie can help it."

The packers had another, even more powerful, ally—time. Summer
adjournment for Congress was only six weeks away. In the days before
air conditioning, most public officials left Washington to escape the
oppressive summer heat. While Congress vacationed, the public would
most likely forget all about *The Jungle,* and as popular outrage dissipated,
so would much of the pressure for reform. Only new and more damaging disclosures could rekindle the fervor that had swept Beveridge's
amendment through the Senate.

So long as the Neill-Reynolds report remained secret, Roosevelt could
save it as the ultimate disclosure to arouse the public. But by the time
the Beveridge bill reached the House, the impatient Upton Sinclair had
reneged on an earlier promise to Roosevelt that he would remain silent
until his accusations had been proven. To goad the president, he published new charges embellished with even more lurid details. Finally,
unable to contain his frustration, he leaked the details of the Neill-
Reynolds report to *The New York Times,* and newspapers across the
country had picked up the story. Having lost its shock value, Roosevelt's
big stick appeared more like a little twig.

at this point, when no accommodation seems possible, the negotiation and compromise begin.

Faced with Roosevelt's demand for quick action on the Beveridge bill and the Wadsworth-Lorimer substitute, the House voted to send both measures to the Agriculture Committee. In doing so, it followed a well-established procedure for reviewing legislation through its committee system. No handbook exists that explains how the committee system works; nor does the Constitution make any mention of it. Congress first established committees to streamline its functioning. Rather than have the entire body deliberate every bill, these smaller groups consider measures relevant to their areas of special interest before making recommendations to the entire House or Senate. A trade bill may go to the Commerce or Foreign Relations Committees, a pork barrel water project to the Rivers and Harbors Committee, and a farm bill to the Agriculture Committee. Those bills encompassing a variety of features have to go through several committees. All bills must eventually pass through the Rules Committee, which establishes parliamentary rules, such as the time allotted for floor debate or the conditions for amendment.

Yet if the committee system promotes efficiency, it also can become an undemocratic process used by a handful of representatives or senators to defeat a popular bill, either by eliminating or amending its central provisions or by refusing to return it to the floor for a vote. In sending the Beveridge bill to the Agriculture Committee, the House had routed it through an enemy stronghold. Wadsworth and Lorimer were both members of the committee; they had only to gain ten of eighteen votes from their colleagues in order to replace the Beveridge bill with their substitute. Other members of the House might never have a chance to vote on the original bill, even if a majority favored it.

Diligently, Wadsworth and Lorimer set out to undermine the Beveridge bill. They opened their attack by holding committee hearings to which they invited only witnesses sympathetic to the packers. Hearings are ostensibly a means to collect information that guides Congress as it formulates legislation. But they can be used for many other purposes—to delay, to discredit opponents, or to gain publicity for committee members. So for four days the Agriculture Committee heard a parade of witnesses defend the packers. The testimony of Thomas Wilson, a leading packer lobbyist, set the tone. Fed leading questions by Lorimer and Wadsworth, he attacked the Neill-Reynolds report as a "compendium of inaccuracies of fact," impugned the two men's competence, and stressed the "non-practical nature" of their background. And though under oath, Wilson swore that no condemned meat ever entered the market! The packers, he explained, were reasonable, public-spirited men. They would support a fair measure, such as Wadsworth and Lorimer had proposed, but not the government interference Beveridge called for.

More moderate committee members finally insisted that the committee hear opposing witnesses as well. That suited Wadsworth and Lorimer, for the longer the hearings lasted, the closer Congress came to adjourning. They also gained an opportunity to confront Neill and Reynolds directly. Neill attempted to refute criticism of his impracticality by stating that "we only reported what we could see, hear, and smell." He soon withered, however, under an unending barrage of hostile questions from the chairman and his crony. Reynolds, the Washington lawyer, was more accustomed to such abusive tactics. He coolly pointed out that, while he had based his conclusions on direct observation, Wilson had relied solely on hearsay gathered from packing house employees.

As the hearings closed on June 9, Wadsworth eked out a narrow margin of victory, his substitute bill passing by only eleven to seven. Four Republicans had been so disgusted by the "bullyragging" aimed at Neill and Reynolds, they had voted against the substitute. The president exploded when he saw Wadsworth's handiwork. The provisions in the new bill struck him as "so bad that . . . if they had been deliberately designed to prevent remedying of the evils complained of, they could not have been worse."

Historians recognize that parties to a negotiation often inflate their initial demands to allow room for compromise. Still, Wadsworth and Lorimer had been unusually brazen in attacking the heart of Beveridge's inspection system. In their substitute, they made no provision for night inspection. Lorimer had also included a clause that waived for one year the civil service requirements for new inspectors. In that year, he could personally control the list of new appointments. The BAI would be saddled with political hacks loyal only to Lorimer and the packers.

Two provisions particularly infuriated Roosevelt. The agriculture department had suggested as a compromise that Congress authorize an annual appropriation, but also grant the secretary standby power to levy a head fee if the appropriation proved inadequate. Lorimer and Wadsworth insisted on an annual sum of $1 million, scarcely enough to meet current costs. And once again, they had shifted final authority under the act from the secretary of agriculture to the federal courts.

The president did not deny that the packers, like any one else, were entitled to "due process." But he also believed that court review should be restricted to a narrow procedural question: Had the secretary been fair in reaching his decision? The committee granted the courts power to rule on substantive questions of fact. "You would have the functions of the Secretary of Agriculture narrowly limited so as to be purely ministerial," Roosevelt told Wadsworth, "and when he declared a given slaughter house unsanitary, or a given product unwholesome, acting upon the judgment of government experts, you would put on a judge, who had no knowledge of conditions, the burden of stating whether the Secretary was right."

Wadsworth refused to be cowed by the president's angry outburst. "You are wrong, very, very wrong in your estimate of the committee's bill," he responded. He even criticized the president for "impugning the sincerity and competency of a Committee of the House of Representatives" and called his substitute measure "as perfect a piece of legislation to carry into effect your own views on this question as was ever prepared by a committee of Congress." Lorimer, too, vowed to continue his defiance of the president.

All that sniping would not deserve so much notice except for one important factor—all of the antagonists belonged to the same party. The meat inspection battle had pitted a popular and powerful Republican president and his Senate friends against the Republican majority in the House. Senator Henry Cabot Lodge of Massachusetts, perhaps the president's closest political friend, had made the intraparty schism that much more public when he denounced the "greedy" packers for their attempt to derail the reform bill. Sensing the growing embarrassment among Republicans, House Democrats sought to deepen the rift. They insisted that the Beveridge bill be given a full vote on the House floor, even though it had not been voted out of the Agriculture Committee. "Czar" Joseph Cannon, the dictatorial Republican speaker, temporarily retrieved the situation for his party by ruling the motion out of order.

Cannon was now the man on the hot seat. The fight among Republican factions threatened to become a donnybrook that might destroy the political empire he had so ruthlessly built and ruled. His personal and political sympathies lay with the packers and conservatives who opposed government regulation of the free enterprise system. His power came, however, not from leading any particular faction, but from bringing together all the elements of his party into a unified machine. As speaker and chairman of the powerful Rules Committee, he had the means to keep unruly congressmen in line because he handed out all committee assignments. Members of Congress prefer to sit on those committees that deal with issues important to their constituents. Industrial state representatives may want Labor or Commerce, while a representative from a mining state like Nevada might prefer Interior. To earn Cannon's favor, many representatives found themselves forced to vote with the speaker and against their consciences.

With his power base shaken, Cannon sought some way to break the impasse between Republican reformers and conservatives. Since Roosevelt, too, had an interest in party unity, the speaker went to see him at the White House. The president proved amenable to a suitable compromise. They agreed that Wisconsin Representative Henry Adams, a moderate and a member of the Agriculture Committee, was the best person to work out the details. Adams had endorsed earlier compromises and, as a former food commissioner and champion of pure foods legislation, he was free of the taint that clung to Wadsworth and Lorimer. Adams, Reynolds, and agriculture department lawyers had soon produced a new bill. From the Wadsworth-Lorimer measure, they dropped the civil service waiver, added a provision for dating canned meats, gave the secretary standby fee authority, and eliminated the section on broad court review. Roosevelt declared their measure "as good as the Beveridge amendment."

All those negotiations took place while Wadsworth and Lorimer were away from Washington, but when they returned, they vowed to reverse the president's apparent victory. Cannon, however, had no appetite for further infighting. He urged the Agriculture Committee to work out yet another compromise. Wadsworth and Lorimer immediately deleted the secretary's standby fee authority from the Adams bill, though they did raise the appropriation to $3 million, more than enough to meet current costs. Their axe next fell on the dating requirement and, in return, they kept out the civil service waiver, while explicitly authorizing inspectors to visit plants "day or night."

One crucial issue remained. What would be the scope of court review? Wadsworth was willing to drop his demand for broad review if the president took out the Senate's phrase giving the secretary "final and conclusive" authority. Roosevelt agreed to that horse trade, which one historian aptly described as "purposeful obscurity." To achieve his larger goal of improved inspection, Roosevelt was willing to let the courts decide the actual scope of judicial review. He regretted the absence of mandatory dating, but did not consider the issue sufficiently important to upset the hard-won compromise. Roosevelt often criticized those diehards who would go down fighting for a "whole loaf," when "half a loaf" was the best they could expect. With the president behind the final committee bill, the entire House passed it on June 19.

The battle was not yet won, however, for Beveridge and the reformers in the Senate continued their fight, threatening to keep the two Houses deadlocked until recess. The Indiana senator had strong support from Redfield Proctor, Chairman of the Senate Agriculture Committee. Though nearly crippled by rheumatism, Proctor had stayed on in Washington to assure passage of an effective meat bill. Like Beveridge, he believed a consumer had the right to know whether canned meats were five days or five years old. And if the government stamp would be worth millions in free advertising for the packers, Proctor thought the industry, not the taxpayer, should bear the cost. The Senate, therefore, voted to reject the House bill in favor of its own.

Once again, process more than substance determined the outcome. When the two Houses pass different versions of the same bill, they create a conference committee to iron out the discrepancies. With time too short for long wrangling over each point, Roosevelt intervened. He first urged the House members to reconsider their position on dating and fees. They refused so vehemently that Roosevelt turned to the Senate conferees instead. Proctor and Beveridge recognized that further resistance meant total defeat. On June 29, the day before adjournment, they raised the white flag "to make sure of the greater good," and the Senate passed the House bill. The next day, after Roosevelt signed, the Meat Inspection Act of 1906 became the law of the land.

OUT OF THE JUNGLE?

We might think that the passage of the new act was cause to uncork the champagne for a celebration. Despite their opposition to certain compromises, Roosevelt and Beveridge had endorsed the final measure as a triumph for reform. If historians let the case rest here, however, they would not know whether to accept Roosevelt and Beveridge's enthusiasm or Knute Nelson's despair. Who, after all, had won this legislative battle? Certainly, reformers would be heartened to see that the old toothless law had been replaced by a system that required "day and night" inspection; banned uninspected meats from interstate commerce; gave the secretary authority to establish sanitary standards; and provided ample funding for the immediate future at least. Yet the final bill contained no provisions for head fees or dating and still left the courts as the final judge of the secretary of agriculture's rulings.

In determining who could claim victory, Roosevelt, Beveridge, and Nelson had to base their judgment only on the provisions of the final act. Yet the real significance of legislation cannot be determined until its effectiveness in practice has been measured. A law must be applied by the executive branch and tested in the courts. In the case of the Meat Inspection Act, future presidents might appoint agriculture secretaries sympathetic to the packers. The standards established might be either too vague or too lax to enforce proper sanitation. More important, the courts might yet call Roosevelt's bluff and interpret their prerogative for review broadly. Only after observing the operation of the new system over time can the historian decide whether the compromises vindicated Roosevelt or proved "half a loaf" worse than none at all.

As it happens, the subsequent history of meat inspection confirms the wisdom of the president's compromise strategy. The $3 million appropriation more than adequately funded the "beefed up" inspection system. By the end of 1907, Secretary Wilson reported that new and more efficient procedures had substantially reduced operating costs. The BAI spent only $2 million the first year, and costs dropped even though the industry grew.

Roosevelt had been shrewdest in his resort to "purposeful obscurity." The packers made no attempt to dismantle the inspection system in the courts—the first important case did not arise for over ten years. Then in 1917, in *United States* v. *Cudahy Packing Co., et al.,* a federal judge affirmed the secretary's authority. Congress, he ruled, could "delegate authority to the proper administrative officer to make effective rules. . . ." Two years later the Supreme Court adopted "narrow" rather than "broad" review. In an opinion for a unanimous Court in the case of *Houston* v. *St. Louis Independent Packing Company,* Justice John Clarke wrote that a decision over proper labelling of meat "is a question of fact, the determination of which is committed to the Secretary of Agriculture . . . , and the law is that the conclusion of the head of an executive department . . . will not be reviewed by the Courts, where it is fairly arrived at with substantial support." After thirteen years, the reformers could finally claim victory, though the outcome by then was scarcely in doubt. Not until 1968 did another generation of reformers spurred by Ralph Nader find it necessary to launch a campaign to strengthen the inspection system. Then, they sought higher standards for meats subject only to state inspection.

The controversy over meat inspection reminds the historian that when a legislative issue involves the disposition of economic and political power, all three branches of government influence the outcome. That does not mean, however, that their roles are equal. In this case a politically shrewd and popular executive had shown greater capacity to affect the political process at critical moments. Roosevelt used the power of his

Following the public outcry, meat packers tried to create a better image of conditions in their plants and the thoroughness of government inspection. In fact, when this picture was taken in 1906, postmortem inspection as shown here had not been at all common.

office, his control over the Republican party, and his ability to generate publicity to overcome opposition on both sides. Beveridge admitted that even in the face of widespread public outrage Congress would not have acted "if the President had not picked up his big stick and smashed the packers and their agents in the House and Senate over the head with it." Yet Roosevelt prevailed in the end only because he recognized compromise as an essential feature of the political process. He had yielded on points he considered less consequential in order to achieve his larger objective.

Just as historians must expand their field of vision to weigh the effects on a law of all three branches of government, so too they must establish the historical context of a bill over time. As we discovered, the meat scandal had a long history before the publication of *The Jungle.* We discovered, too, near-unanimous support for stricter inspection, though little understanding of what form a new bill might take. Only when the bill made its way through the legislative process did we find that the widespread cry for reform masked a deep conflict over the roles of private and public agencies in determining satisfactory standards. The packers wanted the benefits of a new bill without having to relinquish control over any aspect of their business. In addition to chastening the packers, the reformers sought to assert the authority of the federal government to police "corporate arrogance." The success of their efforts remained in doubt until well after the bill's enactment, when the Supreme Court adopted "narrow review."

It becomes clear, then, why the Meat Inspection Act could generate both Beveridge's enthusiasm and Nelson's dismay. All the interested parties had gained some, though not all, of their objectives. With public confidence restored, the packers could anticipate renewed growth for their industry. Reformers could, however, hold them to higher standards of accountability. The Republicans had averted a destructive intraparty battle and had emerged as spokesmen for the public interest, despite Wadsworth and Lorimer. Roosevelt had strengthened his control over the party, while extending the scope of his executive authority. Above all, he had demonstrated a capacity for effective leadership. The public gained, too, for they could sit down to dinner having to worry less what their canned foods contained besides meat.

The Meat Inspection Act of 1906 had been a total victory for neither reformers nor packers. As is so often the case, the political system achieved results only after the visible symbols and myths of public discourse had been negotiated, debated, and compromised in the procedural tangle at the heart of the legislative process. Gone from our analysis are those wonderful symbols of corporate villainy and presidential heroism. But in their place we have a more complex story revealing the political processes that shape our history.

Additional Reading

This chapter grew out of an Early Concentration History Seminar at Yale. To give students their own experience at reconstructing history from primary sources, Mark Lytle put together a package of documents on the Meat Inspection Act of 1906. Many of those students showed remarkable initiative in locating additional materials. In particular, they discovered the section in John Braeman, "The Square Deal in Action: A Case Study in the Growth of the 'National Police Power,' " that discusses the constitutional questions the new meat inspection law raised. That essay appears in Braeman, et al., *Change and Continuity in Twentieth Century America,* vol. 1 (Columbus, Oh., 1964), 34–80.

Any reader interested in a similar exploration of secondary and primary materials might begin with Upton Sinclair, *The Jungle* (New York, 1906) and *The Brass Check* (Pasadena, Calif., 1919), often autobiographical. On Theodore Roosevelt and the politics of progressivism see George Mowry, *The Era of Theodore Roosevelt* (New York, 1958), John Blum, *The Republican Roosevelt* (Cambridge, Mass., 1958), and Gabriel Kolko, *The Triumph of Conservatism* (New York, 1964). After going through the documents for themselves our students concluded that Mowry's cursory treatment missed much of the significant political maneuvering and that Kolko misused documents and misinterpreted the meaning of the act. Another helpful secondary work is Joel Tarr, *Boss Politics* (Chicago, 1964), which examines the career of "Blond Billy" Lorimer. David Thelen, "Not Classes, But Issues," which first appeared in *The Journal of American History,* vol. LVI (September 1969), 323–334, offers a stimulating review of the many explanations of progressivism, as well as a substantial interpretation of his own.

The documents in this case study are available in good research libraries and can be readily assembled. Such newspapers as the *New York Times, Chicago Tribune, Chicago Record-Herald,* and the *Chicago Inter-Ocean* covered the entire controversy, though the Chicago papers did so in greater depth. Much of Roosevelt's thinking can be found in Elting Morison, et al., *The Letters of Theodore Roosevelt,* vol. 5 (Cambridge, Mass., 1953). Access to some contemporary magazines including *Everybody's Magazine, The Lancet, Cosmopolitan,* and specifically J. Ogden Armour, "The Packers and the People," *Saturday Evening Post,* CLXXVII, no. 37 (March 10, 1906)—a key document in Kolko's interpretation —will provide a picture of the debate over meat packing and other muckraking issues.

This chapter drew most heavily on government documents. Readers should see *Congressional Record,* 59th Congress, 1st Session; House Committee on Agriculture, 59th Congress, 1st Session, *Hearings . . . on the So-called "Beveridge Amendment" to the Agriculture Appropriation Bill—H.R. 18537* (Washington, D.C., 1906); Bureau of Animal Industry, *Twenty-third Annual Report* (Washington, D.C., 1906); *House Document 873,* 59th Congress, 1st Session (June 1906)—the Neill-Reynolds Report and Theodore Roosevelt's cover letter; and the Agriculture Committee's minority and majority reports in *House Report* 4935, pts. 1 and 2, 59th Congress, 1st Session (June 14 & 15, 1906) and *House Report,* 3468, pt. 2, 59th Congress, 1st Session (June 15, 1906). Additional materials can be found in the Roosevelt Papers (Harvard University) and Beveridge Papers (University of Indiana).

Finally, thanks go to Stuart Drake, Boris Feldman, William Garfinkel, and other Early Concentration students whose research helped locate relevant documents used in this chapter. Professor Lewis Gould of the University of Texas at Austin generously offered some important revisions. Students interested in the interpretations of progressive reform could profitably read Lewis Gould, ed., *The Progressive Era* (1973).

CHAPTER

TEN

Sacco and Vanzetti

In the years after World War I, crime statistics curved sharply upwards. Armed robberies rose at an alarming rate, and anyone handling large sums of money had reason to exercise caution. On most paydays Frederick Parmenter, paymaster for the Slater and Morrill Shoe Company of South Braintree, Massachusetts, would have used a truck to deliver his money boxes to the lower factory building. Only a few months earlier, in December 1919, a brazen gang of bandits had attempted a daylight payroll heist in nearby Bridgewater. The bandits had fled empty-handed and no one was hurt in the gunfight; still, area businesses were uneasy. On the morning of April 15, 1920, however, the robbery attempt must have been far from Parmenter's mind. It was a mild spring day and he set out on foot for the lower factory building with his assistant, Alessandro Berardelli, walking ahead.

Halfway to their destination, a man approached Berardelli from the side of the road, spoke to him briefly, and then suddenly shot him dead. As Parmenter turned to flee, the bandits fired again, mortally wounding him. A blue Buick pulled out from its parking place. The two assailants and their lookout jumped into the car and fled toward Bridgewater. To discourage any pursuers, the bandits threw tacks onto the streets. Two miles from Braintree they abandoned the Buick and escaped in another car.

Bridgewater Police Chief Michael Stewart thought he recognized a familiar pattern in the Braintree crime. The same foreigners who bungled the December heist, he guessed, had probably pulled off the Braintree job. Stewart's investigation put him on the trail of Mike Boda, an Italian anarchist. Unable to locate Boda, Stewart kept watch on a car Boda had left at Simon Johnson's garage for repairs. Whoever came to get the car would, according to Stewart's theory, become a prime suspect in both crimes.

His expectations were soon rewarded. On May 5, 1920, Boda and three other Italians called for the car. Mrs. Johnson immediately slipped next door to alert the police, but the four men did not wait for her return. Boda and his friend Orciana left on a motorcycle, while their companions walked to a nearby streetcar stop. Apparently nervous, they moved on to another stop a half mile away. There they boarded the trolley for Brockton. As the car moved down Main Street, Police Officer Michael Connolly climbed on. Having spotted the two foreigners, he arrested them. When they asked why, he replied curtly, "suspicious characters."

Thus began the epic story of Nicola Sacco and Bartolomeo Vanzetti, two obscure Italian aliens who became the focal point of one of the most controversial episodes in American history. Within little more than a year after their arrest a jury deliberated for just five hours before convicting both men of robbery and murder. Such a quick decision came as a surprise, particularly in a trial that had lasted seven weeks, heard over 160 witnesses, and gained national attention.

Nor did the controversy end with the jury's decision. Six years of appeals turned a simple incident of robbery and murder into a major international uproar. The Italian government indicated that it had followed the case with interest. Thousands of liberals, criminal lawyers, legal scholars, civil libertarians, radicals, labor leaders, prominent socialites, and spokesmen for immigrant groups rallied to Sacco and Vanzetti's cause. Arrayed against them was an equally imposing collection of the nation's legal, social, academic, and political elite.

The case climaxed on April 9, 1927. Having denied some eight appeals, trial judge Webster Thayer sentenced Sacco and Vanzetti to die in the electric chair. His action triggered months of protests and political activities. Around Charleston Prison and the State House in Boston Sacco and Vanzetti's supporters marched, collected petitions, and walked picket lines. Occasionally violence erupted between protestors and authorities, as mounted police attacked crowds in Boston, clubbed them off the streets in New York. Final appeals were in vain: Governor Alvan Fuller would not grant clemency and the United States Supreme Court refused to stay the execution.

On August 22, the morning before Sacco and Vanzetti were scheduled to die, Governor Fuller fooled few in the gathered crowd with his false cheer as he bounded up the State House steps. All weekend two thousand heavily armed police had patrolled Boston. Planes circled overhead to spot any outbreaks of violence. Charleston Prison, where Sacco and Vanzetti waited, appeared like an embattled fortress. Ropes circled the prison grounds to keep protestors at bay as eight hundred armed guards

Nicola Sacco and Bartolomeo Vanzetti, accused of committing a payroll robbery of the Slater and Morrill Shoe Company in South Braintree, Massachusetts. When police asked witnesses to identify the two men, instead of using a line-up, officers made Sacco and Vanzetti stand alone in the middle of a room and pose as bandits.

walked the walls. That evening 15,000 people gathered in New York's Union Square to stand in silent vigil. Similar crowds stood by in major European cities. All awaited the news of the fate of "a good shoemaker and a poor fish peddler."

The historian confronting that extraordinary event faces some perplexing questions. How did a case of robbery and murder become an international *cause célèbre?* How was it that two Italian immigrants living on the fringe of American society had become the focus of a debate that brought the nation's cherished legal institutions under attack? Or as one legal historian rhetorically posed the question:

Why all this fuss over a couple of 'wops', who after years in this country had not even made application to become citizens; who had not learned to use our language even modestly well; who did not believe in our form of government; . . . who were confessed slackers and claimed to be pacifists but went armed with deadly weapons for the professed purpose of defending their individual personal property in violation of all the principles they preached?

THE LAWYERS' BRIEF: THE LEGAL SYSTEM FAILED

Lawyers reviewing the case might answer those questions by arguing that the Sacco and Vanzetti case raised fundamental doubts about the tradition of Anglo-Saxon justice so venerated in the United States. More specifically, many legal scholars have stated then and since that the trial and appeals process failed to meet the minimum standards of fairness required in a criminal case, particularly one that involved a capital crime placing human lives in jeopardy.

Indeed, it was Felix Frankfurter, an eminent Harvard Law School professor and later Supreme Court Justice, who provoked much of the controversy. In January 1927, with final appeal still pending before the Massachusetts Supreme Judicial Court, Frankfurter published a lengthy article in the *Atlantic Monthly* in which he questioned the proceedings in the original trial, the conduct of Judge Thayer and the prosecutor, and the state's refusal to grant either clemency or a new trial. Sacco and Vanzetti, he argued persuasively, had never been proven guilty. The weight of evidence did not sustain the jury's verdict. In fact, all the evidence indicated that a gang of professional bandits, most still at large, had committed both the bungled holdup at Bridgewater and the crimes at South Braintree.

Even a brief examination of the trial record indicates that the prosecution had a flimsy case, flawed by irregularities in procedure that arose before the trial began. The day Chief Stewart ordered officer Connolly to arrest Sacco and Vanzetti he had no evidence, other than his suspicion of foreign radicals, to associate either man with the crimes. The investigation, however, had at first sustained Stewart's theory. Both suspects carried loaded pistols and extra ammunition. Together with Boda, Orciana, and other Italian anarchists, Sacco and Vanzetti could have formed a gang. Stewart and District Attorney Frederick Katzmann, who first questioned the suspects, knew both had lied about their friends, associates, and reasons for trying to reclaim the car. Vanzetti, for example, at first denied that he knew Boda.

But suspicious behavior was one thing; proof that Sacco and Vanzetti had committed the Braintree murders was another. The district attorney's office and the police had to build a stronger case. In 1920 the conduct of such an investigation permitted far greater latitude than the law does today. The Supreme Court decisions in *Miranda* (1966) and *Escobedo* (1964) established that criminal suspects have the right to maintain silence, to know their rights, and to stand in an impartial lineup for identification. None of those guarantees existed in 1920. All the same, Katzmann and Stewart showed unusual zeal in constructing a case against Sacco and Vanzetti. At no time during the first two days of questioning did they tell either suspect why they had been arrested. Chief Stewart repeatedly asked them not about the robbery, but about their political beliefs. The district attorney did obliquely inquire about their activities on April 15, though he never mentioned the Braintree crimes. Furthermore, when the police asked witnesses to identify the suspects, they did not use a lineup. Instead, they forced Sacco and Vanzetti to stand alone in the middle of a room posing as bandits.

As the investigation continued, the case against Sacco and Vanzetti came close to collapsing for lack of incriminating evidence. Of the five suspected gang members all but Vanzetti could prove they had not been in Bridgewater during the December holdup attempt. Despite an intensive search of the suspects' belongings, including a trunk sent to Italy, Katzmann was never able to trace the money, even among groups with whom they were associated. Nor could he establish that Sacco or Vanzetti had in any way changed lifestyles since the crime. Fingerprint experts found no matches between prints lifted from the abandoned Buick and those taken from the suspects.

Faced with all those gaps in the evidence, Katzmann still decided, first, to prosecute Vanzetti for the December Bridgewater holdup and, second, to charge both Sacco and Vanzetti with the Braintree murders in April. Arguing the Bridgewater case in June 1920 before Judge Webster Thayer, Katzmann presented a weak case against Vanzetti on the charge of assault with intent to rob. Still, he did manage to make the jury aware of Vanzetti's anarchist views and persuade them to convict. Judge Thayer then meted out an unusually severe sentence (twelve to fifteen years) to a defendant with no criminal record for a crime in which no one was hurt and nothing was stolen.

That conviction allowed Katzmann to proceed with the second trial, to be held in the suburban town of Dedham. Since this would be a special session of the superior court, a judge had to be appointed to hear the case. Judge Thayer asked his old college friend, Chief Justice John Aiken, for the assignment, even though he had presided over Vanzetti's earlier trial and could scarcely consider himself impartial. Thus, the second trial opened with a judge who already believed unequivocally in the defendants' guilt.

At Dedham, District Attorney Katzmann built his case around three major categories of evidence: (1) eyewitness identification of Sacco and Vanzetti at the scene; (2) expert ballistics testimony establishing Sacco's gun as the weapon that fired the fatal shot at Berardelli and Vanzetti's gun as one taken from Berardelli during the robbery; (3) the defendants' evasive behavior both before and after arrest as evidence of what is legally termed "consciousness of guilt."

Anyone who examines the trial record closely cannot escape Frankfurter's conclusion that the prosecution never proved either man guilty. In the matter of eyewitness identification the defense successfully impugned the testimony placing Sacco and Vanzetti at the scene. One witness, Mary Splaine, claimed to have observed the shooting from a window in the Slater and Morrill factory for no longer than 3 seconds at a distance of about 60 feet. In that time she watched an unknown man in a car travelling about 18 mph. Immediately after the crime Splaine had difficulty describing any of the bandits, but one year later she picked out Sacco, vividly recalling such details as his "good-sized" left hand. She refused to recant her testimony even after the defense demonstrated that Sacco had relatively small hands.

Louis Pelzer testified for the prosecution that upon hearing shots he had stood for at least a minute at a window from which he observed the crime. He pointed to Sacco as the "dead image" of the man who shot Berardelli. Two defense witnesses completely controverted Pelzer's story. Upon hearing the shots, they recalled, Pelzer had immediately hidden under his workbench—hardly a vantage point from which to make a clear identification. Rather than condemn Pelzer for perjury on this and other points, Katzmann praised him for explaining away his lies.

Lola Andrews, a third witness, claimed that on the morning of the crime she had stopped near the factory to ask directions from a dark-haired man working under a car. She later identified Sacco as that man. Defense lawyers challenged both her testimony and character. A companion, Mrs. Julia Campbell, denied that Andrews had ever spoken to the man under the car. Instead, she had approached a pale, sickly young man who was standing nearby. Other witnesses had recalled the same pale person. A second friend swore that he had heard Andrews say after she returned from police headquarters that "the government took me down and wanted me to recognize those men and I don't know a thing about them." Nor did Andrews's reputation as a streetwalker enhance her credibility. The prosecutor had clearly tampered with this witness. Yet in his summation he told the jury that in eleven years as district attorney he had not "ever before . . . laid eye or given ear to so convincing a witness as Lola Andrews."

Against Katzmann's dubious cast the defense produced seventeen of its own witnesses who provided the defendants with alibis for the day or who had seen the crime, but not Sacco or Vanzetti. One, an official of the Italian Consulate in Boston, confirmed Sacco's claim that he had been in Boston on April 15 acquiring a passport. The official remembered Sacco because he had tried to use a picture over ten inches square for his passport photo. "Since such a large photograph had never been presented before . . . ," the official recalled, "I took it in and showed it to the Secretary of the Consulate. We laughed and talked over the incident. I remember observing the date . . . on a large pad calendar." Others said they had met Sacco at a luncheon banquet that day. Witnesses for Vanzetti claimed to have bought fish from him. Katzmann could only try to persuade the jury that the witnesses had little reason to connect such a mundane event with a specific date.

In the face of contradictory eyewitness testimony, the ballistics evidence should have decided the case. To prove murder, Katzmann had to show that the fatal shot striking Berardelli had come from Sacco's gun. Ballistics specialists can often identify the gun that fired a bullet by characteristic marks, as distinct as fingerprints, that the barrel and hammer make on the projectile and casing. Katzmann brought to the stand Captains William Proctor and Charles Van Amburgh, two experts experienced in police work. Both connected the fatal bullet to a Colt pistol similar to and possibly the same as Sacco's. But neither made a definitive statement. "It is consistent with being fired by that pistol," Proctor replied to Katzmann. Van Amburgh also indicated some ambiguity: "I am inclined to believe that it was fired . . . from this pistol."

For unknown reasons defense attorneys never pursued the equivocation of those testimonies. Instead, the defense called its own ballistics specialists who stated with absolute certainty that the fatal bullet could not have come from Sacco's gun. In addition they controverted the prosecutor's claim that Vanzetti had taken Berardelli's gun during the holdup. Shortly before his murder Berardelli had left his pistol at a repair shop to have the hammer fixed. Shop records, though imprecise, indicated that the gun was .32 caliber, not a .38 such as Vanzetti was carrying. The records also supported Mrs. Berardelli's sworn testimony that her husband had never reclaimed his pistol. The defense then argued that the hammer on Vanzetti's gun had never been repaired.

Since the defense had weakened the ballistics evidence, Katzmann based his case primarily on "consciousness of guilt." He had to persuade the jury that Sacco and Vanzetti, in their behavior before and after arrest, had acted like men guilty of a crime. Evidence in such arguments is generally circumstantial, based on interpretations of individual behavior rather than on facts. Most often prosecutors use "consciousness of guilt" to corroborate other facets of their case, since circumstantial evidence alone does not adequately prove guilt. In the Dedham trial Katzmann used this dimension of his case with telling effect. Both men had been armed when arrested. They had lied about their movements that day, about their associates, and about places they had visited. Neither could deny their strange behavior during the visit to Johnson's garage.

To explain that behavior the defense was forced to introduce the inflammatory issue of the defendants' political radicalism. Both men had adopted an anarchist philosophy and played active roles in the labor unrest of the era. As a result they had been greatly alarmed by the severe government crackdown on radicals that began in 1919. When officer Connolly arrested them, Sacco and Vanzetti assumed that they, too, had been snared in the government's dragnet. Of course they felt guilty, not as criminals, but as alien radicals. Constant questioning about their political beliefs merely confirmed their fears. They lied to protect friends, relatives, and political associates, the defense argued, not to cover up any crime.

Similar fears accounted for their peculiar actions at Johnson's garage. Shortly before his arrest, Vanzetti had conferred with the Italian Defense Committee of New York, then inquiring into the fate of fellow anarchist Andrea Salsedo. The committee knew only that Salsedo was being held by Justice Department agents in a New York jail, and members warned Vanzetti that he and his friends might be in similar danger. Prudence dictated that they dispose of all potentially incriminating political literature. Vanzetti soon discovered the urgency of their advice when he learned that Salsedo had "mysteriously" fallen to his death from a twelfth-floor window. That was when the defendants and their friends had gone to retrieve Boda's car in order to carry away the pamphlets stored in their homes. Wary of police surveillance, they had reason to behave suspiciously.

Sacco and Vanzetti had plausible, though far from persuasive, explanations for being armed. They testified that on the morning of their arrest they had planned to hunt in some nearby woods. Once they had decided to go for the car, they forgot to leave the weapons at home. Both were accustomed to carrying guns. Sacco carried his whenever he worked as a night watchman. Vanzetti explained that in his business he often had to handle large sums of cash, and, therefore, he used a gun for self-protection. In any case, it was not unusual in the 1920s for Americans of any background to carry guns.

The undue importance placed on "consciousness of guilt" became painfully apparent in Katzmann's summation and Judge Thayer's charge to the jury. Katzmann brushed over the weaknesses in eyewitness testimony and implied that his ballistics experts had actually identified Sacco's gun as the murder weapon. He emphasized "consciousness of guilt" as the crux of his case by dwelling on those actions that seemed most damaging to the defendants.

Katzmann might not have swayed the jury so readily had Judge Thayer properly performed his duties. In theory, a judge's charge guides the jury as it interprets conflicting evidence, in separating the relevant from the irrelevant, and in establishing the grounds for an objective verdict. As Felix Frankfurter remarked, "in drawing together the threads of evidence and marshaling the claims on both sides he must exercise a scrupulous regard for relevance and proportion. Misplaced emphasis here and omission there may work more damage than any outspoken comment."

Judge Thayer used his charge to reinforce the prosecution's case. Half his opening remarks were vague legal generalities with no real bearing on the evidence. He dispatched the ballistics testimony in a few brief comments that never addressed the substance of the conflict between the experts. But like Katzmann, he made the erroneous assertion that Proctor and Van Amburgh had actually claimed that Sacco's gun fired the fatal shot. On the issue of eyewitness identification Thayer became evasive. He never mentioned witnesses by name nor discussed inconsistencies in testimony. And he virtually ignored the vital alibi witnesses called by the defense.

Not until he reached "consciousness of guilt" did Thayer become expansive and specific. He lingered over the evidence offered by the police and garage owner, while omitting reference to Sacco and Vanzetti's explanations of their behavior. As Justice Frankfurter commented, "The disproportionate consideration which Judge Thayer gave this issue . . . must have left the impression on the jury that the case turned on 'consciousness of guilt.' "

Frankfurter and other legal critics of the trial have raised many other telling criticisms—excesses in the trial procedures, prejudice on the part of both judge and prosecutor, bungling by defense lawyers, and the injustice inherent in the jury's guilty verdict. And inevitably, the lawyers' perspective and the analysis of legal scholars have influenced the way historians have treated the case. Since the performance of the legal system has been the focus of most debate, the questions many critics raise are those which the law is equipped to answer and predisposed to concentrate on. Thus historians must constantly remind themselves that, from their point of view, those questions, no matter how important, are still relatively narrow ones. They deal largely with the issue of guilt and innocence—or, rather, the issue of *proof* of guilt.

Contrary to much popular opinion, the courts do not determine whether a person is guilty or innocent of a crime. They decide merely whether the prosecutor has assembled sufficient evidence to establish guilt. The judge may even suspect a defendant is guilty, but if the evidence does not meet minimum standards of legal proof, the court must set the accused free. As one court concluded, "the commonwealth demands no victims . . . and it is as much the duty of the district attorney to see that no innocent man suffers, as it is to see that no guilty man escapes."

Thus lawyers tend to focus on narrow, yet admittedly important, questions. They are all the more crucial when human lives are at stake, as was the case with Sacco and Vanzetti. Believing that the legal system maintains vital safeguards of individual rights, lawyers in general seek to ensure that proper legal procedures have been followed, that evidence is submitted according to established rules, and, in accordance with those procedures, that guilt has been adequately determined. A lawyer answering the question, "Why all the fuss?" over the Sacco and Vanzetti case would most likely reply, "Because the trial, by failing to prove guilt beyond reasonable doubt, perpetrated a serious miscarriage of justice." The inability of the defendants to rectify the original injustice through the appeals process only made matters worse. By sentencing Sacco and Vanzetti to death, the system honored the rule of law without similar regard for the spirit of justice.

THE HISTORIANS' BRIEF: BEYOND GUILT OR INNOCENCE

So far in these essays we have considered enough historical methods to understand that history affords far more latitude in weighing and collecting evidence than the legal system. The law attempts to limit the flow of evidence in a trial to what can reasonably be construed as fact. A judge will generally exclude hearsay testimony, speculation about states of mind or motives, conjecture, and vague questions leading witnesses to conclusions. But those are areas of information upon which historians can and do draw in their research. They can afford to speculate more freely, because their conclusions will not send innocent people to jail or let the guilty go free. In one instance, for example, appeals judges refused to act upon defense assertions that Judge Thayer had allowed his prejudices against Sacco and Vanzetti to influence his conduct of the trial. They ruled that remarks made outside the courtroom, no matter how inappropriate, had no bearing on what occurred inside. By contrast, the historian can accept the fact of Judge Thayer's prejudice regardless of where he revealed it.

Given their broader canons of evidence, historians might be tempted to go the lawyers one step further by establishing whether Sacco and Vanzetti did commit the robbery and murders at Braintree. To succeed in such an investigation would at least lay the controversy to its final rest. Yet that approach does not take us beyond the lawyers' questions. We are still dealing with only two men—Sacco and Vanzetti—and one central question—guilty or innocent? In that endeavor we would only be acting more brashly in assuming that the historian can answer a "yes or no" question more persuasively.

We must remember, however, that when historians confront "either/or" questions, they do not have to answer them in just that way. Their overriding obligation is the construction of a hypothesis or interpretation that gives full play to *all* aspects of the subject being investigated, not just the question of guilt or innocence. They must look beyond Sacco and Vanzetti at the actions of the people and society around them. What political currents led the prosecutor to bring those two men to trial? How much were Judge Thayer, District Attorney Katzmann, and the men in the jury box representative of Massachusetts or of American society in general? Of just what crime did the jury actually convict the defendants? In answering those questions, historians must lift their drama out of the Dedham courtroom and establish it in a larger theater of action. In short, we cannot answer our original question, "Why all the fuss?" merely by proving the defendants guilty or innocent. Historians want to know why this case has provoked such sharp controversy for so many years.

Any historian who studies the climate of opinion in the early 1920s cannot help suspecting that those who persecuted Sacco and Vanzetti were far more concerned with who the defendants were and what they believed than with what they might have done. Throughout the nation's history, Americans have periodically expressed vehement hostility toward immigrants and foreign political ideas which were perceived as a threat to the "American way of life." Nativism, as such defensive nationalism has been called, has been a problem at least since the first waves of Irish immigrants came ashore in the first half of the nineteenth century. Until then, the United States had been a largely homogeneous society dominated by white Protestants with a common English heritage. The influx of the Catholic Irish and then political refugees from the 1848 German revolution diversified the nation's population. Native-born Americans became alarmed that immigration threatened their cherished institutions. Successive waves of newcomers from Asia, Mediterranean countries, and eastern Europe deepened their fears.

Going to Join the Indian and Buffalo?

The sturdy old American breed that wrested this country from the wilderness might now try a hard, quick shove toward the middle of the bench

Many "Old Stock" Americans from northern Europe feared that the new flood of immigrants from southeastern Europe would, by sheer force of numbers, displace them from their dominant place in society. Even a progressive like George Creel, who had been sympathetic to immigrants during World War I, turned hostile and referred to the newcomers as "so much slag in the melting pot." Respected academics published research which purported to prove "the intellectual superiority of our Nordic groups over the Alpine, Mediterranean, and negro groups."

In analyzing nativist ideology, historian John Higham has identified three major attitudes: anti-Catholicism, antiradicalism, and Anglo-Saxon nationalism. Anti-Catholicism reflected northern European Protestants' preoccupation with the corruption of the Catholic Church, rejection of its hierarchical and undemocratic structure, and image of the pope as a religious despot. Nativists often viewed Catholic immigrants as papal agents sent to bring the United States under the tyranny of Rome. Antiradicalism stemmed in part from an increasing rejection of America's own revolutionary tradition and in part from the American tendency to associate violence and criminal subversion with Europe's radical political creeds such as Marxism, socialism, and anarchism. Anglo-Saxon nationalism was a more amorphous blend of notions about the racial superiority of the northern European people and pride in the Anglo-Saxon heritage of legal, political, and economic institutions. One of the most cherished has always been the Anglo-Saxon tradition of justice.

The tides of nativism tend to rise and fall with the fortunes of the nation. During periods of prosperity, Americans often welcome immigrants as a vital source of new labor. In the 1860s, for example, many Californians cheered the arrival of the strange Chinese coolies without whom the transcontinental railroad could not have been so quickly completed. In the 1870s, as the nation struggled through a severe industrial depression, nativism became a virulent social disease. The same Californians who once welcomed the Chinese now organized vigilante groups to harass them and clamored for laws to restrict the number of Asian immigrants.

The period following World War I, which Higham labelled the "Tribal Twenties," marked the high tide of nativism. No group more fully embodied the nativist impulse than the reborn Ku Klux Klan. By 1924 it claimed large chapters not only in its traditional southern strongholds but also in major cities, in Oregon, and in the states of the upper middle west—Indiana, Ohio, and Illinois in particular. The Klan's constitution unabashedly advertised the organization's commitment to all three nativist traditions:

> to unite white, male persons, native born gentile citizens of the United States of America, who owe no allegiance of any nature to any foreign government, nation, institution, sect, ruler, person or people; whose morals are good, whose reputations and vocations are exemplary . . . ; to shield the sanctity of white womanhood; to maintain forever white supremacy. . . .

Loyalty to the Church, the pope, a motherland, old world culture, or any other tie outside the United States eliminated almost all immigrants from possible Klan membership.

Several factors accounted for the resurgence of nativism in the 1920s. World War I had temporarily interrupted the flow of immigrants who, since the 1880s, had increasingly included a preponderance of Catholics and Jews from countries with strong radical traditions. In 1914 alone, over 1.2 million Jews came to the United States. By 1918 the number fell to just 110,000 but then rose to 805,000 in 1921, the last year of unrestricted immigration. A similar pattern occured among Italians. In the entire decade of the 1870s only 50,000 Italians came to the United States. In the first fifteen years of the twentieth century almost 2.5 million

The rabid patriotism of the war led to widespread abuses of civil liberties. Here, angry servicemen on the Boston Commons destroy a Socialist party flag seized during a 1918 peace march. The same spirit of intolerance was also reflected in the Red Scare, during which an Indiana jury deliberated only two minutes before acquitting a defendant who had shot and killed a radical for yelling, "To hell with the United States!"

made the crossing. That torrent, which slowed to a trickle during the war years, became swollen again with the return of peace. More than ever, nativists protested that those strange people would destroy cherished institutions, weaken the genetic pool, or in other ways undermine the American way of life.

The Wilson Administration's failure to plan the transition from a wartime to a peacetime economy only aggravated the resentment toward immigrants. Returning veterans expected jobs from a grateful nation; instead, they found crowds of unemployed workers around factory gates. The army had discharged millions of soldiers almost overnight. The government dismissed hundreds of thousands of temporary wartime employees and canceled millions of dollars' worth of contracts with private businesses. As the economy plunged downward, native-born Americans once again looked on new immigrants as a threat to their livelihoods. Organized labor joined other traditional nativist groups in demanding new restriction laws.

Union leaders called for relief on another front. During the war they had cooperated with the government to control inflation by minimizing wage increases. At the same time, high wartime employment had attracted millions of new recruits to the union movement. The government had orchestrated labor-management harmony to ensure uninterrupted production schedules. Once the war ended, labor set out to consolidate its recent gains. Union leaders asked for higher wages, improved working conditions, and the recognition of collective bargaining.

Most businessmen were in no mood to compromise. They had actively resented the assistance the government had given organized labor. In the years after the war, they not only rejected even the mildest union demands but also sought to cripple the labor movement. The Wilson administration swung its support behind the employer groups. Conservative businessmen launched a national campaign to brand all organized labor as Bolsheviks, Reds, and anarchists. They called strikes "crimes against society," "conspiracies against the government," and "plots to establish communism." As the market for manufactures declined, employers had little reason to avoid a showdown. Strikes saved them the problem of laying off unneeded workers.

In 1919 American industry lost more manhours to strikes than ever before in history. March brought 175 significant strikes, followed by 248 in April, 388 in May, 303 in June, 360 in July, and 373 in August. By September, strikes in the coal and steel industries alone had idled over 700,000 workers and led to repeated violence. The average strike lasted thirty-four days, while some exceeded four months. Even employers who made minor concessions on wages or hours refused to yield on the question of collective bargaining.

Radicals played at most a minor role in the postwar labor unrest. Most union leaders were as archly conservative as the employers they confronted. Still, the constant barrage of anti-red propaganda turned public opinion against the unions.

American radicals fed that hostility by adopting highly visible tactics. The success of a small band of Bolsheviks in capturing Russia's tottering government in October 1917 had rekindled their waning hopes, at the same time startling most Americans. The Bolsheviks had further shocked the Allies when they concluded a separate peace with Germany and made Moscow the center of a worker-dominated state dedicated to the cause of worldwide revolution. In 1919 they organized the Third Communist International to carry the revolution to other countries. Communist-led worker uprisings in Hungary and Germany increased conservative anxiety that a similar revolutionary fever might soon infect American workers. Those conservatives shuddered when a Comintern official bragged that the money spent in Germany "was as nothing compared to the funds transmitted to New York for the purpose of spreading Bolshevism in the United States."

Out of the combination of unvented war fervor, economic distress, labor unrest, and renewed immigration from southern and eastern Europe blossomed the first major "Red Scare." In response to the growing clamor for government action, Attorney General A. Mitchell Palmer created an antiradical division in the Justice Department. At its head he placed a resourceful young bureaucrat, J. Edgar Hoover, who turned his anticommunist crusade into a lifelong obsession and his division into the vaunted F.B.I.

For over a year Palmer, Hoover, and their agents raided homes, offices, union halls, and alien organizations. Seldom did the raiders pay even passing attention to civil liberties or constitutional prohibitions against illegal search and seizure. One particularly spectacular outing netted over 4,000 alleged subversives in some thirty-three cities. Most of those arrested, though innocent of any crime, were detained illegally by state authorities either for trial or Labor Department deportation hearings. Police jammed suspects in cramped rooms with inadequate food and sanitation. They refused to honor the suspects' rights to post bail or obtain a writ of habeas corpus.

The public quickly wearied of Palmer and the exaggerated stories of grand revolutionary conspiracies. Not one incident had produced any evidence of a serious plot. Palmer predicted that on May 1, 1920, radicals would launch a massive attempt to overthrow the government. Alerted by the Justice Department, local police and militia girded for the assault. But May Day passed without incident. The heightened surveillance did, however, have profound consequences for Nicola Sacco and Bartolomeo Vanzetti. Both men were on a list of suspects the Justice Department had sent to District Attorney Katzmann and Chief Stewart. Just four days after the May Day scare, Officer Connolly arrested the two aliens.

Sacco and Vanzetti closely fit the stereotypes nativists held of foreigners. Sacco arrived in the United States in 1908 at the age of seventeen. Like so many other Italians he had fled the oppressive poverty of his homeland with no intention of making a permanent home in America. Most of the young men planned to stay only until they had saved enough money to return home and improve their family fortunes. Though born into a modestly well-to-do family, Sacco was no stranger to hard labor. Shortly after his arrival he found steady work in the shoe factories around Milford, Massachusetts.

Sacco's resourcefulness and industry marked him as the kind of foreign worker whose competition American labor feared. Though he lacked formal schooling, Sacco understood that skilled labor commanded steadier work and higher wages and he paid $50 out of his earnings to learn the specialized trade of edge trimming. His wages soon reached as high as $80 per week. By 1917 he had a wife and child, his own home, and $1,500 in savings. His employer at the "3 K" shoe factory described him as an excellent worker and recalled that Sacco often found time, despite his long work days, to put in a few hours each morning and evening in his vegetable garden.

Vanzetti conformed more to the nativist stereotype of shiftless foreigners. After arriving in the United States in 1908, he drifted from job to job around New England before finally settling near Plymouth. There, he sold fish from a cart. Along the way he found time to read and acquire something of a homespun education. Vanzetti was always more sensitive and studious than Sacco. Born in 1888 in the northern Italian village of Villafalletto, he had left home by the age of thirteen to apprentice in a pastry shop. Ninety-hour weeks at hard labor eventually broke his health. He returned home only to find his mother dying of cancer. That tragedy inspired his decision to leave for the United States.

Vanzetti's first years in America tell a grim story of the immigrants' experience. He began work as a dishwasher in hot, stinking kitchens. "We worked twelve hours one day and fourteen the next, with five hours off every other Sunday," he recalled. "Damp food hardly fit for a dog and five or six dollars a week was the pay." Fearing another attack of consumption, Vanzetti migrated to the countryside in search of open air work. "I worked on farms, cut trees, made bricks, dug ditches, and quarried rocks. I worked in a fruit, candy and ice cream store and for a telephone company," he wrote his sister in Italy. By 1914 he had wandered to Plymouth where he took a job in a cordage factory.

If those details told the whole story, Sacco and Vanzetti would not seem likely suspects for Justice Department agents. But there was another side to their lives that brought them together and to the attention of federal and local authorities. Though not a student like Vanzetti, Sacco was something of a rebel. He identified closely with the workers' struggle for better wages and the right to organize. In 1912 he and Vanzetti had independently participated in the violent textile strike at Lawrence, Massachusetts. Three years later plant owners around Plymouth had blacklisted Vanzetti for his role in a local strike. Sacco had walked off his job to express sympathy for the cordage workers. Soon after a local labor leader organized a sympathy strike to support workers in Minnesota, authorities had arrested Sacco and convicted him of disturbing the peace. All this time, he and his wife regularly joined street theater productions performed to raise money for labor and radical groups.

American entry into World War I created a crisis for both men. Their pacifist and anarchist beliefs forced them to oppose the war. Sacco even refused the patriotic pressures to buy war bonds. He quit his job rather than compromise his principles. Both began to dread deportation or, worse yet, the military draft (though in fact as aliens they were ineligible). They decided to join a group of pacifists who in May 1917 fled to Mexico. It was most likely in Mexico that the two first became personal friends. The hard life and absence from his family finally drove Sacco to return home under an alias, though he did resume his name and former job after the war. As postwar nativist hysteria grew, he and Vanzetti continued to preach anarchism among their countrymen living near Boston. Neither had by then made a significant effort to learn English, adopt citizenship, or acculturate in other ways.

Armed with that knowledge of Sacco and Vanzetti's past, as well as awareness of the postwar mood, historians can recognize just how much nativist prejudices affected the legal system's handling of their case. Above all, they can understand that the suspicious behavior, which Katzmann construed as "consciousness of guilt," could indeed stem from the legitimate fear of imminent arrest and deportation. Hundreds of friends and associates had already met such a fate.

Nativism undoubtedly influenced the jury's reaction to the eyewitness testimony. Almost all those people who identified Sacco and Vanzetti were native-born Americans. That they saw a resemblance between the Italian suspects and the foreign-looking criminals proved only, as Felix Frankfurter remarked, that there was much truth in the popular old song, "All Coons Look Alike to Me." On the other hand, almost all the witnesses substantiating the defendants' alibis were Italians who answered through an interpreter. The jury, also all native-born Americans, would likely accept Katzmann's imputation that foreigners stuck together to protect each other from the authorities.

The choice of Fred Moore as chief defense counsel guaranteed that radicalism would become a central issue in the trial. In his earlier trial, Vanzetti had been defended by a conservative criminal lawyer, George Vahey. His conviction persuaded Vanzetti that Vahey had not done all he could. When Vahey entered into a law partnership with Katzmann shortly after the trial, Vanzetti believed his worst suspicions had been confirmed. For the Dedham trial, friends, local labor leaders, and anarchists created a defense fund to see that no similar betrayal by counsel occurred. The committee concluded that radical defendants could be adequately represented only by a lawyer sympathetic to his clients' beliefs. From Elizabeth Gurley Flynn, an Industrial Workers of the World agitator and wife of anarchist publisher Carlo Tresca, the committee learned of Moore, who had participated in the trials of numerous radicals, including two Italian anarchists charged with murder during the Lawrence strike. Only later did the committee learn that Moore had contributed little to the acquittal of the Lawrence defendants.

Moore's participation must have reinforced the impression that Sacco and Vanzetti were dangerous radicals. Moore spent the bulk of defense funds to orchestrate a propaganda campaign dramatizing the plight of his clients and the persecution of radicals. He gave far less attention to planning defense strategy. That was left largely in the hands of two local co-counsels, Thomas and Jeremiah McAnarney.

Yet in the courtroom Moore insisted on playing the major role. The McAnarneys soon despaired of making a favorable impression on the jury: they were convinced that Moore's presence and conduct would lead to a miscarriage of justice against their clients. Most attorneys recognize that judges and juries alike sympathize more with local lawyers than with an interloper; and Moore hailed from California.

Worse still, Moore refused to accommodate local mores. He wore his hair long and sometimes shocked the court by parading around in his shirtsleeves and socks. Rumors abounded about his unorthodox sex life.

And at critical moments he sometimes disappeared for several days. Judge Thayer once became so outraged at Moore that he told a friend, "I'll show them that no long-haired anarchist from California can run this court." Legal scholars have been almost unanimous in characterizing Moore's conduct of the defense as inept. Not until 1924 did he finally withdraw in favor of William Thompson, a respected Massachusetts criminal lawyer.*

Nativism, particularly antiradicalism, obviously prejudiced Judge Thayer and District Attorney Katzmann. We have already seen how Thayer used his charge to the jury to underscore Katzmann's construction of the evidence in the trial. But the two men also collaborated to make the trial a confrontation between patriotism and loyalty on the one side and alien radicalism on the other. Thayer consistently violated the canons of judicial discretion by discussing his views of the case outside the courtroom. George Crocker, who sometimes lunched with Thayer, testified that on many occasions the judge "conveyed to me by his words and manner that he was bound to convict these men because they were 'reds.'" Veteran court reporter Frank Silbey had been forced to stop lunching at the Dedham Inn to avoid Thayer and his indiscreet remarks. Silbey later recalled, "In my thirty-five years I never saw anything like it. . . . His whole attitude seemed to be that the jurors were there to convict these men."

From the moment the trial opened, Thayer and Katzmann missed few opportunities to strike a patriotic pose or to remind the jury that both defendants were draft dodgers. Thayer told the prospective jurors at the outset, "I call upon you to render this service . . . with the same patriotism as was exhibited by our soldier boys across the sea." Katzmann opened his cross-examination of Vanzetti with a cutting statement dressed up as a question: "So you left Plymouth, Mr. Vanzetti, in May 1917 to dodge the draft did you?" Since Vanzetti was charged with murder, not draft evasion, the question served obviously to arouse the jury's patriotic indignation.

Katzmann struck hardest in his questioning of Sacco, whose poor command of English often left him confused or under a misapprehension. Judge Thayer never intervened to restrain the overzealous prosecutor even when it became clear that Sacco could neither follow a question

---

*It is by no means clear that any other lawyer could have won acquittal. Through repeated innuendos, Katzmann had managed to introduce Vanzetti's radicalism into the earlier trial, despite the presence of George Vahey, a conservative criminal lawyer.

nor express his thoughts clearly. Playing once again upon the residual patriotic war fervor, Katzmann hammered away at the defendant's evident disloyalty. A brief sample of the testimony suggests the devastating impact:

> KATZMANN: And in order to show your love for this United States of America when she was about to call upon you to become a soldier you ran away to Mexico. Did you run away to Mexico to avoid being a soldier for the country that you loved?
> SACCO: Yes.
> KATZMANN: And would it be your idea of showing love for your wife that when she needed you, you ran away from her?
> SACCO: I did not run away from her.

When the defense objected, Thayer ruled that this line of questioning would help establish Sacco's character. But instead of showing Sacco's philosophical opposition to war, Katzmann made the defendant appear, as one critic expressed it, "an ingrate and a slacker" who invited the jury's contempt. With such skillful cross-examination Katzmann twisted Sacco's professed love of "a free country" into a preference for high wages, pleasant work, and good food.

The prosecutor summed up his strategy in his final appeal to the jury: "Men of Norfolk do your duty. Do it like men. Stand together you men of Norfolk." There was the case in a nutshell—native American solidarity against alien people and their values. Whether he convicted Sacco and Vanzetti of murder mattered little, for he had proven them guilty of disloyalty. And in case the point was lost, Judge Thayer reiterated it in his charge:

> Although you knew such service would be arduous, painful, and tiresome, yet you, like the true soldier, responded to the call in the spirit of supreme American loyalty. There is no better word in the English language than "loyalty."

And just who were those "men of Norfolk" to whom the judge and prosecutor appealed? Could they put aside inflammatory rhetoric and render a just verdict? As legal historian Edmund M. Morgan observed, it was unlikely in the backwash of wartime patriotic fever that two Italian aliens could receive justice anywhere in America. Dedham was no exception. Not a single foreign name, much less an Italian one, appeared on the juror's list. Because Fred Moore had rejected any "capitalists" during jury selection, a few prospective jurors whom the McAnarneys knew to be fair-minded were kept off the jury. Those jurors selected were drawn from the tradesmen and other respectable Protestants of the town. None would share the defendants' antipathy to capitalism. Few among them could have had any compassion for the plight of Italian immigrants or union men.

In fact the jury foreman, Harry Ripley, revealed such prejudice toward Sacco and Vanzetti that the defense made him the subject of its first appeal. Ripley was a former police chief. Every defense lawyer knows that law enforcement officers make the worst jurors because they tend to assume automatically that the defendant is guilty. Ripley, however, outdid himself in persuading his fellow jurors to convict. He violated basic rules of evidence in a capital case by bringing into the juryroom cartridges similar to those placed in evidence. A short time before, he had told his friend William Daly that he would be on the jury in "the case of the two 'ginneys' charged with murder at South Braintree." When Daly suggested that they might be innocent, Ripley replied, "Damn them, they ought to hang anyway."

By using the concept of nativism to gain a broader perspective, the historian has come to understand the answer to a question lawyers need not even ask: What factors accounted for the conviction of Sacco and Vanzetti where legitimate evidence was so clearly lacking? Nativism explains many prejudices exhibited in the trial record. It also explains why those attitudes were so widespread in 1920–1921. We must accept the truth of Professor Morgan's assertion that it was "almost impossible to secure a verdict which runs counter to the settled convictions of the community." Sacco and Vanzetti symbolized for a majority of Americans and the "men of Norfolk" alien forces that threatened their way of life.

Yet, having answered one important question, the historian still faces another. Granted that a jury convicted two alien radicals of robbery and murder in 1921; "why all the fuss," as we asked earlier, in the years that followed? After all, Sacco and Vanzetti were not sentenced until 1927, long after the virulent nativist mood had passed. Corruption and scandal had by then killed the Klan. Prohibition had closed that infernal den of immigrant iniquity, the saloon. The Immigration Acts of 1921 and 1924 had severely curbed the flow of newcomers from Italy and eastern Europe. The damage from unsuccessful strikes, management opposition, and government hostility had sent organized labor into a decline from which it would not recover until the New Deal years. The historian must still explain how a local case extended its impact beyond Nor-

THE AMERICANESE WALL, AS CONGRESSMAN
BURNETT WOULD BUILD IT.
Uncle Sam: You're welcome in — if you can climb it!

Seeking to screen out those immigrants who were "undesirable," many nativists urged Congress to adopt a literacy test. Although campaigns for such a law had been mounted since the 1890s, only in 1917 did a literacy requirement pass Congress. The cartoon shown here disparages such exclusionist policies but in the 1920s the pressure for even tighter restrictions mounted, to be embodied (as one Minnesota representative put it) in a "genuine 100 per cent American immigration law."

folk County to the nation and even the international community. No single answer, even one so broad as nativism, can account for the notoriety. Certainly, from the beginning the case had sent ripples across the nation. Socially prominent individuals, intellectuals, the American Federation of Labor, immigrant groups, and radicals had all contributed to the defense fund for the Dedham trial. Those people represented a small minority without great political influence. But by tracing out the appeals process, much as we followed the judicial history of the Meat Inspection Act, the historian discovers a series of events that enlarged the significance of the case, heightened the public's awareness of the crucial issues involved, and raised the stakes many groups risked on the judicial outcome.

A GOOD SHOEMAKER AND A POOR FISH PEDDLER STIR A NATION

Most Americans assume that the right to appeal protects defendants against a miscarriage of justice in the court of original jurisdiction. But in 1920 that was not the case in Massachusetts, where the appeals process contained a provision that ultimately proved fatal to Sacco and Vanzetti. Any motion for a retrial based on new evidence had to be granted by the original trial judge. On each of eight motions made by the defense, including substantial evidence of prejudice on the part of the judge, the person who heard that appeal was none other than Webster Thayer! Thayer did not have to determine whether new information proved the men innocent; only if another jury might reasonably reach a different verdict.

The next higher court, the Supreme Judicial Court, had only narrow grounds on which to reverse Thayer's decisions. It could review the law in each case, but not the facts. That meant it could determine only if the procedure conformed to the criteria of a fair trial established under state and federal constitutions. Though it found some irregularities in procedure, the Supreme Judicial Court ruled that they did not prejudice the verdict against the defendants. At no time did that court review the weight of evidence presented at the trial or on appeal. It determined, instead, that a reasonable judge might have acted as Thayer did.

And what of the U.S. Supreme Court, the ultimate safeguard of our civil liberties? On three separate occasions the defense attempted to move the case into the federal courts. Defense attorneys argued that Sacco and Vanzetti had been the victims of a sham trial, particularly given Judge Thayer's overwhelming prejudice. Justice Oliver Wendell Holmes, Jr., long a champion of civil liberties, wrote that the court could rule only on the grounds of constitutional defects in Massachusetts law. Since none existed, he refused in 1927 to grant a writ of *certiorari* allowing the Supreme Court to review the weight of evidence. Thus the appeals procedure created a formidable barrier to rectifying the injustice done at Dedham.

Despite such inequities, the defense spent six years in an effort to overturn the conviction. Between July 1921 and October 1924 it presented five motions for a new trial. The first, as we have seen, involved the behavior of jury foreman Harry Ripley. In response, Thayer completely ignored the affidavit from Ripley's friend William Daly and ruled that Ripley's tampering with evidence had not materially affected the verdict.

Eighteen months later the defense uncovered an important new witness, Roy Gould, who had been shot at, at point blank range, by the fleeing bandits. Gould had told his story to police immediately afterwards, but Katzmann never called him to testify. Eventually defense lawyers uncovered Gould and realized why he had been kept off the stand. Gould had been so close to the escape car that one shot passed through his overcoat; yet he swore that Sacco was not one of the men. Incredibly, Judge Thayer rejected that appeal on the grounds that since Gould's testimony did no more than add to the cumulative weight of evidence, it did not justify a new trial.

On the third and fourth motions, Moore attempted to substantiate the prosecutor's tampering with two key witnesses. Both recanted their courtroom statements and then recanted their recantations. Rather than find Katzmann guilty of impropriety, Thayer condemned Moore for his "bold and cruel attempt to sandbag" witnesses. The fifth motion came after Captain Proctor impeached his own expert ballistics testimony. Proctor signed an affidavit in which he swore that on many occasions he had told Katzmann there was no evidence proving Sacco's gun had fired the fatal shot. He warned the prosecutor that if asked a direct question, he would answer "no." Katzmann had, therefore, examined Proctor with studied ambiguity. By the time Thayer ruled on this motion, Proctor had died. The judge ruled that the jury had understood perfectly what Proctor meant and that Katzmann had not tried to be evasive.

After that setback, the defense embarked on a new course. Moore finally withdrew in favor of William Thompson, a distinguished trial lawyer who devoted the rest of his career to Sacco and Vanzetti's cause. Thompson made the first appeal to the Supreme Judicial Court. He argued that the accumulated weight of exculpatory evidence and the repeated rejection of appeals demonstrated that Thayer had been so moved by his hostility to Moore and the defendants that he had abused his discretionary authority. Unlike historians, who would render judgment on the basis of the totality of evidence, the appeals judges turned down the defense arguments case-by-case, point-by-point. That is, the court never considered the cumulative weight of evidence. Judge Thayer, they found in each separate instance, had acted within his proper authority.

Throughout this drawn-out process, public interest in the case had steadily dwindled. But after November 18, 1925, controversy exploded once again. Sacco received a note from a fellow inmate which read, "I hear by [sic] confess to being in the South Braintree shoe company crime and Sacco and Vanzetti was not in said crime. Celestino F. Medeiros." Medeiros was a young prisoner then facing execution for a murder conviction under appeal.

The defense soon connected Medeiros to the Morelli gang of Providence, Rhode Island. In the spring of 1921, the Morellis badly needed money to fight a pending indictment, and so had ample reason to commit a desperate payroll robbery. All the available details fit them into the prosecutor's case: Joe Morelli carried a .32 Colt pistol and bore a striking resemblance to Sacco. Another gang member carried an automatic pistol, which could account for spent cartridges found at the scene. Mike Morelli had been driving a new Buick, which disappeared after April 15. Another member fit the description of the pale, sickly driver. A number of defense and prosecution witnesses identified Joe Morelli when shown his picture. The New Bedford police had even suspected the Morellis of the Braintree crime.

Here surely was the basis for a new investigation and trial. How then did the legal system react? The District Attorney's office refused to reopen the case. The defense then appealed to Thayer to order a new trial. Once again, Thayer did not have to determine if the evidence conclusively demonstrated Medeiros's guilt or Sacco and Vanzetti's innocence. He had only to decide that a new jury might now reach a different verdict. It took Thayer some 25,000 words to deny this motion.

That decision, more than any other, unleashed the torrent of outrage that surrounded the last months of the Sacco and Vanzetti case. It provoked Professor Frankfurter to publish his attack. "I assert with deep regret but without the slightest fear of disproof," he wrote, "that certainly in modern times Judge Thayer's opinion [on the Medeiros motion] stands unmatched, happily, for discrepancies between what the record discloses and what the opinion conveys." Frankfurter described the document as "a farrago of misquotations, misrepresentations, suppressions, and mutilations." The *Boston Herald* rebuked Thayer for adopting "the tone of the advocate rather than the arbiter." Once a staunch supporter of the prosecution, the *Herald* now called on the Supreme Judicial Court to overturn this ruling. Once again, the court refused to weigh the evidence. It ruled in rejecting the appeal that the defense motion involved questions of fact lying totally within the purview of the trial judge.

That decision, in combination with Frankfurter's blistering attack,

Many artists, intellectuals, and literary figures sympathized with Sacco and Vanzetti. Maxwell Anderson wrote a play, *Gods of the Lightning;* Upton Sinclair, the novel *Boston;* and Edna St. Vincent Millay, a series of sonnets. Artist Ben Shahn, himself an immigrant from Lithuania, received recognition during the 1930s for his series of twenty-three paintings on Sacco and Vanzetti. When the painting shown here is compared with the photograph of the two men (page 273), Shahn's source becomes evident. But the artist transformed the photograph in subtle ways. Given our earlier discussion of photographic evidence, how do the changes lend more force to his painting? (Ben Shahn, *Bartolomeo Vanzetti and Nicola Sacco*, 1931–32)

shifted public sympathy to Sacco and Vanzetti. A mounting body of evidence seemed to indicate that the two men were innocent. Yet, as the courts remained deaf to the defense appeals, more and more reasonable people came to suspect that, indeed, powerful men and institutions were conspiring to destroy two people perceived as a threat to the social order. Such a notion rocked popular faith in the judicial system as a guardian of individual liberties. Thayer's sentence of death by electrocution seemed but a final thread in a web of legal intrigue to commit an injustice.

Sacco and Vanzetti played an important part in winning broad popular support for their cause. Steadfastly, in the face of repeated disappointments, they maintained their innocence with an air of dignity. Sacco, the more simple and direct of the two, suffered deeply as a result of separation from his family. During the first trying years, he went on a hunger strike and suffered a nervous breakdown. From that point on, he stoically awaited the end, more preoccupied with saving his wife further anguish than with saving himself. To assist the defense effort, however, he had begun in 1923 to study English, though with little success. A letter written to his teacher in 1926 best conveys his warm, simple idealism. Sacco had wanted to explain to his teacher why he had been unable to master the language:

> No, it isn't, because I have try with all my passion for the success of this beautiful language, not only for the sake of my family and the promise I have made to you—but for my own individual satisfaction, to know and to be able to read and write correct English. But woe is me! It wasn't so; no, because the sadness of these close and cold walls, the idea to be away from my dear family, for all the beauty and joy of liberty—had more than once exhaust my passion.

Vanzetti was far more intellectual in temperament. His articulate, often eloquent, speeches and letters won him the respect of fellow prisoners, defenders, and the literary figures drawn to the case. A few particularly devoted followers compared Vanzetti to Jesus Christ. Perhaps the best sense of the man was revealed in his speech before Judge Thayer on the day he was sentenced. More than reiterating his innocence, Vanzetti made a passionate defense of human liberty, dignity, and justice:

> Now, I should say that I am not only innocent of all these things, not only have I never committed a real crime in my life—though some sins but not crimes—not only have I struggled all my life to eliminate crimes, the crimes official law and official moral condemns, but also the crime that the official moral and official law sanctions and sanctifies,—the exploitation and the oppression of man by man, and if there is reason why you in a few minutes can doom me, it is this reason and nothing else. . . .
> I would not wish to a dog or to a snake, to the most low and misfortunate creature of the earth—I would not wish to any of them what I have had to suffer for things that I am not guilty of. But my conviction is that I have

suffered for things I am guilty of. I am suffering because I am a radical and indeed I am a radical; I have suffered because I was an Italian, and indeed I am an Italian; I have suffered more for my family and beloved than for myself; but I am so convinced to be right that if you could execute me two times, and if I could be reborn two other times, I would live again to do what I have done already.

Such eloquence stirred much of the nation. The political leadership of Massachusetts saw public support for execution rapidly eroding. Frankfurter's article had undermined the state's credibility. Yet an equally vociferous segment of popular opinion cheered Thayer's sentence as an example to "reds" that they could not subvert the Commonwealth. Governor Alvan Fuller, a successful car dealer, amateur politician, and White House aspirant, thus faced a difficult decision when he received Vanzetti's plea for executive clemency.*

To help him decide, Fuller appointed a blue-ribbon panel to conduct an "impartial" review of the evidence and judicial proceedings. If the creation of a committee showed some official preoccupation with justice, the selection of its members did not. The three men Fuller chose were symbols of the Commonwealth's social and educational elite. Retired Judge Robert Grant proved the worst choice, a socialite often more preoccupied with black-tie parties than public affairs. Samuel Stratton, President of the Massachusetts Institute of Technology, was clearly overshadowed by the committee's designated chairman, A. Lawrence Lowell, pillar of Boston society, a lawyer by training, and the president of Harvard. Lowell had already demonstrated his capacity for ethnocentrism when he introduced formal quotas to limit the number of Jewish students admitted to Harvard. The avowedly liberal *New Republic* remarked of the committee, "the life of an Italian anarchist was as foreign to them as life on Mars."

No more than judge, jury, or prosecutor did those guardians of establishment respectability rise above their inherited prejudices to render an impartial verdict. For over ten days they heard testimony on the evidence—much of it new. On July 23, 1927 the defense submitted a lengthy brief. Four days later, the committee filed its final report, without taking the time necessary to sort out the complex issues. The report upheld both the verdict and sentence against Sacco and Vanzetti. Sympathizers reacted with a mixture of despair and disgust. "What more can

*Sacco refused to sign. Though he agreed with Vanzetti's arguments, he did not want to violate his principles by appealing to government authorities—or to give his wife further vain hopes.

immigrants from Italy expect?" asked editorial writer Haywood Broun. "It's not every prisoner who has the President of Harvard throw the switch for him."

Governor Fuller's evident need to involve the educational and social elite in what had become a politically onerous responsibility indicates to the historian the degree to which the Sacco and Vanzetti case had polarized the nation. It brought to the forefront not only issues of guilt and innocence, justice and injustice but also more fundamental tensions in American society. On one side were arrayed immigrants, workers, and the poor for whom Sacco and Vanzetti stood as powerful symbols. On the other side stood Thayer, the "men of Norfolk," the Protestant establishment, and all those who believed that America should tolerate only certain peoples and ideas.

On the night of August 22, 1927, John Dos Passos, a young writer, stood with the crowd outside Charleston Prison waiting for news of Sacco and Vanzetti's fate. Shortly after midnight word came—the "good shoemaker and poor fish peddler" were dead. Grief and anger raked the crowd. Some wept, others cried out in the name of justice, and many tore their clothes in anguish. The scene outside the prison was repeated in New York and other cities around the world. Years later, Dos Passos expressed the outrage he felt against those who had persecuted Sacco and Vanzetti:

> they have clubbed us off the streets they are stronger they are rich they hire and fire the politicians the newspapereditors the old judges the small men with reputations the collegepresidents the ward heelers (listen collegepresidentsjudges America will not forget her betrayers). . . .
>
> all right you have won you will kill the brave men our friends tonight there is nothing left to do we are beaten. . . .
>
> America our nation has been beaten by strangers who have turned our language inside out who have taken the clean words our Fathers spoke and made them slimy and foul. . . .
>
> they have built the electricchair and hired the executioner to throw the switch
>
> all right we are two nations

Two nations—that was the reason for "all the fuss."

So long as America remains an open, heterogeneous society, fear will nourish bigotry with depressing regularity. The victims may be "new" immigrants, or political dissenters, or racial minorities, or social outcasts, or simply those who flaunt their differences. It is not surprising, therefore, to find that passion and controversy still surround the case of Sacco and Vanzetti. When Massachusetts Governor Michael Dukakis issued a public apology on the fiftieth anniversary of their execution, many citizens and politicians condemned his action. Their response confirmed critic Malcolm Cowley's observation that "the effects of the case continued to operate in a subterranean way, and after a few years they would once again appear on the surface."

All the "fuss" was not just over two Italian aliens, nor a sense of "justice crucified," though both provoked much of the controversy. The historian must suspect that Americans were fighting over the meaning of those "clean words our Fathers spoke." Sacco and Vanzetti forced the nation to ask who in the society of the 1920s best embodied the spiritual legacy of 1776. Neither historians nor lawyers can resolve that question to the satisfaction of a divided nation.

Additional Reading

Novelists often make excellent historians. Though they may play hob with facts or freely mingle real and fictitious characters, they just as often have a keen sense of the temper of the times and the issues facing a society. Thus, someone interested in the Sacco and Vanzetti case in the context of the 1920s might begin by reading the trilogy by John Dos Passos, *U.S.A.*. In volume three, *The Big Money* (New York, 1930), Mary French, an idealistic young liberal, becomes deeply involved in the fight to save Sacco and Vanzetti. More important, Dos Passos writes about the tensions besetting American society and particularly the sense among liberals and radicals that the ruling class had betrayed the nation. This work made Dos Passos a hero to many radicals of the 1930s, though he gravitated steadily to the right.

There are several general histories of the 1920s that make good reading. Among the best are William Leuchtenberg, *The Perils of Prosperity* (Chicago, 1958), Frederick Lewis Allen, *Only Yesterday* (New York, 1931), and Arthur Schlesinger, Jr., *The Crisis of the Old Order* (New York, 1957). All those works treat Sacco and Vanzetti briefly in the context of the time. Richard Pells, *Radical Visions and American Dreams* (New York, 1973) places the case in its intellectual context and explains how reactions among those involved set much of the radical tone of the depression era. John Higham, *Strangers in the Land* (New Brunswick, N.J., 1955) remains not only the outstanding work on nativism but also one of the best monographic treatments of modern American history. On the political repression of labor and radicals, Robert Murray, *Red Scare* (New York, 1955), is a colorful, though not deeply analytical, account.

Like so many controversial episodes in American history, the Sacco and Vanzetti case has become something of a cottage industry for devotees, polemicists, scholars, and writers seeking a provocative subject. To read all the works might take a dedicated person much of a lifetime. Among those works which have sought to establish the guilt of Sacco, Vanzetti, or both, the most forceful presentation is made by Francis Russell, *Tragedy in Dedham* (New York, 1971). To our minds, the following works have made a far stronger case. Readers might best start with Felix Frankfurter, *The Case of Sacco and Vanzetti* (New York, 1962), a reprint of his famous *Atlantic Monthly* critique of the case. It reveals why the establishment reacted so violently—to the extent that the Justice Department tapped his phone until after the execution. The trial transcripts, though available in some libraries in five volumes, may be found in adequate length in Robert Weeks, ed., *The Sacco-Vanzetti Case* (Englewood Cliffs, N.J., 1959), though unfortunately this edition is recently out of print.

One work which recognized that this case had a social as well as legal side is Edmund M. Morgan and Louis Joughlin, *The Legacy of Sacco and Vanzetti* (New York, 1948). Morgan, like Frankfurter a Harvard law professor, used his expertise on rules of evidence to analyze the legal issues, while Joughlin, an English professor, traced the strong effects of the case on intellectuals and writers. Another compelling treatment of the evidence, trial, and appeals procedure is Herbert Ehrmann, *The Case That Will Not Die* (Boston, 1969). Erhmann entered the case as an assistant to William Thompson. His first assignment was to research the Medeiros confession. From that experience he developed a lifelong commitment to establish Sacco and Vanzetti's innocence. Any reader who wishes to encounter Sacco and Vanzetti through their own words can read Marion Frankfurter and Gardner Means, eds., *The Letters of Sacco and Vanzetti* (New York, 1960).

Those who doubt that the case still engages writers' passions might look at Roberta Feuerlicht, *Justice Crucified* (New York, 1977). This most recent attempt to prove Sacco and Vanzetti innocent is flawed by the author's bias and poor grasp of history. Finally, we encourage students of the case to consult, as we did, a lawyer familiar with criminal procedures. Our two lawyers, Tom Frost of Rhinebeck, N.Y., and Mary Keller of the Texas Civil Liberties Union, made us realize that much of the trial, which we found extraordinary, was in fact common courtroom practice. Without that perspective it is impossible to evaluate the legal issues in the case.

CHAPTER

ELEVEN

❖

Huey Generis

Franklin Roosevelt called him one of the two most dangerous men in America. Other contemporaries casting a troubled eye toward Hitler's Nazi Germany and Mussolini's Italy feared he might lead an American fascist movement. Folks back home in Winnfield, Louisiana, remembered him more simply as a smart aleck kid always butting into someone else's business. Many political foes hated him as the political boss who had overwhelmed their entrenched machine only to replace it with a more powerful one of his own. Southerners recognized him as one of those colorful demagogues like Cole Blease, James K. Vardemann, or Theodore Bilbo, who periodically played upon the deep-seated economic grievances and racial hatreds of poor whites. His supporters cheered him as a statesman—a politician who made promises, then delivered. To millions of poor Americans he appeared as a potential savior in the darkest days of the depression.

Whatever people called him, Huey Long took second place to no one. In school, he challenged his teachers. In the courtroom he swung judge and jury to his view of a case. When he first appeared before a committee of the Louisiana legislature, the members heaped abuse on the unknown twenty-two-year-old attorney. Then suddenly, they found themselves charged as the "henchmen and attorneys for the interests." Soon, with a mixture of vituperation and skillful argument, the upstart backed them into a political corner. They had little choice but to pass Huey's amendments to strengthen the state's workman's compensation laws.

Even routine affairs of state afforded the "Kingfish," as he liked to be called, an opportunity to capture headlines. He once turned a visit from the commander of a German warship into an international incident. Eager to meet the political phenomenon from Louisiana, the stiff officer was jolted to find the "Kingfish" casually attired in lime green pajamas. The chagrin of Germany proved the delight of backwoods Louisiana.

Even Franklin Roosevelt found himself occasionally overshadowed by Huey. In 1933 H.G. Wells, the noted British historian and writer, came to Washington to observe the new political rage—Huey Long, not the president. Gertrude Stein, who earlier had "discovered" the lost generation in Paris, found Huey as well. To her, he was "not boring the way Harding, President Roosevelt, and Al Smith have been boring."

As much as the president, Long mastered the new art of media and mass communications. Millions of Americans would gather eagerly around their radios when they heard, "Hello friends, this is Huey Long speaking." Suddenly the mood would brighten in anticipation of some

"Hello, friends, this is Huey Long speaking." Thus commenced the refrain of Long's popular radio show. Huey knew how to build his audience, too. "Before I begin," he would inform his curious listeners, "I want you to do me a favor. I am going to talk about four or five minutes. While I am doing that I want you to go to the telephone and call up five of your friends and tell them Huey Long is on the air, and he has some very important revelations to make." After the interlude, Huey would be off and running with more political fun and mayhem.

political fun: Huey was off and running, regaling his audience with funny stories and playing upon their fears, prejudices, and anger. His enemies were their enemies—the lying newspapers, the selfish rich, and the greedy corporations with their corrupt political allies. At least for two enjoyable hours, Huey's millions could dream of striking back at those who left them poor and desperate.

Physical presence could hardly explain Long's power. His unkempt red hair fell loosely across his broad forehead. His pug nose and dimpled chin emphasized his round, fleshy face. Over the years, rich food and late-night carousing settled a noticeable paunch on his otherwise average frame. It was the eyes that revealed the difference. Sharp and intense, they sparked with the demonic energy of the man. They were a hater's eyes. Huey never forgave an insult or a political treachery. Unlike his brother Earl, who hated with an unbridled fury that often led to loss of control and physical violence, Huey hated with a cold, calculating intensity that warned friend or foe that he might destroy them when it served his purpose. His fear of physical confrontation, advertised by the constant presence of burly state policemen, led many people to call him a coward, but in politics he never ran from a fight: "Once disappointed over a political undertaking, I could never cast it from my mind. I awaited the opportunity of a political contest."

Personal style set Long apart from other politicians. He had the common touch without ever appearing common. One minute he could play the "good ol' boy" full of easy-going down-home charm; the next minute he would rage with fury at his enemies. As with most mass leaders and celebrities, his mere presence could excite a crowd. Plain folks loved his flair. New York sophisticates might laugh at the lavender shirts, pink ties, shiny suits, and jaunty straw hat, but to Huey and millions of small farmers, workers, and downtrodden Americans, his outlandish garb seemed the height of elegance.

Whether flailing the ruling classes or chiding the president for refusing to redistribute wealth, Long never lost touch with his audience. He would try out a series of ideas or themes until he evoked the right response. He talked the people's language, but with an eloquence that gave their hopes and fears special meaning. Once when asked to compare the Hoover and Roosevelt administrations, Huey likened Hoover to a hoot owl and Roosevelt to a scrootch owl. To catch a hen, he explained, a hoot owl knocked her off the roost and grabbed her as she fell. The scrootch owl was much smoother. He "scrootches up to the hen and talks softly to her, and the hen just falls in love with him, and the next thing you know, there ain't no hen."

Anyone who met Long recognized immediately that he had an extraordinary mind and almost inhuman energy. His near-photographic memory enabled him to recall an infinite number of names, faces, and details of even the most mundane matters. As a lawyer, Huey won the praise of Chief Justice William Howard Taft, who described him as one of the best legal minds to appear before the United States Supreme Court. One writer recalled a typical political conference held in Huey's hotel bedroom. There was Huey lounging drowsily in the notorious lime green pajamas. Then suddenly, an issue fired his imagination. He exploded from bed waving his arms in windmill fashion, shouting at his henchmen, while pointing a finger and pounding them with his fist for emphasis. No matter what the topic—whether to build a drainage ditch at a parish hospital or how to run the next campaign—Huey knew as much or more about it than anyone in the room. Raymond Moley, a member of FDR's braintrust, admitted, "I have never known a mind that moved with more clarity, decisiveness or force." But as one of Long's many critics, Moley regretted the way in which he thought Long "misused his fine mind, battered it, as a child mistreats a toy the value of which he could not understand."

Like Long's contemporaries, historians have been divided in their judgments on the "Kingfish." Arthur Schlesinger, Jr., a fervent champion of the liberalism of Franklin Roosevelt and John Kennedy, recognized Long's talents, but portrayed him as a vicious and dangerous man. Finding Long devoid of any larger social or political vision, Schlesinger banished him from the ranks of both liberal reformers and fascist dictators. "The Messiah of the Rednecks," as Schlesinger condescendingly labelled Long, belonged in the company of such petty politicians as the corrupt dictators of South American "banana republics." "Like them," Schlesinger concluded, "he stood in some muddled way for economic modernization and social justice; like them, he was most threatened by his own arrogance and cupidity, his weakness for soft living and his rage for personal power."

Less doctrinaire in his liberalism, William Leuchtenberg, another leading New Deal historian, treated Long with a bit more sympathy and respect. He recognized that the backwoods buffoon which Long displayed in public was a cleverly conceived act. "A shrewd, intelligent lawyer," Leuchtenberg noted, "Huey cultivated the impression he was an ignoramus. Yet at the same time he lampooned the serious social thinkers of the day." In the end, though, Leuchtenberg dismissed Long as an overblown phenomenon, seriously threatening neither to FDR's reelection in 1936 nor the survival of liberal democracy. His pledge to

"Share Our Wealth" linked Long to the "Pied Piper" as he led the poor masses on a futile quest.

In contrast to both Leuchtenberg and Schlesinger, Long's chief biographer, T. Harry Williams, found much to admire in the "Kingfish" and his legacy. That Williams studied Long from an office at Louisiana State University might cause cynics to doubt his impartiality. Yet even the most hostile of Long's detractors must agree with Williams that Huey Long was no ordinary man. Whatever the label—dictator, demagogue, fascist, populist, liberal reformer, political boss, or revolutionary—Williams concluded that Long "was undeniably a great leader, one of those breed who has to move and drive ordinary men, one of those who break the pattern of their time and shape it anew."

"GREAT MAN" THEORY

Over the centuries, historians and philosophers have debated the influence of "great men"* in shaping the course of human history. At one extreme stands the nineteenth-century romantic philosopher Thomas Carlyle, who argued that the actions of great leaders have determined history. "Universal history," he wrote, "the history of what man has accomplished in this world, is at bottom the history of the Great Men who have worked here." At the other extreme stand the social determinists, followers of Hegel, Marx, and Darwin, who argued that great leaders do not make history. They are products of the times, a reflection of spiritual or material forces, that call forth the heroes demanded by the unfolding of historical laws. As Marx's collaborator Frederick Engels argued, "That Napoleon . . . should have been the military dictator made necessary by the exhausting wars of the French Revolution—that was a matter of chance. But in default of Napoleon, another would have filled his place, that is established by the fact that whenever a great man was necessary, he has always been found: Caesar, Augustus, Cromwell."

Between those extremes—heroes who stand above and direct the social forces of the day and heroes who act as instruments of historical laws—there are, of course, other points of view. Many social Darwinists, for example, saw great leaders as the product of chance brought

*The term unfortunately displays its male bias. Since the historians and others we quote have traditionally used it, we make grudging acknowledgment of the tradition. But hereafter we will prefer the more impartial phrase "great leaders."

forth through the process of natural variation. Once these "mutants" arrived, the social environment acted as a selective mechanism by providing the opportunities for those actions that demonstrated their heroic nature. William James, the father of American pragmatist philosophy, suggested, "The mutations of society from generation to generation are in the main due directly or indirectly to the acts or examples of individuals whose genius was so adapted to the receptivities of the moment, or whose accidental position of authority was so critical that they became ferments, initiators of movement, setters of precedent or fashion, centers of corruption, or destroyers of persons whose gifts, had they had free play, would have led society in another direction." In short, James concluded that the "receptivities of the moment" mediate between genius and society. Many potentially great leaders may have died in obscurity because the times or the presence of another dominant figure did not permit them to realize their talents.

T. Harry Williams's sense of Huey Long as a great leader is reflective of the position defined by philosopher Sidney Hook. As a liberal and disillusioned Marxist, Hook took pains to reject the social determinists' view that individuals had little impact on history. "The hero in history," he wrote, "is the individual to whom we can attribute preponderant influence in determining an issue or event whose consequences would have been profoundly different if he had not acted as he did." Hook's heroes are limited neither to the world of public affairs nor politics. They may be men or women of science, the arts, literature, or any other field. Nor must they be people whose actions history approves. Hitler, Rasputin, and Napoleon have been as crucial as Joan of Arc, George Washington, or Einstein.

Heroes appear for Hook at the "forking point of history." Antecedent events have prepared the stage for their entrances and decisive acts, choices, or discoveries. Such a conception forces Hook to distinguish between what he calls the "eventful" hero and the "event-making" hero. Paul Revere exemplifies the "eventful" man, a person who commits a critical act, but through chance, rather than personal achievement. Anybody who could ride a horse, tell the difference between one or two lanterns, find the road to Concord and Lexington, and yell, "The Redcoats are coming!" could have filled Revere's heroic shoes. Still, his actions were of grave importance, for history might have taken a different course had he fallen off along the way.

By contrast, the "event-making" person is a hero for who and what he is as well as what he does. He not only leads people at the "fork in the road"; he also helps create that fork. His quality of leadership will then sweep aside potential opposition to assure that people accept the alternate road he has chosen. Surely George Washington's imposing presence as the first president helped assure the survival of republican government when others sought a monarch or benevolent dictator. Another measure of his greatness is his significant "imprint" still visible long after his death. Americans for almost two hundred years have treated the "Farewell Address" as historical verity carved in stone. His character has served as a model for generations of school children and national leaders. Who else has sanctified as many inns and bedrooms by his choice of accommodations? Washington clearly exemplifies the "event-making" hero.

Was Huey Long another "event-making" hero? Is T. Harry Williams correct when he asserts that Long fulfilled the definition of such men offered by historian Jacob Burckhardt? "He appears complete in every situation," Burckhardt wrote, "but every situation seems to cramp him. He does not merely fill it. He may shatter it. . . . Confronted with parliaments, senates, assemblies, press, public opinion, he knows at any moment how far they are real or only imaginary, and makes frank use of them. . . ."

Modern historians have moved steadily away from Carlyle's romantic view toward the social determinists' opinion of great leaders. It becomes increasingly attractive to dismiss the notion of "heroes" and "heroic" abilities as irrelevant or of little consequence in directing the course of history. Certainly the worldwide magnitude of the Great Depression and its devasting impact on industrial nations underscores the large impersonal forces that affect modern society and that mock the efforts of individuals to understand, much less control them. Around the world factories stood idle and food rotted in the fields while millions of unemployed workers faced growing poverty and even starvation. The political and business leadership that took so much credit for American prosperity in the 1920s now stood impotent in the face of spiraling disaster. President Herbert Hoover symbolized the bankruptcy of leaders and ideas with his much-heralded "no business" conferences. Business leaders paraded to the White House for talks that led to further inaction. The subsequent history of the 1930s would seem to confirm the social determinists' view that perilous times evoke great leaders. That single decade brought forth an almost unprecedented generation of political giants, among them Franklin D. Roosevelt, Winston Churchill, Adolf Hitler, Joseph Stalin, and Mao Zedong.

LONG'S LOUISIANA

Louisiana, too, seemed fertile ground for the emergence of a leader who would attack the corrupt political alliance that had held the people in the thralls of poverty, ignorance, debt, and disease. In the 1920s, the state had only 331 miles of paved roads. Among the forty-eight states it had one of the lowest expenditures for education and ranked forty-seven out of forty-eight in literacy. A good 16 percent of the population could neither read nor write. A state as poor as Louisiana could scarcely afford the health, educational, and other social services the poor so desperately needed.

But Louisiana was poor by choice as well as circumstances. Through corruption, police intimidation, and fraud, the Old Regulars and their allies in the Choctaw Club, the political machine that ran New Orleans, assured victory for their chosen candidates. Across the state the conservative business and planter classes and their henchmen used the political system to preserve their special privileges. Louisiana had the same combination of cotton planters, merchants, and professional politicians who feasted regularly at the public trough all across the South. Together they thwarted any efforts to raise taxes or divert state resources to programs for the poor. "We were secure. We were the old families," one prominent society matron recalled. "We had what we wanted. We didn't bother anybody. All we wanted was to keep it."

One corporation in particular, Standard Oil of Louisiana, dominated the economic and political life of the state. It paid almost nothing for the right to drain Louisiana's oil riches. Standard joined with the conservative hierarchy to ensure a favorable climate for business at great expense to the workers and the poor. Citizens of New Orleans, for example, paid among the highest utility rates in the nation, while business taxes were among the lowest. From the Civil War to the 1920s such self-serving greed and class interest kept Louisiana in a condition comparable to feudalism.

Several peculiarities explain the plight of Louisiana's lower classes. Besides cotton planters, the state had a powerful block of sugar planters to reinforce the conservative hierarchy. The Old Regulars and Choctaws constituted the only powerful urban machine in southern politics. That combination of planters and urban bosses had long managed to rule the state without serious challenge. Briefly during the populist uprising of the 1890s poor blacks and whites had joined to demand redress for their manifold economic grievances. But the conservatives had an issue along with race-baiting to keep the poor divided. Most of southern Louisiana was Catholic, while the poor northern hill farmers were largely Protestant. No one outside the conservative hierarchy had ever found a way to unite the two groups.

Mired in poverty, exploited by the wealthy few, and without a political voice, the masses of Louisiana were indeed ripe for a popular leader. Yet, since the Civil War, the conservatives had crushed or absorbed anyone who sought to upset the state's balance. A "good ol' boy" might come around preaching the politics of discontent to farmers along the creek forks, upland hills, or bayous, but sooner or later he would lose his fire and sell out to the interests.

Huey Long was different. His claim to greatness as an "event-making" leader rests largely on the capacity he demonstrated to redefine the rules and goals of politics at almost every stage of his career. Even a brief summary of that career suggests why T. Harry Williams could claim Long as an example of the great leaders who redirect the course of history. Huey was born in 1893 at the beginning of a severe national depression and died forty-two years later in the middle of an even worse economic disaster. Those who seek the roots of character in childhood will find potential confirmation of Long's greatness in his early years. Even before walking at just nine months, Long showed signs of the electric energy and devilish curiosity that set him apart. His sisters recalled that if left alone, he might roll off the porch, crawl to the fence, and unlatch the gate, so that he could sit by the road and watch the people passing.

By the age of twenty-five, Long had accomplished more than many people achieve in a lifetime. He moved with the sense of urgency and destiny historians often discover in the lives of great leaders. After turning the local Winnfield schools upside down with his irrepressible antics, he embarked at age seventeen on a brief career as a salesman. Though he earned little, he gained valuable experience dealing with the public and learning to survive by his wits. Five years after high school, he had been through several jobs, a brief stint at the University of Oklahoma, marriage, a year at Tulane University Law School, and the Louisiana bar exam. Over the next three years, he established a successful law practice, became the father of two children (one a future senator), and won his first election to public office.

Such a fast-moving, ambitious young man was bound to experience frustration and a few failures along his way. At the age of thirty-one, he lost his first race for the governorship. Four years later, in 1928, he came back to beat the odds and the conservative hierarchy to become one of the youngest governors ever elected. He still had to withstand an impeachment effort before he could count on keeping his office out of the clutches of his enemies. That unsuccessful effort to destroy his political career seemed to have hardened his ambition to smash anyone who stood in his way. He allowed the shattered remnants of the Standard Oil, cotton and sugar planter, and urban Choctaw machine alliance to survive because he understood that in politics such enemies make useful scapegoats. Whenever he needed to arouse his followers or justify the ruthlessness of his politics he could flail the conservative oligarchy. Under Long, Louisiana became the one southern state that had something resembling a two-party system, though his dictatorial power made political opposition virtually meaningless.

Preoccupied with the state's economic and social injustice, Long avoided the traditional southern demagogues' passion for race baiting and religious bigotry. Instead, he made Louisianans face up to the real sources of their poverty: inequitable income distribution, regressive taxation, poor education, paucity of social services, and the domination of corporate interests. As one critic of his dictatorship conceded, "Huey Pierce Long has the distinction of having injected more realism into southern politics than any man of his generation."

In 1930, while still governor, Long began his ascent into national politics. He was just thirty-seven when elected senator from Louisiana. For one year he refused to leave the state to assume his seat until he had found a successor he could trust to mind the store in his absence. It was that same year that the notorious "green pajamas" episode with the German naval commander helped project him into the national limelight. In the Senate, he associated himself with a small band of hopelessly outnumbered progressives, centered around George Norris of Nebraska. He soon broke with the stodgy and conservative Democratic leadership of Arkansas's Joe Robinson. In 1932 he began his troubled association with Franklin Roosevelt, when at Norris's urging, he helped the New York governor win the 1932 Democratic presidential nomination. Long then stumped effectively for Roosevelt and, one suspects, for himself in the few midwestern states where Roosevelt's wary campaign managers dared to send him. The raves from enthusiastic local party leaders astounded Roosevelt's advisors. "We never again underrated him," recalled campaign chief Jim Farley.

Before Roosevelt had completed the spectacular first "hundred days," the Kingfish had bolted from the New Deal. Long charged that Roosevelt was too much the captive of the special interests to confront the real issue facing the United States—maldistribution of wealth. "When one man decided he must have more goods to wear for himself and his family than any other ninety-nine people," Long explained, "then the condition results that instead of one hundred people sharing the things on earth for one hundred people, that one man through his greed, takes over ninety-nine parts for himself and leaves one part for ninety-nine." While Frank-lin De-La-No-Roo-Se-Velt, as Long twittingly pronounced the president's name, catered to bankers and took money from veterans to plant trees, the hard-working middle class of America was disappearing into poverty.

A buoyant Kingfish celebrates the 1934 election-night victory of one of his allies, James P. O'Connor (left), along with Governor O.K. Allen (right). Less than a year later, Long was gunned down in the Louisiana state capitol building by an irate physician. Reeling down the corridor, Long slumped into the arms of O'Connor, who had come running to investigate the commotion. "Jimmy, my boy, I've been shot," gasped Long. Governor Allen, also present, reportedly seized a pistol and dashed down the corridor toward the assassin shouting, "If there's shooting I want to be in on it!"

Long countered the president's reformism with a grandiose scheme for sharing wealth. He proposed to tax away income over $1 million and inheritance over $5 million. With little regard for economic realities, Long began to promise his followers some remarkable benefits. Every family would receive a $5,000 homestead allowance and a guaranteed income of $2,000 a year. He offered additional support for labor, farmers, the elderly, and the young. If someone suggested that Long's plan sounded like Hitler's or Lenin's, he referred the heckler to his true source—the Bible. "It's all in the scriptures," he would claim and then cite Leviticus, Deuteronomy, or Isaiah.

The real cause of Long's dissatisfaction, most historians would agree, was that Franklin Roosevelt's success blocked his own road to national power. The Kingfish had grown too accustomed to solo performances to play second violin to Roosevelt. By 1934 he had begun organizing his own political base outside the Democratic Party. With his slogan "every man a king, but no man wears a crown," he attracted perhaps as many as seven million members to his Share Our Wealth Clubs. But whether Long could have translated membership into enough votes to mount a serious threat to Roosevelt's reelection in either 1936 or 1940 can never be known. On a whirlwind trip to tend to business in Louisiana, his career ended tragically. Carl Weiss, a brilliant surgeon and son-in-law of a disappointed officeholder, mortally wounded the Kingfish in the corridor of the state capitol building. Weiss died immediately in a hail of gunfire.

Death at an early age left Long's promise unfulfilled. "God don't let me die," friends around his deathbed heard him whisper. "I have so much to do." The circumstance of his death evokes an eerie resemblance to Hegel's description of great leaders as instruments of history to be discarded when their work is done. "Their whole life is labor and trouble . . . ," Hegel wrote, "They die early like Alexander; they are murdered like Caesar. . . ."

THE GREATNESS OF HUEY LONG

Long's tragic death has made it impossible for historians to measure his potential for national leadership. When he died, he was on the verge of greatness, but he had held office only as the governor and senator from a relatively backward southern state. He demonstrated a capacity for dynamic leadership at the state level and for using his flamboyant personality to attract a national audience of uncertain political persuasion. In that light he would stand in the second tier of political leaders and invite comparison to such regional aspirants for national office as Dixiecrat Strom Thurmond of South Carolina or former Governor George Wallace of Alabama. Wallace, like Long, dramatized working- and lower-middle-class discontent without proving that he could establish the broad-based national coalition needed to win the presidency. It is impossible to determine if Long could have lured many followers away from Franklin Roosevelt and his popular New Deal programs. At the time of Long's death, federal investigations into the corruption in Louisiana threatened to weaken or destroy the machine that served as his political base.

Since actual events cannot sufficiently measure Long's potential as a great national and international leader, historians must search for alternatives to the standard biographical practice of chronicling a subject's many achievements. One method that appealed to many of Long's contemporaries was to draw comparisons between the Kingfish and other great political leaders. The ruthlessness with which Long dominated Louisiana in the 1930s inevitably suggested parallels with Nazi dictator Adolf Hitler. Many of the conditions that accompanied Hitler's rise to power existed in the United States: an increasingly impoverished middle class, growing radical political groups, a leadership that often failed to respond to popular fears and suffering, and huge inequities of power and wealth created by capitalism. Some people predicted that if Roosevelt faltered in his efforts to bring the country out of the depression or to provide a measure of security, Long stood lurking in the wings to "Hitlerize America."

Upon closer analysis the comparison breaks down. In at least two important particulars, Long rejected Hitler's program. He was not anti-intellectual nor was he a religious or racial bigot. The growth in size and quality of Louisiana State University remained one of his proudest accomplishments. And when a reporter once tried to compare him to Hitler, Long shot back, "Don't liken me to that sonofabitch. Anybody that lets his public policies be mixed up with his religious prejudices is a plain goddamned fool." As a hard-bitten political realist, Long never indulged in Hitler's sometimes dreamy forays into romantic fantasy. Both Hitler and Mussolini dabbled in social thought and evolved theories of the state as the end point of politics. Beyond his scheme to redistribute wealth, Long generated few political ideas.

Still, Long's potential appeal to mass discontent gave special cause for concern. Raymond Graham Swing, the commentator who most fully explored the parallels to Hitler, worried over the remark of a young Louisiana State University professor. "There are many things Huey does

I don't approve of," the professor admitted. "But on the whole he has done a great deal of good. And if I had to choose between him without democracy and going back to the old crowd . . . I should choose Huey. After all, democracy isn't any good if it doesn't work. Do you really think freedom is so important?"

More fruitful comparisons can be drawn between Long and politicians of a homegrown variety. Among other senators in the twentieth century who built a national following, Robert LaFollette and Joseph McCarthy, both from Wisconsin, offer the historian some interesting parallels. Comparison to LaFollette brings out Long's capacity for constructive and innovative politics, while the link to McCarthy illuminates his disruptive tactics and his facility for exploiting institutional and human weaknesses. All three careers provide insight into the nature of national leadership below the presidential level.

Though not as politically precocious as Long, "Battle Bob" turned early in his life from law to politics. At age twenty-five, just seven months out of college and recently admitted to the bar, LaFollette defied the local machine boss to win election as district attorney. Soon, like Long, he had built a reputation as a champion of the little guy and foe of the interests. In 1885, he began the first of his three terms in Congress and by 1900 after two unsuccessful bids he was elected governor of Wisconsin. He brought to public office the same burning ambition that set Long apart from most men. His enemies were Long's enemies: corrupt political machines, large corporations, greedy bankers, and concentrated wealth. His first electoral defeat at the hands of the entrenched interests led him, like Long, to declare war on the machine. In its place he constructed an equally powerful organization loyal to himself, but one which for forty years earned a well-deserved reputation for efficient, honest, and progressive government.

It was not just progressive zeal that differentiated LaFollette from Long. "Battle Bob" possessed little of the common touch. His stern Calvinist soul, intense convictions, and unbending nature led him to champion minority causes and to set his eye on what was right rather than expedient. Where Long used his barbed wit, biting invective, and homespun ebullience to win an audience, LaFollette preferred the power of truth and moral rectitude to persuade his followers. Such political asceticism could never achieve the broad mass appeal that attracted millions to Long. And LaFollette, too, had his Roosevelt—in this case the popular Teddy Roosevelt—who for a season blocked any aspirations he might have had for national leadership.

A comparison to Senator Joseph McCarthy must dwell on the dark side

of Long's political nature—his capacity for hate, his wanton destructive-
ness, and his disregard for rules of fair play or responsible politics. What
Euripedes said of the demagogue in *Orestes* might apply equally well at
times to either McCarthy or Long: "A man of loose tongue, intemperate,
trusting in tumult, leading the population to mischief with empty
words." Long drew his followers from the millions suffering the fear and
deprivations of the depression. McCarthy exploited the cold war fear of
communism to wreak havoc on the apparatus of American foreign
policymaking. His goal, as far as historians can judge, was neither a safer
America nor the eradication of domestic communism, but a prominent
place in the public limelight. He relished his ability to generate headlines
and confusion among his political foes.

Like Long, McCarthy was something of a political innovator. While
Long perfected the devices of the state political machine, McCarthy
mastered the "multiple untruth," a falsehood so large, hyperbolic, and
complex that it defied refutation. "The Multiple Untruth," observed
McCarthy's biographer Richard Rovere, "places an unbearable burden
of disproof on the challenger. The work of refutation is always inconclu-
sive, confusing, and—most important of all, perhaps—boring to the
public." No one, either friend or foe, ever found Long or McCarthy
boring. Still, McCarthy relied even more than Long on the measure of
public gullibility. Americans love facts and McCarthy seemed weighted
down with them. His briefcase, bulging with documents, photostats, and
transcripts, lent an air of credibility to his extravagant accusations. Close
examination usually proved that his documents had little relevance to the
charges he raised. McCarthy, too, matched his public excesses with a
private passion for voluptuous living. Boozing, womanizing, and late
nights (possibly drug addiction as well) took their toll just as they did
for Long.

For all the parallels, "Tail-gunner Joe" differed from Long in at least
one critical aspect. McCarthy never tried to direct his popularity into a
political organization. Rovere described him as a leader with a following
but no movement. He did not employ the demagogue's practice of
tempting his audience with a vision of a better tomorrow but dwelt,
instead, on their darkest fears and insecurities. When the Senate cen-
sured him for his misconduct, he did not whip his followers into frenzied
outrage, as Long surely would have. McCarthy had no program and
possibly no ambition other than to sustain his capacity to dominate the
headlines.

Since Long built a stronger national political organization than either
LaFollette or McCarthy, it might be more productive to compare him to
the popular presidents rather than senators. Abraham Lincoln, Lyndon

Johnson, and Harry Truman among others followed Long's path from modest beginnings and political obscurity in remote rural communities to the top and center of American politics. But none of those men who achieved more in politics moved so far outside traditional channels or advanced as rapidly at such a young age. The presidents who did achieve their ambitions early, Theodore Roosevelt and John Kennedy, both started with the advantages of wealth and prominence. Their road to the White House was shorter than that of any president save, perhaps, John Quincy Adams. Each faced obstacles, nonetheless, as formidable as any Long encountered. Roosevelt had to overcome the prejudice of patricians against politics and of professional politicians against patricians. Kennedy surmounted the deep-seated American prejudice against Catholics. It is improbable, though certainly not impossible, that Long could have conquered the national bias that kept southerners out of the White House until Lyndon Johnson's victory in 1964.

INSTANCES OF GREATNESS?

The attempt to find adequate parallels in the lives of other national leaders proves ultimately as unsatisfactory as contemporaries' efforts to fix Long with an accurate political label. Just as his program defied precise definition, his brand of politics was unique. He had elements of the demagogue, populist, liberal reformer, radical, and native fascist, but he conformed to no particular type. Once again, historians are forced to accept the label Long pinned on himself; he was indeed *sui generis.* To measure his potential as a great leader, historians must look closely at some of the critical moments in his career. We can then better judge whether Long brought circumstances to a "forking point" and then, through the force of his character, determined the path history followed. Or we might conclude that Long was little more than an instrument of larger political forces at work in that turbulent era in the history of Louisiana and the United States.

One of the first key episodes in Long's public life occurred before he formally embarked on his career in politics. As a struggling young lawyer, he had come under the benevolent wing of a successful Winnfield politician, State Senator S. J. Harper. True to the dissenting heritage of Winnfield County politics, Harper adopted a body of unorthodox, even eccentric ideas. He opposed war, Wall Street bankers, liquor, the microbe theory, and high heels for women. It was in support of Harper's workman's compensation amendments that Long first spoke before the Louisiana legislature. When the United States entered World War I in

1917, Harper demanded that Congress finance the war effort by con-scripting wealth. He later elaborated his views in a pamphlet denouncing war profiteers, bankers, and Wall Street. His outburst incurred the wrath of state officials who, along with most Americans caught in the contagion of war fever, had lost all tolerance for dissent. A federal grand jury indicted Harper for violating the Espionage Act.

Despite the popular furor, Long made the risky decision to serve as Harper's attorney. He understood that the government's case amounted to a political vendetta and, therefore, politicized the defense by denouncing the indictment at a press conference. By defusing some of the hostility, Long shifted opinion in favor of his client and thereby reduced the personal risk of committing political suicide prematurely. As the case came to trial, Huey was unwilling merely to stand by and let the law take its course. While his brother Julius prepared the legal side of the defense, Huey worked behind the scenes to shift the odds in Harper's favor. He soon learned that government agents were shad-owing all the prospective jurors. As openly as possible, he contacted all those who might be hostile to Harper and engaged them in drinks and conversation. The agents duly reported those friendly encounters, though Huey, in fact, had never mentioned the case. When each of those compromised jurors was called, suspicious government attorneys excused them. Huey had virtually cleared the jury of potentially un-sympathetic elements.

T. Harry Williams has persuasively argued that Long's antics had little to do with Harper's acquittal. The government's weak case simply fell apart in the courtroom. But what does impress the student of "great leaders" is a certain characteristic behavior that recurs throughout Long's career. First, Long perceived in an apparently damaging case an opportunity to advance his own political fortunes and earn the gratitude of an ally as well. Second, he showed his cleverness at redefining the rules to suit his own purpose. Tampering with the jury violated the spirit, if not the letter of the law. Third, his decision to attack the prosecution involved a cardinal rule of American politics, later perfected in Califor-nia by campaign strategist Murray Chotiner and his apt student, Richard Nixon. Do not defend yourself and let the public know where you stand. Attack your opponents and let the public know where they stand, while revealing as little about yourself as possible. Once attention is focused on what voters resent in your opponents, they will be on the defensive. Americans, Long understood, are as likely to decide *against* candidates and issues as they are *for* them. Long would use those tactics—pro-jecting himself to the public, redefining the rules of the game, and

mastering the attack—to win victories even when defeat seemed virtually inevitable.

The most dramatic instance of Long's talent for improvisation and
survival came during his 1929 impeachment case. Conservative leaders,
outraged by his attempt to tax Standard Oil; by his progressive textbook,
road, and welfare programs; and by his high-handed political methods,
formed the "Dynamite Squad" to impeach the governor before he became too popular with the masses. The most serious charge leveled
against him was that he had tried to bribe his former bodyguard, "Bat-
tling" Harry Bozeman, to murder J. Y. Sanders, Jr., leader of the conservative anti-Long faction in the State Senate. Other charges referred
to Long misusing state funds, abusing the powers of his office, and
attempting to influence judges, legislators, and other officials through
bribery, political pressures, and intimidation. Beginning in April 1929,
the Dynamite Squad met daily in Sanders's office to mastermind impeachment strategy. They started with all the advantages on their side
—initiative, an eager staff, and ample volunteer legal assistance.

Momentarily stunned by the strength and organization of the opposition, Long realized he had reached the crossroads of his political career.
Out of habit, he did what he knew best—attacked. For two months he
flooded the state with almost a million copies of circulars he composed
himself (and had delivered by off-duty state police and other state workers). He laid the impeachment fight on the doorstep of his favorite
villain, Standard Oil. The real contest, he charged repeatedly, pitted
Huey Long, champion of the people, against a corporation and its henchmen determined to keep Louisiana in bondage.

Once on the offensive, Long defeated his enemies by using his infinite
energy, his organizational skills, and his political and legal shrewdness.
Since the Dynamite Squad needed a two-thirds majority in the senate to
impeach, Long required support from just fourteen senators to block
them. He and his allies crossed and recrossed the state rounding up
support and rousing the voters to bring pressure to bear on reluctant
legislators. Where those pressures failed, both sides resorted to all manner of argument, including bribery and promises of patronage.

Long's masterstroke came when he adopted a tactic used in 1919 by
senate Republicans to frustrate Woodrow Wilson's attempt to offer them
a "Democratic" Versailles peace treaty. During the negotiations, thirty-
nine, or more than enough to prevent a two-thirds majority, had signed
a round robin letter expressing their opposition to the treaty as then
written. Huey or some member of his inner circle had proposed the same
strategy to win the impeachment fight. As the Louisiana Senate met to

hear the evidence against the governor, a pro-Long senator rose to announce that he and fourteen others, in light of the "unconstitutionality and invalidity" of the charges, had signed a round robin in which they pledged to vote against all articles of impeachment. No matter what evidence the Dynamite Squad hoped to present, no matter how they villified the fifteen pro-Long senators, they had already lost. In stunned silence the legislature agreed to adjourn.

Over the years many of Long's opponents reaped the whirlwind of failure, for Huey always revenged himself against his enemies. Some he drove from office; some he denied patronage; and a few he simply ruined. And just as he never forgave his enemies, he never forgot his

Whenever Huey Long rallied support in a campaign or a debate over legislative issues, he flooded Louisiana with circulars and posters. He often prepared them himself and then used his army of political supporters and government employees to spread the materials around the state. This photograph was taken by Ben Shahn, who painted the portrait of Sacco and Vanzetti on page 297. From 1933 through 1938 Shahn was one of about a dozen photographers who created a pictorial record of rural life during the Depression on behalf of the Farm Security Administration.

supporters. Once five years later, when his successor O. K. Allen claimed he had no position to give an old Long loyalist, Huey shouted at him, "That's one of my old friends who signed the 'Round Robin' to keep them from impeaching me. What do you mean, you haven't got a job?" On such reciprocal loyalties, Long understood, successful organizations were built.

Among his many political skills none surpassed Long's genius as a campaigner. Few politicians have ever had his capacity to organize and conduct a successful race. One of his greatest electoral achievements did not even come on his own behalf, but in the incredible upset he engineered for Hattie Caraway of Arkansas, the first woman elected to the United States Senate. Mrs. Caraway had originally filled her husband's seat after he died in office. Arkansas Democrats apparently expected her to retire gracefully at the end of her term, but Mrs. Caraway had ideas of her own. While in Washington she had met and become friends with the junior senator from Louisiana, Huey Long. Appreciative of the courage she showed in voting regularly with the outnumbered progressives, Long began to act as an informal advisor.

As the new election approached, leading Arkansas Democrats vied to replace Mrs. Caraway. Few noticed, or even cared, when she announced in July that she too would be a candidate in the August 9 election. Not only was she a woman in a region that frowned on women in politics, but she also had no organization, no financial support, and no significant backers. Analysts predicted that at most she would receive 1 percent of the vote. They had not anticipated that Huey would come to campaign for his friend.* Even after he announced his intention, Arkansas politicians scoffed, for Long had just six days to salvage the weakest candidate in the race. Without the advantages of mass communications like television, he would be hard-pressed to reach a substantial number of voters in such a rural state.

Huey gave those smug Arkansas politicians a lesson they did not soon forget. With his sound trucks and circulars, he treated the state to what one observer described as a "circus hitched to a tornado." When it was over, he had given thirty-nine speeches, covered over 2,000 miles, and spoken to some 200,000 people. His campaign rhetoric was vintage Long—maldistribution of wealth, politicians under Wall Street's thumb,

---

*T. Harry Williams has argued convincingly that friendship could hardly have been Long's primary motive. Success in Arkansas would enhance his prestige, increase his public exposure, and frighten his arch political enemy, Joe Robinson, leader of the conservative Senate Democrats and the senior senator from Arkansas.

and the unnecessary suffering from the depression. At the end of each speech he would praise Hattie Caraway for courageously fighting on behalf of the common people. When the cyclone had subsided, Mrs. Caraway won a smashing victory with more votes than the combined totals of her six opponents. Out of the seventy-five counties in Arkansas, Huey had campaigned in thirty-one and Hattie carried twenty-nine of those.

Once again Long had confounded the political professionals. He showed that he understood the mood of the electorate far better than they. His vote-getting tactics presaged a new era in American politics. Out in California the public relations firm of Whitaker and Baxter was already perfecting the "Madison Avenue" blend of media, image, and packaging that has come to dominate election campaigns. Huey had proven as well that his popular appeal was not confined to his native Louisiana. Once aware of his awesome vote-getting talents, national political leaders could no longer dismiss him as a backwoods buffoon.

No historian would build a case for a "great leader" around three isolated successes. In Long's case that is not necessary. His political triumphs were legion. He turned a minor office on the moribund state railroad commission into a major public platform. To win the governorship he became the first candidate outside the old machine who gained broad support in both the Protestant north and the Catholic south. He then welded those factions into a tight organization. As a senator, he showed similar disregard for convention when he attacked one of the most popular and powerful presidents in the nation's history—and from his own party, no less! Many historians agree that his campaign to redistribute wealth forced Roosevelt to propose his own radical tax measure, which led to the Wealth Tax Act of 1935.

At each stage of his career Long had shown that through the force of his charismatic personality and his political savvy he could force others to adopt his agenda for public debate. Whether he could have had that same impact on the U.S. Senate and the national political agenda is open to serious question. During the depression most politicians or parties with a single issue or a narrow constituency flourished briefly and then disappeared. Roosevelt and the New Deal often co-opted their issues, or frustration pushed them further into the extremes of the political spectrum, from which they could not attract a significant following. Corruption, too, whether from wealth or power, took a heavy toll among the political aspirants of the era. Long was vulnerable to all those forces —cooptation, frustration, and corruption. Yet repeatedly, he had proven the experts and their conventional wisdom wrong. He was more forceful, dynamic, and charismatic than most of them recognized. No matter what the yardstick, Sidney Hook's "event-making" hero or Jacob Burkhardt's "great leader," Long met their criteria.

What remains uncertain is what role such persons play in determining the course of history. Long seems to offer some confirmation to both the social determinists and the "great man" theorists. Along with Father Coughlin, Hitler, Franklin Roosevelt, and the California media moguls, Long taught Americans what a charismatic leader could accomplish with the aid of modern mass communications. Still, it seems inevitable that politicians would have learned that lesson even without him. In Louisiana, he redefined state politics and threw the bums out. But soon after he died, his followers had equalled the Old Regulars' reputation for

The Kingfish lives on: a poster tacked to the wall of a Louisiana farmhouse, and caught by another Farm Security Administration photographer, Russell Lee.

venality, inefficiency, and catering to special interests. On the national level, his plan to redistribute wealth died with him. Only World War II led to tax policies that in a small measure shifted wealth from one class to another. Since then, however, the inequities of income and wealth have remained a fixed part of American life.

How then did Huey Long, a great man, redirect the course of history? While historians might agree that he was far more than "The Messiah of the Rednecks," they could not determine what would have happened if Long had never entered politics or had lived to sixty-five. Such speculation takes them into the realm of seers, metaphysicians, and theologians. Those are grounds on which the modern historian treads lightly, if at all.

Additional Reading

Writing in the 1940s, when the presence of Hitler, Roosevelt, Churchill, Stalin, and Mussolini naturally focused attention on the topic, Sidney Hook composed *The Hero in History* (New York, 1943), a clear survey of almost 150 years' historical and philosophical debate over great leaders in history. Since Hook is no particular partisan of the Marxist tradition, a reader might want to give Marx his due by reading Karl Marx and Frederick Engels, *The German Ideology* (New York, 1970).

The issue of the great leader in history is the interpretive framework adopted by T. Harry Williams, *Huey Long* (New York, 1969). Williams set out to write the definitive Long biography, but despite the length and rich detail in his book, he fell short. He records and respects Long's achievements as well as some of the blemishes without fully analyzing the consequences of either. Aside from Williams, Long has had few biographers who did not make use of either a hatchet or kid gloves. Probably the most balanced appraisal comes in Hugh Davis Graham, ed., *Huey Long* (Englewood Cliffs, N.J., 1970), a volume in the "Great Lives Observed" series. Graham provides a mix of documents, contemporary views, and historical perspectives, including Arthur Schlesinger, Jr.'s "Messiah of the Rednecks." That selection is from *The Politics of Upheaval* (New York, 1960), 42–69. Graham also includes a selection from Huey Pierce Long, *Every Man a King* (Baton Rouge, La., 1933), Long's autobiography that became the bible of his Share Our Wealth Clubs. Alan Brinkley, *Voices of Protest* (New York, 1982) has produced the most persuasive interpretation of Long (as well as the "Radio Priest," Father Charles Coughlin) yet written. Placing the Kingfish in the mainstream of the American political tradition, Brinkley debunks the idea that Long threatened to bring fascism to the United States. He was, in Brinkley's eyes, if not a "great man," at least a remarkable politician who gave voice to the desire of millions of Americans "to defend the autonomy of the individual and the independence of the community against encroachments from the modern industrial state."

The best work on the New Deal includes one of the best short sketches of Long yet written—William Leuchtenberg, *Franklin D. Roosevelt and the New Deal* (New York, 1963), 96–99. Otherwise, the reader has to turn to scholars who have studied Long's politics more than his personality. One good place to begin is V. O. Key, *Southern Politics in State and Nation* (New York, 1950) or Allan Sindler, *Huey Long's Louisiana* (Baltimore, 1956). Among the best Long biographies produced by his contemporaries are Forrest Davis, *Huey Long: A Candid*

Biography (New York, 1935) and Carleton Beals, *The Story of Huey P. Long* (Philadelphia, 1935).

In the previous chapter we expressed our opinion that novelists are often excellent historians. Robert Penn Warren, *All the King's Men* (New York, 1946) certainly vindicates that judgment. Critic Robert Alter called it the best political novel of the century and we agree. Warren did not write a novel about Huey Long, but he wrote about the nature of good and evil and the uses and abuses of power. Still, anyone who wants a feeling for Long's Louisiana could find no better source than *All the King's Men*.

The Decision to Drop the Bomb

Just before dawn on July 16, 1945, only a few clouds hung over the still New Mexico desert. The air possessed that lucid clarity which skews all sense of distance and space. There were several large towers erected far out on the desert, yet from the perspective of the blockhouse, they appeared as little more than a few spikes stuck in the sand.

Suddenly, at one of the towers, a brilliant fireball lit up the sky, searing the air and instantly replacing the dawn's subtle pastels with a blazing radiance. With the radiance came heat: an incredible, scorching heat that rolled outward in waves. Where seconds before the sand had stretched cool and level in every direction, now it fused into glass pellets. The concussion from the fireball completely vaporized the tower at its center, created a crater a quarter of a mile wide, and obliterated another forty-ton steel tower one-half mile away. Above the fireball an ominous cloud formed, shooting upwards, outwards, then back upon itself to form the shape of a mushroom, expanding until it had reached eight miles into the air. The effects of the fireball continued outward from its center: the light, followed by the waves of heat, and then the deadening roar of the concussion, sharp enough to break a window over 125 miles away. Light; heat; concussion—but first and foremost, the brilliance of the fireball's light. At the edge of the desert a blind woman was facing the explosion. She saw the light.

In the blockhouse where scientists watched, feelings of joy and relief were mixed with foreboding. The bomb had worked. Theory had been turned into practice. Devastating as the explosion appeared, the resulting fireball had not ignited the earth's atmosphere, as some scientists had predicted. But the foreboding was impossible to shake. Humankind now had in its hands unprecedented destructive powers.

General Leslie R. Groves, director of the atom bomb project, wired the news halfway around the globe to President Harry Truman, then meeting with allied leaders at Potsdam outside Berlin: "The test was successful beyond the most optimistic expectations of anyone." Buoyed by the report, Truman returned to the conference a changed man. British Prime Minister Winston Churchill noticed Truman's sudden self-confidence. "He stood up to the Russians in a most decisive and emphatic manner," Churchill remarked. "He told the Russians just where they got on and got off and generally bossed the whole meeting." Since the British were partners on the bomb project, Churchill soon learned from Groves's report what had so lifted Truman's spirits.

Less than three weeks later, on August 6, 1945, a second mushroom cloud rose, this time above Hiroshima in Japan. That explosion destroyed an entire city, left almost 100,000 people dead and thousands of others dying from radiation poisoning. Along with a second bomb that levelled Nagasaki, it ended the bloodiest and most costly war in history. Ever since, the world has lived with the stark reality that the human race in its imperfection might unleash that atomic horror in a final apocalyptic moment.

The New Mexico test of the first atom bomb marked the successful conclusion of the Manhattan Project, a code name for one of the largest scientific and industrial efforts ever undertaken. Between 1942 and 1945 the United States spent over $2 billion to build three atom bombs. Twenty years earlier that would have equalled the total federal budget. The project required some thirty-seven factories and laboratories in nineteen states and Canada, employed more than 120,000 people, and monopolized many of the nation's top scientists and engineers during a period when their skills were considered essential to national survival. Some of the nation's largest corporations—DuPont, Eastman Kodak, and General Electric—as well as leading universities devoted substantial resources to the Manhattan Project. It received the highest priority from President Roosevelt as he mobilized the country to fight militarism around the world.

Nothing could better illustrate how war had altered the character of scientific research and development than the contrast between the Manhattan Project and the original experiment that made it possible. In 1938, working with relatively primitive equipment on an old kitchen table, German physicist Otto Hahn had exposed uranium (U-238), the heaviest known element, to slow neutrons. Among the products of the reaction he found elements with a mass half that of uranium. Unable to account for the results, he wrote to Lise Meitner, a former colleague.

At 0815 hours August 6, 1945, the bomber Enola Gay and its flight crew received weather clearance and proceeded toward Hiroshima. An hour later, flying at 328 miles per hour, it dropped its bomb directly over the city, from 31,000 feet. It then turned and dove sharply in order to gain speed. The bomb detonated at about 2,000 feet above Hiroshima in order to increase the effective radius of its blast; the resulting cloud, photographed by a nearby observation plane, reached 50,000 feet into the air and was visible for 390 miles. The final statistic: approximately 100,000 people killed and thousands dying from radiation poisoning.

Meitner understood, perhaps too well, what Hahn had observed. Uranium atoms, when struck by a neutron, split into lighter atoms with an enormous release of energy. Physicists around the world began to speculate that with sufficient neutrons they might be able to touch off a multiplying chain reaction. The energy released could conceivably drive turbines, heat buildings, or set off an immense explosion. The Hahn-Meitner discovery assumed a sinister cast in September 1939 as Hitler's blitzkrieg overwhelmed Poland. Science would surely be enlisted in the war that soon engulfed much of the world.

Historians have learned that wars do not create change so much as they accelerate changes already underway. Even before the Manhattan Project, physicists and other scientists had experienced the trend in modern industrial society for ever more of human work, creativity, and important decisions to take place in large organizations. Scientists of the nineteenth century, much like artists, generally worked alone or in small groups with relatively simple equipment. But World War I had demonstrated that organized, well-funded science could be vital to national security. During the war, scientists joined in large research projects to develop new optical glass, explosives, poison gases, airplane instruments, and submarine detection devices. In less than two years, physicists and electrical engineers had doubled the advances of radio technology over the previous ten years. The government, for the first time, funded research on a large scale. But scientists, as much committed to laissez-faire as the most conservative robber baron, learned what it meant to have the imperatives of war rather than their own curiosity determine the nature of their research.

The end of the war halted government interference and financial support. Still, like most Americans, scientists shared in the prosperity of the 1920s. Economic boom meant increases in budgets available for research. Success in the laboratory attracted contributions from private foundations and wealthy individuals. American science began to approach the quality of science in Europe. A few scientists became minor celebrities. When Albert Einstein visited the United States in 1921, large crowds gathered to pay him tribute, though few people understood the significance of either the special or general theories of relativity.

The depression of the 1930s forced scientists to tighten their belts and lower their expectations. The government, though seldom an important source of funding, drastically cut the budgets for its scientific bureaus. Even when the New Deal created jobs for scientists, it did so primarily to stimulate employment, not research. But by the late 1930s, private foundations had resumed their earlier levels of support. Now, however, a preoccupation with social utility shifted their emphasis from the physical sciences to biomedical fields.

Such difficulties did not seriously hamper the work of physicist Ernest Lawrence, who emerged in the 1930s as the most famous American scientist. When Lawrence took a position in 1929 at the University of California, Berkeley, physicists had zeroed in on the structure of the nucleus as their most urgent area of research. It became Lawrence's dream to create a machine of sufficient power to penetrate the nucleus's protective shell and unlock its secrets. By 1932, Lawrence and his associates had built what he called a cyclotron, which could accelerate atomic particles in a focused beam to unprecedented energies. But the obsession with perfecting his machine at first distracted Lawrence from realizing its experimental potential. English physicists working with far less powerful equipment achieved earlier successes.

Soon, however, Lawrence and his laboratory staff showed what the cyclotron could do. In anticipation of the 1933 Chicago World's Fair, they conducted a wide range of experiments that no one else could duplicate, for no one else had a machine as powerful. To an impressed crowd, Lawrence described how he had transmuted elements, released power from deuterium (heavy water, widely used in fission research), and begun to penetrate the innermost secrets of the neutron. Newspapers spread Lawrence's fame across the nation. Radio comedians made jokes about heavy water. Lawrence soon became an internationally known scientific figure and by 1939 added the Nobel Prize to his long list of honors.

He had not achieved his fame alone. His work in big-machine physics required elaborate equipment, an extensive staff, and large sums of money to maintain the program. As his reputation grew and the cyclotron produced impressive discoveries, Lawrence increased his capacity to raise money and acquire assistants. Equally important, he and his brother John, a specialist in internal medicine, demonstrated that the cyclotron held out hope for radical new treatment of cancer. Lawrence could thus tap sources of money unavailable to other researchers in the physical sciences.

Early on, physicists at Berkeley complained that Lawrence's obsession with bigger machines was crowding them out of the laboratory. To accommodate his first large cyclotron, Lawrence acquired an old shack behind the lab and raised $10,000 to build a million-volt machine with a two-ton magnet. Soon the radiation lab, as his facility was called, began to dwarf the entire physics department. By 1939 his work went on in a

$300,000 lab, while he set out to raise $1.5 million to construct a 100-million-volt cyclotron with a 2,000-ton magnet. His success in raising money reflected his prestige, not the soundness of his physics, for leading theoretical physicists had determined that "Lawrence's project for a hundred million volts was no more practical than a time machine."

Lawrence's big-machine physics helped establish the trend toward large-scale research projects, undertaken by groups of researchers and technicians, working with expensive equipment. Still, the historian must avoid overemphasizing the extent to which science had become organized, bureaucratized, and institutionalized in those days before the Manhattan Project. One physicist who had worked with Lawrence remarked, "I try to live now the way we did in those days. . . . No forms to fill out. No organization charts. Not even one secretary." Compared to the $600 million the Manhattan Project later invested in Lawrence's process for electromagnetic separation of the isotope U-235, his request for $1.5 million seems paltry. In creating the bomb, scientists who once had difficulty spending thousands of dollars over a year learned to spend millions overnight.

Cultural historians have recognized that trends in one field usually have parallels throughout a society. The movement toward organization and bureaucracy in science was no exception. As Lawrence built his laboratory at Berkeley, the New Deal established a wide array of regulatory agencies, social welfare programs, and other government organizations to extend its reach into many areas of daily life. Much that the New Deal did through government and politics in the 1930s, large corporations had accomplished in the preceding era. Centralized slaughter houses with a distribution of railroads, refrigerated warehouses, and trucks replaced the local butcher to put meat on American tables. What Armour and Swift did for meatpacking, Heinz did for the pickle, Henry Ford for the automobile, and other corporations for the multitude of goods used in American homes and industry. To study the modern era, historians must understand how large organizations work.

THE NEED FOR MODELS

The study of organizations forces historians to adopt new interpretive tools. Ideas that may adequately describe the motives or actions of individuals may not explain the functioning of groups. Yet historians have traditionally tended to equate the actions of governments with the purposeful behavior of individuals. The history of the Meat Inspection Act has already demonstrated the tendency to personalize issues in the political arena, where newspaper cartoons and the rhetoric of politics paint issues in terms of personal actors and their motives. Obviously, as the complexity of modern bureaucracies increases, such simplified explanations conceal more and more of institutional realities.

Thus, it is convenient to talk about the United States government as a single entity or to say, for example, that "Truman dropped the atom bomb to win the war," when what we really mean is that an American airplane, armed with a single atom bomb, designed and built by Manhattan Project scientists and technicians, under the authority of the War Department, followed the orders of the president, conveyed through the military chain of command, to proceed to its target in Japan, selected by the secretary of war, in consultation with his military advisers, in order to destroy a Japanese city and thereby hasten the end of the war. The difference in meaning between "Truman dropped" and what actually happened encapsulates the modern historian's dilemma. The first explanation is coherent, clear, and human. The second is cumbersome and confusing but more comprehensive and accurate.

To enhance their analytical powers, historians, like most social scientists, must work with interpretive models. For many people the term "model" might bring to mind an object like a small plastic airplane or an electric train. For social scientists a model, not unlike the small plane, reduces the scale of reality and increases their capacity to describe the characteristics of what they observe. Even though the plastic model has no instruments or engines, it has the same shape, proportions, and external details as an actual plane. Models often have the additional virtue of being less complex than the real object. But in that way models also limit our understanding. We cannot judge from an electric train how all the parts in a real train interact. The observer gains insight into several features or components, while acquiring a false or incomplete sense of the whole. Models allow historians to isolate certain factors critical to the understanding of a complex reality. They do not, however, enable them to see the "whole truth."

The phrase "Truman dropped" typifies the application of what might be termed a "rational actor" model, the interpretive framework historians most often adopt. As indicated before, the rational actor model equates the behavior of governments with the purposeful actions of individuals. It assumes that government leaders pursue the course of action best suited to solve a given problem and that their significant actions have equally significant causes. If victory in war is the objective, leaders consider the various possible strategies compatible with their resources, consider the pros and cons of each option, and then select the one that offers the highest probability of success at the lowest cost. The critical assumptions behind this model are rationality and value-maximizing. Rationality demands that the government-actor always choose the best course of action, which, in turn, requires value-maximizing—that is, choosing the optimum means to achieve the optimum ends. Motives such as desire for personal aggrandizement or glory seldom play an important part in rational actor models.

The appeal of this model lies in its predictive powers and its capacity to allow the analyst to make bold inductive leaps. If historians know what a nation did without knowing why, they can still explain its actions with a minimum of evidence by applying the rules of rationality and value-maximizing. In short, historians can determine a nation's ends, once they know the means it adopted, and vice versa. Historians, for example, do not know for certain what made President Roosevelt decide to undertake the Manhattan Project. The rational actor model suggests that he recognized the military potential of nuclear fission, calculated that the United States had the financial, industrial, and scientific resources needed, and concluded that the nation's security demanded full-scale research and development.

There are of course serious weaknesses with this model. We have already seen that rationality alone cannot fully explain human behavior; a whole range of attitudes and emotions must be considered. In addition, this model supposes in the absence of contrary evidence that the actor recognizes all the important options and their possible consequences. Yet we also know that traditions, habits, national cultures, ideologies, and many intangible factors act as blinders that obscure some possible strategies, eliminate others, or prevent the actor or nation from choosing the most effective.

Despite those limitations the rational actor model does account fairly well for the American decision to build an atom bomb. The Manhattan Project owed its beginnings to the concern of physicists, primarily refugees from fascist Germany and Italy, who feared that the Hahn-Meitner research would allow the Nazis to develop a weapon of unparalleled destructive force. In March 1939 Enrico Fermi, a refugee and Nobel Prize winning physicist, paid his own way to Washington to warn the military. Fermi himself had been on the verge of discovering fission reactions in 1934. His failure to recognize the meaning of his results denied the fascist powers the first chance to tap fission for military use. Though Fermi had become an American citizen and a faculty member at Columbia University, Navy technical experts refused to heed his warning. Other refugee physicists, led by Leo Szilard, joined the campaign. Szilard persuaded Albert Einstein, the world's most admired scientist, to lend his name to a letter explaining their concern to President Roosevelt. Alexander Sachs, an economic adviser to the president, acted as their emissary. After Roosevelt read the letter and heard Sachs out, he remarked, "Alex, what you are after is to see they don't blow us up."

The president immediately ordered the formation of a Uranium Committee to promote American research on a fission bomb. Despite his support, the project got underway slowly. Other more promising experimental efforts competed for research funds that were particularly scarce since the United States was not yet at war. The bomb remained a remote theoretical possibility. Given open access to the resources of the Army and Navy scientific bureaus, the Uranium Committee asked for just $6,000 during its first year. But at the same time, restrictions barring refugees from top-priority military projects left them free to experiment on fission. Two German emigrés working in England, Otto Frisch and Rudolph Peierls, used that opportunity to devise an explanation of how a "superbomb" might work. They also suggested ways to separate the fissionable isotope U-235 from Uranium-238 and predicted the radiation effects of a nuclear bomb. American researchers were far behind. Since they could not guarantee that a bomb would be available for wartime use, they could not attract the money for vital chain-reaction experiments. Despite the president's interest, government science administrators steered their funds into other projects.

The British research gave the rational actor—in this case President Roosevelt—sufficient cause to commit the United States to a full-scale project. Frisch and Peierls had gone on to determine that either pure U-235 or plutonium would produce the fast neutrons that would set off an explosive chain reaction. The quantity of fissionable material would be small enough to fit into a bomb that existing aircraft could carry. Such a bomb, the British informed the National Defense Research Committee (NDRC), could be built in two years. The head of NDRC, Vannevar Bush, told Roosevelt, "If such an explosive were made it would be thousands of times more powerful than existing explosives, and its use might be determining."

Since the Germans with their high-quality physics had made similar discoveries and might be as much as two years ahead in their research, the atom bomb project now became a matter of national survival. Many scientists came to believe that they, even more than the military, were responsible for saving the nation and the world from a fascist victory. To accelerate the research effort, Roosevelt replaced the ineffectual Uranium Committee with a group called S-1. The membership of the committee reflected the new priority of the bomb project. It included Bush, now the head of the Office of Scientific Research and Development, Vice President Henry Wallace, as liaison to the president, Secretary of War Henry Stimson, Chief of Staff General George Marshall, upon whom both Roosevelt and Stimson leaned heavily for military advice, and James Conant, president of Harvard and successor to Bush at NDRC. Until the bomb neared completion in the spring of 1945, Bush and Conant assumed primary responsibility for overseeing the project and keeping the president informed. In 1942, they were joined by General Leslie Groves, who had been appointed to command construction and operation of the Manhattan Project's vast facilities. Groves was already familiar with the new symbols of organization and bureaucracy, for he had supervised construction of the nearly completed Pentagon.

For three years, American, British, and emigré scientists raced against time and what they feared was an insurmountable German lead. At first, research focused on the work of scientists at the Chicago Metallurgical Lab (another code name). There, on a squash court under the old University of Chicago football stadium, Fermi and his associates achieved the first self-sustaining chain reaction. The next goal was the separation of enough pure U-235 or sufficient plutonium to build a bomb. That required the construction of huge plants at Oak Ridge, Tennessee, and Hanford, Washington. Actual design of the bomb took place at a remote desert site near Los Alamos, New Mexico. Here in the desert he so deeply loved, physicist Robert Oppenheimer skillfully directed the most outstanding collection of experimental and theoretical physicists, mathematicians, chemists, and engineers ever assembled. Nobel Prize winners rubbed elbows with graduate students hastily recruited to pursue the Project's deathly mission.

As the bomb neared completion in early 1945, scientists found themselves in a different race. They knew that the war against Germany was won and that German physicists had long since given up hope of building a bomb. But the war against Japan seemed far from over. President Roosevelt had travelled to the Yalta Conference in February 1945 determined to secure Stalin's help in defeating the Japanese. Yet the president was reluctant to draw a potentially expansionist Soviet Union into Japan. If the bomb could win the war for the United States, all the sacrifices of time, personnel, money, and materials would not have been in vain.

Thus the rational actor model explains adequately the progression of events that brought about development of the bomb: 1) physicists saw the potential of nuclear fission and warned the president; 2) the president ordered the necessary research; 3) new advances led to greater certainty of eventual success and, in turn, the president gave bomb research top priority; 4) the race with Germany, and then Japanese resistance in the Far East encouraged scientists to push on toward success.

While the decision to build a bomb was one matter that lends itself to rational actor analysis, historians have come to see the decision to drop the bomb as quite another. The attacks on Hiroshima and Nagasaki raise four difficult questions that have long been the center of historical controversy. Did the military situation justify the surprise attack with atom bombs? Would a nonmilitary demonstration have persuaded the Japanese to surrender? Why did the United States drop a second bomb so soon after the first? And, finally, who did the United States really want to shock, Japan or the Soviet Union? For each of those questions, rational actor analysis has allowed historians to offer and defend contradictory answers.

One difficulty for historians lies in determining what, in the summer of 1945, was the major problem facing the rational actor. Between President Roosevelt's untimely death in April 1945 and the Japanese surrender in August, military and diplomatic planning underwent a transition from war to peace. During that transition, decision makers were preoccupied both with defeating Japan and with finding ways to make the Russians more cooperative at the bargaining table. Japan posed the greatest problem in war; the Soviet Union seemed the greatest threat to the peace. A wartime demonstration of the bomb might impress the Russians with American military power. Which of those concerns, then, most influenced the decision to drop two atom bombs on Japan?

Resolution of the historical debate has profound significance for the way Americans feel about their responsibility and morality as a nation. If the Soviet Union more than Japan was the target, then Truman may have wantonly incinerated hundreds of thousands of Japanese. He placed on the United States the moral burden of introducing the world to this awful weapon without adequate justification. And if Russian cooperation was his goal, Truman seriously erred, for the Soviet Union became, if anything, more intractable after Japan's surrender. Failure to achieve a nuclear arms control agreement with Stalin, while the United States and Britain had a monopoly on atomic weapons, led to a postwar arms race. Possession of the atom bomb resulted finally in a decrease in American security and a loss of moral stature. Those are not the desired results of rational decision making.

When applied at the level of presidential decision making, rational actor analysis reveals that the decision to drop the bomb was consistent with perceived American goals. In the summer of 1945, American policymakers sought above all to end the war against Japan as quickly as possible with a minimum number of casualties. Resolution of Soviet-American differences was a secondary goal, though rapidly becoming the Truman administration's chief preoccupation. The United States also hoped that the United Nations and the threat of nuclear annihilation would eliminate wars of aggression as instruments of international politics. As a final and far less consequential concern, the Roosevelt and Truman administrations wanted to avoid any scandals over the wartime allocation of money and resources, including the $2 billion spent on the Manhattan Project. The bombing of Hiroshima and Nagasaki appeared to be the optimum way to reach their primary objective with the additional virtue of promoting secondary goals as well.

Until his death in April 1945 President Roosevelt had been the final arbiter of matters related to the development of the bomb and its use. His decision to build it involved an implicit assumption that it would be used. "At no time," recalled former Secretary of War Stimson, "did I ever hear it suggested by the President, or by any other responsible member of the government, that atomic energy should not be used in the war." Robert Oppenheimer, whose leadership at Los Alamos played a critical role in the success of the Project, confirmed Stimson's point: ". . . we always assumed if they were needed, they would be used." In September 1944 at Hyde Park Roosevelt and British Prime Minister Churchill signed a memorandum which summarized their attitudes about the bomb. They agreed that the bomb would be kept a secret from the Russians, thereby indicating that they saw it as an important lever in postwar negotiations. The exclusive Anglo-American monopoly would continue after the defeat of Japan. Finally, they decided that after "mature" deliberation and adequate warning, the bomb *might* be used against Japan.

When Roosevelt died, none of his military and diplomatic advisers was aware of the Hyde Park memorandum or its contents. Responsibility for atomic policy shifted largely to Secretary Stimson, the cabinet officer in charge of the Manhattan Project. The new president, Harry Truman, knew nothing about the bomb or most other critical diplomatic and military matters. Roosevelt had seldom consulted him or even met with him. Once as a Senate Committee head, Truman sought to inquire into the vast sums spent on some unknown project, only to be persuaded by Stimson that secrecy should prevail. As the war rapidly approached its end and Truman faced a host of critical decisions, Stimson cautiously introduced him to the bomb. "I mentioned it to you shortly after you took office," the secretary explained, "but have not urged it since on account of the pressure you have been under. It, however, has such bearing on our present foreign relations . . . I think you ought to know about it without further delay."

To present his case, Stimson prepared a memorandum which defined his two most pressing concerns. He wanted Truman to recognize the monumental importance of the bomb for postwar relations, particularly with the Soviet Union, as well as the capacity of the bomb to shorten the war. He mentioned no qualms about using the bomb against Japan and considered no steps to avert a postwar nuclear arms race. The two men agreed that Stimson should form a committee to formulate further policy options.

The "Interim" Committee, as the group was known, met three times to weigh bomb policy. Its members included Stimson, representatives

J. Robert Oppenheimer directed the construction, completion, and testing of the first atomic bomb, at a remote desert site near Los Alamos, New Mexico. He was an intense, introspective man and a chain smoker early in his career—who confessed he found it nearly impossible to think without a cigarette in his hand. The burden of the Manhattan Project took its toll on him: the chain smoking commenced again and his weight, normally only 130 pounds, dropped to 116.

from the State and Navy departments, and three leading science administrators. The Interim Committee, in turn, created a scientific panel including Oppenheimer, Fermi, Lawrence, and Arthur Compton (head of the
Chicago Lab) to advise the committee. During its meetings, the committee scarcely touched the question of whether to drop the bomb on Japan.
"It seemed to be a foregone conclusion," Arthur Compton recalled,
"that the bomb would be used. It was regarding only the details of
strategy and tactics that differing views were expressed." When the issue
did arise, some members of the committee briefly considered whether
a nonmilitary demonstration might be preferable to a surprise military
attack. Since the bomb had yet to be tested, Oppenheimer could only
estimate its destructive force. He felt he could not conceive any demonstration that would have the impact of an attack on a real target of
factories and buildings. Furthermore the bomb might fizzle and make the
test a fiasco. Any warning might allow the Japanese to prepare their
defenses or move American prisoners of war to likely bombing targets.

Several assumptions seem to have predetermined the committee's
recommendations. Above all, they considered the military leadership of
Japan so fanatic that only a profound shock such as the bomb could
deliver would persuade them to surrender. Kamikaze attacks and other
resistance continued to claim a heavy toll of American lives. General
Douglas MacArthur, who had led the Western Pacific campaign against
Japan, discounted the effectiveness of either a naval blockade of the
home islands or continued air raids with conventional bombs. Only
invasion, first of Kyushu and then the main island of Honshu, MacArthur
argued, would bring to bear the weight of American naval, air, and
ground forces needed to force surrender. Trained in the uses of conventional weapons, military planners were unable or unwilling to place too
much reliance on an untested and unproven weapon, no matter what its
potential. They continued to organize an invasion for November 1, in
which they anticipated as many as a half million American casualties.

The committee members had by 1945 become somewhat inured to
the idea of killing enemy soldiers or civilians. Conventional firebombing
had already proven as brutal as the atom bomb promised to be. In one
incendiary raid on Tokyo, American bombers had leveled one quarter
of Tokyo, left 83,000 people dead, and wounded another 40,000. Having lived with the fear that the Germans might use an atom bomb against
the United States, the members had ample reason to see it as a potential
weapon against the Japanese. Since it promised to save many American
lives, the committee sensed that the public would want, even demand,
combat use. And finally, though the members were far from agreed, the

committee decided that a combat demonstration would facilitate negotiations with the Russians. From those assumptions they reached three conclusions: (1) the bomb should be used as quickly as possible against Japan; (2) to maximize the shock value, the target should be a war plant surrounded by workers' homes; (3) no warning should be given. When Stimson communicated those views to Truman, he included a recommendation that both bombs scheduled for completion by August should be dropped in separate raids to maximize the shock and convince Japanese leaders that further resistance meant certain destruction.

In only one small but vital way did Truman deviate from the committee's determination of how and why to use the bomb. A group of scientists at the Chicago laboratory, led by Leo Szilard, had become persuaded that combat use of the bomb without warning would lead to a postwar Soviet-American arms race. They urged Truman and his advisers to tell the Russians about the bomb and to plan a demonstration before using it in combat. In a concession to Szilard and his colleagues, the Interim Committee recommended that Truman disclose the bomb to Stalin to gain his cooperation after the war. But at Potsdam, Truman chose not to discuss the bomb or atomic energy. He made only an oblique reference to Stalin "that we had a weapon of unusual destructive force." Stalin was equally cryptic in reply. "He was glad to hear it and hoped we would make 'good use of it' against the Japanese," the president recalled.

What little evidence exists has persuaded Martin Sherwin, the leading historian of atomic diplomacy, that Stalin treated Truman's comment as a thinly veiled threat against the Soviet Union. As a result, the moment passed when the bomb might have served to foster trust among the wartime Allies. Sherwin, however, came to an even more startling conclusion, "that *neither* bomb may have been necessary; and certainly that the second was not." He reached that conclusion by applying rational actor analysis to Japanese and Russian decision making as well as to the Americans'. Like most historians, Sherwin benefited from the advantages of hindsight and greater detachment. He did not share the pressures facing Truman and advisers who had to plan simultaneously for war and peace. Still, Sherwin was fair in his judgment, because the evidence he used was available to Truman when he chose to bomb Hiroshima and Nagasaki without explicit warning to either the Russians or Japanese.

As Sherwin reconstructed the decision-making process he became convinced that both Roosevelt and Truman knew that, despite extensive efforts to maintain complete secrecy, Russian spies had learned about the Manhattan Project. They were aware also that the Soviet Union had physicists capable of building an atom bomb independently. Roosevelt chose, nonetheless, to accept Churchill's demand that the atom bomb remain a closed Anglo-American monopoly. Entreaties from the eminent Nobel Prize-winning physicist Neils Bohr to seek an international control agreement before using the bomb did not change either Churchill's or Roosevelt's minds. Instead, they began to suspect Bohr's loyalty.

By the time Roosevelt died and Truman became president, Soviet-American relations had deteriorated. Truman and his closest advisers believed that the bomb monopoly would be vital to win concessions from the Russians on thorny postwar issues. They wanted the Hiroshima attack to shock the Russians as well as the Japanese. And yet, they recognized that Stalin's territorial and political ambitions reflected a preoccupation with future Russian security. In that context, the Anglo-American monopoly promised to harden, not soften, Stalin's resolve to protect Russian interests.

There is no doubt either that by the summer of 1945, Japan was a defeated nation and the Americans knew it. The U.S. Navy had established a tight blockade that isolated the large Manchurian Army from the home islands and cut off delivery of any vital raw materials. Allied land-based bombers conducted regular raids without opposition from Japanese fighters. What they had done to Tokyo, they could do to other cities almost at will. The only salvation for Japan by July 1945 lay with the remote possibility the Russians might agree to mediate an armistice. The main concession the Japanese hoped to gain was some guarantee of the survival of the emperor and the imperial institution. Had the Americans dropped their demand for "unconditional surrender" and given some assurances to the emperor, Japan might well have capitulated before the United States dropped the bomb or before an invasion became necessary.

Truman and his advisers knew that the Japanese had made overtures to Moscow. On July 13, 1945, the Japanese Foreign Minister told his peace emissary in Moscow, "Unconditional surrender is the only obstacle to peace. . . ." American intelligence, which even before Pearl Harbor had cracked the Japanese code, intercepted that message and forwarded it to Truman. Clearly the president understood that Japanese leaders recognized their desperate military plight. And he knew, too, that the Russians would never assist Japan, for Stalin had already promised Roosevelt at Yalta to declare war three months after Germany surrendered. Russian entry, alone, might prove a sufficient shock to force a Japanese surrender.

Truman, nonetheless, proved unwilling to deviate from Roosevelt's policy on unconditional surrender. From Potsdam the Allies issued a vaguely worded proclamation that warned the Japanese of certain destruction if they fought on. Nowhere did the proclamation hint at Allied plans for the emperor, though considerable sentiment existed to retain him in some capacity. When the Japanese ignored the warning, the Americans concluded that Japan had resolved to continue fanatic resistance. In fact, the emperor himself had taken an unprecedented, though slow and cautious, step to undermine the war party. The bombing of Hiroshima, on August 6th, followed two days later by a Russian declaration of war, threw the Japanese government into confusion. Before they could digest the double shock, Nagasaki had been levelled on August 9th. Even then, the Japanese surrendered only when the United States made an implicit commitment to retain the emperor.

A MODEL OF ORGANIZATIONAL PROCESSES

Why, many critics have asked, did the United States not make a greater effort to explore the peace initiatives? And why, when the United States was eventually willing to compromise on "unconditional surrender," did it wait until 150,000 Japanese had died needlessly? Using rational actor analysis, those critics have argued that since Japan was clearly defeated before Hiroshima, the United States had another target—the Soviet Union. Had the Russians' declaration of war, rather than the bomb, forced a surrender, Truman feared that Stalin might demand a larger role in the Japanese peace negotiations. The most cynical critics charge that the second bomb was dropped to minimize the impact of the Russian declaration of war the day before.

Rational actor analysis alone cannot adequately answer the questions historians have raised about the decision to drop the bomb. Other models are needed to explain why the United States dropped the second bomb so soon, why policymakers ruled out a demonstration, why they failed to tell the Russians about the bomb, and how they chose the targets. We need a model that recognizes that governments are more than the leaders who determine policy on the basis of rational calculation. Decision makers stand atop a pyramid of organizations and political actors who participate in the formulation and application of government policies. Large actions at the center require a myriad of smaller activities at various levels of bureaucracy. If we looked at a government as a clock, rational actor analysis would define the telling of time as the visible movements of the hands controlled by a closed box. A model representing organizational processes, on the other hand, takes us inside the clock to observe the complex of gears and levers that move the hands. It allows the historian to analyze internal mechanisms that help determine external action.

Observation instructs us, however, that people in organizations are less predictable than gears in a clock and that government agencies seldom approach such a degree of coordinated activity. Often the organizations that comprise a government work at cross purposes or pursue conflicting objectives. While the Surgeon General's office warns that cigarette smoking "may be hazardous," the Department of Agriculture produces films on the virtues of American tobacco. To understand better the difference between rational actor and organizational process models, imagine yourself in the stands at a football game. We see the players moving in coordinated patterns in an effort to control the movement of the ball. Rational actor analysis suggests that the coach, or another centralized decision maker, has selected the strategies best suited to win the game. That larger strategy, in turn, determines the plays that the offense and defense will use.

After closer observation, we begin to sense that the play is not as centrally coordinated as we anticipated. Different groups of players move in patterns determined by their positions as well as the team strategy. Linemen block, ends run pass patterns, and quarterbacks hand off the ball. We come to understand that the team is made up of subunits that have regularly assigned tasks. In each situation, the players do not try to think of the best imaginable play, but rather they repeat those actions they have been trained to perform. Thus, a halfback will generally advance the ball by running and leave the passing to the quarterback. On many plays, we observe that some players' actions seem inappropriate. A halfback runs when he should be blocking. Where the rational actor might attribute that move to some purposeful attempt at deception, an organizational process analysis might define it as a breakdown of coordination among subunits. What one model treats as planned, the other treats as a mistake.

Thus the organizational process model leads the historian to treat government behavior not as centralized acts and choices, but as the actions of bureaucracies functioning in relatively predictable patterns. Organizations begin by breaking problems into parts, which are parcelled out to the appropriate subunits. The subunits usually respond according to established procedures or routines without necessarily having any sense of the larger problem. A lineman, for example, does not need to know who will run the ball, only whether to block his opponent to the left or right. Standard operating procedures (SOP's) allow organizations to coordinate the independent activities of many groups and individuals. Each group contributes to the final outcome by doing those things it has been trained and assigned to do. Failure to perform any one task may undermine the entire operation. If just one of seven linemen misses his block, the runner may be tackled without advancing the ball.

While SOP's make coordination possible, they also define and limit the actions of organizations. Specialization both within and among organizations restricts the number of tasks they can perform. Available equipment, training, and information make it difficult to deviate from regular routines. The weather bureau could not easily shift from predicting rain to predicting fluctuations in the economy. And where the rational actor weighs all available choices to find the best one, SOP's determine the range and pattern of choices that organizations consider. They are generally content to choose standardized and previously determined policies rather than searching for the optimum one.

Since organizations are generally more preoccupied with avoiding failure than with gambling on success, they tend to be conservative. Where the rational actor might decide, after weighing the potential benefits against possible consequences, to make a bold new departure, organizations change in small, incremental steps. Corporations, for example, like to test market a product before they risk investing in expensive new plants, distribution networks, and advertising. Though such caution may cost several years of profitable sales, it reduces the risk of flooding the market with Edsels and electric forks.

Reward structures in organizations reinforce their conservatism. Those who do their jobs properly day after day continue to work. Those who make errors lose their jobs or fail to win promotions. Individuals have little incentive to take risks. Critical decisions are generally made in committees so that no individual assumes sole responsibility if a venture fails. But committees take much longer to act and often adopt unwieldy compromises. (An old adage defines a camel as a horse designed by a committee.) As a further hedge against failure, goals and responsibilities are set well within the individual or groups' performance capabilities. People are given eight hours to do four hours' work. Such practices stifle individual initiative and encourage inefficiency. Mountains of paperwork and miles of red tape are the ultimate symbol of organizational caution and conservatism.

By treating the decision to drop the bomb not as a single act but as the outcome of many organizational routines, historians can gain new insight into old issues. In the first place, the decision to build a bomb first required the creation of new organizations and the reorientation of existing ones. Before the Manhattan Project no organization had ever applied scientific research to weapons development on such a giant scale. Had the emigré scientists approached the United States government solely through normal organizational channels the bomb might not have been built during World War II. Navy bureaucrats did not even understand Fermi when he delivered his warning in 1939. Other scientific bureaus had neither the capacity nor the incentive to undertake such a large and risky venture. But by circumventing the standard organizational channels and going right to President Roosevelt, the scientists attracted the support needed to initiate atomic weapons research.

To get the project under way, Roosevelt had to create an *ad hoc* committee to investigate the military potential of nuclear fission. His decision to appoint Lyman Briggs, a government physicist, as head of the Uranium Committee may have delayed the project by at least a year. As the director of the Bureau of Standards, Briggs knew little about nuclear physics. He was by temperament "slow, conservative, methodical"— ideal bureaucratic qualities totally unsuited to the bold departure Roosevelt sought. Not until Roosevelt created the National Defense Research Committee did nuclear physics gain adequate support. Roosevelt gave NDRC responsibility for applying science to the military demands of the impending war. As chairman of NDRC, Vannevar Bush made the farsighted decision to keep his organization independent of the military bureaucracies. He knew generals and admirals would fight against civilian interference and that scientists would balk at military regulation of their research. Under Bush, scientists remained free to pursue the research they and not the military thought was important. Traditional definitions of missions and military needs would not cut off funds or new research projects.

Even so, atomic research moved slowly until Roosevelt replaced the ineffectual Uranium Committee with the S-1 Committee, where the presence of the highest ranking bureaucrats guaranteed a high priority for the project. Roosevelt's desire to keep abreast of its progress allowed the three top administrators, Bush, Conant, and General Groves, direct access to the White House. As Bush worked to organize the project, he decided to operate where necessary under the War Department rather than the Navy.*

---

*At that time the Army and Navy had separate organizations. The head of each held a cabinet post. The Marines were a branch of the Navy, the Air Corps a branch of

The Navy had repeatedly shown either indifference or hostility to advice from civilian scientists. The Army and particularly its Air Corps branch proved far more receptive to new research. Consequently, the atom bomb was developed with the Army's mission and organizational routines in mind. Such skillful administrative negotiation of organizational minefields accounted in part for the project's success.

In other areas, administrative and organizational conflict delayed the project. President Roosevelt had established two incompatible priorities for Bush: speed and security. The scientists felt speed should come before security; military administrators like Groves opted for security over speed. Military SOP demanded strict adherence to a chain of command and rigid compartmentalization of all tasks. A military officer who had taken Szilard's approach of going to the president over his superiors' heads might well find himself court-martialed or assigned to some remote Aleutian Island.

The conflict between speed and security became particularly acute at Los Alamos. To maximize security Groves tried to place the laboratory under military control. All the scientists would don uniforms and receive ranks based on their importance. Scientists, however, feared that military regulations would undermine their traditional autonomy to pursue research as they saw fit. Oppenheimer could not recruit many scientists to come to Los Alamos until he demilitarized the project.

Compartmentalization, another Groves scheme, seriously inhibited research. Physicists believed their work required access to all relevant information. They thought best when they understood the wider ramifications of their work. Groves disdained their habit of engaging in free-wheeling discussions that regularly drifted far afield of the topic at hand. He could not appreciate the creative dimension of scientific work. Scientists should stick to their jobs and receive information solely on a "need to know" basis. "Just as outfielders should not think about the manager's job of changing pitchers," Groves said to justify his system, ". . . each scientist had to be made to do his own work." While compartmentalization promoted security, it denied scientists vital information from other areas of the project. Some scientists, like Szilard, avoided the problem by violating security procedures. Oppenheimer eased the problem at Los Alamos by conducting seminars where his staff could exchange ideas and information, but information never flowed freely among the many research and production sites.

---

the Army. Congress created the unified defense structure under a single secretary in 1947.

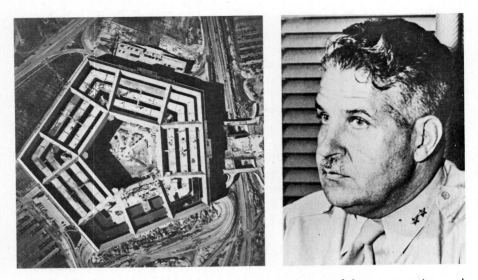

In 1942 **General Leslie Groves** was placed in charge of the construction and operation of the Manhattan Project. He got the job in part because he was a good organizer, having supervised the construction of the Pentagon, still unfinished in this 1942 photo. The building became the largest office facility in the world, containing 16 miles of corridors, 600,000 square feet of office space, and a capacity to house 32,000 workers. As historian Warren Susman recognized, it also became a symbol of its era: "For the age it climaxed indeed the triumph of order, science, reason. . . . And yet, for the age being born it was the home of the atom bomb and a frightening bureaucratic structure, the beginning of a brave new world of anxiety."

Security procedures indicate, too, that long before the war ended many policymakers saw the Soviet Union as their chief enemy. Few precautions were designed against Japanese or even German agents. Military intelligence concentrated its counterespionage against Soviet and communist spies. Known communists or scientists with communist associations were kept under constant surveillance. Had intelligence officers prevailed, they would have barred Oppenheimer from the project because of his previous involvement with communist front organizations. To his credit, Groves overruled the nearsighted sleuths in Army intelligence and saved the project's most valuable member. In the meantime, security precautions against a wartime ally continued to work to the advantage of the Nazis by delaying the project.

The military was not solely responsible for project bottlenecks. The procedures of organized science added to the difficulties as well. Scientists recruited from private industry did not share their academic colleagues' preoccupation with speed. Work in industry had conditioned them to move cautiously, with an eye toward efficiency, permanence, and low risk. Academic scientists felt such industrial values "led to a considerable retardation of the program." But the traditions of academic science also slowed the project. The bulk of research money had most often been directed to the celebrities in each field. Ernest Lawrence's reputation made him a magnet for grants and contributions. Manhattan Project administrators automatically turned to him as they sought methods to refine the pure U-235 needed for the bomb. Much of the money spent at Oak Ridge, Tennessee, went into Lawrence's electromagnetic process based on the Berkeley cyclotron.

Lawrence's program proved to be one of the most conspicuous failures of the Manhattan Project. By 1944, Oppenheimer had the design for a uranium bomb, but scarcely any U-235. In desperation he looked toward a process of gas-diffusion developed four years before by a young and relatively unknown physicist named John Dunning. Lawrence had been so persuaded of the superiority of his own method that he had steered attention and money away from Dunning. Compartmentalization prevented other physicists from learning more about Dunning's work. In 1944 Oppenheimer changed the priorities and the gas-diffusion process began to produce refined U-235 at a far greater rate than Lawrence's cyclotron. Physicists soon acknowledged that electromagnetic separation was obsolete, but in the meantime, the completion of the Uranium bomb, "Little Boy," was delayed until July 1945.

The organizational process model gives historians an even more startling insight into the choice of targets and the decision to bomb Nagasaki just three days after Hiroshima. To select the targets, Groves appointed a Target Committee composed of scientists and ordnance specialists. Their priorities reflected both the military's desire to end the war quickly and the scientists' hope to transmit a dramatic warning to the world. They sought cities that included military installations and a larger concentration of structures subject to the blast in case the bomb missed its primary target. Kyoto, the ancient cultural and political center of Japan, topped their list.

Secretary of War Stimson vetoed that choice. As a former secretary of state and a man of broad cultural and political experience, he believed that the destruction of Kyoto would engender in the Japanese an undying bitterness toward the United States. Any hopes of integrating a revitalized and reformed Japan into a healthy postwar Asia might die with Kyoto. Stimson's position near the top of the organizational hierarchy gave him a different perspective from lower-level planners who weighed other issues. On the final target list Hiroshima ranked first, Nagasaki ranked fourth, and Kyoto not at all.

It was the weather, and not diplomatic or military strategy, that sealed Nagasaki's fate. After the bombing of Hiroshima and the Russian declaration of war, Japanese leaders had decided to sue for peace. Advocates of surrender just needed enough time to work out acceptable terms and to reconcile the military diehards to the inevitable. As the Japanese discussed policy, the Americans followed standard military procedure. Control shifted from the commander in Washington, President Truman, to the commander of the bomber squadron on the island of Tinian in the Pacific. Plans called for "Fat Man," a plutonium bomb, to be ready by August 11. Since work went faster than expected, the bomb crew advanced the date to the 10th. The forecast called for clear skies on the 9th, followed by five days of bad weather. Urged on by the squadron commander, the crew had "Fat Man" armed and loaded on the morning of the 9th. And again following military SOP, the pilot shifted his attack to Nagasaki, when clouds obscured his primary target.

The timing of that attack on Nagasaki could only be explained through the application of the organizational process model. Had the original plan been followed, Japan might well have surrendered before the weather cleared. Nagasaki would have been spared. The man who ordered the attack had little appreciation of the larger military picture that made Nagasaki a target or that made the Soviet Union a diplomatic problem connected with the atom bomb. He acted according to the SOP's of the organization that trained him and placed him in a position of authority. He weighed factors important to a bomb squadron commander, not to diplomats or political leaders.

A MODEL OF INTERNAL POLITICS

Secretary Stimson's decision to veto the Target Committee's recommendation suggests that a third model of organizational policymaking was at work as well. Powerful individuals or groups can overrule bureaucratic procedures and rationally conceived choices. Thus the historian must also appreciate government decisions as the result of internal institutional politics. So now, when we return to our vantage point in the football stadium, we perceive another pattern to the decisions that determine the players' actions. Before each play coaches confer on the sidelines, while the players huddle on the field. The play finally chosen may not reflect rational choice or routines, but bargaining and compromise

"Fat Man," also familiarly known to scientists working on the project as "Fat Boy." The graffiti on the tail include the notation, "Chicago is represented in here more than once."

among the players and coaches. On third down and five yards to go, either a pass or a run might achieve the desired outcome—a first down. The quarterback and ends argue for a pass which will enhance their importance to the team, improve their personal statistics, and perhaps allow them to demand higher salaries. For the same reason the backs suggest a run, the kicking team a field goal, and the defense a quick kick which will put them back in the game.

The analyst must recognize that the parties to this negotiation do not have an equal role in determining the outcome. Final authority may rest with a coach or the quarterback. Other players, such as a star halfback, gain influence and prestige from the skill with which they play their position. And to minimize conflict and promote team spirit, all the participants prefer to reach a decision acceptable to as many of the players as possible. Teams, like other organizations, seek consensus rather than confrontation. We are not surprised, then, to see the team execute a quarterback option that permits a pass, run, or lateral to another back.

A historian applying those insights, in what might be called a government politics model, recognizes that an official position as defined by an organizational hierarchy does not alone determine the bargaining power of participants in decision making. According to an organizational flow chart, the most influential members of the executive branch, after the president, would be the secretaries of state, defense (war and navy), and treasury. Yet American history abounds with examples where power has moved outside the normal bureaucratic channels. Sometimes a political actor, through astute jockeying, may convert a relatively less influential office into an important command post, as Henry Kissinger did when he was Richard Nixon's national security adviser. Kissinger, through forceful advocacy, shaped foreign policy far more than Secretary of State William Rogers. Colonel Edward M. House, who proved to be the most influential adviser to Woodrow Wilson, held no formal position at all. House achieved his prestige and power by maintaining a low profile and offering the president seemingly objective counsel. As secretary of commerce under Calvin Coolidge, Herbert Hoover turned his traditionally moribund department into the most dynamic center of the government. Many observers considered the "Boy Wonder," as Coolidge dubbed him, the real head of the administration. Family ties, rather than Robert Kennedy's position as attorney general, gave him a prominent voice in his brother's administration.

In applying the government politics model the historian must first recognize the impact of President Roosevelt's untimely death on atom bomb policy. Few members of Roosevelt's administration had as little access to information and decision-making channels as Vice President Truman. In most vital policy areas, Roosevelt made all the important decisions with the help of a few trusted advisers. Officials like Secretary Stimson had extensive administrative responsibilities without much capacity to determine policy. Ignorance of Roosevelt's policies forced the new president to rely far more heavily on a wider circle of advisers. Stimson, for one, suddenly found that for several months the need to initiate Truman into the secrets of S-1 or the Manhattan Project greatly enhanced his influence.

The atom bomb, like most major policy areas, did not present decision makers with clear-cut choices. Often in such situations leaders face the prospect of selecting the least dangerous rather than the best option. Under those conditions, the power, prestige, and skill of advocates may become more important than the options they back. When the Truman administration weighed the use of the bomb, the players dealt largely with unknowns. Would a Soviet entry into the war force Japan to surrender? Could a blockade or bombing raids bring the war to an end without using the bomb? Did Japan's peace initiatives indicate victory was at hand? Would a compromise on unconditional surrender, specifically a guarantee for the emperor, end the war? Or would a demonstration of the bomb shock the Japanese into suing for peace? All those options presented advisers with reasons to avoid dropping the bomb which, as historian Barton Bernstein pointed out, was "precisely what they were *not* trying to do." But critics of the decision to bomb Hiroshima and Nagasaki charge that those choices should have been tried and that each one had significant advocates within government circles. By applying the government politics model, a historian can better explain why those who proposed alternatives failed to change Truman's decision.

The chief advocates for continued conventional warfare were from the navy. From the beginning, navy leaders had been skeptical of nuclear fission's military potential. Admiral William Leahy, the senior navy representative on the Joint Chiefs of Staff and also an expert on explosives, always doubted the bomb would have anywhere near the force scientists predicted. The Alamogordo test laid his argument to rest. Chief of Naval Operations, Admiral Ernest King, believed a naval blockade would successfully end the war. King had no qualms about the bomb, but as a loyal navy man he hated to see the air force end a war that his service had dominated for four years. He knew, too, that the bomb might undermine the navy's defense role after the war.

Among military men, Admirals Leahy and King had somewhat less influence than General George Marshall, Army Chief of Staff. Marshall, along with General Douglas MacArthur, felt further delay would necessitate an invasion and an unacceptable loss of American lives. Since they favored using the bomb instead, the navy lost that round.

Some members of the State Department, led by acting secretary of state Joseph Grew, believed that diplomacy, either as modification of "unconditional surrender" or response to Japanese peace feelers, would end the war. As a former ambassador to Japan, Grew knew more about Japanese politics and culture than the other major figures in the Truman administration. On the other hand, as a career foreign service officer often far from Washington, Grew had little political influence beyond what he could bring to bear personally. He would remain acting secretary only until the Senate confirmed James Byrnes. By contrast to Grew, Byrnes was largely ignorant of foreign policy matters. His position reflected his consummate skill at domestic politics.

The letter outlining SOP for dropping the bomb. It authorized the "509 Composite Group, 20th Air Force" to "deliver its first special bomb as soon as weather will permit visual bombing after about 3 August 1945 on one of the targets: Hiroshima, Kokura, Niigata and Nagasaki." In a reflection of protocol, as well as a hint of the rivalry between the army and navy, the letter instructs General Spaatz, in paragraph four, to inform General MacArthur and Admiral Nimitz of the decision personally.

During the war, many people considered him second in importance to Roosevelt. Although Truman had risen to prominence as Byrnes's protégé and repaid his political mentor with the appointment to head the State Department, many people believed that Byrnes never conquered his resentment that Truman rather than he had succeeded Roosevelt in the White House.

As early as April 1945, Grew had urged administration officials to extend some guarantee that the imperial throne would not be destroyed. Without that assurance, he felt, the peace party could never overcome the military's determination to fight on. At first Grew had no significant supporters. Even within the State Department, Assistant Secretaries Dean Acheson and Archibald MacLeish, both more influential than Grew, opposed his position. They considered the emperor as the symbol and embodiment of the feudal military tradition they hoped to see destroyed. By the time of the Potsdam Conference, Grew had made just one convert—Secretary Stimson—and a partial convert—Harry Truman. "There was [sic] pretty strong feelings," Stimson recalled, "that it would be deplorable if we have to go through the military program with all its stubborn fighting to the finish." Truman showed sufficient interest to arrange talks between Grew and the military chiefs, but he did not feel he could bring congressional and public opinion in line with Grew's position on the emperor.

The ghost of Franklin Roosevelt proved to be Grew's major opponent. Lacking Roosevelt's prestige, popularity, and mastery of government, Truman felt obliged to pursue many of FDR's policies. A move away from "unconditional surrender" policy posed political risks at home and military risks abroad that Truman did not feel strong enough to take. Acheson and MacLeish reminded their colleagues that Hirohito, Emperor of Japan, had become as despicable to Americans as Hitler. The Joint Chiefs of Staff argued that premature compromise might reduce the emperor's incentive to cooperate in subduing the military diehards after the armistice.

James Byrnes emerged as the leading spokesman against modifying "unconditional surrender." Like Truman, Byrnes sensed the political dangers in such a step. But more important, Byrnes among all the advisers was most preoccupied with postwar Soviet-American relations. By the time of the meeting at Potsdam, he was convinced that by using the atom bomb to end the war quickly the United States could minimize Russian demands for territorial and political concessions in Asia. And he, more than most advisers, believed that successful use of the bomb would strengthen the United States' hand during the postwar negotiations.

Since Byrnes's chief opponents, Grew and Stimson, were old and near retirement, and since he had strong support in both the military and State Department, his position carried the day. At Potsdam, he even deleted a provision in the Allied Declaration that would have guaranteed the imperial institution.

The Japanese peace feelers never constituted a substantial alternative. They consisted largely of messages from the foreign minister to his emissary in Moscow. During the Potsdam Conference, Byrnes and Truman received the messages from military intelligence. They believed, however, that the peace party could not prevail unless American attacks persuaded the military that resistance was insane. Nothing in the messages changed their views, for the minister suggested only vague and general terms that fell far short of American demands. At no time did the Japanese peace advocates make a direct approach to the United States, and no one high in American government ever gave them serious consideration.

By now it must be obvious why none of Truman's advisers wanted to depend on the Soviet Union's declaration of war to force Japan's surrender. At Yalta in February 1945, Roosevelt had made significant concessions on China to win Stalin's commitment to enter the Pacific war. But the shift in military fortunes between Yalta and Potsdam, the following July, made Soviet entry unnecessary. Without shipping, Japan could neither supply its industrial plant nor hope to bring the powerful Manchurian Army back to defend the homeland. Possession of the atom bomb laid to rest any further argument about the need for an invasion.

Some critics suggest that Byrnes and Truman avoided telling Stalin about the bomb at Potsdam to keep the Russians from moving in on Japan more quickly, as well as to make the first combat use of the bomb a dramatic warning about the possible consequences of postwar expansionism. Historians do not have enough evidence to refute or confirm that charge. Yet one thing is certain: no influential adviser ever advocated any strategy to delay surrender in order to allow use of the bomb in combat. Policymakers always weighed strategies with an eye to ending the war as soon as possible.

The government politics model also helps reveal why American policymakers did not demonstrate the bomb to international observers before using it in combat. Pressure for a noncombat demonstration came largely from the scientists working at the Chicago Metallurgical Laboratory. Scientists there had been the first group to finish their work on the bomb. While the Los Alamos lab rushed to complete the designs for "Little Boy" and "Fat Man," scientists at Chicago began discussing the postwar implications of nuclear weapons. The eminent scientist Neils Bohr had already raised those issues with President Roosevelt and British Prime Minister Churchill. Yet, as we have seen, Churchill and Roosevelt had agreed at their 1944 Hyde Park meeting that the bomb might be used to give the Anglo-American powers an advantage in any postwar rivalry with the Russians.

Unaware of the Churchill-Roosevelt Hyde Park agreement, scientists continued to seek a voice in the decisions over how the bomb would be used. As if to underline the irony in human history, Leo Szilard in 1945 organized scientific opposition to an atomic attack on Japan. Just six years before, Szilard played the key role in launching the Manhattan Project. Now he openly violated security rules and the chain of command to take his appeal to Spartansburg, South Carolina, where he saw Secretary designate Byrnes. Byrnes could not have been less sympathetic. He had little understanding of the potential danger nuclear weapons posed. His determination to use the bomb against Japan and to shock the Russians led Szilard to conclude that the United States was headed into an arms race.

Scientists at Chicago continued, nonetheless, to speak out on bomb policy. Chicago Lab head Arthur Compton had organized a series of committees to make further studies and recommendations, the most important of which was headed by emigré James Franck. The Franck Committee concluded that a surprise attack against Japan would destroy the trust and goodwill of other nations for the United States and "precipitate the race for armaments, and prejudice the possibility of reaching an international agreement on the future control of such weapons." When Franck went to present the report to Stimson, the secretary avoided a meeting. The Interim Committee then steered the report to their Scientific Panel of Karl Compton, Fermi, Lawrence, and Oppenheimer. Those scientists, all of whom had greater prestige and influence, concluded that they could "propose no technical demonstration likely to bring an end to the war . . . and no acceptable alternative to direct military use."

That conclusion came before the first test, and Oppenheimer later regretted the panel's shortsightedness. The first explosion so profoundly moved him that its eerie glow recalled an image from the *Bhagavad-Gita:* "I am become death, the shatterer of worlds." Perhaps after Alamagordo, the Scientific Panel might have concluded that a demonstration would be worthwhile, but by then the time for deciding had passed. The momentum of organized bureaucracy now proceeded inexorably toward the Hiroshima-Nagasaki holocausts. The scientists did not have enough political influence to alter the assumptions of leading policymakers, nor were they capable, from their vantage point, of appreciating the difficulties policymakers faced. The scientists had hoped that the force of their argument would compensate for their position of political weakness, but the disagreement among them diluted the persuasiveness of the Franck Committee's report.

So the bomb was dropped and the world entered a new age.

If historians based their interpretations on a single model they would never satisfy their desire to understand the sequence of events leading to Hiroshima. Each model has imbedded in it a single perspective. The use of several models allows the historian the same advantage enjoyed by writers of fiction who employ more than one narrator. Each narrator, like every model, affords the writer a new vantage point from which to tell the story. The facts may not change, but the reader will see them in another light. Old information may take on new significance. Thus, as organizations grow more complex, models afford historians multiple perspectives from which to interpret the same reality.

And yet, we must remind ourselves that models do not work miracles. Like computers, they are tools that help us reduce unwieldy data to more manageable forms. But they are no more revealing than the people who build and apply them. If poorly applied, they may be even worse than more traditional methods: for models, like reams of computer printouts, convey a sense of empirical legitimacy. Data specialists have coined the acronym, "GIGO," to suggest the limits of such mechanical devices— "garbage in, garbage out."

In the end historians must remember that organizations are open systems existing within a broader historical and cultural context. Models often oversimplify because they ignore the external realities that shape the way organizations and the individuals within them perceive the significance of their own actions. Personal values or group ideologies may upset the most carefully constructed organizational flow chart.

Most important, historians must always appreciate the limitations of using a single interpretive point of view. Events of the magnitude of Hiroshima never lend themselves to simple explanation. The mushroom clouds over Japan did more than vindicate the decision to build the bomb. They did more than bring World War II to a close. They shattered a sense of security that Americans had enjoyed for almost 150 years. Who in 1945 could have appreciated that consequence with anything more than a vague sense of foreboding? Every model, by scaling down reality into a series of more easily comprehended components, inevitably reduces the complexities of history. Even when our models have accounted for goals, strategies, SOPs, political influence, and out-

The reaction of scientists watching the detonation of the first atomic bomb in New Mexico was recalled by Robert Oppenheimer: "A few people laughed, a few people cried, most people were silent. There floated through my mind a line from the *Bhagavad-Gita* in which Krishna is trying to persuade the Prince that he should do his duty: 'I am become death, the shatterer of worlds.' I think we all had this feeling, more or less." The photograph is of an atomic blast detonated at Bikini Island in July 1946.

comes, there remain behind those pieces of the picture which are still irreducible: from Robert Oppenheimer's uneasy, almost mystical vision out of the *Bhagavad-Gita* to the strictly inanimate, yet equally complex, meteorological forces which combined to dissipate the clouds over Hiroshima and Nagasaki in August 1945. Some elements of history will always remain stubbornly intractable, beyond the reach of the model builders.

Additional Reading

During the 1950s most historians and political analysts accepted the official government position that Hiroshima had been an inevitable consequence of World War II. Although some policymakers had always questioned the wisdom of dropping the bomb, the first extended public debate came with the publication of Gar Alperovitz, *Atomic Diplomacy* (New York, 1965; rev. ed., 1985). Alperovitz argued that the Soviet Union, not Japan, was the real object behind Truman's decision to drop the bomb. His accusations led Herbert Feis, a former State Department official, to write a defense of the government's policy in *The Atomic Bomb and the End of World War II* (Princeton, N.J., 1966).

As a graduate student doing research during the late 1960s on the cold war era, Mark Lytle began to explore various aspects of the issue in government archives and the private papers of leading policymakers. The papers of Henry L. Stimson at Yale University led him to question the substance of Alperovitz's attack and hence to take Feis more seriously. Stimson's papers give no indication that he saw the bomb as anything but a means to end the war quickly. A reader may well reach similar conclusions by examining Henry Stimson and McGeorge Bundy, *On Active Service in Peace and War* (New York, 1947), or Elting Morison, *Turmoil and Tradition* (Boston, 1960). In addition, anyone fortunate enough to visit the Roosevelt Library, Hyde Park, N.Y., can explore the documents in relevant presidential files, especially those originally kept in the White House "Map Room." Those files contain a large amount of secret wartime material, including correspondence between Churchill and Roosevelt. Other documents are available through the Modern Military Records Branch in the National Archives in Washington.

It is not necessary for readers to do their own research to understand the decision-making process that led to the dropping of the bomb. Martin Sherwin, *A World Destroyed* (New York, 1975) provides an excellent and insightful account of atomic energy policy during World War II. Sherwin appreciates the importance of government bureaucratic processes and their influence on policy-making as he discusses the scientific development of the bomb as well as plans for its use. Briefer, but valuable treatments of the same issues, are Barton Bernstein, "Roosevelt, Truman, and the Atomic Bomb: A Reinterpretation," *Political Science Quarterly,* 90 (Spring 1975), 23–69, and "The Quest for Security: American Foreign Policy and International Control of Atomic Energy," *Journal of American History,* LX (March 1974), 1003–1044.

A number of scholars have properly recognized that scientific research takes place in an institutional setting. Daniel Kevles, *The Physicists* (New York, 1978) explains the impact of individual scientists, institutions, and larger historical and cultural trends on the evolution of physics as a discipline and on major scientific discoveries. One of the most enjoyable accounts of physicists and their work is Nuell Pharr Davis, *Lawrence and Oppenheimer* (New York, 1968). Davis treats the personal and professional lives of the two men most directly responsible for American success in achieving a workable bomb. Other important sources for understanding the bomb project are Arthur Compton, *Atomic Quest* (New York, 1956), Leslie Groves, *Now It Can Be Told* (New York, 1962), and Richard Hewlett and Oscar Anderson, *The New World* (College Park, Pa., 1962), the official history of the Manhattan Project.

Organizational theory is an area of the social sciences with a long history and an enormous literature. The casual student might best use the work upon which this essay was modelled, Graham Allison, *The Essence of Decision* (Boston, 1971). Allison used the three models outlined in our chapter to interpret the Cuban Missile Crisis in a way which is both exciting and informative. His models are built on a wide survey of existing literature in organizational theory, and thus serve as a useful guide to further investigation into the art of model building.

From Rosie to Lucy

It was 1957. Betty Friedan was not just complaining; she was angry—for herself and uncounted other women like her. For some time, she had sensed she was not alone. Now she was certain, as she read the results of a questionnaire she and about 200 graduates of Smith College had completed. The alumni office, no doubt, had been seeking responses designed to show how well a college education fitted Smith students for their roles in later life. But many of the women who answered, it seemed, were frustrated with their lives. They resented the wide disparity between the idealized image society held of them as housewives and mothers and the realities of their daily routines.

True, most were materially well off. The majority had families, a house in the suburbs, and the amenities of an affluent society. But amid that good fortune they felt fragmented, almost as if they had no identity of their own. And it was not only college graduates. "I've tried everything women are supposed to do," one woman confessed to Friedan; "hobbies, gardening, pickling, canning, being very social with my neighbors, joining committees, running PTA teas. I can do it all, and I like it, but it doesn't leave you anything to think about—any feeling of who you are. . . . I love the kids and Bob and my home. There's no problem you can even put a name to. But I'm desperate. I begin to feel I have no personality. I'm a server of food and putter-on of pants and a bedmaker, somebody who can be called on when you want something. But who am I?" A similar sense of incompleteness haunted Friedan. "I, like other women, thought there was something wrong with me because I didn't have an orgasm waxing the kitchen floor," she recalled with some bitterness.

A growing sense of doubt led to a period of questioning. Why, she wondered, had she chosen fifteen years earlier to give up a promising career in psychology for marriage and motherhood? What was it that kept women from using the rights and prerogatives that were theirs? What made them feel guilty for anything they did in their own right rather than as their husbands' wives or children's mothers? Women in the 1950s, it seemed to Friedan, were not behaving quite the way they had a decade earlier. During World War II the popular press extolled the virtues of women like "Rosie the Riveter"—those who left homes and families to join the work force. Now, Rosie was no longer a heroine. The media lavished their praise on women who devoted themselves to family and home. In the closing scene of one 1957 *Redbook* story, the heroine, "Junior" (a "little freckle-faced brunette" who had decided to give up her job), nurses her baby at two in the morning sighing, "I'm glad, glad, glad I'm just a housewife." What had happened? "When did women decide to give up the world and go back home?" Friedan asked herself.

That question might engage a historian in the 1980s, but it was not one housewives of the 1950s were encouraged to ask. For a red-blooded American to doubt something as sacred as the role of housewives and mothers was to show symptoms of mental distress rather than a skeptical or inquiring mind. Whatever the label attached to such feelings—neurosis, anxiety, or depression—most people assumed that women like Friedan needed an analyst, not a historian, to explain their discontent. The malaise was a problem with individuals, not with society. To cure themselves, they needed only to become better adjusted to who and what they were.

Friedan, however, was no ordinary housewife. Before starting her family, she had worked as a newspaper reporter; even after her children came, she wrote regularly for the major women's magazines. By 1957 she was fed up with the endless stories about breast-feeding, the preparation of gourmet snails, and similar domestic fare that was the staple of *Redbook, McCall's,* and *Ladies' Home Journal.* She had noticed, too, that many women like herself who worked outside the home, even part time, felt guilty because their jobs threatened their husbands' roles as providers or took time away from their children. Thus Friedan began to wonder not only about herself as a woman, a wife, and a mother but also about the role society had shaped women to play.

Having seen the results of the Smith questionnaire, Friedan's reportorial instincts took over. She sensed she was onto a story bigger than anything she had written. But when she circulated an article describing the plight so many women were experiencing, the male editors at the women's magazines turned it down flat. It couldn't be true, they insisted; women could not possibly feel as guilty or discontented as Friedan

A Happy Housewife with a Week's Work. By 1947 many women laborers were back in the home full-time and the baby boom was under way. *Life* magazine celebrated the labors of a typical housewife by laying out a week's worth of bedmaking, ironing, washing, grocery shopping, and dishwashing for a family of four. An incomplete tally shows over 250 plates being washed and thirty-five quarts of milk consumed a week. Did the wife drink the majority of the six cups of coffee which seem to have been consumed per day? (Nina Leen, *Life* magazine, © 1947 Time Inc.)

claimed. The problem must be hers. "Betty has gone off her rocker," an editor at *Redbook* told her agent. "She has always done a good job for us, but this time only the most neurotic housewife could identify."

Friedan was not deterred. If the magazines would not print her story, she would do it as a book. For five years, she researched and wrote, describing the "feminine mystique" that she saw American culture promoting.

> The new mystique makes the housewife-mother, who never had a chance to be anything else, the model for all women . . . it simply makes certain concrete, finite, domestic aspects of feminine existence—as it was lived by women whose lives were confined by necessity to cooking, cleaning, washing, bearing children—into a religion, a pattern by which all women must now live or deny their femininity.

By the time Friedan was finished, the book had become a crusade. "I have never experienced anything as powerful, truly mystical, as the forces that seemed to overtake me as I wrote *The Feminine Mystique*," she later admitted. Published in 1963, the book soon joined the ranks of truly consequential books in American history. What Harriet Beecher Stowe did for slaves in *Uncle Tom's Cabin,* Jacob Riis for the urban poor in *How the Other Half Lives,* Upton Sinclair for public health in *The Jungle,* or Rachel Carson for the environment in *Silent Spring,* Friedan did for women. No longer would they bear their dissatisfaction in silence as they confronted the gap between their personal aspirations and the limited avenues society had left open to them. Friedan helped inspire a generation of middle-class women to demand the equal rights and opportunities men routinely claimed. Together with other activists, she founded the National Organization for Women (NOW) in 1965 to press for reforms on an institutional level, donating royalties from her book to support it.

RETREAT FROM REVOLUTION: A DEMOGRAPHIC PROFILE

The feminist movement that blossomed from the actions of NOW and other women's groups had a profound impact on the study of history as well. After all, many of the questions Friedan raised were the sort that historians are trained to explore. Why hadn't women followed up on the gains in employment they experienced during World War II? What caused society in postwar America to place so much emphasis on home and family? What was the image of women that the mass media, scholars, and other opinion makers presented? In seeking answers,

Friedan adopted many methods common to both history and the social sciences. She canvassed articles in popular women's magazines, studied the recent scholarship, and talked to psychologists, sociologists, and marriage counselors who regularly treated women. She conducted in-depth interviews with women of varying ages, backgrounds, and social classes.

It was not so much her methods that affected the study of history, however, as the subjects she chose to probe. Prior to the 1970s, history as a discipline gave slight attention to the experience of women, even though they constituted over half the world's population. The vast majority of studies (most of which were written by men anyway) concentrated on topics in the public arena. Politics, business, intellectual life, diplomacy, war—all were areas in which males defined the terms of action. The few women who did enter the history books were there most often because, like Eleanor Roosevelt, they had lived a public life; like Jane Addams, they initiated political reform; like Margaret Mead, they contributed in major ways to the social sciences; or like Willa Cather, they stood among the nation's leading writers and artists. Those were exceptional women, and it was the exceptional, not the commonplace, that historians generally preferred to study.

Still, history has by no means been confined to the rich, powerful, and famous—as we have seen in earlier chapters. And particularly for the twentieth century, there are documentary materials that make it possible to study ordinary people, either on a small scale, focusing on the personalities and motivations of individuals, or in a macrocosmic sense, looking at the actions of millions of people in the aggregate. The latter approach in particular is possible because of today's modern bureaucracies. Whether they are governmental, private, or academic, all are designed to collect data and store it in systematic ways. The New Deal, which expanded the role of government in so many areas, provided a prime impetus for the collection of statistics. Accustomed as we are to periodic reports on the gross national product, employment, and trade deficits, it is easy to forget that when the Great Depression struck in 1929, the Hoover administration had no way of knowing how many Americans had been put out of work by the crash. No department was charged with collecting such statistics, and one way the government made unemployment estimates was to fan out in several cities, count the number of people waiting in breadlines, and multiply by 10. With the New Deal, government agencies proliferated—and so did their statisticians.

The 1930s was also the decade when George Gallup began developing sophisticated polling operations to determine mass opinions on a multitude of issues. Polling had been done before Gallup began his work, but he and his rivals undertook it much more systematically, devising better ways of recording opinions, more sophisticated techniques for minimizing margins of error, and more scientific means of asking questions. In the academic world, the expansion of social science theory enlarged the kinds of information people thought worth having as well as the means for collecting such data. And as we have seen in the previous chapter, the scientific bureaucracy grew rapidly during this era. Thus when historians began investigating women's status in the mid-twentieth century, they could draw upon a good deal of statistical information. The data they found in some ways challenged Friedan's picture of women being pushed out of the work force, but in other ways her view was strikingly confirmed.

Census data and other governmental records indeed show that many women entered higher-paying and more skilled jobs as early as World War I. But those gains were short-lived. With the return of peace, women faced layoffs, renewed wage discrimination, and segregation into female-only jobs, such as secretarial and clerical work. They made little headway over the next decade, despite the hoopla about the emancipated "new woman" of the twenties. Behind the stereotype of the smart-talking flapper with her cigarette, bobbed hair, and boyish clothes, traditional ideas about women and their proper roles prevailed in the labor marketplace. In 1920, 23 percent of women worked; by 1930, the figure was only 24 percent. Access to the professions, while increased, remained heavily restricted. For example, women earned over 30 percent of all graduate degrees but accounted for only 4 percent of full professors on college faculties. Most women workers toiled at unskilled jobs; most were young, single, and without children. Between 1920 and 1930, the percentage of women in manufacturing fell from 22.6 (the same as 1910) to 17.5, while percentages of women in both domestic service and clerical work—the lowest-paying jobs—rose.

Real gains for women came during World War II. A rapidly expanding war economy absorbed most of the reserve labor force of under- or unemployed male workers. The military alone siphoned off some 15 million men and women. That left married women as the single largest untapped labor reserve. Suddenly, the propaganda machinery that had once discouraged women from competing with men for jobs urged them to enlist in the work force. The patriotic appeal had the desired effect. What faithful wife could sit at home when the media warned that her husband in the service might die from the lack of ammunition? "Commando Mary" and "Rosie the Riveter" became symbols of women who heeded their country's call.

Patriotism by itself did not explain the willingness of married women to take jobs. Many found higher war wages an attractive inducement. Indeed, with so many husbands earning low military pay, families needed additional income to survive. Absent husbands also meant a lower birthrate and fewer demands for household services. That left women more time and opportunity for work outside the home. And wartime restrictions on leisure activities made jobs a more attractive outlet for women's energies. Whether stated as raw numbers or percentages, the statistical gains for women were impressive. From 1940 to 1945, some 6.5 million women entered the work force, over half of them for the first time. Women accounted for just 25 percent of workers in 1940 but 36 percent in 1945.

Women of the *Saturday Evening Post,* **Part One.** In the midst of the war, the *Post's* "cover girl" was this nonchalant and confident Rosie, patriotic buttons across her chest, goggles over her eyes, macho watchband around the wrist, and biceps calculated to make Charles Atlas envious. As one real-life Rosie commented about welding, "We were happy to be doing it. We felt terrific. Lunch hour would find us spread out on the sidewalk. Women welders with our outfits on, and usually a quart of milk in one hand and a salami sandwich in another. It was an experience that none of us had ever had before."

Perhaps more significant were the kinds of women who now found employment outside the home. Young, single women no longer dominated. By 1950 married women were a majority of the female work force, compared with only a third in 1940. Similarly, older women between ages fifty-five and sixty-four became a major group, rising from 17 percent in 1940 to 35 percent by 1960. It was not only the numbers of working women that soared but also the quality of their jobs. Women had an opportunity to work in skilled areas of manufacturing and to earn much higher wages. Black women in particular, who had been concentrated in low-paying farm and domestic jobs, rushed to the factories that offered higher pay and better hours. Women on the assembly lines— shaping sheet metal, building airplanes, and performing a host of skilled tasks—shattered many stereotypes about traditional male and female roles.

Yet for all these undeniable gains, the situation brought about by a world at war was a special case, and most Americans perceived it that way. The men returning home intended to pick up their jobs, while most assumed that women would return to their traditional household duties. As a result, the war led to few structural changes affecting women's economic roles. For example, working mothers needed some form of day care for their young children. The government was slow to provide it and, even where it existed, many mothers were reluctant to use it. They or other family members continued to have primary responsibility for children. One result was a much higher absentee rate for working mothers. In addition, those mothers worked shorter hours. For them, the responsibilities of the job were secondary to those of the home.

Most professions continued to maintain barriers against women. Although female workers flooded government bureaucracies and factories, few received managerial status. And many employers found ways to avoid government regulations requiring equal pay for men and women. General Motors, for example, simply changed its job classifications from overtly segregated male–female categories to "heavy–light," thus leaving women in the "light," lower-paying categories. Fearful that rapidly rising wages would spur inflation, the government was slow to enforce its own rules protecting women from discrimination.

Certain social trends seemed to underscore the traditional resistance to working mothers. Statistics indicated that wartime stresses threatened to undermine the family. Alcohol abuse, divorce, and juvenile delinquency all increased, and some observers blamed those problems on working mothers. In fact, there was no clear evidence that the families of those women had any disadvantage over those whose mothers stayed home. Extraordinary wartime mobility, not the fact that the mothers worked, seems to have accounted for many of those problems. The sudden rush of workers, both male and female, to industrial centers overtaxed all manner of public services, including housing and schools, which were of particular importance to families with young children. The war disrupted families whether mothers worked or not.

What is striking is that by 1945, despite all the gains women had made, most attitudes about women and work had not changed substantially. Surveys showed that Americans, whether male or female, continued to believe that child rearing was a woman's primary job. Thus the marked demographic shift of women into the work force was revolutionary in import, but it brought no revolution in cultural attitudes toward sex roles. As historian William Chafe commented, "The events of the war years suggested that most Americans would accept a significant shift in women's economic activities as long as the shift was viewed as 'temporary' and did not entail a conscious commitment to approve the goals of a sexual revolution."

Despite the general expectation that women would return to the home after the war, female laborers did not simply drop their wrenches and pick up frying pans. Many continued to work outside the home, although mostly to support their families, not to find career alternatives. As peace came in 1945, polls indicated that over 75 percent of all working women wanted to continue at their jobs. About 88 percent of high school girls surveyed said they hoped for a career as well as the role of homemaker. Though employment for women did shrink slightly, a significantly higher percentage of women were working in 1950 than in 1940 (28 percent versus 24). Even more striking, that figure continued to rise, reaching 36 percent by 1960. Those numbers included older women, married women with children, and women of all social classes.

Such statistics would seem at first to undercut Friedan's notion that the vast majority of American women accepted the ideal of total fulfillment through housework and child rearing. Some 2.25 million women did voluntarily return home after the war and another million were laid off by 1946. At the same time, 2.75 million women entered the job market by 1947, leaving a net loss of only half a million.

But if Friedan was mistaken in seeing a mass female exodus from the work force, a significant shift did take place in the types of work performed. When women who had been laid off managed to return to work, they often lost their seniority and had to accept reduced pay in lower job categories. Employment in almost all the professions had decreased by

1960. Despite gains in some areas, women were concentrated in jobs that were primarily extensions of their traditional responsibility for managing the family's physical and emotional well-being: they were nurses, not doctors; teachers, not principals; tellers, not bankers. Far more worked in service jobs (as maids or waitresses, for example) than in manufacturing. Overwhelmingly, job opportunities were segregated by gender. About 75 percent of all women workers held female-only jobs. In fact, gender segregation in the workplace was worse in 1960 than in 1900—and even worse than segregation by race. Thus, even though women's participation in the work force remained comparatively high, it did not inspire a corresponding revolution in attitudes about women's roles in society.

RETREAT FROM REVOLUTION: THE ROLE OF MASS MEDIA

Attitudes, of course, were at the center of Friedan's concerns in *The Feminine Mystique;* and the demographic profile we have sketched underlines the reason for her focus. If the percentage of women holding jobs continued to increase during the 1950s and young women, when polled, said they hoped to combine work in some way with motherhood, how did the cult of the "feminine mystique" become so firmly enshrined? If wartime laboring conditions produced a kind of revolution in fact but not in spirit, what elements of American culture reined in that revolution and kept it from running its course?

As Friedan was well aware, economic and demographic factors played a crucial role in renewing the concern with home and family living. During the war, millions of American men fought overseas, which meant that, correspondingly, millions of wives at home could not have children. Even before the war, the hard times of the depression had discouraged couples from starting large families. But in 1945, when the home front saw the return of peace and prosperity and GIs were eager to do more than kiss their wives hello, the well-nigh inevitable pressures set off a postwar baby boom. For the next fifteen years the United States had one of the highest birthrates in the world, rising from an average of 1.9 to 2.3 children for each woman of childbearing age. Large families became the norm. The number of parents with three children tripled, while those with four quadrupled. Women also married younger. The average age of marriage dropped from 22 in 1900 to 20.3 in 1962. With the highest rate of marriage of any nation in the world, American men and women clearly chose to organize their lives around family.*

Clearly, material conditions not only pushed women out of the workplace as GIs rejoined the peacetime economy but also pulled women back into the home as the birthrate rose. Friedan acknowledged these changes but noted that the birthrates of other economically developed nations—such as France, Norway, and Sweden—had begun to decline by 1955. Even more striking, the sharpest rise in the United States came among women aged fifteen to nineteen. In Great Britain, Canada, and Germany, on the other hand, the rise was more equally distributed among age groups. What was it that made so many American "teen brides" give up the chance of college and a career for early marriage and homemaking?

Friedan's answer was to look more closely at the mass media. Magazines, radio, movies, television—all these had come to play a predominant role in modern culture. They exposed Americans by the millions to powerfully presented messages conveying the standards and ideals of the culture. The media, observed sociologist Harold Lasswell in 1948, had come to perform many of the tasks that, in medieval Europe, were assumed by the Catholic church. Like the church, the media possessed the capacity to send the same message to all classes at the same time, with confidence in their authority to speak and to be heard universally. Friedan, for her part, found it significant that in the postwar era the media's message about women—what they could dream of, set their sights on, and accomplish—underwent a marked shift. The purveyors of popular culture suddenly seemed determined to persuade women that they should not just accept but actually embrace the idealized image of women as wives and mothers.

Having written for the mass-circulation women's magazines, Friedan already knew the part they played in promoting the feminine mystique. What surprised her was how much the image of women had changed. In the 1930s, the woman most likely to appear in a magazine story had a career and was as much concerned with a goal of her own as with getting her man. The heroine of a typical *Ladies' Home Journal* story in 1939 is a nurse who has "strength in her hands, pride in her carriage and nobility in the lift of her chin. . . . She had been on her own ever since she left training, nine years ago. She had earned her way, she need consider nothing but her heart." And unlike the heroines of the 1950s,

---

*At the same time, the United States had the world's highest divorce rate. Enthusiasm for marriage was apparently no guarantee of success.

these women did not have to choose invariably between marriage and career. If they held strongly to their dreams, they could have both. Beginning in the 1950s, however, new heroines appeared. These, Friedan noted, were most often "young and frivolous, almost childlike; fluffy and feminine; passive; gaily content in a world of bedroom and kitchen, sex, babies, and home." The new women did not work "except housework and work to keep their bodies beautiful and to get and keep a man." "Where," Friedan asked rhetorically, "is the world of thought and ideas, the life of the mind and the spirit?"

Talking with some of the few remaining editors from the 1930s, Friedan discovered one reason for the change. "Most of the material used to come from women writers," one explained. "As the young men returned from the war, a great many women writers stopped writing. The new writers were all men, back from the war, who had been dreaming about home, and a cozy domestic life." Male editors, when queried, defended themselves by contending that their readers no longer identified with career women, no longer read serious fiction, and had lost almost all interest in public issues except perhaps those that affected the price of groceries. "You just can't write about ideas or broad issues of the day for women," one remarked.

Just as the image of women changed in mass magazines, so too did women's fashions follow Rosie the Riveter out of the factory. As historian Lois Banner has observed, in the 1930s only a movie star like Katherine Hepburn could get away with wearing slacks. During the 1940s, however, a boyish or mannish look for women became popular. Narrow skirts, padded shoulders, and suits all had a vogue. That ended in 1947, when Parisian designer Christian Dior introduced the "new look." Dior-inspired fashion emphasized femininity. Narrow waistlines drew attention to shapely hips and a fully defined bosom. Most women had to wear foundation garments to achieve the necessary look. The new styles reached their extreme in the "baby doll" fashions, with cinched-in waists that set off full bosoms and bouffant skirts held out by crinoline petticoats. Women's shoes ushered in a bonanza for podiatrists. Toes became pointier and heels rose ever higher, until it became dangerous for women to walk. Banner concluded that "not since the Victorian era had women's fashions been so confining." That fashion was a male image of the ideal feminine look.

In the 1930s, magazines and movies had set the fashion. By the 1950s, both those media had begun to lose their audience to television. Women who had once gone to the matinee stayed home to watch the latest episode of *As the World Turns.* In 1951, cities with television networks reported a 20 to 40 percent decline in movie attendance. Almost over-night, television became the preeminent mass medium, carrying images —feminine or otherwise—of American culture into the home. By 1949 there were about a million sets and 108 licensed stations, most in large urban markets. By 1952, 15 million Americans had bought sets; by 1955, the figure had jumped to 30 million; by 1960, television had entered 46 million homes. In fact, more American homes had television sets than had bathrooms! Obviously, if we are to understand how the mass media of the 1950s shaped the image of women, television must be at the center of our focus.*

And indeed, television portrayed women of the fifties in predictable ways. Most often they were seen in domestic dramas or comedies, in which Mom and Dad were found living happily with their two or three cute children and possibly a live-in maid or relative to provide additional comic situations. The homes in which they lived, even that of blue-collar airplane riveter Chester Riley (*The Life of Riley,* 1949–50, 1953–58), were cheerfully middle class, with the antiseptic look of a furniture showroom. As for Mom herself, she never worked outside the home and seldom seemed to do much more than wave a dust cloth or whip up a three-course meal at a moment's notice. Sometimes, as in *The Adventures of Ozzie and Harriet* (1955–66), she is competent, cool, and collected. Ozzie, in fact, often seems rather a lost soul when he is turned loose in his own castle, having to be guided gently through the current week's predicament by Harriet. In other series, such as *The Burns and Allen Show* (1950–58), women like Gracie Allen and her friend Blanche played more the role of "dizzy dames," unable to balance checkbooks and sublimely oblivious to the realities of the business world. When Harry Morton announces to his wife Blanche, "I've got great news for you!" (he's been offered a new job), Blanche replies, "When can I wear it?"

Perhaps the domestic comedy that best portrayed the archetypical family woman was *Father Knows Best* (1954–62). The title says it all: Robert Young, playing Jim Anderson, never lacks a sane head, while his wife Margaret is devoted, though something of a cipher. She lacks Gra-cie Allen's originality yet still can be counted on as a source of genial

---

*The technology of broadcasting had been available in the 1920s, but only after World War II did commercial application begin in earnest. As secretary of commerce, Herbert Hoover had his image transmitted in 1927, making him the first president to have appeared on television, although this occurred before his election in 1928. "Trivial Pursuit" buffs will recall that Franklin Roosevelt was, in 1939, the first president in office to appear on television.

Women of the *Saturday Evening Post,* **Part Two.** Biceps and riveting guns had deserted *Post* covers by 1956. Instead, these two women—like Margaret in *Father Knows Best*—can barely get their cars out the driveway, let alone down the street. No doubt, however, they could stir up a mean Jell-O salad.

humor as she tries vainly, for instance, to learn to drive the family car. Warmhearted, attractive, submissive, competent only within the sphere of her limited domain, she is the fifties housewife personified.

In one sense, then, Friedan does have a case. The mass media of the 1950s, television prime among them, saturated the American public with the image of the new feminine mystique. But to establish that merely raises a much thornier issue: What sort of relationship is there between the media and reality? Friedan is arguing not merely that the institutions of mass communication promoted the feminine mystique. She is suggesting that, through their influence and pervasiveness, the media were actually able to stifle women's aspirations and shape their attitudes. In that case, it becomes much more understandable why women's gains during the war were not translated into a revolution of the spirit.

REFLECTION VERSUS MANIPULATION

What effect do the mass media have on real life? Obviously, that is a complex question. But in sorting out the possible answers, we can see that there are two sharply contrasting ways of responding. On the one hand, it is possible to argue that, in fact, the media have very little effect on the real world, since they merely reflect tastes and opinions that mass audiences already hold. Confronted with a need to attract the largest number of consumers, media executives select programs that have the broadest appeal. Advertisers seek less to alter values than to channel existing ones toward a specific choice. Americans already value romantic love; once Lever Brothers has its way, they brush with "Close-Up" to achieve it. In the most extreme form, this "reflection hypothesis" would see the media as essentially passive—a simple mirror to society. And in that case, a good deal of Friedan's examination of female imagery might be instructive but beside the point. Women of the fifties were portrayed the way they were because, for whatever reasons, they had been transformed by the conditions of postwar culture.

But that extreme form of the reflection hypothesis breaks down for several reasons. First, if we argue that the mass media are merely reflections, then what are they reflecting? Surely not "real life" pure and simple. Only in commercials do the people who brush with Close-Up make their mates swoon. The parents on *Father Knows Best* are happily married, with two children, hardly the statistical norm in America even then. Divorced, single-parent mothers were unknown in sitcom land. Black families were virtually nonexistent. Obviously, while the media reflect certain aspects of real life, the reflection hypothesis must be modified to admit that a good deal of what is reflected comprises idealized values—what people would like to be rather than what they really are.

But if mass communications reflect ideals as much as reality, whose ideals are these? As Friedan pointed out, most of the editors, producers, directors, and writers of the 1950s were men. If male rather than female ideals and aspirations were being communicated (or, for that matter, white rather than black, middle-class rather than lower-class, or the ideals of any limited group), then it again becomes legitimate to ask how much the ideals of one segment of America are shaping those of a far wider audience.

Of course, many of the people involved in producing mass culture would argue that in the matter of dreams and ideals, they are not selling their own—merely giving the audience what it wants. But do audiences know what they really want? Surely they do sometimes. But they may also be influenced, cajoled, and swayed. Persuasion, after all, is at the heart of modern advertising. A fifties marketing executive made the point quite freely, noting that

> In a free enterprise economy, we have to develop the need for new products. And to do that we have to liberate women to desire these new products. We help them rediscover that homemaking is more creative than to compete with men. This can be manipulated. We sell them what they ought to want, speed up the unconscious, move it along.

Perhaps the most obvious case of an audience susceptible to persuasion is that made up of children. Psychological research has indicated that among children, a process called "modeling" occurs,

> simply by watching others, without any direct reinforcement for learning and without any overt practice. The child imitates the model without being induced or compelled to do so. That learning can occur in the absence of direct reinforcement is a radical departure from earlier theories that regarded reward or punishment as indispensable to learning. There is now considerable evidence that children do learn by watching and listening to others even in the absence of reinforcement and overt practice.

Obviously, if young girls learn week in and week out that father does indeed know best and that a woman's place *is* in the home, the potential for manipulation is strong.

The hypothesis that the media may be manipulative contrasts sharply with the theory that they are only reflective. More realistically, though, the two alternatives are best seen as the poles of a continuum. In its extreme form, the reflection hypothesis sees the media as entirely passive, with no influence whatever. In its extreme form, the manipulative hypothesis sees the media as highly controlling, "brainwashing" viewers (to use a term popular in the anticommunist fifties) into believing and acting in ways they never would have on their own. But a young girl, no matter how long she watches television, is also shaped by what she learns from her parents, schoolteachers, religious instructors, and a host of other influences. Given those contending factors, how decisive a role can the media play?

Ironically, the more extreme forms of the manipulative hypothesis have been supported by both the left and right of the political spectrum. During the 1950s, for example, with worries of foreign subversion running high, conservative ideologues warned that communists had come to rely "more on radio and TV than on the press and motion pictures as 'belts' to transmit pro-Sovietism to the American public." On the other hand, liberal intellectuals charged that mass culture, at its worst, threatened "not merely to cretinize our taste, but to brutalize our senses by paving the way to totalitarianism."

Historians have stepped only gingerly into the debate over media influence. In part this may be because, like most scholars, they tend not to be heavy consumers of mass culture themselves. Preferring a symphony by Strauss to MTV or Madonna, Federico Fellini's *8 1/2* to Burt Reynolds's *Smokey and the Bandit, Part 6,* or *Masterpiece Theater* to *The A-Team,* their instinctive reaction is to deem popular fare "worthy of attention only if it is created by unpaid folk and 'serious' artists who do not appear to think about making a living," as sociologist Herbert Gans has tartly remarked.

By temperament and training, most historians are also more comfortable with the traditional print media. When they seek to explicate a document, book, or diary, they can readily find the text and use common critical strategies to identify major thematic, symbolic, or cultural content. Insofar as the "author" of the document is sensitive to issues that concern some significant sector of society, the text can be said to reflect on social reality.

But what if the "text" is a series of commercials plugging the virtues of a toothpaste or a year's worth of *Guiding Light* soap operas? In that case, historians confront two difficulties. A vast amount of broadcast material is ephemeral—not permanently recorded at the time it was broadcast and recoverable now only in the vast reaches of outer space, where the signals are still radiating, ready either to bore or boggle the minds of another galaxy. The actual content of many broadcasts can be reconstructed only from file scripts or memories of viewers or participants, if at all. Even where television material has been saved and can be analyzed for its cultural content, a knowledge of how the audience received a program or commercial is crucial. As Herbert Gans has insisted, "cultural values cannot be determined from cultural content, until we know why people chose it." Do they watch a program intensely, or do they turn it on only because it's the best of a bad lot? Historians seldom have the means to answer those questions satisfactorily.

Sociologists are the allies most likely to help historians determine the effect of the media—particularly television—in modern life. But while sociologists have run a number of interesting studies involving the effect of television violence and racial stereotypes on viewers, much less systematic evidence has been gathered on television's effect on women. The most promising work has centered on what is known in the trade as content analysis. A content-analysis researcher examines a body of evidence, scanning it systematically in order to answer a few objective questions. How often are sex and violence linked in network crime shows? The researcher picks a sample group of shows, views them on a regular basis, and counts the number of incidents that include sex and violence. The results, of course, are descriptive within fairly limited bounds. They can tell us, for example, how often women appear in certain roles, but not how the audience perceives or values those roles. Nor can we know, except indirectly, what the shows' producers actually intended. If women are always portrayed in inferior positions, we can infer that the producers saw women as inferior; but the inference remains unproved.

Content analysis of early television programming has led sociologist Gaye Tuchman to conclude that television practiced the "symbolic annihilation of women." By that she meant that women were "demeaned, trivialized, or simply ignored." Surveys of television programs revealed that women, who were over half the population, accounted for just 32 percent of the characters in prime-time dramas. Most of the women who did appear were concentrated in comedy series. Children's cartoons had even fewer female characters. Even where women appeared most often—daytime soap operas—they still held inferior positions. A 1963 survey showed, in fact, that men held 80 percent of all jobs in prime-time shows.

Women were demeaned in other ways. They were most often the victims of violence, not the perpetrators. Single women were attacked more frequently than married women. The most favorably portrayed women were either courting or in a family role. In the 1950s, two-thirds of all the women characters on television shows were married, had been married, or were engaged. Even in soap operas, usually set in homes where women might presumably be allowed to act as leaders, women's roles were trivialized, for it was usually men who found the solutions to emotional problems.

Much early content-analysis research was not designed to focus specifically on women. But studies analyzing the settings of shows and the psychological characteristics of heroes, villains, and supporting characters indirectly support Tuchman's conclusion, since they show that the

world of television drama was overwhelmingly white, middle-class, suburban, family-centered, and male-dominated. In eighty-six prime-time
dramas aired during 1953, men outnumbered women 2 to 1. The very
young (under twenty) and the old (over sixty) were underrepresented.
The characters were largely of courting or childbearing age and employed or employable. High white-collar or professional positions were
overrepresented at the expense of routine white- or blue-collar jobs.
Most characters were sane, law-abiding, healthy, and white (over 80
percent). Blacks, who accounted for 12 percent of the population, appeared in only 2 percent of the roles. Heroes outnumbered heroines 2
to 1; and since heroic foreigners were more likely to be women, that left
three American heroes for each American heroine.

In these same eighty-six shows, male villains outnumbered female
villains. On the one hand, feminists might take heart at this more positive
presentation of women. On the other, villains had many traits that
Americans admired. While more unattractive, dishonest, disloyal, dirty,
stingy, and unkind, they were also brave, strong, sharper or harder than
most heroes, and had inner strength. Thus they were effective even if
undesirable. By minimizing women as villains, television denied them
yet another effective role. Similarly, television dramas presented the
most favorable stereotypes of professions in which men dominated. Journalists, doctors, and entertainers all had positive images, while teachers
—a large majority of whom were women—were treated as the slowest,
weakest, and softest professionals (though clean and fair).

So far as content analysis is able to go, then, it confirms that television
did systematically reinforce the feminine mystique Betty Friedan found
so prevalent elsewhere. But along with the advantages of content analysis come limits. To be rigorous, the method of measuring must be
standardized and the questions asked must be fairly limited and objective. For example, one content analyst described her approach in this
way:

Between March 18 and March 31, 1975, I watched and coded the shows,
according to pretested categories. Using a specially prepared timer, I
examined the first verbal or nonverbal interaction clearly between two
people in thirty seconds of one-minute segments of the programs. I recorded who was dominant, dominated, or equal in each interaction and
noted the relevant occupation status, sex, race, and family role of each
participant.

This is admirably systematic, but it leaves little room for more qualitative judgments—for evaluating the nuances of an image as well as its overt content. Sociologists, of course, would say that such subjective analysis is precisely what they are trying to avoid, because any "nuances" are likely to incorporate the prejudices of the researcher. As we know by now, however, historians have traditionally felt that this was a risk worth taking in order to examine documents for what they hint at or even do *not* say as much as for what they do. Since we are not in a position to undertake field research on how audiences of the fifties were affected by programs involving women, let us instead resort to a subjective analysis of television's product itself and see what its leading characters and dramatic themes reveal.

MALE FRAMES AND FEMALE ENERGIES

The most promising programs for exploring gender issues are the situation comedies, or "sitcoms." As we have seen, other genres popular in the 1950s—crime shows, westerns, quiz programs, and network news—tended to ignore women or place them in secondary roles. A majority of the sitcoms, however, take place in a domestic or family setting in which women are central figures. The plots regularly turn on misunderstandings between men and women over their relationships or the proper definition of gender roles. As a consequence, of all television programs, sitcoms had the most formative influence on the image of women.

As a genre, sitcoms had their roots in radio shows like *Jack Benny, Burns and Allen,* and *Amos 'n' Andy*—an influence that helps explain why their comedy came to be more verbal than that of film, which blended physical and verbal humor.* Sitcoms derived most of their laughs from puns, repartee, or irony. What the camera added was the visual delivery of the comedians: a raised eyebrow, a curled lip, or a frown. Thus closeups and reaction shots were key to the humor, especially since the small television screen limited the detail that could be shown. "You know what your mother said the day we were married, Alice?" grumps the obese Ralph Kramden on *The Honeymooners.* [A close-up, here, for

*Amos 'n' Andy, a show about a taxicab company operated by blacks, presented a special crossover problem. The white radio actors who started in the show were hardly appropriate for a visual medium.

emphasis; the double-chin juts in disdain.] "You know what she said? I'm not losing a daughter; I'm gaining a ton." Or another time, when Ralph's vanity gets the better of him, he brags, "Alice, when I was younger, the girls crowded around me at the beach." "Of course, Ralph," replies Alice, "that's because they wanted to sit in the shade." [Cut to Ralph's bulging eyes.]

From the historian's point of view, the more intriguing sitcoms are not the predictable ones like *The Adventures of Ozzie and Harriet* or *Father Knows Best* but those that do not seem to fit the standard mold. It is here —where the familiar conventions come closest to being broken—that the tensions and contradictions of the genre appear most clearly. In different ways, *Our Miss Brooks, I Love Lucy,* and *The Honeymooners* all feature unconventional characters and unusual plot situations. *Our Miss Brooks* stars Eve Arden as an aging, unmarried schoolteacher whose biting humor makes her a threat to the bumbling men around her. *I Love Lucy,* with Lucille Ball, follows the wacky attempts of Lucy Ricardo to break out of her narrow domesticity into the larger world of show business or into some moneymaking venture. Though the Ricardos had a child midway through the series, he was not often featured in the show. *The Honeymooners* was perhaps the most offbeat sitcom of the fifties. It featured the Kramdens, a childless couple, who lived in a dreary Brooklyn flat with their neighbors Ed and Trixie Norton, also childless. Ralph, a bus driver, and Ed, a sewer worker, seem unlikely subjects to reinforce the middle-class values of Friedan's feminine mystique.

Despite their unusual formats, all three sitcoms were among the most popular shows of the fifties, and *Lucy* stayed at the top of the ratings for almost the entire decade. By looking at them, we can better understand on what basis a show could deviate from traditional forms and still remain successful.

As it happens, none of these shows is as exceptional as it might first seem. All incorporate elements of the traditional family show structure, with male authority remaining dominant, middle-class values applauded, and the proper order of society prevailing by the end of each episode. Still, there is more to them than the simple triumph of the feminine mystique. The three leading female characters—Connie Brooks, Lucy Ricardo, and Alice Kramden—reveal through the force of their comic personas certain tensions that slick production styles and pat plot resolutions cannot hide. We see glimpses of women's discontent as well as women's strength in coping with adversity.

The comic tensions in *Our Miss Brooks* arise from two primary sources:

Connie constantly clashes with her authoritarian and pompous principal, Osgood Conklin, and—at the same time—has her amorous eye on the biology teacher, Mr. Boynton. He seems oblivious to her sexual overtures yet is the best prospect to save her from spinsterhood. In one show she walks in with her arms full of packages. "Can I hold something?" he asks. "Sure, as soon as I put these packages down," she cracks. He overlooks the sexual innuendo that she is forced to use in her constant attempts to stir his interest.

Miss Brooks is oppressed on several levels. She recognizes that society places little value on her role as a teacher. There is no future in her job, where she is bullied, exploited, and underpaid. Marriage offers the only way out, but since she is superior in intellect and personality to the men and no longer young and fresh, her prospects are dim. Thus she faces a future in which she cannot fulfill the feminine mystique. Her only hope is to use her wiles to trick Mr. Boynton into marriage. She must be passive-aggressive, because convention prevents her from taking the initiative. At the same time, she must accept an economic role that is far beneath her talents. Rather than challenge the system that demeans her, she survives by treating it as comical and transcending it through the force of her superior character.

The first episode of the series establishes many of those themes as well as a somewhat irreverent style. Connie gets an idea that she can arouse Mr. Boynton's interest by starting a fight. That leads to a number of laughs as Boynton ducks each of her attempts at provocation. Before she makes headway, she is called on the carpet by Mr. Conklin, the principal. In his office, he radiates authority, glowering from behind his desk and treating her with disdain. But Miss Brooks hardly folds before the onslaught. She tricks him into reminiscing about his youth and, as he becomes more mellow (and human), she assumes greater familiarity, until she is sitting casually on the corner of his desk. By the end of the meeting, Connie has sent Mr. Conklin on a wild goose chase that leads to his arrest by the police. In his absence, she becomes acting principal and clearly relishes the sense of authority she gains sitting in the seat of power. The duly constituted hierarchy has been bearded and stood on its head. Of course, all is set right in the end, but before order returns, we have had a glimpse of a world where women have power.

The liberties taken in the show, however, amount to scarcely more than shore leave. Even if Miss Brooks is unmarried, the show does have a kind of surrogate family structure. Despite her relatively advanced age, Connie's real role is more that of an impish teen daughter. She lives in

386 AFTER THE FACT

an apartment with a remarkably maternal housekeeper. One of the students at school, Walter (who these days would be classified as an eminent nerd), serves as a surrogate son, while Mr. Conklin, of course, is the father figure. That leaves Mr. Boynton to be paired off as Miss Brooks's reticent steady. As for Connie's challenges to Mr. Conklin's male authority, they are allowed only because the principal is pompous, arbitrary, or abusive of his position. And Mr. Boynton turns out not to be as dumb as he acts; indeed, at the end of the first episode, as Miss Brooks waits eagerly for a kiss that will demonstrate his interest, he holds back, his wink to the audience indicating that he can dish it out too. With Mr. Conklin back in charge and Mr. Boynton clearly in control, the male frame is reestablished, Connie has been chastened for her presumption, and the normal order of things restored.

Similar tensions operate in the *I Love Lucy* show. Lucy's efforts to escape the confines of domesticity threaten her husband Ricky and the well-being of the family. The plot generally thickens as Lucy cons her neighbor Ethel Mertz into joining her escapades. Ethel and Lucy then become rivals of their husbands. In an episode that could have generated biting commentary, Lucy and Ethel challenge Fred Mertz and Ricky to exchange roles. The women will be the breadwinners, the men the housekeepers. Both, of course, prove equally inept in the others' domain. Ethel and Lucy discover they have no significant job skills. After much frustration, they end up working in a chocolate factory under a woman who is far more domineering and arbitrary than Mr. Conklin ever was. In a parody of Charlie Chaplin's *Modern Times,* they fall hopelessly behind as they pack candies off a relentless conveyor belt. By the end of the day they are emotionally drained, humbled, and thwarted.

In the meantime, Ricky and Fred have virtually destroyed the apartment. How much rice do they need for dinner? They decide on several pounds, so that the kitchen is soon awash. Just as Ethel and Lucy are relieved to return home, Fred and Ricky are overjoyed to escape the toils of domestic life. Each side learns a new regard for the difficulties faced by the other.

Despite the schmaltzy ending, there is a real tension in the structure of this episode and the series as a whole. Within the orthodox framework (Lucy and Ricky are firmly middle class, worrying about money, friends, schools, and a house in the suburbs), the energy and spark of the show comes precisely because Lucy, like Miss Brooks, consistently refuses to recognize the male limits prescribed for her. Although Ricky manages to rein her in by the end of each episode, the audience realizes full well that she is too restless, too much restricted by four walls and a broom,

Fred Mertz (William Frawley) gropes in his pockets for lost tickets while other anxious members of the "I Love Lucy" cast—Lucy (Lucille Ball), Ethel Mertz (Vivian Vance), and Lucy's husband Ricky Ricardo (Desi Arnaz) look on anxiously. For all her zaniness Lucy generally appeared dressed in the latest fashion and her apartment reflected tasteful middle-class decor.

and far too vivacious to accept the cult of domesticity. She will be off and running again the following week in another attempt to break loose.*

*The show's most successful moment might also serve as a model of 1950s family life. In its early years, television honored all the middle-class sexual mores. Even married couples slept in separate beds and the word "pregnant" was taboo (since it implied that a couple had been sexually active—at least once). The producers of *Lucy* thus faced a terrible dilemma when they learned that their star was indeed with child. What to do? They made the bold decision to incorporate Lucille Ball's pregnancy into the show. For months, television audiences watched Lucy become bigger and more uncomfortable. On January 19, 1952, the big day arrived. The episode "Lucy Has Her Baby" (filmed earlier in anticipation of the blessed event) scored the highest

More than any sitcom of the 1950s, *The Honeymooners* seems to deviate from middle-American stereotypes. As lower-class, childless couples living in stark apartments, the Nortons and Kramdens would scarcely seem ideal reflections of an affluent, family-centered society. Ralph and Alice struggle to get by on his $67.50 a week salary as a bus driver. Sewer worker Ed Norton and his wife Trixie live off credit. Whenever their appliances or furniture are repossessed, Ed starts over at another store. The Kramdens have no television set, telephone, vacuum cleaner, or other modern appliance. Their living room/kitchen, the main set for the show, had only a bureau, a table and chairs, a standing sink, an icebox (literally), and a stove. It had the look of the depression era, not the 1950s.

The show turns on Ralph's obsession with money and status. He is forever trying to get rich quick, earn respect, and move up in the world. All that saves him from himself and disaster is Alice's stoic forbearance. She has had to live through all his efforts to assert his authority—"I'm the boss, Alice and don't you ever forget it!"—and to resist his harebrained schemes (diet pizza parlors, wallpaper that glows in the dark to save electricity). And it is Alice who cushions his fall when each new dream turns to ashes. Like most middle-class American couples, Ralph and Alice bicker over money. Ralph is a cheapskate, not by nature but to mask his failure as a breadwinner. Alice must use her feminine wiles to persuade him to buy anything, even a TV or a telephone. To protect his pride, Ralph accuses her of being a spendthrift. Their battles have far more bite than those seen in any other sitcom of that era. In no other show do the characters so regularly lay marriage, ego, or livelihood on the line.

Why, then, did the audience like this show? For one thing, it is very funny. Ed Norton's irrepressible deadpan is a perfect foil to Ralph's manic intensity. It is a delight to watch Norton take forever to shuffle the cards while Ralph does a slow burn. And Alice's alternately tolerant and spirited rejoinders complete the chemistry. In addition, there is a quality to the Kramdens' apartment that separates it in time and space from the world in which middle-class viewers live. The mass audience is more willing to confront serious questions if such issues are raised in distant times or places. Death on *Gunsmoke* does not have the same implications as a death on *Lassie*. Divorce for Henry VIII is one thing;

---

rating (68.8 percent) of any show of the decade. News of the birth of Desi Arnaz, Jr., rivaled the headlines for the inauguration of Dwight D. Eisenhower, which occurred the following morning.

In a typical scene from the "Honeymooners," Ralph Kramden (Jackie Gleason) adopts his usual pompous pose before his skeptical wife Alice (Audrey Meadows) and her anxious friend Trixie Norton (Joyce Randolph), while his friend Ed Norton (Art Carney) looks on with bug-eyed disbelief. Inevitably Ralph's confidence shattered in the face of his bungling attempts to get rich quick, leaving Alice to pick up the pieces and put him back together again.

even a hint of it for Ozzie and Harriet would be something quite different. Thus the Depression look of the Kramdens' apartment gives the audience the spatial and temporal distance it needs to separate itself from the sources of conflict between Ralph and Alice. The audience can look on with a sense of its material and social superiority as Alice and Ralph go at it:

> RALPH: You want this place to be Disneyland.
> ALICE: This place is a regular Disneyland. You see out there, Ralph? The back of the Chinese restaurant, old man Grogan's long underwear on the line, the alley? That's my Fantasyland. You see that sink over there? That's my Adventureland. The stove and the icebox, Ralph, that's

Frontierland. The only thing that's missing is the World of Tomorrow.
RALPH (doing his slow burn): You want Tomorrowland, Alice? You want
Tomorrowland? Well, pack your bags, because you're going to the
moon! [Menaces her with his raised fist.]*

Underneath it all, however, *The Honeymooners* is still a middle-class
family sitcom. Alice and Trixie don't have children; they have Ralph and
Ed. In one episode Trixie says to Alice, "You know those men we're
married to? You have to treat them like children." A trick of social class
makes this arrangement work without threatening the ideal of male
authority. Since the middle classes have always equated the behavior of
the poor with that of children—and Ralph and Ed are poor—no one is
surprised by their childish antics. Trixie and Alice, both having married
beneath them, maintain middle-class standards. At the end of almost
every episode, Alice brings Ralph back into the fold after one of his
schemes fails. Surrounding her in an embrace, he rewards her with his
puppydog devotion: "Baby, you're the greatest."

One episode in particular reveals the price Alice paid to keep her
man-child, marriage, and selfhood intact. A telegram arrives announcing, "I'm coming to visit. Love, Mom." Ralph explodes at the idea of
sharing his apartment with his dreaded mother-in-law, for her disap-
proval and insults wound his brittle pride whenever she visits. There are
numerous jokes at Ralph's expense as well as some cutting commentary
on mothers-in-law, after which Ralph moves in with the Nortons up-
stairs, where he sparks a similar fight between them. Finally, marriage
and family prevail over wounded pride. An unrepentant Ralph returns
home, only to find out that "mother" is Mother Kramden, whom Alice,
of course, is treating with the very warmth Ralph denies *her* mother. He
is once again reduced to a shamefaced puppy.

Alice's victory is so complete that it threatens to destroy her relationship with Ralph. As if to soften the blow, she sits down to deliver her
victory speech. She lowers her eyes, drops her shoulders, and speaks in
tones of resignation rather than triumph, finally reading to Ralph a letter
in praise of mothers-in-law, who have the "hardest job in the world."
It turns out to be a letter Ralph wrote fifteen years earlier to Alice's
mother. The sentiments are so sappy that they virtually destroy the
comedy. Like Ralph, the producers must have thought it better to eat

---

*Similarly a show like *M*A*S*H* could more easily explore topical issues like racism
because it was set in Korea, not the United States, and in the 1950s, not the present,
even though the issues were contemporary.

crow than leave a residue of bitterness or social criticism. They must have recognized that their material had been too extreme, the humor too sharp, and the mother-in-law jokes too cruel for middle-American tastes.

Even after its apology, the show ends with what appears to be an unintentional image of Alice in a domestic prison. Mother Kramden has gone off to "freshen up." A penitent Ralph admits his defeat, then announces he is going out for some air—in essence to pull himself back together. But what of Alice? She is left holding nothing more than she had before—dominion over her dreary kitchen. Her responsibility to Ralph's mother prevents her from escaping also, and she is no better off than before the battle began. Her slumped posture suggests that she understands all too well the hollowness of her triumph. We must believe that many women in videoland identified with Alice.

The Honeymooners, I Love Lucy, and *Our Miss Brooks* all suggest that, while the male characters in the series maintain their ultimate authority, the "symbolic annihilation" of women that Gaye Tuchman spoke of is, in these comedies at least, not total. A battle between the sexes would not be funny unless the two sides were evenly matched; and setting sitcoms in the home placed women in a better position to spar. Further, where men's roles gave them the advantage in terms of social position, rank, and authority, women like Connie, Lucy, and Alice vied equally through the sheer strength of their comedic personalities. The producers, of course, were not closet feminists in permitting this to occur; the circumstances simply made for popular shows. And their ratings were high, we would argue, partly because they hinted at the discontent felt by many women, whether its strength was recognized or not.

If that conclusion is correct, it suggests a common weakness in the ways both the reflective and manipulative hypotheses treat the mass media. At bottom, the extreme forms of each explanation slight one of the constants in historical explanation: change over time. If the mass communications industries simply reflected public taste and never influenced it, they would become nonentities—multimillion-dollar ciphers in any explanation that seeks to account for change. On the other hand, if we assign too manipulative a role to the media, it becomes difficult to explain any change at all. How was it that hundreds of thousands of girls who watched themselves being symbolically annihilated during the 1950s supplied so many converts to the women's movement of the sixties?

The mass media, in other words, while influential forces in modern society, are perhaps not as monolithic in outlook as they sometimes seem. The comparison to the medieval church is apt so long as we remember that the church, too, was hardly able to impose its will universally. Even where orthodoxy reigned, schismatic movements were always springing up. Today's heretics may be feminists rather than Anabaptists, but they are responding to pressures growing within society. From a feminist point of view, we may not have reached utopia merely because, by 1984, a female television producer could launch the series *Cagney and Lacey,* in which two female career police officers energetically catch murderers as well as live through the traumas of being diagnosed for breast cancer. All the same, there is change. Lucy is not Lacey, any more than Rosie was Gracie. And the same mass culture industry that threatened women with symbolic annihilation also published *The Feminine Mystique.*

Additional Reading

This chapter draws on material from three different fields—women's history, social history and popular culture, and the history of television. For overviews of the decade covering all three areas, we recommend James Gilbert, *Another Chance* (New York, 1982); Richard Polenberg, *One Nation Divisible* (New York, 1980); and Godfrey Hodgson, *America in Our Time* (New York, 1976). For overviews of the image of women in our culture, see Lois Banner, *American Beauty* (New York, 1983); Anne Douglas, *The Feminization of American Culture* (New York, 1977); and Mollie Haskell, *From Reverence to Rape* (New York, 1974). Haskell's study of the image of women in movies confirms what we learn from examining other areas of popular culture. A most intriguing strategy for decoding gender signs in the mass media is Erving Goffman, *Gender Advertisements* (New York, 1976).

For readers more concerned with the feminist movement and women's history, Betty Friedan, *The Feminine Mystique* (New York, 1963) is one place to start. Her book retains the vitality that spurred its wide popularity and remains an interesting social history of the 1950s. Kate Millett's *Sexual Politics* (New York, 1970) is another important feminist essay. For an overview of women in twentieth-century America, see Lois Banner, *Women in Modern America* (New York, 1974). In this brief history, Banner resists the argument of two leading male historians writing on women—Carl Degler, *At Odds* (New York, 1980) and William Chafe, *The American Woman* (New York, 1972)—who both stress demographic and economic patterns to explain changing roles for women. Banner gives more credit to the political efforts women have exerted.

The explosion of thinking and writing in women's history makes it impossible to mention more than a few valuable studies. Carroll Smith-Rosenberg has been a leader among women historians; her article "The New Woman and the New History," *Feminist Studies,* 3 (1975–76), 185–98, offers useful perspectives. Similarly, Rosalind Rosenberg, *Beyond Separate Spheres: The Roots of Modern Feminism* (New Haven, 1982) is worthwhile. In addition to Chafe and Degler on women, work, and politics, we found useful Ruth Schwartz Cowan, *More Work for Mother: The Ironies of Household Technologies from Open Hearth to Microwave* (New York, 1983); Eleanor Flexner, *A Century of Struggle,* rev. ed. (Cambridge, Mass., 1975); Susan Estabrook Kennedy, *If All We Did Was to Weep at Home: A History of White Working-Class Women in America* (Bloomington, Ind., 1981); and Barbara M. Wertheimer, *We Were There: The Story of Working Women in*

America (New York, 1977). For anyone curious about the European scene, we recommend John C. Fout, ed., *German Women in the Nineteenth Century* (New York, 1984) because it reveals a variety of methodologies and includes a comprehensive bibliography of women's history.

As we mentioned, historians have not written extensively about television. Clearly, the best place to begin is Eric Barnouw, *Tube of Plenty* (New York, 1975), which is a condensed version of his three-volume history of television and broadcasting. His study *The Sponsor* (New York, 1978) takes a highly critical look at TV advertising. Several collections of essays are quite interesting: John O'Connor, ed., *American History/American Television* (New York, 1983); Horace Newcomb, ed., *Television: The Critical View* (New York, 1976); E. Ann Kaplan, ed., *Regarding Television* (Los Angeles, 1983); and Alan Wells, ed., *Mass Media and Society* (Palo Alto, Calif., 1972) all contain useful historical and critical materials. Raymond Williams, *Television: Technology and Cultural Form* (New York, 1975) has some of the most interesting insights into the evolution of television and its impact on society. David Marc, *Demographic Vistas: Television in American Culture* (Philadelphia, 1984) and Robert Sklar, *Prime Time America* (New York, 1980) are two critical essays on television.

When we turned to sociology and the fields of popular culture, we found a rich though uneven literature. Gaye Tuchman, Arlene Kaplan Daniels, and James Benet, eds., *Hearth and Home: Images of Women in the Mass Media* (New York, 1978) is an invaluable source of statistics and ideas. The often sharp debate over popular culture in the 1950s still makes lively reading in the essay collection edited by Bernard Rosenberg and David White, *Mass Culture* (New York, 1957). Herbert Gans, *High Culture and Popular Culture* (New York, 1974) may have gotten in the final and most persuasive word for the functional school of sociological thought. Charles Wright, *Mass Communications* (New York, 1959), provides a sociological approach to the mass media in the 1950s, while Klaus Krippendorff, *Content Analysis* (London, 1980), covers the tonic named.

In preparing this essay we tried to concentrate on 1950s programs still in syndicated reruns, such as *I Love Lucy* and *The Honeymooners*. It was our hope that students could in that way do some checking on our interpretations as well as striking out on their own. For anyone interested in television history, a visit to the Museum of Broadcasting in New York City is a must. Its video archives are available to the public and contain the most comprehensive collection of old programming. We spent many a happy hour there reliving *Life With Father, Gunsmoke, The $64,000 Question,* and *Topper* as well as the sitcoms we discussed.

FOURTEEN

❖

Instant Watergate

At 2:30 in the morning on Saturday, June 17, 1972, police arrested five men who had broken into Washington headquarters of the Democratic National Committee, located in the plush Watergate apartment complex. The men were a rather strange set of burglars. They wore business suits and rubber surgical gloves, and carried with them a walkie-talkie, forty rolls of unexposed film, two cameras, lock picks, two pen-size tear gas guns, and several bugging devices. Far from stealing into the complex in the dead of night, the burglars had dined earlier on lobster in a Watergate restaurant. Police discovered that among them, the five men carried $2,300, mostly in the form of hundred-dollar bills with sequential serial numbers.

When Bob Woodward of the *Washington Post* received a phone call from the paper requesting him to cover the story that Saturday morning, he had no knowledge of the case's puzzling aspects. To him, it seemed just another burglary assignment handed a cub reporter. He had joined the staff of the *Washington Post* only nine months earlier. That the editors rated the story as minor was confirmed when they allowed Carl Bernstein onto the case. Bernstein, another young reporter, covered the local ups-and-downs of Virginia politics.

But as the day wore on, the appearance of the burglary grew curiouser and curiouser. At the preliminary hearing for the five burglars, their spokesman, one James McCord, was asked his occupation. "Security consultant," he answered quietly. Woodward, covering the hearing, moved to the front row to hear better. McCord was saying that he had recently left a job with the government. Where in government, asked the judge. "CIA," whispered McCord.

Sunday night another *Post* reporter relayed Woodward the information that the police had found two address books on one of the suspects. Each listed the name Howard Hunt, with a telephone number listed as

"W. H." in one book and "W. House" in the other. The next day Woodward called the White House and discovered that indeed, a man named E. Howard Hunt was a White House consultant. Woodward finally reached Hunt and asked him what his name was doing in the address book of two Watergate burglars. "Good God!" responded Hunt. He issued a quick no-comment and hung up. Official White House response was equally swift. Presidential Press Secretary Ronald Ziegler called the break-in "a third-rate burglary attempt" and warned, "certain elements may try to stretch this beyond what it is."

In the months that followed, Woodward and Bernstein began digging for more information. Both reporters assembled their own master lists

E. Howard Hunt, one of the convicted Watergate burglars, testifying at the Senate Watergate hearings. Hunt, a former CIA agent, possessed a flair for the dramatic. He had published a series of James Bond style spy novels, and apparently attempted to live a similar life in his own career. On one secret mission for the White House, he flew to Denver, disguising himself with what one Justice Department official later described as "a cheap, dime-store, reddish colored wig." A similar wig was found in the Watergate hotel the day after the arrest of the burglars.

of key telephone numbers: several hundred contacts who were each called at least twice a week. All notes, records of phone conversations, and first drafts of articles went into a filing system that soon filled four cabinets.

Increasingly, the information they pieced together linked the Watergate burglary with officials in the Nixon re-election campaign, known as the Committee to Re-elect the President, or more popularly, CREEP. One of the burglars, it turned out, had opened a checking account containing $89,000. The money had come from checks which were traced back to fund-raising efforts by the re-election committee. Apparently CREEP Finance Chairman Maurice Stans had gone on a money-raising tour in the spring of 1972. To preserve contributors' anonymity, he "laundered" the funds through a Mexican bank. Somehow, some of the donations had turned up in the burglar's bank account.

Further investigation indicated that in addition to money spent for legitimate purposes, CREEP had a secret "slush fund" of over $350,000 that could be used for clandestine projects. Even more serious, use of the funds had been cleared by high-level White House officials, including Maurice Stans, the former secretary of the treasury; John Mitchell, former attorney general; and H. R. Haldeman, White House chief of staff. The two reporters also uncovered information indicating that the Watergate burglary was only one incident in a larger undercover effort to discredit the campaigns of various Democratic presidential candidates. That effort was coordinated by Donald Segretti; *Post* articles noted that Segretti's minions had been

> following members of Democratic candidates' families; assembling dossiers of their personal lives; forging letters and distributing them under the candidates' letterheads; leaking false and manufactured items to the press; throwing campaign schedules into disarray; seizing confidential campaign files and investigating the lives of dozens of Democratic campaign workers.

Although Segretti himself behaved much like a college prankster out on a romp, he had been hired directly by Dwight Chapin, President Nixon's personal appointments secretary.

Despite Woodward and Bernstein's exposés, the Watergate scandal had little effect on the Nixon re-election campaign. The president himself announced in August that White House counsel John Dean had conducted an investigation into the burglary and that "no one on the White House staff . . . was involved in this very bizarre situation. What really hurts in matters of this sort is not the fact that they occur," the president continued, " What really hurts is if you try to cover it up." In the closing days of the campaign, White House officials accused the *Post* of being little more than an appendage of the McGovern organization. "This is a political effort by the *Washington Post,"* complained Ziegler, "well conceived and coordinated, to discredit this administration and individuals in it."

On election day Richard Nixon received nearly 61 percent of the popular vote, one of the largest majorities in American presidential elections. At the same time Woodward and Bernstein were finding it increasingly difficult to come up with new leads in their investigation. Ben Bradlee, the *Post*'s flamboyant editor, recalled in frustration that he had been "ready to hold both Woodward's and Bernstein's heads in a pail of water until they came up with another story."

The decisive break in the case came not from any investigative reporting, but from pressures arising out of the burglars' trial held in January 1973. Despite an extensive investigation, officials chose to prosecute only the five burglars, plus Howard Hunt and G. Gordon Liddy, a former FBI agent and finance counsel for CREEP, who had helped Hunt. The trial was concluded within a month, and the jury took less than an hour and a half to find all seven defendants guilty.

But the presiding judge, John Sirica, remained unsatisfied. None of the seven men had explained adequately why they had acted as they did and where they got their money. "These hundred dollar bills," Sirica complained of the bank account funds, "were floating around like coupons." He criticized the prosecution's handling of the case and concluded, "I have not been satisfied, and I am still not satisfied that all the pertinent facts that might be available—I say *might* be available—have been produced before an American jury." He set bond for McCord and Liddy at $100,000 each and threatened to impose particularly stiff sentences on them.

In March, McCord apparently decided not to chance the harsh sentence. He wrote Judge Sirica a letter maintaining that the burglars had been under political pressure to plead guilty, and so avoid any protracted questioning during the trial. Some witnesses had perjured themselves, he claimed; the names of others involved in the conspiracy had been kept out of the trial.

During March and April the prosecutors investigated McCord's claims. As the threat of exposure increased, some campaign officials scrambled for lawyers; others approached the prosecutors with their own revised stories. By April new disclosures had forced President Nixon to accept reluctantly the resignations of his two closest aides, H. R. Haldeman and John Ehrlichman, as well as Richard Kleindienst, the attorney general. The President also fired his White House counsel, John Dean, who had agreed to cooperate fully with the prosecutors.

Watergate stories were breaking daily throughout the spring of 1973; as spring turned to summer Americans got a firsthand look at the controversy when a special Senate committee, chaired by Senator Sam Ervin of North Carolina, convened to hear testimony about Watergate. During televised hearings, viewers saw a parade of witnesses testify that Attorney General John Mitchell, the highest law enforcement officer in the land, had been present at meetings where Gordon Liddy outlined his proposals for the Watergate burglary and other espionage attempts. Others testified that McCord, Liddy, and their associates had worked directly for John Ehrlichman as part of a security group called "the

Former White House Counsel John Dean consults a portion of his testimony, as Senator Sam Ervin (left) speaks with Dean's lawyers. Dean's low-key manner, meticulous testimony, and remarkable memory impressed many listeners, but until the existence of the tapes became known, it was Dean's word against the president's.

Plumbers," which investigated leaks to the press. The Plumbers, it was revealed, had burglarized the office of a psychiatrist to obtain damaging information about Daniel Ellsberg, a former government official being prosecuted for leaking a secret Pentagon study about the conduct of the Vietnam war.

The most astonishing witness to appear before the Ervin committee was John Dean. In a quiet, monotonous voice Dean testified that the president himself had maintained the cover-up as recently as April 1973. When McCord had threatened to tell prosecutors what he knew, Dean met with the president and his aides on March 21 and approved "hush money" of up to a million dollars to buy the Watergate burglars' silence. Of all the witnesses, only Dean claimed that Richard Nixon had participated in the cover-up. It was his word against the president's. Then came the most stunning revelation of all. Alexander Butterfield, an aide to H. R. Haldeman, informed committee members that for years a secret White House taping system had routinely recorded all presidential conversations. If the committee could listen to those tapes, it would no longer have to weigh one witness's word against another's. The tapes could tell all.

But obtaining that evidence did not prove easy. Archibald Cox, who in May had been appointed as special prosecutor to investigate the new Watergate disclosures, subpoenaed relevant tapes. When the courts backed Cox in his request, the president fired him on Saturday, October 20. Reaction was swift and vehement. Attorney General Elliot Richardson and his immediate subordinate resigned in protest. Reporters dubbed the firing and resignations the "Saturday Night Massacre." In Congress, twenty-two separate bills were introduced calling for possible impeachment of the president, and Representative Peter Rodino, chairman of the House Judiciary Committee, began deliberations on the matter.

Under immense pressure, President Nixon named a new special prosecutor, Leon Jaworski of Texas, and released the subpoenaed tapes to Judge Sirica. Then came yet another jolt. White House counsel J. Fred Buzhardt told the court that some sections of the requested tapes were missing. One tape contained a crucial eighteen-and-a-half-minute "gap." Experts testified that the missing materials had been deliberately erased. Alexander Haig, the president's new chief of staff, could only suggest lamely to Sirica that "some sinister force" was at work. By April 1974, Special Prosecutor Jaworski and the House Judiciary Committee had requested additional tapes. At first the president refused; then he grudgingly agreed to supply edited transcripts. White House secretaries typed up over 1,200 pages, which the president with a show of virtue made public.

The transcripts were damaging. They revealed a president who was often vindictive, vulgar, and small-minded. The pivotal meeting with John Dean, on March 21, 1973, showed him discussing in detail how his aides might, as he put it, "take care of the jackasses who are in jail." "How much money do you need?" Nixon asked Dean. "I would say these people are going to cost a million dollars," Dean estimated. "We could get that," replied the president. " . . . You could get a million dollars. And you could get it in cash. I know where it could be gotten. I mean it's not easy, but it could be done."

In the following months events moved swiftly. Neither the Judiciary Committee nor Jaworski was satisfied with edited transcripts, and Jaworski appealed directly to the Supreme Court. In July, the Court voted unanimously to order the president to produce the tapes. The same month, the Judiciary Committee passed three articles of impeachment, accusing the president of obstructing justice, misusing his presidential powers, and refusing to comply with the committee's requests for evidence. In August, the president's lawyers, J. Fred Buzhardt and James St. Clair, insisted that the president release transcripts of conversations recorded on June 23, 1972, only a few days after the Watergate burglary. The tapes demonstrated beyond all doubt that from the beginning the president had known of the burglars' connection to the White House and had acted to limit the FBI investigation. Even the president's staunchest supporters in Congress refused to defend him.

Bowing to the inevitable, Richard Nixon appeared on national television and announced his resignation, effective the following day at noon. On August 9 the new president, Gerald Ford, took the oath of office. "The Constitution works," he announced. "Our long national nightmare is over."

TWO JOURNALISTS IN SEARCH OF A HISTORY

At every turn in its two years of unwinding, the Watergate drama grew beyond the expectations of those who pursued its story. What had begun as a routine burglary assigned to a couple of young reporters had ended with the first resignation of a president of the United States. Woodward and Bernstein had fought to stay on top of events as they grew. When the *Post*'s national desk sought to take over the story, the two reporters successfully defended their claim to cover the case. For months it was their investigations and their by-line that advanced public knowledge of the scandal. Yet even they were overtaken by the flood of events. In the months after McCord's letter to Sirica, when every day brought a new participant willing to tell his own version of events, Woodward and Bernstein's articles were joined by a host of others from major newspapers and newsweeklies.

Still, the two reporters recognized that from the beginning they had been as close as any reporters to the unfolding drama. Why not write a book about Watergate? Even in October 1972, before the election, Woodward and Bernstein pursued the idea with representatives of Simon and Schuster. The result of these conferences was *All the President's Men,* published in mid-1974 at the height of the Watergate crisis. It became an immediate bestseller.

All the President's Men was popular not merely because of its timing but also because it was an exciting, well-written detective story. The book's main characters were not really the president's men so much as the *Washington Post*'s—Woodward and Bernstein themselves. The narrative outlined, day by day, the extensive, exhausting, and sometimes suspenseful maneuvers undertaken by the two reporters to get their story. It recounted late-night visits to CREEP accountants, clandestine attempts (of dubious legality) to obtain information from grand jurors hearing the Watergate case, and Woodward's periodic cloak-and-dagger visits to a source high in the Nixon administration, identified in the book only by the nickname "Deep Throat." On most occasions, Deep Throat agreed to meet only at two in the morning in a parking garage, and only after Woodward had taken two separate cabs in order to elude any possible tails. This emphasis on the reporters' own story made good sense. The detective work was worth describing, and in any case, Woodward and Bernstein remained very much outsiders: investigators trying to penetrate the secrets of the Palace Guard.

The two reporters probably recognized that this approach left the end of their book dangling. If the story was going to be about their detective work, then the unique part of the tale ended, for the most part, once the host of other journalists had joined them in the hue and cry. Thus 95 percent of *All the President's Men* describes events previous to April 1973; the book ends with the Watergate crisis itself unresolved. While it was only natural, then, that the two reporters would consider writing a second book, such a sequel would necessarily have to focus not on the reporters, but on the main participants in Watergate itself. It would be history, not autobiography.

Within a week of the Nixon resignation, Woodward and Bernstein began work on an account of the president's last days in office. Starting with their already impressive number of contacts, they interviewed anyone who had a part in the drama—from secretaries of state to secretaries of offices and presidential barbers. Within six months, they and two other research assistants had talked with 394 people. They collected unpublished notes, memos, diaries, transcripts, logs, and correspondence. In the spring of 1976 the fruits of this labor appeared in a voluminous account titled *The Final Days.*

Once again, the two reporters had a hit on their hands. Eager readers scrambled for the serialized excerpts in *Newsweek* magazine to discover the lurid, yet-untold highlights of the drama. And lurid highlights there were. The book's portrait of Richard Nixon revealed a leader obsessed with Watergate, largely incapable of concentrating on other matters, and at times driven to heavy drinking. At one point, the book told of the president's son-in-law, Edward Cox, sighting the president in the White House hallways late at night, talking to the pictures on the wall. The most dramatic moment of the book came when the president, having made his decision to resign, summoned Secretary of State Henry Kissinger to the Lincoln Room of the White House. As the two men talked, Nixon broke down and sobbed. "Henry, you are not a very orthodox Jew, and I am not an orthodox Quaker, but we need to pray." With both men on their knees, the president prayed for peace, rest, and love. And then, still sobbing, Nixon leaned over and struck his fist on the carpet, crying, "What have I done? What has happened?"

Given such riveting material, *The Final Days* sold well; yet praise from the press was much less overwhelming than it had been for *All the President's Men.* Most critics took exception to both the book's narrative style and its research techniques. In *All the President's Men,* where Woodward and Bernstein had written autobiographically, they dealt primarily with firsthand experiences. In crossing the line from autobiography to history, they had to reconstruct the activities of the president and his inner circle from a variety of documents and interviews. And this presented a problem. Most scholars undertaking such a project would have provided readers with footnotes, indicating which sources contributed to which sections of the narrative. But Woodward and Bernstein conducted all of their interviews "on background," with the understanding that the information would be used only if the source's identity remained confidential. Thus the book was written without footnotes.

"Hell, I trust Woodward and Bernstein," wrote Richard Reeves in his *New York Times* review (headlined "Lots of Footwork, No Footnotes"). "But how do you evaluate material this important without a guide to the

sources?" Historian Max Lerner made the same point in an article entitled "Writing 'Hot History.' " "The self-interest of many of [the book's]
sources—their public face, their desire to rid themselves of the Watergate taint and get a better role in the drama of history—seem to me an
insurmountable obstacle, unless the reader knows who the sources are
and can make his own assessment of them." In the *New Republic,* John
Osborne angrily observed that Woodward and Bernstein "never once
attribute a statement to the source or sources of the statement." Osborne
called *The Final Days* "on the whole the worst job of nationally noted
reporting that I've observed during 49 years in the business."*

The widespread reaction of journalists against the missing footnotes
may be partly explained by another feature of *The Final Days*: its "omniscient" narrative perspective. The book's characters are never made to
say anything "according to reliable sources," or "based on a participant's
notes made shortly after the meeting." Words are instead placed in their
mouths as if the two inquiring reporters from the *Post* were invisibly
present at all the crucial meetings. Such a style may pretend to omniscience, the critics argued, but Woodward, Bernstein, and Ben Bradlee
were hardly Father, Son, and Holy Ghost.

At first glance, it would appear that professional historians might share
the critics' disdain for *The Final Days*. As we have already seen, one of
the prime requirements of historical research is the necessity of evaluating the perspectives of all primary sources. It is scant consolation to know
that Woodward and Bernstein have pledged to deposit their notes and
interviews in a library, to be made public at some distant future date.

---

*Osborne and Lerner were more adept at mustering righteous indignation than being
consistent. Osborne admitted that his own writings were full of unattributed statements—"by preference" even—but weakly argued that Woodward and Bernstein's
"piling statement upon unattributed statement for 450 pages" gave "a good method
a bad name." The rest of the review was replete with rebuttals that began, "I was
told recently on excellent authority. . . ." Lerner, for his part, attacked Woodward
and Bernstein for claiming that Chief Justice Warren Burger's Supreme Court opinion on the Nixon tapes was so inadequate that Justice Potter Stewart undertook to
co-author it. "As it happens," Lerner announced in his most authoritative deadpan,
"I tried out this assertion on the Chief Justice, who was astounded by it. He told me
that the process of shaping a unanimous opinion was a long one, but that he had been
in charge all along and had no 'co-authors.' " Despite Lerner's own admonition that
Watergate participants might distort their recollections in order to "get a better role
in the drama of history," he apparently felt that if his friend the Chief Justice said it
ain't so, that settled the case.

Their book is available to historians now; and the need to evaluate it exists now.

Yet historians are likely to judge the two reporters less severely than their colleagues in journalism, if only because historians are all too eager to obtain data from any quarter. Readers will recall that early on in our explorations we examined another piece of "hot history"—Captain John Smith's *Generall Historie of Virginia.* No doubt Smith's account would have been lambasted by today's reporters for the same reasons they chastised Woodward and Bernstein's. The captain includes no footnotes. He writes with an "omniscient" perspective, even referring to himself in the third person. Furthermore, he often blithely borrows passages from other published works, silently incorporating them in his own narrative as if he had written them himself. Smith gets terrible marks on all these counts, yet historians of early Virginia depend on his account continually.

And they do so without surrendering their ability to judge the material critically. Smith may not have left behind footnotes, but historians have their own ways of evaluating his prose. Henry Adams, we saw, questioned Smith's Pocohontas story by comparing the *Generall Historie* with earlier published versions of it. In our own investigation, we were able to judge Smith's stories of Indian life critically by making ourselves aware of the narrative's characteristic perspectives.

By the same token, historians reading *The Final Days* are not left quite as helpless by the lack of footnotes as journalists apparently believe. For the fact is, Woodward and Bernstein tell readers a good deal more about the identity of their sources than first appears. Their "omniscient" prose, like Smith's, is readily susceptible to analysis. It is worth examining how such an analysis might proceed.

BEHIND THE OMNISCIENT NARRATIVE

Even the casual reader of *The Final Days* can guess the approximate source of information in many of the book's passages. When we read that Special Prosecutor Leon Jaworski considered compromising with the White House on access to the tapes, we cannot guarantee that Jaworski himself was the source, but the text says he "called a meeting of his most trusted assistants" to discuss the problem, and the book then goes on to recount the debate. Obviously, one or more of the assistants are prime candidates. All the major figures in the Watergate

James St. Clair, special counsel to the president for Watergate, surrounded by his entourage. Although there are smiles on all the faces, the narrative perspectives in *The Final Days* suggest that while St. Clair refused to talk with Woodward and Bernstein, several of his hard-worked, disgruntled staff unburdened themselves to the two reporters.

drama commanded their own entourage of aides, associates, and secretaries whom Woodward and Bernstein went to work on. It is the time-honored tactic, after all: start with the minnows and work slowly up to the big fish. Jaworski used it himself when he was investigating the cover-up.

But knowing the approximate source of information is not good enough. The more a story is passed ear to ear, the more likely it is distorted. Furthermore, different perspectives yield different accounts. James St. Clair is unlikely to narrate the challenges of his appearances before the House Judiciary Committee quite in the same manner as his disgruntled research assistant. So it is important to determine, wherever possible, which of the major characters are willing firsthand sources, and which appear only through the filtered accounts of either their subordinates or other major protagonists. The task is by no means easy.

But is the prose of *The Final Days* all that omniscient? Consider the realm of fiction. Novelists, who possess absolute control over their creations, have the license to be as omniscient as they please. Their writing does not require either the historian's footnote or the journalist's attributive clause. Yet they do not always exercise their prerogative. Charles Dickens, for instance, opens his novel, *Bleak House,* with a chapter that omnisciently enters the minds of all the characters and explains their thoughts. But then in chapter II Dickens decides to write with only partial omniscience. "We still use his eyes," E. M. Forster has noted, "but for some reason they begin to grow weak: he can explain Sir Leicester Dedlock to us, part of Lady Dedlock but not all, and nothing of Mr. Tulkinghorn. In Chapter III he is even more reprehensible: he goes straight across into the dramatic method and inhabits a young lady, Esther Summerson. . . . Logically, *Bleak House* is all to pieces, but Dickens bounces us, so that we do not mind the shiftings of the view-point."

Woodward and Bernstein are equally good bouncers, but for different reasons. Dickens keeps quiet about Lady Dedlock's inner thoughts because the plot demands it; Woodward and Bernstein keep quiet because they simply don't have certain information. But they are such good storytellers that, like Dickens, they keep us from noticing their elegant sleights of hand.

Take, for example, Edward Cox's well-publicized phone call to Senator Robert Griffin of Michigan, during which Cox anxiously reported that President Nixon had been walking the halls talking to pictures. Here is the way *The Final Days* introduces the episode:

> Griffin was worried. His call for resignation, a difficult thing for him to do, had fizzled. In his office that afternoon, he was notified that Ed Cox was on the phone. . . . He picked up the phone and found a very disturbed young man on the other end of the line.

It all seems perfectly omniscient. But the passage does take a point of view. Woodward and Bernstein might just as easily have written it this way:

> Ed Cox was worried. Late the previous evening while walking the corridors of the White House, he had witnessed something that disturbed him intensely. Now he picked up the phone and asked the operator to get him Senator Robert Griffin.

A novelist's option, certainly, and also the most direct approach. But it was not the phrasing Woodward and Bernstein chose, we may reasonably conclude, because their information came either from Griffin or an aide in his office. The reporters naturally retold the story from the same perspective that it came to them.

One example surely will not demonstrate that Cox refused to talk to Woodward and Bernstein. But when a similar pattern emerges (indeed, all of Cox's worries about the president's mental state are described from the far end of the telephone), then we begin to be on the lookout. We notice, for instance, that when relating Nixon family conversations, *The Final Days* appears much more omniscient about the thoughts of David Eisenhower than those of Ed Cox. We constantly learn what David felt directly (he *realized* he was doing a lot of repeating, he *sensed* the president was going to resign); whereas with Ed, we are often told only how an observer thought he felt: "Ed *appeared* irritated;" "He weighed both sides carefully, *as if* he were going to make a presentation." (Not, "*because he intended* to make a presentation. . . .") And the facade slips a little when the book refers to Ed Cox primarily as "Cox," but to David Eisenhower as "David."

It is often easier to discover who did not talk than it is to establish conclusively who did. Just because the text says, "David *thought*," it does not follow that Eisenhower was necessarily a firsthand source. "At no point in the book do we describe someone's thought processes," argued Bernstein in an interview. He cited Buzhardt as an example. "There's a sentence [in there] that says that Buzhardt thought that the President was the most transparent liar he had ever seen. That's not describing the thought process. That's not attributing thoughts to someone's head which were unexpressed. That's a statement Buzhardt said to a good number of people." In the case of David Eisenhower, *The Final Days* reports that he constantly confided in his close friend, Brooks Harrington. And of course Eisenhower also talked with other friends of the family like Pat Buchanan. So we must concede that the Eisenhower material may be secondhand, at least until we find other ways to pin down its origins.*

To identify sources more precisely, then, we must isolate material in the text that could have come from one person and one person only. Henry Kissinger's final meeting with the president in the Lincoln Room

*Eisenhower has admitted that he contributed material, but we are concerned here not simply with who talked, but with the evidence that can be deduced from the text of *The Final Days* alone.

has attracted so much notice, in part, precisely because it fits this category. Nixon didn't talk, so Kissinger must have—to someone. Yet (as everyone has also pointed out) he *did* talk—to two of his aides, Brent Scowcroft and Lawrence Eagleburger, right after the meeting. The book comes right out and says so. And Scowcroft and Eagleburger would have to have possessed the resolution of saints to keep from retelling the story to a few trusted friends. With an event of such magnitude, it is only natural to expect word to spread.

So natural, in fact, that the curious footnote-hunters in the popular press ought to have kicked themselves for not making the final logical inference. If the big, dramatic stories are the ones passed from ear to ear, then the way to isolate the sources of *The Final Days* is to go back and look for the events so undramatic, so minuscule that *nobody* would bother to tell anyone else about them.

In a book jammed with dramatic events, the minuscule is hard to come

J. Fred Buzhardt, Special White House Counsel for Watergate, wearing the telltale West Point class ring. Internal evidence indicates that Buzhardt was Woodward and Bernstein's most extensive source.

by. But it is there, even as the curtain rings up on White House lawyers Fred Buzhardt and Leonard Garment winging their way south on Eastern Flight 177 to recommend that the president resign:

> For most of the travellers, the flight was an occasion for relaxation, the beginning of a vacation. But Buzhardt and Garment were grim and tense as they rehearsed their presentation. . . .
>
> Buzhardt nervously tapped his hand on the armrest. His West Point class ring struck the metal. The "1946" was nearly worn from the setting. A slightly hunched figure with thick glasses and a slow, deliberate manner, Buzhardt came out of the political stable of Senator Strom Thurmond. . . .

It is all done so well, so quickly, that we hardly stop to think that only two people saw that ring tapping the metal armrest. And chances are, even Buzhardt was unaware of his mannerism. But in either case, it is not the sort of fact that anyone would bother to pass along to an aide (or for that matter, the sort of fact aides would be likely to remember if they ever had been told). No, the tapping ring provides a good indication that either Buzhardt or Garment (and most probably Garment) spoke with Woodward and Bernstein.

Other such revealing details are sprinkled through the book. Attorney General Elliot Richardson might well confide to his aides that he had written a letter of resignation over the Archibald Cox affair, but would he mention that as he wrote, he could barely hear "the rush of the Potomac River" in the distance? Buzhardt would tell his friends that he guessed the president would resign by Friday, August 2, but would he bother to tell them that he also made that guess to his wife? And who but presidential speechwriter Pat Buchanan would know that Alexander Haig's office called just as Buchanan had "laced up his new blue-and-white track shoes"? Who would know that, as he went jogging that day, "he slowed down only at the guard post on West Executive Avenue between the White House and the EOB"? The probabilities are high that in each case, Richardson, Buzhardt, and Buchanan told those parts of the story directly to Woodward and Bernstein; doubly high if other supporting evidence can be found.

Critical readers might object that these conclusions depend too heavily on the assumption that Woodward and Bernstein are not indulging in what they might regard as innocent embellishment: making up details like the ring-tapping to dramatize the story. Certainly some reporters are not above fabrication. Journalist Richard Reeves admits to inventing secret sources to protect his information and regards it as so well-established a practice that he even doubts the existence of Deep Throat. But there are reporters and there are reporters; and each journalist deserves to be judged on his or her own merits. Maybe Woodward and Bernstein did take a little license with the ring-tapping or the jogging, but if so, why not embellish more consistently? Some narrative passages are so spare (as we shall shortly see) that they nearly beg for some imaginative, lively detail. That is simply not Woodward and Bernstein's style. When they lack information, they pass by in unnoticed silence. When they do have information, they print it—even when its actual value is marginal, as in a largely irrelevant presidential conversation with Milton Pitts, Nixon's barber.

In any case, the small telltale details are not so much proofs in themselves as indicators of larger confirming patterns embedded in the book's narrative perspectives.

Such patterns can be found, to take one example, in the syntax of the many conversations recorded in *The Final Days.* The human memory is both fallible and selective. It does not, like the tape recorder, indiscriminately record every syllable of a conversation. If Alexander Haig spends two hours alone with the president, and then comes out and gives a blow-by-blow account to his friend Buzhardt, Haig's account will be at best only a partial retelling. He may quote a few phrases verbatim, mention the president's more dramatic gestures, and paraphrase the remaining points. If Haig keeps a diary, he may be able to record the conversation with a fair amount of detail, but nothing approaching a verbatim report. Buzhardt too may keep a diary, but his record of Haig's meeting will suffer from the disadvantage of having to select highlights from highlights, rather than from the complete two-hour conversation. Thus Buzhardt's entry will be less detailed and much briefer.

Now, as can be seen, any presidential conversation may produce several types of records. And each type will tend to leave behind characteristic trademarks in Woodward and Bernstein's apparently omniscient prose.

If a tape transcript of the actual meeting is available, Woodward and Bernstein can quote extended passages of conversation. More important, they will quote it in the style of the mechanical recorder, which remembers each phrase exactly, complete with missteps, stutters, stops, and backtrackings. When we come to the conversation between Nixon and

Ziegler on June 4, 1973, we hardly need a footnote to realize the account is based on a transcript:

> "That's the tragedy of the whole thing [says the President]. Mitchell would never step up to this. Well, I suppose, would you? No, no. Former Attorney General step up and say you bugged? Shit, I wouldn't. What I would step up and say—'Look, I haven't approved a goddam thing and so forth, but I take responsibility for it—bah, bah, bah, bah, you know—and I'm going to take, uh, take, you know, a suspended sentence or misdemeanor slapped in the face or whatever the hell it's going to be.' But once denied—under oath—he was stuck. See? God damn."

This speech is set in the middle of a four-page, back-and-forth dialogue between Ziegler and Nixon—a dialogue no one could possibly remember in its entirety, not to mention all the *uhs, you knows,* and *bah, bah, bahs* of this particular passage.

Perhaps the most interesting example of "transcript syntax" occurs near the end of the drama, when Nixon is about to go before the cameras and announce his resignation. For two full pages, *The Final Days* presents a back-and-forth conversation between a nervous, distraught president and a nervous, uneasy television crew. All the little transcript stumbles are there, such as Nixon correcting himself when he mispronounces photographer Ollie Atkins's name. When the president laughs nervously or clears his throat, we are told; so also when his voice quavers. And when the lights shine in his eyes, we even learn he squinted. Yet the White House taping system was no longer in operation. What was the source of the transcript? The historian is inevitably led to conclude that the television crew was already videotaping as they tested lighting and microphone levels. Somehow the tape was never erased, and Woodward and Bernstein managed to view a copy of it.*

Transcripts are not often available, of course. Thus when Buzhardt first informs the president of his discovery of the famous eighteen-minute gap (Haig present also), the account is less detailed than a transcript but long enough to suggest that it is based on recollections and records of someone who was actually there. Questions and answers are related in a back-and-forth manner, but not, for the most part, enclosed in quotation marks.

*Through an element of serendipity, we learned while writing this that such a videotape does indeed exist, although we have not viewed it.

The President appeared concerned but calm as Buzhardt described the sounds of the two tones [during the gap].

What did he think might have happened? the President asked.

Buzhardt said he had no answers.

What had been on the tape?

Buzhardt didn't know that either.

Nixon said he could not recall what had occurred in the conversation. He had tried, but. . . .

The construction of the account implies that one of the participants recorded its substance shortly after, but (naturally enough) did not include any verbatim statements. Sometimes *The Final Days* makes the presence of such notes even more explicit: "Buzhardt jotted furiously on his own legal pad as Nixon read from his notes" of the March 21st conversation. "Richardson gathered his assistants at the Justice Department" to try and resolve the conflict between Nixon and Archibald Cox: "An initial draft was made: 'A Proposal—ELR #1.'"

In contrast to the longer descriptions, notice this account of lawyer James St. Clair's meeting with the president, just after St. Clair appeared before the Justices of the Supreme Court:

St. Clair had met with Nixon for forty minutes that afternoon. It had gone well, he told the President, very well. They had a good chance. He firmly believed it.

A forty-minute meeting, immediately after an appearance of momentous consequence for both Nixon and St. Clair, and the narrative lasts only four sentences. A log of some sort has likely indicated the duration of the meeting, but the only substance reported is the kind of cautious digest St. Clair might have given to another of the principals after the conference. If St. Clair spoke with Woodward and Bernstein, he surely refused them any information about this meeting.

Taken singly, none of these inferences conclusively indicates who contributed material to *The Final Days*. But when the entire text of the book is subjected to a similarly close contextual reading, patterns emerge that permit the historian to conjecture with fair probability the identities of *The Final Days'* principal sources. Since neither historian nor journalist has yet, to our knowledge, undertaken such an effort, it may be useful to present our major findings.

Henry Kissinger contributed virtually nothing. When *The Final Days* first appeared the press devoted a great deal of attention to the Kissinger

The video camera (right) is the source of "transcript syntax" in the following excerpt from *The Final Days,* which describes President Nixon before his resignation speech. Note the characteristic transcript patterns, as well as the additional visual cues:

  The President pointed to the backup camera. "That's an NBC camera, I presume?"

  "No, they're both CBS cameras."

  "Standard joke," the President said and laughed nervously. He cleared his throat loudly.

  "Let me see, did you get these lights properly?" They were shining in his eyes. He squinted. "My eyes always have . . . you'll find they get past sixty . . ." his voice trailed off.

material, primarily because the book's revelations about him were almost as shocking as the revelations about Nixon. But the secretary plays a remarkably small role in the entire drama. He doesn't appear center stage until Chapters 14, 16, and 17, and then disappears again for all practical purposes until his final dramatic return. Furthermore, chapters

14, 16, and 17 contain none of the extended conversations present in other parts of *The Final Days;* only a series of facts, opinions, and quotations that could easily have been strung together from immediate aides to Kissinger like Eagleburger and Scowcroft, and from minor assistants and secretaries.

For the fact of the matter is, the secretary of state left behind a wide trail of evidence generated by his system for monitoring and recording phone conversations. The system was elaborate enough to require a small army of transcribers to keep it going, and for sheer complexity, put to shame Richard Nixon's jerry-rigged Oval Office recorders. "On some calls," note Woodward and Bernstein, "the unsuspecting party might be talking simultaneously to Kissinger, Haig, a transcribing secretary, and the appointments secretary." And in Kissinger's basement office at the White House, eight other phones could monitor the direct line with Nixon. When the transcribing volume got too large for the regular secretaries, a night crew was put on the job. Thus, although Kissinger took great pains to conceal his true feelings from his commander-in-chief, there were plenty of secretaries and aides within transcribing distance, enough of them sufficiently disgruntled to remember and report any off-the-cuff retorts, as when the secretary reportedly referred to his superior as "our meatball President."

In addition, Kissinger seems to have enjoyed talking to his immediate subordinates about the manipulation of power and about his own power politics in particular. Much material in the Kissinger chapters is explicitly attributed to assistants. The secretary could control Nixon on his Cambodia policy, he "boasted to his aides." The president couldn't be pushed too far, he "warned his associates." Deviousness was a part of the job, he "counseled his aides." Indeed, when it comes right down to it, virtually all the material in these sections is either explicitly or implicitly critical of Kissinger. No secretary of state with an I. Q. above 75 would willingly volunteer any of it, especially while still in office.

David Eisenhower and Pat Buchanan are key sources for Nixon family material. Eisenhower admitted to having two interview sessions with Woodward and Bernstein. But even had he denied it, the book makes his contribution clear. His point of view dominates many of the family narratives, as we have seen. Some of his opinions and feelings could have been reported secondhand by Harrington and other friends (to his credit, Eisenhower appears to be one of the few family members at once loyal and yet willing to voice differing opinions). Still, many of the family conversations are detailed enough to suggest a firsthand source. On Friday, August 2, the president is seen with his feet up on an ottoman;

David sits with his back to the fireplace and is thus able to see "the flames reflected in Nixon's glazed eyes."

Speechwriter Pat Buchanan, with his sharp, journalist's eye, flavors his accounts with the small details that a firsthand source is privy to: the exact route he jogs, the sneakers he wears, his wife's white lie that he is already asleep when Julie Eisenhower tries to reach him. More to the point, the narrative often assumes the Buchanan point of view during family debates, especially the sequence on Saturday morning, August 3. We meet Buchanan, 9:30 at the office, and follow him along to the White House where we get a detailed reconstruction of the family meeting (aided also by Eisenhower's recollections). Buchanan's perspective is ever-present: "Buchanan sipped his coffee. . . . Buchanan understood. . . . Buchanan shifted uneasily. . . . Buchanan was swallowing hard. . . . Buchanan paused, searching for the right words."

When the discussion is over and Buchanan leaves, do we stay to hear the family's reaction? No, the narrator obediently trails Buchanan down the hall and observes a chat with Rosemary Woods. Then Rebozo comes along and he and Buchanan decide to see Haig. Haig is busy. They try the president. No response there, either, so Rebozo goes his own way. Do we go with Rebozo? No, back to the office with Buchanan, then come along to lunch in the senior staff mess. Finally, off to Buzhardt's office for a conference. Is it only coincidence that we shadow Buchanan from scene to scene the whole morning?

St. Clair kept his counsel. The extended conversations in which he participates either are a matter of public record (his Supreme Court and Judiciary Committee presentations) or are seen from an aide's point of view ("Presenting the transcript at this late date would be a public relations disaster, Speakes felt, but St. Clair was a $300,000-a-year lawyer and he must know what he was doing.") In the case of St. Clair's relations with the president, detailed conversations are reported only when Woodward and Bernstein sources are also present. Other times, as after the Supreme Court decision, we get either silence or a curt summary: "St. Clair met with Nixon and Haig for nearly two hours and spent the rest of the day preparing." St. Clair's silence may have been principled or it may have been pragmatic, but whichever, it surely resulted in his being on the receiving end of the book's biggest hatchet job.

Alexander Haig did not talk. This is perhaps the most surprising conclusion of them all; not because Haig would be expected to talk, but simply because he is the focus of so much of *The Final Days.* Even in *Newsweek,* where *The Final Days* first appeared, the book reviewer assumed that the general had contributed. Yet however much we see of Haig, we miss even more. If he talked, why is there silence at so many key points? During the Richardson negotiations over the fate of Archibald Cox, Haig goes to Nixon's office to persuade the president to keep Cox. We wait back with everyone else in Haig's office. He returns: the scene with Nixon has been "bloody, bloody," he says. But once again, we get no details. The same pattern appears throughout the book. (Page 62: "Haig said he would present the idea to the President. Within an hour he was back on the phone with good news for Richardson." Page 264: "The general had gone to the residence 45 minutes earlier to brief the President and had just come back, his mouth set in a tight line.")

Small wonder, then, that when the first excerpts appeared in *Newsweek,* Haig sent a telegram to Nixon denying any participation and noting that he was "genuinely shocked by the excerpts." In their quest for material, Woodward and Bernstein had pursued him all the way to the Netherlands, where he had been stationed, and still the loyal general remained silent. Suddenly he was confronted with an account so detailed, it approached a minute-by-minute narrative of his actions—indeed, sometimes even presented his thoughts in the same omniscient way it did David Eisenhower's. Haig may be forgiven for wondering ruefully whether the *Post* reporters had somehow stumbled onto his obliging double.

In fact, they had stumbled onto his double, or the nearest thing to it. The man who very likely contributed more to *The Final Days* than any other major participant was the man also closest to Alexander Haig: White House lawyer Fred Buzhardt.

The Loquacious J. Fred Buzhardt. Buzhardt admitted that he talked to Woodward and Bernstein but did not let on just how much. Internal evidence indicates that he was a key contributor. The small, personal details are there, the extended paraphrases of presidential conversations, the blow-by-blow accounts of Buzhardt's first hearing of the tapes.

And the larger narrative pattern is equally revealing. The detailed accounts of White House strategy sessions among Nixon, Haig, and White House lawyers decrease significantly after Buzhardt suffers a heart attack in mid-June 1974. They do not resume until he is back on the job later in the summer. Where in earlier sections, much light is shed on the president's wavering resolution to surrender the tapes, we hear little about the July decision to provide the Judiciary Committee with an additional snippet of exonerating evidence. Did the president object to release as much as he did with the earlier transcripts? Who discovered the exonerating evidence? How much did Nixon want to edit the transcript? These kinds of questions, which the book readily answers when Buzhardt is on the scene, are now silently passed over. The absence goes unnoticed because the Kissinger chapters are conveniently introduced at the point of Buzhardt's illness, and personal glimpses of the president are inserted based on the Eisenhower-Harrington material.

Because Buzhardt is such a helpful source, Woodward and Bernstein can fill in many details about Haig's attitudes, even though Haig himself remained silent. Both aides were West Point graduates. Both decided early on that they were treading slippery ground and thus "sought each other's counsel." "They could protect themselves," Haig is said to suggest, "if they trusted each other totally. But no one else." So the two men "began meeting regularly in the general's office to debate the ethics of the situation and calculate their next moves." This close relationship enables Woodward and Bernstein on several occasions to re-create private conversations between the president and Haig, since Buzhardt got a replay of the action immediately afterwards. (E.g., Thursday, August 1: "When Haig got back to his office, Buzhardt was there waiting for him.")

Fred Buzhardt's vantage point, in other words, functions as one of the major narrative perspectives within *The Final Days*—perhaps the most dominant perspective of all, at least for the political and legal portions of the book. Woodward and Bernstein indicate that while "dozens of persons volunteered information freely," one person "was interviewed seventeen times." Buzhardt surely seems to run a strong race for that top position.

THE BOUNDARIES OF HISTORY

Critics who decry the lack of footnotes, then, are perhaps being a bit ungenerous as well as unrealistic. Ungenerous, because Woodward and Bernstein are straightforward enough in their narrative approach to enable careful readers to deduce the book's major sources. Unrealistic, because under the circumstances only a promise of anonymity enabled Woodward and Bernstein to get as much information as they did.

In part, however, the resentment of some critics seems to be focused on a different issue: the book's implicit pretension to being history. In crossing the line from the autobiographical prose of *All the President's Men* into the historical narrative of *The Final Days,* Woodward and

Bernstein committed the cardinal sin of not knowing their place. They attempted a production beyond their means, and the result was "hot" history. So the critics would have us believe.

Is *The Final Days* history? Or to rephrase the question, are Woodward and Bernstein "doing" history? Since the bulk of this volume has been spent watching historians go about their business, we are in a better than usual position to answer.

The two reporters readily surmount the first and easiest hurdle. History is a narrative reconstruction of past events. The events of the Nixon presidency are past; *The Final Days* is a narrative reconstruction. So far, so good. But as has become clear, the key word in that definition is "reconstruction." It is reconstruction—the act of gathering, analyzing, and shaping raw information—that is at the heart of history. So let us look a little more closely, first, at the raw information gathered by Woodward and Bernstein; and second, at the analyzing and shaping they do.

In terms of raw information, Woodward and Bernstein have gathered reasonably well. They make use of many of the sorts of documents that historians of the Nixon years will continue to draw upon: logs, memoranda, diaries, notes. There is, of course, a good deal of information the reporters did not gather because they could not. Classified materials were not available. Some actors in the drama refused to cooperate, including Alexander Haig, Henry Kissinger, and the man at the center of the action, Richard Nixon.

In the area of oral evidence, however, Woodward and Bernstein have collected more and better raw information than most historians could ever hope to find. As the case of the slave narratives collection demonstrated, oral evidence can be extremely valuable. Historians have made excellent use of the freedmen's stories, even though some may have been distorted by hindsight or blurred by time. In the case of *The Final Days,* interviews were conducted with subjects whose recollections were fresh, vivid, and close to the event—the ideal of oral historians. Indeed, the reporters recognized this closeness as their strong suit. They began interviewing only a week after the Nixon resignation because, as they put it, "We didn't want to give people a chance at hindsight."

The quality of Woodward and Bernstein's information is also noteworthy in terms of the people interviewed. Throughout this work we have seen historians expanding their research beyond the narrow coverage of society's elite to include the perspectives of middle and "bottom rail" people: the tobacco hands of Virginia, the villagers of Salem, the freedmen of Carolina, the white and blue collar Americans of Dedham and Braintree. In political history too, historians have moved beyond an analysis that focuses solely on "rational actors" and major decision makers to a recognition that anonymous bureaucrats and bureaucratic structures affect the political process.

Woodward and Bernstein have incorporated such perspectives into their narrative. Scores of secretaries, legal assistants, sub-cabinet officers, and personal aides have, in effect, left behind their own memoirs in *The Final Days.* The vast majority of such people would never publish recollections; yet their perspectives are important for historians wishing to piece together the dynamics of political Washington. Max Lerner notwithstanding, it may be valuable to know what the law clerks of Potter Stewart (not to mention Stewart himself) thought of Warren Burger's attempt to write a majority opinion on the Nixon tapes case. Similarly, it will be helpful to know how Henry Kissinger dealt with the inertial bureaucracy of the State Department—from the bureaucracy's point of view as well as the secretary's. And in terms of status dynamics and conspicuous consumption, we certainly are unlikely to learn from Ronald Ziegler's official memoirs that he demanded his coffee be served in a cup and saucer identical to the president's—cream-colored Lenox china with a silver presidential seal. Woodward and Bernstein's technique of beginning with the smaller fish and working up to the bigger ones has paid perhaps unanticipated dividends.

That raises the second part of our question—did the two reporters fully anticipate the dividends? History springs not from the raw material itself, but from the historian's ability to see its potential and shape it. How does *The Final Days* make use of its materials? What questions does it ask of them in order to extort significance? Throughout this book we have seen historians constantly analyzing individual documents and records. They have asked questions about perspective; about a document's context; or how its predispositions might affect its value as evidence.

Again, Woodward and Bernstein demonstrate that they have taken such questions into account. "In the course of over three years of reporting on the Nixon Administration," they note,

> we had learned to place extraordinary trust in the accuracy and candor of some sources. We had also talked regularly over the same period with a small number of people who consistently sought to give versions of events that were slanted, self-serving, or otherwise untrustworthy; we used information from them only when we were convinced by more reliable sources of its accuracy.

The prose of *The Final Days* confirms this assertion. For example, Ronald Ziegler appears to have contributed some material; yet Woodward and Bernstein obviously distrust his perceptions. Inevitably, some readers will disagree with the reporters' evaluation of their sources, but that is a matter of judgment. Such disagreements are everyday occurrences in the historical profession.

On a larger scale, however, Woodward and Bernstein's narrative asks relatively limited questions. This work has made clear that the broader concerns of historical inquiry are shaped by the theoretical concepts that historians bring to bear on an investigation. We have examined the pattern of land speculation and settlement in Tennessee because Frederick Jackson Turner asked provocative questions about the relation between democracy and the American frontier. We have gone beyond the question of guilt or innocence in the Sacco and Vanzetti case because John Higham and other historians have made us sensitive to the conflicts between immigrants and native-born Americans. We have explored the bureaucratic features of scientific research in the 1930s and 1940s because decision-making theories suggest that we may learn more that way about how the atomic bomb came to be used. Questions of such broad scope are not often suggested by the raw information itself. They are brought to the material by the historian.

This is where Woodward and Bernstein least resemble the researchers we have followed throughout this book. *The Final Days* is narrative history in its narrower sense, concerned primarily with laying out the who-what-where and describing it in a vivid, readable way. These are commendable goals, and ones not easily attained. But the broader questions remain unasked. What significance, for example, does the Watergate controversy have for the development of American political institutions? Perhaps Watergate should be regarded merely as one of the periodic scandals that embarrass administrations—like Teapot Dome of the twenties or the Credit Mobilier frauds of the Grant administration. On the other hand, President Nixon's behavior raises important questions about the constitutional division of power among the branches of the federal government. The Nixon administration continued a trend, begun during the New Deal years, of consolidating executive initiative and power at the expense of Congress and the courts. The president defied the Democratic-controlled Congress by refusing to spend money that Congress had appropriated for programs he disapproved. He engaged in wire-tapping and other clandestine intelligence activities for political gain as well as for national security.

Woodward and Bernstein discuss none of the issues raised by these

Carl Bernstein and Bob Woodward (right) of the *Washington Post.* "Yesterday was for the history books. . . ."

actions, most likely because at heart, they are indeed journalists. The word itself reflects their perspective, sharing its Latin root with the French *jour,* or day. For the journalist, each day is a new deadline. *Washington Post* editors were in the habit of asking their reporters, "What have you done for me *today*?" Woodward and Bernstein were willing to write by that philosophy. "Yesterday was for the history books," they note in *All the President's Men,* "not newspapers." It was only natural that they were not inclined to step back and examine larger issues.

From the historian's point of view their decision, conscious or not, was wisely made. For we have seen that contemporary observers are usually not particularly well-positioned to evaluate the larger issues of their day. Was Teddy Roosevelt's compromise with the packing industry an astute bargain or a sellout? The question was impossible to answer without knowing how the court ruled in later challenges to the Meat Inspection Act. Will the reform legislation passed during the aftermath of Watergate adequately restrain an imperial Presidency? Even a trained historian would be loath to answer without hedging. Woodward and Bernstein chose to do the kind of history they knew best—an up-close, day-by-day narrative rather than detached, magisterial analysis.

To say that *The Final Days,* then, is only one kind of history is not to slight the book; merely to recognize the discipline's immense variety. History, after all, is perhaps the only profession that has the audacity to define its boundaries in terms of time rather than subject matter—to cast its gaze on anything that happened in the past. There is plenty of elbow room in this discipline; sufficient space for members to be catholic in their choice of both subject matter and method.

Indeed, the variety of methods even more than the range of subjects is what lends history its breadth. This is seen most obviously in the willingness, even the downright avidity, of recent historians to adopt the many approaches of the social sciences. Psychology, sociology, economics, anthropology, organizational theory—each of these disciplines has formulated characteristic ways of analyzing human behavior and reducing a mass of particular facts to coherent and general laws. Historians have applied those formulations to their own investigations in order to derive similar general truths about the past.

Yet to our way of thinking, history owes its breadth as much to what it does *not* borrow from the social sciences. We have already noted our belief that good history begins with a good story; that the narrative tradition remains central to the discipline. To insist upon this is to affirm that history is equally concerned with the uniqueness of an event, with its particulars, as with general laws that can be derived from theory. When we look at the sequence of decisions that led to the dropping of the atom bomb at Hiroshima, general models of bureaucratic behavior help explain how the decision came to be made—indeed, such models are indispensable. But the story would not be complete—in fact its heart would be missing—without an appreciation of the individual burdens carried by the Manhattan Project scientists, or the palpable tension at the

Los Alamos blockhouse that early morning of July 16. Robert Oppenheimer's vision from the *Bhagavad-Gita* is not readily susceptible to generalization, yet it remains inseparable from the Los Alamos story, an irreducible part of the narrative. So it should be, for good history is always humanistic as well as scientific.

In the end, however, the metaphor of depth rather than breadth most convincingly explains history's relevance. The urge to construct histories runs deep in human character. It is one of the oldest and most basic ways of organizing human knowledge. In our personal lives, the histories begin with tales of family, place, and ancestral roots, passed from father to daughter, from mother to son, from older sister to younger brother. The tales are most often passed orally, although thanks to George Eastman, they are also conveyed by photographs and family albums. Throughout our lives we continually construct our own histories as well as interpret the histories of others. Carl Becker, himself an accomplished scholar, insisted that we are all historians in one guise or another: the farmer down the road, tracing caterpiller plagues in the rings of a tree; or Sam Mitchell, recounting the day the guns thundered freedom over the Carolina Sea Islands; or Bartolomeo Vanzetti, impelled to consider whether he would repeat the actions that brought him to final sentencing; or Bob Woodward and Carl Bernstein, journalists who became historians despite their honorable intentions of leaving yesterday "for the history books." All of these people found that history enlarged their present through the experiences of the past.

Carl Becker was right: we all do history. Those of us who are fortunate enough to make our living at it should heartily encourage those who join us, whether the recruits arrive through the traditional front door of the library, or via an early-morning call to investigate a third-rate burglary. Whatever one's personal path to the past, once there, it is an intriguing place to spend time. And the only self-respecting way back to the present leaves each of us with the responsibility of fashioning our own route out.

Additional Reading

Woodward and Bernstein narrate their own pursuit of the cover-up in *All the President's Men* (New York, 1974), an account which focuses primarily on events through April 1973. *The Final Days* (New York, 1976) picks up chronologically where the first book left off. Press reaction to *The Final Days* can be found in the daily newspapers and newsmagazines of April 1976, as well as in book reviews and commentary such as Max Lerner, "Writing 'Hot History,' " *Saturday Review*, May 29, 1976; and John Osborne, "The Woodstein Flap," *New Republic*, April 24, 1976.

For another example of "hot history," readers may wish to compare Theodore White's *Breach of Faith* (New York, 1975) and Jonathan Schell's more interpretive study of the Nixon years, *The Time of Illusion* (New York, 1976). Some of the larger issues skirted by Woodward and Bernstein are aired in Frederick C. Mosher, *Watergate: Implications for Responsible Government* (New York, 1974); Ralph K. Winter, *Watergate and the Law* (Washington, D.C., 1974); and Philip B. Kurland, *Watergate and the Constitution* (Chicago, 1978).

Most accounts of Watergate that have appeared thus far are by the participants themselves, occasionally helped along by the ever-obliging "as-told-to" ghost writers. From the ranks of the co-conspirators have come the following books, listed roughly in diminishing order of administrative rank: *The Memoirs of Richard Nixon* (New York, 1978), in which Richard Nixon, after many pages, still seems puzzled over what the fuss was about; Harry R. Haldeman, *The Ends of Power* (New York, 1978); John Dean, *Blind Ambition: The White House Years* (New York, 1976), one of the more perceptive accounts; Charles Colson, *Born Again* (Old Tappan, N. J., 1976); Jeb Magruder, *An American Life* (New York, 1974); E. Howard Hunt, *Undercover: Memoirs of an American Secret Agent* (New York, 1974); James McCord, *A Piece of the Tape* (Rockville, Md., 1974); and G. Gordon Liddy, *Will* (New York, 1980). The last account seems to confirm the president's own assessment of Liddy. ("He just isn't well screwed on, is he?")

Other areas of the Watergate story have been recounted by those who brought the malfeasants to justice. "Maximum John" Sirica, as he was known in legal circles, gives the bench's perspective in *To Set the Record Straight* (New York, 1979). For the Ervin Committee, there is Senator Sam's version itself, perhaps somewhat ambitiously titled *The Whole Truth* (New York, 1981), as well as Samuel Dash, *Chief Counsel: Inside the Ervin Committee* (New York, 1976), and Minority Counsel Fred D. Thompson's *At that Point in Time* (New York, 1975). For the Special Prosecutor's office, see Leon Jaworski, *The Right and the Power* (New York, 1976); Richard Ben-Veniste and George Frampton, Jr., *Stonewall* (New York, 1977); and James Doyle, *Not Above the Law* (New York, 1977). Howard Fields, *High Crimes and Misdemeanors* (New York, 1978), covers the impeachment proceedings, as does a large part of Elizabeth Drew's perceptive *Washington Journal: the Events of 1973–1974* (New York, 1975).

We have not discussed the thorny and familiar issue of who Bob Woodward's most famous source, "Deep Throat," was, since he appears only in *All the President's Men* and not *The Final Days*. We admit to having our own theories, though they require more legwork and researching to substantiate than we have had time, as yet, to spare. Perhaps a later edition of this book will have an epilogue. In the meantime, the most thorough detective work on the problem has been done by John Dean, in his book *Lost Honor* (Los Angeles, 1982). His choice for Deep Throat: Alexander Haig.

For readers wishing to investigate some of the primary documents of Watergate, several sourcebooks are available which make the task easier. *The End of a Presidency* (New York, 1974), edited by the staff of the *New York Times,* includes a detailed chronology of events, an aid to keeping names, dates, and places straight. For excerpts from the Ervin Committee hearings, consult *The Watergate Hearings* (New York, 1973), again assembled by The *New York Times,* or else the full version issued by the Senate Select Committee on Presidential Campaign Activities, *Hearings, Watergate and Related Activities* (Washington, D.C., 1973). For the impeachment proceedings, see the House Committee on the Judiciary's *Impeachment of Richard Nixon, President of the United States* (Washington, D.C., 1974).

Then, of course, there are the most notorious primary sources of the drama, the White House tapes and transcripts. The transcripts are available in convenient form either in *The Presidential Transcripts* (New York, 1974), as issued by the *Washington Post,* or in *The White House Transcripts* (New York, 1974), by the *New York Times.* Both texts are copied in full from the more unwieldy typescript edition issued by the Government Printing Office. But as *The Final Days* makes clear, the transcripts have been sometimes severely edited. A number of the relevant tapes, now stored at the National Archives, are available in unexpurgated form. When we listened to one of them, we found the quality uneven, but for the most part quite understandable with the help of FBI transcripts provided at the Archives. The opportunity to analyze political decision-making in terms of a blow-by-blow conversation, with inflection of voice to be weighed as well as syntax and content, makes these tapes an absolutely unprecedented source in the history of presidential politics.

Finally, those readers who would like to try their hand at analyzing narrative perspectives might turn to Bob Woodward's later study of the Supreme Court, co-authored by Scott Armstrong and titled *The Brethren* (New York, 1979). Once again, the subject is controversial, the sources are confidential, and the narrative perspective is "omniscient." Happy footnote hunting!

INDEX

i

Palmer, Paul C., 29
Parkman, Francis, 106
Parliament, xxix–xxx, 74–76, 80–81, 90
Parmenter, Frederick, 271
Parris, Samuel, 29–30, 49–51
Parry, Lewis, 114
Pattie, James Ohio, 120
Pearl Harbor, 344
Pells, William, 302
Perkins, Simon, 151
Perspective: embedded in facts, 6–10, 17; and freedmen, 181–85, 188–201, 202–3; and selection of facts, xvii, xxi, 3, 217–18. *See also* Documents; Evidence; Theory
Phillips, Wendell, 174
Philosophes, 78
Phips, Sir William, 32
Photography: and family albums, 224–26, 423; historical development of, 216, 219, 224; and "reality," 208–18, 228–29; 216–24, 236–37; reveals urban slum conditions, 216, 219–21, 226–35. *See also* Pictorial evidence, Television
Pictorial evidence, ix, 216–17, 221–22, 297. *See also* Cartoons; Photography
Plants, 121; European vs. American, 135; and Indian use of, 121–24, 135, 138–39; trees as resource, 138–39
Plumbers, the, 399
Pocahontas, 4, 26, 405
Polenberg, Richard, 393
Political history: and courts, 265–68; and legislative process, 254–65; and role of institutions, 248–53; and symbolic overtones, 240, 244–48, 260
Pope, Alexander, 78
Population, of precontact America, 125–29

Populism, 51, 244
Potsdam Conference, 330, 343, 344, 357–59
Pottawatomie Massacre, 154–55, 159
Potter, David, 114
Powhatan, 4
Primary sources. *See* Documents; Evidence; Perspective; Theory
Proctor, Elizabeth, 33, 36, 51
Proctor, John, 51
Proctor, Redfield, 265
Proctor, William, 277, 279, 295
Progressivism, 102, 105, 252–55
Psychoanalysis. *See* Freud, Sigmund; Psychohistory
Psychohistory: and Andrew Jackson, 106–10, 111–12, 114; and conversion hysteria, 40–44, 86, 87; and insanity, 158; and psychoanalytic theory, 159–61, 165–74, 175–76; as social explanation, 44; and witchcraft, 40–44. *See also* Freud, Sigmund
Pure Food and Drug Act, 255
Puritans, 33, 39, 51

Radicalism, 285–86, 288, 289, 293
Radio. *See* Mass media
Randolph, Joyce, 389
"Rational actor" model, 335–46
Rebozo, Bebe, 416
Reconstruction, 209. *See also* Blacks; Freedman's Bureau
Redbook, 365, 366
Red Scare, 286–87
Reeves, Richard, 403, 410
Remini, Robert, 113
Republican party, 149–50, 156, 242, 262–65, 321
Revere, Paul, 309
Reynolds, James, 255–57, 261–62. *See also* Neill-Reynolds report
Richardson, Elliot, 400, 413, 416
Riis, Jacob, 367; background, 214–16; bias of, 221–37; and children,

About the Authors

JAMES WEST DAVIDSON is a writer and historian. He was educated at Haverford College and at Yale University, where he received his Ph.D. in 1973. Davidson's books include *The Complete Wilderness Paddler* (with John Rugge, 1976) and *The Logic of Millennial Thought* (1977).

MARK HAMILTON LYTLE is Associate Professor of History at Bard College. He was granted a B.A. from Cornell University and his Ph.D. from Yale University in 1973. He has written (with Davidson) *The United States: A History of the Republic* (1981); *Shang* (with Dixon Merkt, 1984) and *The Origins of the Iranian-American Alliance, 1941–1953* (1986).

A Note on the Design of This Book

The text of this book was set via computer-driven cathode
ray tube in a type face known as Garamond.
Its design is based on letterforms
originally created by Claude Garamond, 1510-1561.
Garamond was a pupil of Geoffrey Troy and
may have patterned his letterforms on Venetian
models. To this day, the type face that
bears his name is one of the most attractive
used in book composition, and the intervening years
have caused it to lose little of its
freshness or beauty.